MENTAL HEALTH AND THE LAW

Edward B. Beis, LL.B.

AN ASPEN PUBLICATION®
Aspen Systems Corporation
Rockville, Maryland
Royal Tunbridge Wells
1984

Library of Congress Cataloging in Publication Data

Beis, Edward B.
Mental health and the law.

An Aspen publication.

Includes index.
1. Mental health laws—United States. 2. Mental health personnel—
Malpractice—United States. 3. Psychiatrists—Malpractice—United
States. 4. Evidence, Expert—United States. 5. Witnesses—United
States. I. Title. [DNLM: 1. Mental health—United States—
Legislation. 2. Patient advocacy. 3. Malpractice—United States—
Legislation. WM 33 AA1B42m]
KF3828.B44   1984   344.73'044   83-15825
ISBN: 0-89443-893-X   347.30444

Publisher: John Marozsan
Editor-in-Chief: Michael Brown
Executive Managing Editor: Margot Raphael
Editorial Services: Scott Ballotin
Printing and Manufacturing: Debbie Collins

Library of Congress Catalog Card Number: 83-15825
ISBN: 0-89443-893-X

Printed in the United States of America

2 3 4 5

With love
to my wife Marilyn
and to my children
Douglas and Julia

Table of Contents

Preface

The goals of this book are threefold: (1) to explain in lay terms the legal aspects of the mental health system and the legal responsibilities of those working in the mental health care field, including governing board members, administrators, psychiatrists, psychologists, psychiatric social workers, and nurses; (2) to provide to those responsible for quality assurance and risk management a guide to the standards of care and treatment required by law; and (3) to improve the effectiveness of mental health professionals in their roles as expert witnesses. Additionally, while it is not intended as an in-depth research tool, the book does provide citations to authorities, making it useful to lawyers.

Traditionally, few lawsuits have been filed against mental health professionals because patients are often reluctant to sue a psychiatrist or psychologist. Commentators attribute this reluctance to several factors, among them fear of admitting to being treated for mental illness, transference phenomenon, and lack of legal precedent. In recent years, however, the number of lawsuits against mental health professionals, including a very few against psychiatric nurses and social workers, has increased. Public mental health institutions have become embroiled in a flood of litigation, and the number of suits against private institutions is increasing. People have become more aware of their legal rights. Judges are more willing to impose liability against professionals who do not live up to required standards. Legislators have passed more laws expanding patients' rights.

Given this growth in lawsuits, knowledge of legal responsibilities and rights becomes increasingly important to the individual practitioner and to those who provide institutional services.

Part I of the book is introductory. It sketches the legal trends in mental health and provides a general explanation of the law.

Part II discusses various legal concepts of liability and sources of duties. Part III applies these concepts to outpatient settings. Subjects covered include abuse of the therapist-patient relationship in psychotherapy, treatment by medication, abandonment, confidentiality, and the right to community treatment.

Part IV discusses issues related to inpatient settings, including responsibilities of governing boards, chief executive officers, and medical staffs; quality assurance/risk management; patient medical records; admission of patients; diagnosis and treatment, including medication and electroconvulsive therapy; patients' rights; protection of patients; and discharge of patients.

Part V discusses the roles of expert witnesses, including psychiatrists, psychologists, and psychiatric nurses, in court proceedings. It also discusses the legal standards applied in civil and criminal actions in which expert witnesses commonly testify. The civil actions include guardianship, property matters (such as wills and contracts), family cases, Social Security disability, and special education. The criminal actions include fitness to stand trial and criminal responsibility (insanity defense, diminished capacity, guilty but mentally ill and mentally disordered sex offenders). Therapists who do not testify as expert witnesses should have a general knowledge of these legal standards because their patients are often the subjects of such proceedings.

Finally, a note on terminology in this book. The words "patient" and "client" are used interchangeably. Generally, in practice, "patient" refers to a person hospitalized or receiving the care of a psychiatrist, while "client" refers to a person under the care of a therapist who is a social worker, a psychologist, a psychiatric nurse or some other practitioner licensed to provide independent services. The term "patient" is used to cover all of these situations.

Edward B. Beis

Part I

Introduction

Chapter 1

Mental Health and the Law: Historical Perspectives and Modern Trends

In colonial America,[1] no institutions existed for the mentally disabled. The family was expected to care for such persons. Mentally disabled persons who had no assets and no family faced great difficulties. Unable to support themselves in a society that equated work with a good moral life and whose laws tended to compel work rather than provide necessities,[2] they were forced to rove from town to town with bands composed of mentally and physically disabled persons and those who refused to work. Townspeople resented the itinerant poor, fearing they would have to support them.

PROTECTION FOR THE COMMUNITY

Community action in the late 1600s tended to assist the families of the mentally disabled. In 1676 a Pennsylvania man filed an action with a court stating that his son was mad and that he could not support him. The court ordered three or four people to build a blockhouse in which to confine the madman. In 1689, a Massachusetts community voted to construct a small building to confine a woman. Her brother was ordered to provide for her, but the town voted to pay the expenses of her care. Other communities made maintenance payments to persons unrelated to mentally disabled persons who cared for them. The settlers viewed such actions as devices to remedy community nuisances rather than to assist the mentally disabled.[3]

If mentally disabled persons were dangerous the sheriff or constable detained and forcibly restrained them. In some instances the town itself requested police to take such measures. In 1676, Massachusetts enacted a statute ordering the selectmen of towns having dangerously disturbed persons to take care of them so "that they do not damnify others."

Communities took action to restrain the violent, not to treat them. Medical knowledge provided no mode of treatment. If a person's mental disability and violent tendencies were readily apparent, and the disabled person was without family, no objections were raised to commitment.[4]

3

The first hospitals for treatment of the mentally disabled developed during the eighteenth century. In May 1751, in response to a petition by Benjamin Franklin, the Pennsylvania Assembly authorized the establishment of a general hospital to cure the mentally disabled as well as the sick poor. Certification by one physician was required for commitment. In 1773, Virginia established its first hospital devoted exclusively to the mentally disabled. It remained the only one of its kind until 1824, when Kentucky established the Eastern Lunatic Asylum.[5]

A statute enacted by New York in 1788 authorized two or more justices to issue warrants directing constables to apprehend and lock up persons who were lunatics or mad and "so far disoriented in their senses that they may be too dangerous to be permitted to go abroad." The statute provided that a warrant should not be interpreted to restrain or abridge the power of the chancellor as it pertained to lunatics or to prevent any friends or relatives of lunatics from taking them under their own care and protection. Asylums were to be used primarily for the care of violent persons who could not be cared for privately.[6]

Property rights of the mentally disabled were protected by appointment of a guardian by the chancellor. A jury inquired into the mental condition of an individual. If the jury believed that the individual was incompetent, the chancellor appointed a guardian. The guardian could also request an opportunity to examine the individual. Adequate notice to the individual was necessary. Under its civil law system, Louisiana declared that people could not be deprived of the right to manage their own affairs on *ex parte* evidence and that mentally disabled persons should have the opportunity to cross-examine witnesses as in any other lawsuit.[7] The common law right of *habeas corpus* was available to test detention of mentally disabled persons.

Gradually, as more asylums were built, the number of persons committed increased, and confinement was not limited to the obviously dangerous. Court decisions of the time reflected a change in attitude. In the *Oakes* case in Massachusetts, a petition for a writ of *habeas corpus* was filed in 1845 on behalf of Josiah Oakes, who sought release from an asylum in Massachusetts on the grounds that he had been illegally committed by his family. The court held:

> [T]he right to restrain an insane person of his liberty is found in that great law of humanity, which makes it necessary to confine those whose going at large would be dangerous to themselves or others. . . . And the necessity which creates the law creates the limitation of the law. The question must then arise in each particular case, whether a patient's own safety, or that of others, requires that he should be restrained for a certain time and *whether restraint is necessary for his restoration* or will be conducive thereto. The restraint can continue as long as the necessity continues. This is the limitation, and the proper limitation.[8]

Oakes was not a dangerous person. He had been held on the allegations that he suffered from hallucinations and showed unsoundness of mind in managing his business affairs. The allegations were based on the fact that Oakes, an elderly and responsible person, had become engaged to a young woman of blemished character shortly after the death of his wife. This case is cited as the first in the United States to justify confinement for treatment.

A case in Philadelphia in 1849 illustrated the necessity for protection of hospital officials acting in good faith. A patient instituted a civil suit for wrongful detention against his mother, his sister, his cousin, the physicians of the asylum, and the physician who signed the commitment certificate, thereby recovering a large sum of money. In reporting the case Isaac Ray stated that the evidence showed beyond a doubt that the patient was violently and dangerously insane.[9]

REFORM MOVEMENT

As part of a reform movement, 13 hospital superintendents met in Philadelphia in 1844 and founded The American Psychiatric Association (APA). Two of the founding members were Benjamin Rush, the father of American psychiatry, and Isaac Ray, an authority on psychiatry and the law. The APA, Dr. Rush, and Dr. Ray called for changes in view of the advances of medical science.

Other early reform advocates included Mrs. E.P.W. Packard, who advocated reforming commitment procedures, and Dorothea Dix, who stressed the inadequate conditions of treatment facilities. Packard had been committed to a state hospital in Illinois on her husband's petition pursuant to a statute that allowed married women and infants to be admitted involuntarily upon the request of a husband or guardian without the presentation of evidence that the statutory standard had been met. Upon her release after three years' hospitalization, Packard began a campaign for new legislation that would prohibit a person from being confined solely on the basis of opinions expressed. Instead confinement would be based on erratic conduct that indicates that the individual is unable to function. She portrayed in her books and lectures the horror of being wrongfully placed in a mental institution. Largely because of her efforts, Illinois required that a jury determine whether a person should be committed to a mental institution.[10]

Dix, a Massachusetts schoolteacher who later became Superintendent of Nurses for the Union forces in the Civil War, was appalled at the lack of adequate facilities for the mentally disabled. She spent 50 years of her life crusading for improved hospital conditions. As a result of her efforts, 32 hospitals in the United States and abroad were founded, and at least 20 states responded to her appeals by establishing and enlarging mental hospitals.[11]

Fearing high welfare costs, the states prohibited voluntary admissions to public mental institutions until the end of the nineteenth century. This policy kept many people out of institutions. Then in 1881, Massachusetts enacted the first voluntary admission statute, limited to paying patients only. By the 1920s, some 28 states permitted voluntary admission.[12] Of course, almost all states do now.

MODERN TRENDS

From the mid-1800s until the 1960s, the criteria for commitment gradually broadened, with many statutes specifying that the need for treatment—a need that was to be determined by a psychiatrist or another physician—was sufficient to justify commitment. A 1951 Pennsylvania statute permitted the confinement of anyone who suffered from a mental disability that "lessened the capacity of the person to use his customary self-control, judgment and discretion in the conduct of his affairs and social relations." The Draft Act for the hospitalization of the mentally disabled, suggested as a model for states in 1952, provided for the involuntary admission of those who are "in need of care or treatment and lack sufficient capacity to evaluate such need responsibly."[13] This trend toward liberalization of standards for confinement continued until the late 1960s.

In 1958, Michael Hakeem questioned expansion of the use of psychiatry in the criminal process.[14] Morton Birnbaum proposed a constitutional right to treatment in 1960.[15] In *The Myth of Mental Illness*, one of two books published in 1961 important to the mental health field, Thomas Szasz questioned the existence of mental illness and argued that psychiatrists had become jailer-custodians of those who deviated from accepted moral and social values. Health values had replaced social values; social engineering had been disguised as mental health. He questioned psychiatric labels, pointed out the involuntary nature of voluntary admissions, and became a leading spokesman against involuntary admission. In the other important publication of that year, *Asylums*, Erving Goffman analyzed the environment of and the various roles played in mental hospitals. His analysis led to many sociological studies of mental institutions.[16]

In 1963, Congress enacted the Community Mental Health Centers Act, which initiated a program of federal financial support to induce states to provide local mental health services,[17] and, in the early 1960s, it amended the Medicare/Medicaid law to eliminate reimbursement for inpatient care for persons aged 21 through 65. These developments seeded substantial changes in the 1970s and 1980s.

Beginning in the early 1970s, mental health law began to undergo substantial changes due in part to reform efforts of public interest and legal aid lawyers filing lawsuits and engaging in legislative advocacy. These activities resulted in more restrictive involuntary admission procedures and standards, primarily reducing the number of admissions to state hospitals. Patients' rights have been expanded in most states.

In 1972, in *Lessard v. Schmidt*,[18] a Wisconsin federal court handed down a sweeping opinion requiring more stringent procedural protections for persons subjected to involuntary admissions. In 1975, the United States Supreme Court held in *O'Connor v. Donaldson*[19] that evidence of mental illness alone is not sufficient to admit a person involuntarily to a mental hospital. Rather, a showing of dangerousness or inability to care for oneself in the community is necessary.

In 1979, the court in *Parham v. J. R.*[20] ruled on the kind of inquiry for the involuntary admission of minors required by the United States Constitution. During the 1970s, most states revised their admission statutes.

Lower courts have held that patients in state institutions have constitutional rights to treatment and to refuse treatment, particularly medication. Conditions in state hospitals have been the targets of these lawsuits. In 1971, a federal district court in *Wyatt v. Stickney*[21] held that patients have a constitutional right to treatment.

By 1975 these cases began reaching the Supreme Court for review. In 1982, the high court remanded *Mills v. Rogers*[22] to an appeals court to decide whether patients have a constitutional right to refuse medication under Massachusetts law.

Litigation over the side effects of psychotropic drugs has increased. Former patients and some mental health professionals are attacking electroconvulsive therapy (ECT). In Berkeley, California, a referendum has made the administration of ECT a criminal offense.

Numerous judicial opinions have considered patients' rights. In 1982, the Supreme Court held in *Youngsboro v. Romeo*[23] that patients have a constitutional right to protection from unreasonable bodily restraints. In 1981, Congress enacted the Mental Health Systems, which includes a patient's Bill of Rights[24] that is advisory only to states. This Bill of Rights contains the sweeping changes that occurred during the previous decade. (See Appendix D.)

In the 1970s, the accuracy and validity of psychiatric and psychological opinions were questioned in a number of contexts. The prediction of dangerousness in involuntary admission proceedings has been challenged. The accuracy of psychiatric opinions on the sanity of defendants has been repeatedly attacked. Similarly, the accuracy of opinions on which the release of patients is based has been questioned. Finally, it has been argued that therapists have no duty to protect third parties from harm threatened by a patient because dangerousness cannot be predicted with accuracy, an argument rejected by courts that have ruled on the issue.

A tremendous flood of litigation continues, involving a host of mental health issues. While many mental health professionals find such extensive involvement of the law in the mental health system objectionable, this trend is not likely to change in the foreseeable future.

NOTES

1. For an excellent summary of mental health law from antiquity to the late 1960s, *see* S. Brakel and R. Rock, *The Mentally Disabled and the Law* (Chicago: University of Chicago Press, 1971) [hereinafter cited as Brakel and Rock], and Nicholas N. Kittrie, *The Right to be Different* (Baltimore: Johns Hopkins Press, 1971) [hereinafter cited as Kittrie], and primary sources collected therein.

2. Brakel and Rock, *supra* note 1, at 4.

3. *Id.*

4. *Id.* at 5, 6.

5. *Id.*

6. *Id.* at 6.

7. *Id.*

8. Matter of Josiah Oakes, 8 Law Rep. 123, 125 (Mass. 1845).

9. Brakel and Rock, *supra* note 1, at 7.

10. *Id.* at 7, 8.

11. *Id.* at 8.

12. Kittrie, *supra* note 1, at 70.

13. *Id.* at 67.

14. Michael Hakeem, "A Critique of the Psychiatric Approach to Crime and Corrections," 23 *Law and Contemporary Problems* 650 (1958).

15. Morton Birnbaum, "The Right to Treatment," 46 A.B.A.J. 499 (1960).

16. For a discussion of these developments, *see* Jonas Robitscher, *The Powers of Psychiatry* (Boston: Houghton Mifflin Co., 1980), Ch. 8.

17. 42 U.S.C. §§ 2681–87.

18. 349 F. Supp. 1078 (E.D. Wis. 1972).

19. 422 U.S. 563 (1975).

20. 442 U.S. 584 (1979).

21. 325 F. Supp. 781 (M.D. Ala. 1971).

22. 102 S. Ct. 2442 (1982).

23. 102 S. Ct. 2452 (1982).

24. 42 U.S.C. § 9501.

Chapter 2

Introduction to Mental Health Law

While the number of lawyers specializing in mental health law is very small in comparison to other law specialties, there has been a virtual explosion of activity in the field since the early 1970s. In 1973 the American Bar Association recognized the importance of mental health law by establishing the Commission on the Mentally Disabled to work for the reform of mental health laws. Most law schools now offer a course in this area.

WHAT IS MENTAL HEALTH LAW?

Mental health professionals perform a variety of functions. They diagnose, test, and treat clients in private practice, hospitals, outpatient clinics, and special education programs, among others. They give expert opinions in numerous legal proceedings on such topics as appointment of a guardian or whether an individual meets the standard for involuntary admission, is eligible for special education, is disabled within the meaning of the Social Security disability law, or meets the insanity or fitness-to-stand-trial standards in criminal actions. They also opine on malpractice and negligence actions.

No other health area is so dominated by law.

The Nature of Law

Law has been defined many ways. The essence, however, is that law is a system of principles and processes by which people who live in a society seek to solve or settle their disputes and problems without resort to the use of force. Law governs the relationships of private individuals and organizations both to other private individuals and to the government, the paramount authority of the society. Law that deals with the relationships between private parties is termed "private law," while "public law" describes law dealing with the relationships between private parties and government. With the increasing complexity of society and life in the United States has come a corresponding increase in the scope of public law. Regulating private persons and institutions for the purpose of dealing with the many problems within society has become pervasive.

One important segment of public law is state mental health codes, which govern the admission, treatment, other rights, and discharge of patients in both private and public mental health facilities. Another is state confidentiality acts, which control the flow of information concerning patients. Still another important segment of public law is criminal law, which proscribes conduct deemed injurious to the public order and provides for punishment of those found to have engaged in proscribed conduct.

Public law consists also of an enormous variety and amount of regulation designed to advance societal objectives by requiring private individuals and organizations to adopt specified courses of action in connection with their activities and undertakings. While much of such public law contains criminal provisions applicable to those individuals and organizations who do not abide by the regulations established, the aim of most public law is to secure what are deemed valid public goals.

The formulation of public policy with regard to mental health care has thrust mental health professionals into the arena of legislative debate about admission standards, duty to warn provisions, right to treatment, insanity defenses, and other important topics. The object of public law at both the federal and state level is to deal with societal problems of a broad nature.

Private law concerns the recognition and enforcement of rights and duties of private individuals and organizations. Legal actions between private parties are of two basic types: tort and contract. In a tort action one party asserts that wrongful conduct on the part of the other has caused harm, and compensation for harm suffered is sought. Examples are malpractice and negligence actions. In a contract action one party asserts that the other party has, in failing to fulfill an obligation, breached the contract, and either compensation or performance of the obligation is sought as remedy. One example is an action by a mental health professional whose clinical privileges have been reduced or terminated in violation of an implied contract between the professional and a hospital.

The first type of action that usually comes to mind when considering private law in a hospital setting is the patient's right to sue for injuries caused by the malpractice or negligence of hospital employees or members of a medical staff. It is much more than that, however; it includes not only the many possible applications of negligence law, but also the laws of confidentiality, consent, competency, property, privacy, contract, and other facets of the legal relationships between a mental health facility and all the patients, employees, and other individuals with whom it has contact.

In daily life the law serves as a guide to conduct, for most disputes or controversies are resolved without resort to either lawyers or the courts. The existence of the legal system is thus a stimulus to orderly private resolution of disputes and serves as a reinforcement of the compromises reached. The likelihood of success in court affects the willingness of parties to negotiate private settlements. Therefore, knowledge of the sources and application of law is important for those who may become involved in disputes or controversies.

Sources of Law

Law encompasses principles and rules derived from several sources: the United States Constitution and state constitutions, statutes enacted by Congress and state legislatures, regulations promulgated by administrative agencies to implement statutory law, and judicial opinions of state and federal courts.

The Constitution of the United States, as adopted at the Constitutional Convention of 1789 and ratified by the states, together with the duly ratified amendments to the Constitution, has the highest position in the hierarchy of enacted law. Article VI of the Constitution declares, "This Constitution, and the Laws of the United States which shall be made in pursuance thereof; and all Treaties made, or which shall be made, under the authority of the United States, shall be the supreme Law of the land. . . ." The clear import here is that the Constitution, federal law, and treaties take precedence over the constitutions and laws of the various states.

The United States Supreme Court is the final court of review of all appeals from federal courts of appeal and state supreme courts (in some states, the court of appeals is the highest court). Generally, federal courts interpret the U.S. Constitution and federal statutes and regulations. State courts interpret the U.S. Constitution and state constitutions, state statutes and regulations, and state common law.

Many of the legal principles and rules applied by the courts in the United States are the product of the common law first developed in England. The term "common law" is applied to the body of principles that evolves from court decisions resolving controversies and that is continually adapted and expanded. During the colonial period, English common law applied uniformly; however, after the Revolution each state provided for the adoption of part or all of the then-existing English common law. All subsequent common law in the United States has been developed on a state basis; thus, the common law on specific subjects may differ from state to state.

The rights offered to some parties by common law will sometimes prove inadequate. Because it is based on the accumulation of judicial precedent, the common law takes time to adapt and adjust to changing conditions and new techniques. This hiatus may leave some parties without adequate legal remedies under common law. Legislators, both federal and state, will occasionally act to override or supplement common law to provide adequate remedies. For example, state common law generally governs malpractice and negligence actions. Nevertheless, legislatures have supplemented common law by enacting statutes placing limitations on the time in which a party must file an action and, in some states, a limit on the amount of damages that can be recovered in a medical malpractice action.

With regard to the law applicable to specific controversies, courts usually adhere to the concept of *stare decisis*, which is frequently described as "following precedent." By referring to a similar case previously decided and applying to the same rules and principles, a court arrives at the same ruling in the current case. However, factual differences may provide a basis for recognizing distinctions between precedent and the current case. Additionally, a court may conclude, even when such differences are absent, that a particular common law is no longer in accord with the needs of society and may depart from precedent. One clear example of this departure from precedent was the reconsideration and elimination in nearly every state of the principle of charitable immunity, which had provided nonprofit hospitals with virtual freedom from liability for harm to patients resulting from wrongful conduct, including the negligent provision of health services.

Not all judicial decisions are given equal weight nor are the courts bound by decisions from other circuits or states. Decisions of the U.S. Supreme Court and the state supreme court must be followed by all appellate courts and trial courts within a state, but state courts are not bound by federal and state court decisions from outside the state. Within a state, a trial court is not bound by a decision of another trial court. Often, two appellate courts within a state will hand down conflicting decisions on a particular issue. Trial courts are free to follow either decision until the state supreme court resolves the conflict.

Similarly, federal district courts are bound by decisions of the U.S. Supreme Court and the circuit courts of appeal. If a conflict exists on an issue between circuits, the district court is bound by the decision of its circuit court of appeals until the U.S. Supreme Court resolves the issue.

Of course, lawyers are free to cite opinions from other courts. However, they cite the opinions for their persuasiveness and not because the court hearing a particular case is bound by the "foreign" decision. Such decisions are cited particularly where a case of first impression exists, that is, the issue has not been decided in that jurisdiction.

Whether of statutory or common law origin, the principles of substantive law are subject to change. Statutory law may be amended, repealed, or expanded by legislative action; common law principles may be modified, abrogated, or newly created by subsequent court decisions. Thus, the law affecting mental health professionals and hospitals—which includes the regulations and decisions of administrative agencies, in addition to statutory and common laws—is not static, but rather is in a continuing process of growth and modification.

Substantive and Procedural Law

Most of the law discussed in this book is substantive law, which is the collection of principles and rulings about the subject matter of actual issues. An example is the law of malpractice, which deals with whether a mental health professional has provided care that meets professional standards.

Note, however, that many court actions actually turn on procedural issues, such as rules of evidence and statutes of limitations. Far from being "mere technicalities," the laws of process and procedure are designed to assure fairness in settling substantive issues. They are important for obtaining a just and binding outcome in a lawsuit. The following are examples of procedural law.

Statute of Limitations. Whether a suit for malpractice or negligence can be brought against a mental health professional often depends upon whether the action is filed within a time specified by the applicable statute of limitations. This subject is covered in more detail in Chapter 3.

Charitable Immunity. The story of the rise and fall of the doctrine of charitable immunity is an interesting example of the relationship between court and social developments. A century ago a Massachusetts court applied the doctrine to protect hospitals and other charitable institutions from lawsuits that might diminish their assets. Loss of assets intended for charitable purposes was considered against public policy. The courts of many states and even some legislatures followed this precedent until relatively recently. Nearly every state has now abolished the doctrine, recognizing that charitable institutions, like other business organizations, have a social obligation to compensate persons for injuries caused by them. Additionally, as the courts have noted, liability insurance is now available to charitable institutions, thus eliminating the need for the doctrine of charitable immunity.

Governmental Immunity. Sovereign immunity had its beginning in the English common-law concept that the King could do no wrong and was thus not subject to suit for the alleged wrongs committed by himself and his subordinates. This ancient doctrine is the basis for today's governmental immunity. Therefore, in the absence of express consent to suit, federal and state governments are immune from liability arising out of the negligence of their officers, agents, and employees.

Governmental hospitals are granted immunity because they are engaged in carrying out a government function, the protection and promotion of the health and welfare of the citizenry. Governmental hospital immunity depends upon the immunity of the governmental unit establishing and operating it. Because of this dependent feature, the general rule regarding governmental hospitals is subject to many exceptions. These exceptions stem from federal, state, and local statutes that waive the immunity, as well as from judicial decisions that hold the doctrine inapplicable in certain situations. Federal hospitals, for example, are not totally immune from suit, as explained in the discussion of the Federal Tort Claims Act in Chapter 3.

Many states maintain the doctrine of governmental immunity as it applies to state and local facilities as a defense in actions arising against them for the negligence of officers, agents, and employees of state hospitals. In other states, legislative action or judicial decision has established liability within defined limits.

Counties, cities, and special authorities of the state enjoy immunity to a lesser extent. Where immunity applies it is an extension of the immunity of the state because counties and municipalities are creatures of the state. A distinction exists, however, between the governmental and proprietary (that is, nongovernmental) functions of county and municipal hospitals. If the operation of a county or municipal hospital is deemed a governmental function, immunity will usually attach. However, should the operation of the facility be deemed a proprietary function, no immunity will exist.

The rules applied to determine whether the operation of a state facility is governmental or proprietary are inconsistent, indicating a reluctance to grant total immunity. They are also difficult to apply. For example, some say governmental functions are those that are exercised for the good of the public as a whole, while proprietary functions are those in which the entity might compete with private institutions. Applying these standards to specific activities and institutions has resulted in some dubious distinctions. The courts make a further distinction based on whether the statute authorizing the creation of the hospital is mandatory or permissive. If the wording of the statute imposes a duty on the political subdivision, it is considered mandatory because the subdivision has no choice in deciding whether to operate a hospital; consequently, governmental immunity will follow. A permissive statute is one that merely authorizes the operation of a hospital, leaving the final decision with the subdivision. In some states, hospitals established under a permissive statute do not enjoy governmental immunity.

A determination that the operation of a hospital is not a governmental function and therefore not protected by governmental immunity will sometimes be made if the hospital admits patients who pay. Some courts consider that the admission of paying patients renders the operation of the hospital a proprietary function. Other courts have considered the operation of a governmental hospital as proprietary only with respect to the paying patients. This determination results in the withdrawal of governmental immunity in actions by paying patients only. Another position maintained by courts in several jurisdictions is that the question of payment for hospital care does not affect the applicability of governmental immunity because the test of a governmental function is whether the activity is for the common benefit of the public.

Frequently plaintiffs have urged courts not to permit the defense to interpose the doctrine of governmental immunity when the political subdivision or hospital carries liability insurance. While most jurisdictions will not let the presence of insurance affect immunity, some states, by court decision or by statute, allow recovery to the limit of the insurance coverage. The statutes provide that if a state or political subdivision has purchased liability insurance, the defense of governmental immunity can be raised neither by the insured nor the insurer in a suit for personal injuries. Also the cloak of immunity does not extend to the negligent employee's liability as an individual, unless the legislation specifically so provides.

Many states have intensely reexamined the public policy basis upon which governmental immunity rests. A departure from the doctrine of charitable immunity has often presaged a restriction of governmental immunity. The expansion of governmental activities into fields formerly left to private individuals and organizations may also speed the end of governmental immunity. Many courts are unwilling, however, to assume the initiative in abrogating the doctrine; they prefer to leave this matter of potentially great financial consequences to legislative action. Legislatures may delineate the areas in which government is to accept responsibility for the various actions of its employees and may spell out monetary limitations and notice requirements. Where a legislature has already acted toward a partial abrogation of the doctrine of governmental immunity, the courts are reluctant to overthrow the doctrine totally.

Physician-Patient Privilege. Strictly speaking, the familiar rule known as the physician-patient privilege is a courtroom rule of evidence rather than a general principle of confidentiality. Indeed, it does not even exist in some states and is inapplicable to many situations (such as child abuse and criminal cases) in most other states. By definition, the privilege is a statutory right of patients to object to their physicians' testifying in legal proceedings about matters related to their medical treatment. While the reason for the privilege is to promote personal trust between patients and doctors, the matters covered by the privilege have been extended to medical and hospital records, including entire entries made by nurses and others associated with the patient. Whether to divulge the information found in a patient's record is the right of the patient, not the privilege of the physician or hospital.

Applications of this privilege vary. For example, the very act of suing a mental health professional or a hospital for negligent treatment may constitute a waiver of the right. Also, in most states the presiding judge can suspend the privilege when the testimony would be in the public interest, such as a case involving the illegal use of drugs. The effect of the privilege rule on medical records is discussed in greater detail in a later chapter.

Hearsay. Another familiar rule that affects the introduction of evidence is the hearsay rule. This rule is intended to promote accuracy and validity in courtroom testimony by limiting the use of statements and other declarations made outside the courtroom. Many exceptions of this rule have been devised as necessary to the rational and orderly conduct of legal proceedings. One such exception is for business records. Any regular records made at or near the time of a transaction in the ordinary course of business are generally considered admissible as evidence, if they are relevant and material to the legal proceeding. Thus, hospital records are generally not excluded by the hearsay rule, if they are prepared in a customary manner.

Standards of Proof. The standard of proof required in a legal action depends on the type of proceeding. In a malpractice or negligence action against a mental health professional, the patient must prove the case by a "preponderance of the evidence," which the courts have defined as evidence that is of greater weight or more convincing than the evidence that is offered in opposition to it. Another way of defining it is that it is evidence which as a whole shows that the fact sought to be proved is more probable than not.

In an involuntary admission proceeding the U.S. Supreme Court has held that the state must prove that an individual meets the state statutory standard for admission by "clear and convincing evidence"—a standard higher than "preponderance of the evidence." "Clear and convincing evidence" is defined as proof beyond a reasonable, well-founded doubt. It must produce in the judge or jury a firm belief or conviction as to the allegations sought to be established.

In a criminal proceeding, the state must prove "beyond a reasonable doubt" that the defendant committed the alleged crime. To meet the standard of "beyond a reasonable doubt," the judge or jury must be fully satisfied, entirely convinced, or satisfied to a moral certainty concerning the facts supporting the allegation.

Finally, in a proceeding to review an administrative decision, the state must show that substantial evidence, that is, evidence that has been defined as that which a reasonable mind might accept as adequate to support a conclusion, supports the decision.

Reference Material

In the other chapters of this book are many citations and references to judicial opinions and statutes. The citation to a court opinion contains the names of the parties to the action, the volume of the law reporter in which the opinion can be found, the name of the reporter, the page number at which the case can be found, and the year in which the opinion came down. Take, for example, *O'Connor v. Donaldson*, 422 U.S. 563 (1975). O'Connor and Donaldson are the names of the parties; 422 is the volume number; U.S. is an abbreviation for *United States Reporter*; 563 is the page number of the decision; and 1975 is the year in which the decision was made.

Statute citations contain the chapter number, identification of the statute as federal or state, the section number, and the year of the set of statutes cited (not the year of passage). For example, the federal Civil Rights Act is cited 42 U.S.C. § 1983 (1980). The first number, 42, is the chapter number; U.S.C. is the abbreviation for United States Code; § 1983 is the section number; and 1980 is the year of the set of statutes cited. An example of a state statute is: Mass. General Laws Ann., ch. 123, § 23 (West Supp. 1982). The statute is identified, followed by the chapter, section, and year of supplement.[1]

PROCEDURAL OUTLINE OF A LEGAL ACTION

The purpose of the rules of procedure and evidence is to ensure that a judge or jury hears all the relevant facts on both sides of a dispute. The judge runs the trial, deciding whether an expert witness is qualified to testify, whether a document is admissible, what questions may be asked witnesses, and what instructions should be given jurors. Before a dispute goes to trial, both sides engage in preparation of facts called "discovery." What follows is an outline of a legal action.

Complaint

The first step in the process is to file a complaint that sets out general allegations of the facts that support the elements of a cause of action, for example, facts that support a claim that a therapist-patient relationship existed and that the treatment by the defendant-therapist fell below the required standard of care; the below-standard care was the proximate cause of injury to the plaintiff-patient. A demand for a money judgment is included. A summons is prepared and served on the defendant, along with a copy of the complaint. As discussed in Chapter 3, a notice must be sent to federal officials if the action is against a Veterans' Administration or military facility and may have to be sent to state officials if the action is against a state government entity. The complaint must be filed within the time provided in the statute of limitations.

Motions

Motions are requests to the court for various forms of relief, such as clarification of the complaint. The defendant may file a motion to dismiss the complaint; that is, assuming for the purpose of the motion that all the allegations are true, such claim is not recognized by law.

Answer

If the defendant does not file a motion to dismiss or if such a motion is denied, then the defendant must file an answer. An answer is a written response to each specific allegation made by the plaintiff in the complaint. The answer may also include affirmative defenses, such as failure of the plaintiff to file the complaint within the time allowed by the statute of limitations, failure to give notice to a federal or state agency under the Federal Tort Claims Act or a state statute requiring notice, and contributory or comparative negligence.

Reply

Some states allow a plaintiff to file a reply to the affirmative defenses of the defendant. Others do not, simply assuming that the plaintiff denies such defenses.

Discovery

While both sides will have informally investigated the subject matter of the action prior to filing, discovery refers to a formal investigation under the rules of civil practice. Through discovery each side pins down the other's story of what happened. Discovery takes several forms.

Written Interrogatories. Each party may require the opposing party to answer written questions relevant to the action in writing and under oath. The basic facts are obtained.

Oral Depositions. Both the plaintiff's and the defendant's attorneys may require the other party and nonparty witnesses to answer questions orally under oath. A court reporter makes a verbatim transcript of the questions and answers. Generally, crucial facts are obtained through depositions, where the person answering the question does not have the time to think about an answer as with interrogatories.

Production of Documents. One party may serve notice for the production of relevant documents and objects for inspection on the other party. Generally, copies of all relevant documents are provided.

Physical and Mental Examinations. Where the action involves a dispute as to the physical or mental condition of a party, such as the extent of an injury, the court can order the plaintiff to submit to a mental or physical examination.

Request for Admission of Facts. A party may request the admission of relevant facts, including the genuineness of documents. If the party served with the request fails to respond, the facts are taken as true. If the party served denies the facts and the serving party proves they are true, the party served must bear the expenses for proof of the matter in question.

Pretrial Conference

Some jurisdictions require a pretrial conference. The judge, the attorneys, and, sometimes, the parties attend. Settlement possibilities are discussed. If settlement is not possible, methods of simplifying the trial, such as stipulation to facts, are discussed.

Trial

The following is a sketch of the major stages of a civil jury trial:

Selection of Jury. Twelve impartial jurors, sometimes fewer, are selected by the process called *voir dire* ("to tell the truth"). By questioning prospective jurors, attorneys for each party seek jurors who they think they can convince of their view of the dispute. Generally, panels of 12 prospective jurors are questioned. A prospective juror may be challenged for cause or by peremptory challenge. A challenge for cause may be exercised where the answers to questions indicate that a juror is incapable of reaching a fair decision. Peremptory challenges may be exercised for any reason. The number of peremptory challenges is limited.

Opening Statements. Counsel for both sides make opening statements in which they summarize what each expects to prove by the evidence. The statements are an overview of each party's side of the dispute.

Testimony of Witnesses and Introduction of Other Evidence. The plaintiff's witnesses always appear first because the plaintiff has the burden of proving the case. The plaintiff's attorney conducts direct examination, followed by cross-examination by counsel for the defendant. This may be followed by redirect and recross-examination to clarify the facts. Tangible evidence such as medical records, EKG reports, or equipment (for example, electroconvulsive equipment) may be introduced into evidence. The judge rules upon objections to questions, qualifications of expert witnesses, and introduction of tangible evidence. When the plaintiff has completed offering evidence, the defendant introduces evidence. A transcript is made of the proceeding.

Motion for Directed Verdict by Defendant. The defendant may move for a directed verdict at the end of the plaintiff's case. The motion will be granted only if there is no factual dispute to be resolved. In other words, the undisputed facts proved by the plaintiff do not make out a case of liability under law. If the motion is denied, the defense will commence its case.

Rebuttal Evidence by the Plaintiff. After the defendant's case has ended, the plaintiff may introduce evidence to rebut matters introduced by the defendant.

Renewal of Motion for Directed Verdict. After all the evidence has been introduced by both sides, the defendant may renew this motion for a directed verdict. The judge may rule or delay the ruling until after the verdict of the jury. A verdict for the defendant renders the motion moot.

Closing Argument. Each side argues its case, stressing its strengths and the other side's weaknesses. Counsel for the plaintiff goes first. After counsel for the defendant makes a closing argument, counsel for the plaintiff may respond.

Jury Instructions. The judge instructs the jury as to the applicable law to be applied to the case. The instructions involve the elements that the plaintiff must prove. The judge also explains the computation of damages in the event the verdict is for the plaintiff. Instructions include directions for a verdict for the defendant if the elements of an affirmative defense are proved.

Jury Decision. The jury usually returns a verdict for one of the parties. If it cannot decide, it is a hung jury. In some jurisdictions, the verdict must be unanimous, while in others only a majority vote is required.

Post-Trial Motions. After the verdict, the losing side may move for a verdict notwithstanding the jury verdict. The judge will grant this only if the jury verdict was legally unjustified. The losing side may move for a new trial on grounds that there were errors in rulings on objections to evidence at trial. If post-trial motions are denied, the losing side must consider an appeal to a higher court to have the case reviewed.

NOTE

1. For more information on citations, *see A Uniform System of Citation* (13th ed.) (Cambridge, Mass.: The Harvard Law Review Association, 1981). For the best source of current information on mental health law, *see Mental Health Disability Reporter*, published bimonthly by the American Bar Association's Commission on the Mentally Disabled.

Part II

Concepts of Liability

Chapter 3

Bases of Liability

Public policy requires that mental health practitioners have a duty[1] to be able and careful, and to use their best judgment in the care and treatment of patients. This policy is rooted in the state's responsibility to protect the welfare and safety of its citizens. Violation of this duty exposes the practitioner to liability for malpractice, a specialized form of negligence.

Hospitals have a duty to ensure that reasonable care is provided to patients. This includes ensuring that employees, both professionals and nonprofessionals, are competent. It also includes a responsibility to ensure that patients are protected and that facilities and equipment are safe. Violation of these duties can leave a hospital liable for negligence.

Practitioners, hospitals, and clinics must observe the statutory and constitutional rights of patients. Violation of this duty subjects the culpable party to monetary damages and restraining orders in state court, or, if a hospital or clinic is public, to damages, restraining orders, and attorney's fees in federal court under the Civil Rights Act. In some situations, an individual practitioner acting for the state may be sued under the Civil Rights Act.

Practitioners also may be subject to suspension or even license revocation by state agencies and loss of membership in professional associations.

Boards of directors and hospital medical staffs should provide for effective credentialing committees, peer review committees, and quality assurance/risk management programs to ensure appropriate care to patients. Practitioners should carry an adequate level of insurance for protection against liability. Most hospitals require it.

MALPRACTICE AND NEGLIGENCE

Practitioners

Mental health practitioners—psychiatrists, psychologists, psychiatric nurses, and social workers—have a duty to provide appropriate care based on the stand-

23

ards of their professions and the standards set by law. A breach of this duty to a patient by a practitioner that is the proximate cause of injury to the patient is characterized as "malpractice."

In the absence of any state statutes, common law is the basis of liability for injuries to patients caused by acts of malpractice and negligence of individual practitioners.[2] Common law is the body of principles and rules of action relating to the government and security of persons and property that derives its authority from judicial judgments and decrees.[3] In other words, common law is law based upon legal precedent rather than any express action of the legislature.

Negligence has been characterized as the failure "to do something which a reasonable man, guided by those ordinary considerations which ordinarily regulate human affairs, would do, or doing something which a prudent and reasonable man would not do."[4] Any person may be negligent. In contrast, malpractice is a specialized form of negligence applicable only to professionals.[5] Malpractice has been defined as:

> [T]he failure of one rendering professional services to exercise that degree of skill and learning commonly applied under all the circumstances in the community by the average prudent reputable member of the profession with the result of injury, loss, or damage to the recipient of those services or to those entitled to rely upon them.[6]

Psychiatrists, psychologists, psychiatric nurses (in some jurisdictions), social workers, and other therapists licensed or sanctioned by the state are held to professional standards and subject to malpractice actions.[7] Nonprofessional therapists, such as lay leaders of encounter groups, family counselors unlicensed and unsanctioned by the state,[8] nurses performing acts administrative or ministerial in nature,[9] practical nurses, student nurses, nurse's aides, and technicians[10] are subject to negligence actions.

Courts often use the terms "malpractice" and "negligence" interchangeably. Where the action is characterized as malpractice, the breach of the duty will be framed in terms of deviation from a professional standard. When the term negligence is used, the violation of the duty will be framed in terms of what a reasonably prudent psychiatrist (psychologist, psychiatric nurse) would have done in the same or similar circumstances. Therefore, whether the conduct complained of by the patient is called malpractice or negligence generally will make no difference.[11] Deviation from a professional standard or failure to act as a reasonably prudent mental health professional alone will not result in liability. There must be a deviation or failure to act that is the proximate cause of injury to the patient.

Standards of Care

Mental health professionals—psychiatrists, psychologists, and psychiatric nurses and social workers—have a duty to possess, and, using their best judgment, apply with reasonable care, the degree of skill and learning ordinarily possessed and used by members of their profession in good standing engaged in the same type of practice in the community in which they practice or in a similar community.[12]

Specialists, such as psychiatrists and psychiatric nurses, are bound to higher standards of care in their fields of expertise than nonspecialists, general physicians, and general nurses, because they are regarded as having a higher degree of skill and knowledge.[13]

What constitutes reasonable care? Historically, this standard of care encompassed a "community measurement," comparing the physician's care and skill with that of other physicians in his or her immediate area.[14] The duty of care has developed to include "the degree of care which a professional of ordinary prudence and skill, practicing in the same or similar community, would have exercised in the same or similar circumstances."[15] The basis for the locality rule is a recognition of varying levels of competence relating to education and experience.[16] In jurisdictions where courts have retained the historical locality rule, it is justified on the basis that a physician practicing in a large metropolitan area has greater access to seminars, lectures, and other continuing education programs than would a doctor practicing in a rural area.[17]

Nevertheless, the trend is toward a more broadly based standard. For example, the Supreme Court of Utah has held that physicians who profess to be experts should be held to the same standard of care exercised by experts in the same field in cities of comparable size, and concluded that the testimony of an expert from Los Angeles should have been allowed in Salt Lake City.[18] In Stamford, Connecticut, the locale or pertinent area for purposes of determining the standard of care is at least the entire state of Connecticut.[19] This trend toward a broader base is the result of modern communications and other information dissemination techniques that tend to minimize the difference in education.

Psychiatrists in public institutions are not necessarily held to the same professional standard as those in private institutions in the same or similar geographic communities. In a class-action lawsuit alleging medical malpractice by the staff of a state institution for the mentally ill, a federal court in Massachusetts held that allowance would be made for the type of institution in which the physicians practiced when determining the degree of skill expected of the average qualified practitioner. Factors considered were medical resources available, whether the physician was a general practitioner or a specialist, and the fact that the institution had a difficult time attracting qualified physicians due to a low salary structure and an outdated physical plant.[20] This court seemed to say that public institution practitioners will be held to a lower standard because those institutions cannot attract practitioners as qualified as those in private institutions.

The standard to which mental health professionals must adhere is not the average among all known practitioners from the best to the worst and from the most to the least experienced, but rather the reasonable average merit among ordinarily good practitioners. A California court stated that the standard of care to be exercised by a physician or surgeon is not determined by aggregating "into a common class the quacks, the young men [and women] who have no practice, the old ones who have dropped out of practice, the good and the very best, and then strike an average between them. This method would evidently place the standard too low."[21] Yet the utmost degree of care and skill attainable or known to the profession is not required. Nor are professionals required to exercise their best skill and ability at all times for no one can always be at his or her best.[22]

The professional standard of care to be exercised when conducting psychotherapy is difficult to establish with certainty considering the numerous modes of treatment. More than 200 varieties of psychotherapy exist.[23] The standard of care may be that held by a respected minority of specialists in the profession.[24] This is called the doctrine of respected minorities. That is, a practitioner is entitled to be judged according to the standards of his or her school of therapy. There are limits, however, to this "school rule." This school must be a recognized school of good standing, which has established rules and principles of practice for the guidance of all its members, with regard to the diagnosis and treatment that each member should observe in any given case.[25] The limits on this doctrine may be significant in malpractice actions involving nontraditional psychotherapy.

In addition to professional standards, mental health practitioners must also meet numerous legal standards found in mental health and confidentiality statutes and judicial opinions. For example, many states have statutes that set standards and procedures for the use of restraints and seclusion.

Establishing the Therapist-Patient Relationship

The first element to be established in a malpractice or negligence action is the therapist-patient relationship created by an express or implied agreement.[26] While a therapist is under no obligation to practice, when professional services of a therapist are accepted by another person for the purpose of treatment, a therapist-patient relationship is created. This relationship is consensual: patients willingly seek the assistance of a therapist and the therapist knowingly accepts them as patients. Whether or not this relationship exists is a question of fact. One considers whether the patient placed himself or herself in the care of the therapist and whether the therapist accepted the case. When the patient accepts the treatment provided by the therapist, there is a *prima facie* presumption that a therapist-patient relationship is created.[27]

A therapist-patient relationship may be created even though services are performed without fee and at the request of a third party. A student and his parents sought to recover in a malpractice action from a psychiatrist retained by a school district to determine whether the student was emotionally handicapped. The student alleged that the psychiatrist had disclosed information acquired in attending the patient in a professional capacity. The court recognized that the physician-patient relationship does not require payment of a fee nor that the psychiatrist be retained by the patient himself. Nevertheless, the court held that no therapist-patient relationship was created, stating that had the parents sincerely believed that the relationship existed they would have asserted their claim of privilege before the hearing officer. Their failure to do so indicated a recognition that no therapist-patient relationship was created, the court ruled.[28]

A physician-patient relationship was created where an "on call" physician at a hospital emergency room refused to treat a particular patient. The court held that the physician by assenting to the bylaws, rules, and regulations of the hospital to act as the "on call" emergency room doctor was obligated by contract to treat a patient who was suffering from acute hyperglycemia.[29]

A court held that the issue of whether a physician-patient relationship was created should be heard when the physician, on inactive courtesy staff, had allowed his name to be used to admit a patient for emergency treatment by the general staff doctors. He did not treat the patient, but allowed the patient to be admitted in his name because the patient could not procure medical care or hospitalization.[30]

Generally, when a therapist is conducting an examination, but not providing treatment, no therapist-patient relationship is created. Examples of such a situation would be when a physician or therapist conducts an examination of a claimant for workers' compensation,[31] insurance,[32] or employment.[33] However, if the therapist treats the patient, a therapist-patient relationship may be created. A physician who was employed to administer annual x-ray checkups to employees advised an employee concerning a lung infection, referred the employee to a consultant, and then, after the consultation, provided further advice. The court held that a physician-patient relationship had been created, stating that one who assumes to act, even though gratuitously, must act carefully.[34]

In general, no therapist-patient relationship is created for purposes of a malpractice action when a therapist conducts an evaluation of the mental status of a person on behalf of the state.[35] The therapist is not held to the same degree of care that would be owed a patient and is only liable for acts performed in bad faith. However, the Texas Supreme Court recently held that a cause of action for "misdiagnosis-medical malpractice" could be maintained by a respondent in a civil commitment proceeding against three psychiatrists who certified in reports that she was mentally ill and dangerous.[36] The plaintiff-respondent obtained a writ of *habeas corpus* releasing her and the malpractice action was filed. The Court of Appeals affirmed the lower court's dismissal stating that the reports were privileged. In reversing, the Texas Supreme Court agreed that the reports could not serve as a basis for a defamation action, no matter how negligently made. Nevertheless, the court said that a cause of action for malpractice was stated, reasoning that a Texas statute protected "all persons acting in good faith, reasonably and without negligence" from civil or criminal liability in examination and certification of persons held under the mental health statute. The court analyzed the elements of a negligence action without discussion of whether a therapist-patient relationship was created. The court overruled a recent Texas case granting blanket immunity to a psychiatrist testifying in mental health proceedings.[37]

When a psychologist advised a woman not to permit her ex-husband to visit their 2½-year-old son after the wife expressed concern over possible sexual molestation, the court dismissed a malpractice action because no therapist-patient relationship existed. The psychologist did not examine the husband, had never seen him, and the diagnosis reached was for the child not the husband.[38]

Establishing the Standard of Care

The second element that a plaintiff must establish in a malpractice action is the standard of care by which the judge or jury will measure the acts complained of. Generally, the standard is established by the expert testimony of psychiatrists, psychologists, and nurses.[39] Exceptions to the expert witness rule have been made in cases where the lack of skill or care is grossly apparent or the treatment is so common as to be within the comprehension of the lay person and requires only common knowledge and experience to understand and judge.[40] For example, where there is no consent, no expert is generally needed, the argument being that a patient who had been informed would not have consented.[41] In a rare case, a patient in New York sued her psychiatrist for using beatings in a continuing course of treatment by psychotherapy. The court ruled that no expert testimony was necessary to establish that the standard of care with respect to psychotherapy does not include beatings.[42]

The practitioner who testifies as an expert generally must be of the same school of therapy as the defendant practitioner, but a practitioner from one school may testify concerning the standard of another when the schools have similar techniques and modes of therapy for a particular ailment.[43]

The expert witness must be familiar with the standard of care and treatment in local hospitals or in similar hospitals in similar communities, whichever is required by state law. In a Connecticut case, the psychiatrists who appeared testified that they were familiar with the standard of psychiatric care practiced at general hospitals in that state at the time the incident occurred.[44] One registered nurse who testified in the same case said that she was familiar with the "Yale Model" at the time the incident occurred. Previous testimony had indicated that the hospital relied on the "Yale Model" for its standard of care for nurses. Two other nurses testified that they "had personal knowledge of the care, skill and diligence ordinarily possessed and exercised by registered nurses, licensed practical nurses, and psychiatric nurses in psychiatric units of general hospitals in the State of Connecticut" at the time of the incident.[45]

Additional evidence of standards are specific state statutes or regulations that contain objective standards mental health professionals must follow. The bylaws, regulations, rules, or policies of a hospital set out objective standards for psychiatrists (and sometimes psychologists) who hold privileges, and for psychiatric nurses and other employees.[46] Ethical statements of professional associations and the Joint Commission on Accreditation of Hospitals (JCAH) have promulgated standards for psychiatric programs.[47] Generally, an expert witness would testify making reference to these standards.

Treatises and other professional literature may be introduced into evidence in some states to establish the standard.[48] Traditionally, such literature was used only to discredit or support expert testimony, but several jurisdictions, including the federal courts, have now abolished this traditional limitation and admit learned treatises to prove the truth of the statements contained within them.[49] However, the states are inconsistent on this point. In Illinois, for example, scientific works generally cannot be used as direct evidence, but they may be used to cross-examine an expert witness.[50]

Deviation from the Standard

After establishing a therapist-patient relationship and the standard of care required, a patient must prove that the practitioner deviated from that standard. Generally, expert testimony must establish a deviation from the standard, but there are exceptions. As an Illinois court said: "[E]xpert testimony is not required if the . . . [deviation] is so grossly apparent or the treatment is of such a common occurrence that a layman would have no difficulty in appraising it."[51] For example, an expert witness is not necessary to establish that not obtaining written consent from a patient for the administration of ECT is a deviation from the standard. However, an expert witness may be needed to establish that a deviation occurred if the consent was not *informed*.

An unsuccessful result does not mean that the care and treatment provided fell below the required standard; a practitioner may do everything expected of a competent specialist and not achieve success.[52] Nor is a bona fide error of judgment a deviation from the standard. Practitioners must base their professional decisions on skill and careful study of the case, but when the decision requires the exercise of judgment, the law requires only that the judgment be bona fide. Practitioners need not guarantee that their judgment is correct.[53] They need only exercise the reasonable degree of skill and diligence ordinarily exercised by specialists in the profession.

Psychiatry (or clinical psychology) is not an exact science. Rather, it is a profession that calls for the exercise of individual judgment within a framework of established procedures, and differences of opinion are consistent with exercise of due care.[54] Hence, the testimony of another mental health professional that he or she would have acted differently does not establish a deviation from a standard.

The facts underlying a deviation from a standard may be difficult to establish. An individual patient who makes claims of abuse or incompetence, but who is characterized as mentally ill, may not be believed. One patient succeeded in establishing that her therapist had engaged in sexual relations with her only after several other women came forward and testified that the therapist had had sexual relations with them during the same period of time.[55] It is rare for such witnesses to come forward voluntarily. Such information would not be available in pretrial discovery because of the right of confidentiality.[56]

Proximate Cause of Injury

Proof of a practitioner's deviation from the standard or failure to act as a reasonably prudent mental health professional does not automatically entitle the patient to damages from the practitioner or hospital. The patient must also prove that the wrongful act was a proximate cause of the injury. In other words, proof of a causal connection between the deviation and the patient's injuries must exist, and the injury must have been foreseeable as a consequence of the act of malpractice or negligence. Proximate cause need not be established with certainty, but while probability is sufficient, possibility is not.[57] When an alleged injury may have been due to one of several causes, the patient must show that the deviation from the standard caused the injury.

In the context of diagnosis and treatment of mental illness, the cause of injury is not always easy to establish. For example, in an Oklahoma case a psychiatrist prescribed tranquilizers and antidepressants for a patient with a schizophrenic condition, even though the psychiatrist knew that a general practitioner was prescribing antihistamines and Carbrital at the same time. The general practitioner did not prescribe a Carbrital refill, but a pharmacist provided it anyway. The patient committed suicide by consuming pills from the Carbrital refill. Both physicians and the pharmacist were sued. The court held that the physicians did not cause the patient's death because they did not prescribe the particular pills he ingested to commit suicide.[58] In other words, there was an intervening cause.

In addition, the court said that a reasonably skillful psychiatrist would not have regarded the patient as a suicidal risk who should not have been allowed to possess large quantities of sleeping pills. Therefore, he had no duty to contact the physician and direct him to limit the number of sleeping pills prescribed. The patient had threatened suicide only once, nine years previously. There was no deviation from the standard of care. The pharmacist was found not liable because the purpose of the statute violated (filling a nonrefillable prescription) was not to protect a patient from suicide. The pharmacist had no knowledge that the patient intended to kill himself. Suicide is "not a result naturally and reasonably" to be expected, solely from the sale of medication.

A court reached a different conclusion in a case where a physician had prescribed an "extreme" amount of Valium to a patient without an adequate history and without checking clinical records. The patient took the medication, drank alcohol, and caused a head-on automobile collision. The court held that the negligence was the proximate cause of the accident.

> The proximate cause rule in Alabama is that a person is responsible for all the reasonably foreseeable consequences of his negligent act. . . . Obviously, a foreseeable consequence of prescribing Valium to a serviceman without checking to see if he has a history of psychiatric problems is that the serviceman will in fact have psychiatric problems. It is also foreseeable that a serviceman suffering from depression will drink. And finally, it is foreseeable that a person with mental problems, who has ingested Valium and alcohol, will cause injury to others. Thus, [the physician's] . . . negligence in prescribing the Valium must be considered a proximate cause of the plaintiffs' . . . injuries.[59]

A patient who is in no worse a position after a deviation than before the deviation occurred has suffered no legally recognizable harm. For example, in a New Jersey case[60] a physician breached the duty of reasonable care he owed to the patient. The physician certified the patient as insane in support of an application for an order of commitment. He did not, however, personally examine the patient within the time required by the state commitment statute. Nevertheless, he was not liable for damages, the court having reasoned that there was no injury because the evidence was clear that the patient needed the hospitalization and treatment she received. In other words, the patient was in no worse a position as a result of the doctor's breach of duty; she would have been committed even if the doctor had exercised reasonable care.

Damages

A mental health professional is liable only for those damages that are the approximate result of his or her deviation from the standard. The measure of damages is the reasonable compensation for the mental and/or physical suffering and for any permanent disability resulting in the patient's inability to work. A husband may recover damages for the loss of the services of his wife. Some recent cases also allow a wife to recover for the loss of services of her husband.

Punitive damages may be recovered for a willful and wanton act, that is, one that intentionally causes injury or one committed under circumstances exhibiting a reckless disregard for the safety of others.[61] Some states use "conscious disregard" as the standard. A Florida court held that the behavior of a psychiatrist did not raise the presumption of conscious indifference to the consequences of ECT treatment so as to permit punitive damages for the dislocation and fracturing of the patient's shoulder. The court reached this conclusion even though the psychiatrist failed to warn the patient of the danger of shoulder fracture during administration of the treatment. The psychiatrist did not administer a muscle relaxant, minimized the importance of the patient's complaint of extreme pain in the shoulder following one treatment, and convinced the patient to proceed with another treatment on the following day.[62]

In a Pennsylvania case a patient recovered damages from a psychiatrist for negligent treatment, "principally by engaging in a sexual relationship with her in the course of therapy and by improperly administering drugs."[63] The jury awarded the patient $275,000 in compensatory damages, $90,000 for future psychiatric care, and $300,000 in punitive damages. In a motion to set aside the verdict, the psychiatrist argued that the record did not support the award for future psychiatric treatment. The court reduced the verdict by $90,000 because the patient failed to demonstrate the probability that she would undergo treatment in the future.[64]

Hospitals

Hospitals have a corporate duty to ensure that patients receive reasonable care. Generally, a hospital is not responsible for the acts of malpractice or negligence of members of the medical staff who are not employees or agents of the hospital. A trend exists toward one exception to this general rule. Fourteen states have held that a hospital has "a direct and independent responsibility to its patients of insuring the competency of its medical staff and the quality of medical care through the prudent selection, review and continuing evaluation of the physicians granted staff privileges."[65] Presumably, a hospital has a similar responsibility for psychologists appointed to the medical staff, although there are no judicial opinions on this issue. A hospital is, of course, responsible for its employees and agents, professional and nonprofessional. A breach of these duties that proximately causes injury to a patient is negligence.

Standards of Care

The standard of reasonable care for hospitals is that level of care provided by other hospitals with psychiatric programs in the same community or in similar communities. Other sources of standards include state mental health and confidentiality codes, bylaws, rules, regulations and policies of the hospital, and standards of the JCAH.[66]

A hospital's standard of care manifests itself in numerous ways. For example, the building itself must be suitable for the care of the types of patients in residence.[67] Seclusion rooms must be properly designed and furnished.[68]

The hospital must also exercise reasonable care in the provision, selection, and maintenance of equipment, and must see that it is fit for its intended use. Reasonable care requires the hospital to provide the usual and customary equipment, not the newest or the best.[69]

Hospitals providing mental health care have certain additional duties. They must protect patients from foreseeable harm both from themselves and from other patients. Both the hospital and its staff must exercise due care to assure patient safety in light of what is or ought to be known about the patients. If a psychiatric hospital neglects to take proper measures either to act on knowledge or to obtain knowledge, the hospital may be liable for resulting patient injuries.[70] In addition, a hospital may be liable to third parties for the negligent release of a dangerous patient if the patient subsequently harms someone.

While hospitals traditionally have been protected from liability by charitable or governmental immunity, it has long been recognized that they are vicariously responsible for acts of malpractice or negligence committed by their employees acting within the scope of their employment. This is characterized as the doctrine of *respondeat superior*, which means "Let the Master Answer."[71]

If a master-servant relationship exists between a hospital and its nurses, that is, if the nurses are employees of the hospital and the hospital exercises control and supervision over their acts under the concept of *respondeat superior*, the hospital is liable to patients for its nurses' acts of negligence or malpractice.[72] In determining whether a nurse is an employee over whom the hospital has supervision and control, many states in the past first determined whether the nurse's injury-causing act was administrative or clerical, as opposed to medical. Under this approach, the hospital would be held liable for administrative or clerical acts, but not for a medical act. A nurse performing an act considered medical was treated as an independent contractor and therefore not an agent of the hospital. "The doctrine of *respondeat superior* is not applicable to nurses engaged in professional tasks in the treatment of patients in a hospital."[73] Now courts in most states determine whether the hospital is responsible on the basis of simple agency rules: Was the nurse acting as an agent of the hospital when an act of negligence or malpractice was committed? If so, the hospital is liable to the patient for injuries caused by the acts of the nurse.[74]

This does not mean that the employee is absolved of liability for the wrongful act. The injured party may sue the employee directly, and the employer may seek indemnification from such employee, that is, recover for the financial loss to the employer resulting from liability for the employee's wrongful act. Because the employee is primarily responsible for the loss, the law does not relieve the employee's liability when the hospital is held liable through the application of *respondeat superior*.

Administrators and supervisory personnel generally are not liable for staff members' negligence or malpractice. No employer-employee or master-servant relationship exists; therefore, *respondeat superior* does not apply.[75] Nevertheless, where a supervisor has knowledge or should have knowledge of wrongful acts and takes no corrective steps, liability may be imposed. In other words, a supervisor is liable for negligence in failing to carry out supervisory duties.

Hospitals traditionally were viewed as mere physical structures where physicians worked, and thus could not be held liable for malpractice because they did not practice medicine.[76] Hospitals were merely concerned with administrative matters, while medical care was the exclusive concern of the medical staff. This view is changing. A California court summarized the situation:

> [T]he concept that a hospital does not undertake to treat patients, does not undertake to act through its doctors and nurses, but only procures them to act solely upon their own responsibility, no longer reflects the fact. The complex manner of operation of the modern-day medical institution clearly demonstrates that they furnish far more than mere facilities for treatment. They appoint physicians and surgeons to their medical staffs, as well as regularly employing on a salary basis resident physicians and surgeons, nurses, administrative and manual workers and they charge patients for medical diagnosis, care, treatment and therapy, receiving payment for such services through privately financed medical insurance policies and government financed programs known as Medicare and Medicaid. Certainly, the person who avails himself of our modern "hospital facilities" (frequently a medical teaching institution) expects that the hospital staff will do all it reasonably can to cure him and does not anticipate that its nurses, doctors and other employees will be acting solely on their own responsibility.[77]

This shift in the role of hospitals has resulted in a trend to impose a duty on hospitals to ensure that the medical staff is competent:

> A hospital has a duty to know the qualifications and the standard of performance of the physicians who practice on its premises. To permit a physician on its staff who the hospital knows or should have known is unqualified or negligent is a breach of the hospital's duty of care to its patients.[78]

Courts in 14 states have held that hospitals have such a duty.[79] The significance of such a duty is that hospitals must exercise reasonable care in the appointment and reappointment of medical staff members. In addition, when information comes to the attention of the administration or medical staff that reflects negatively on the competence of a member of the medical staff, there may be a responsibility for the peer review committee to review the current competence of the staff member.[80]

Two cases illustrate hospital liability. In Connecticut, a hospital was found liable for injuries caused by the negligence of its employees to a patient placed in seclusion:

Having established the applicable standard, the plaintiff then introduced an abundance of evidence that under the circumstances in this case the defendant violated that standard. The defendant's staff recognized the need to remove the steel frame bed for the plaintiff's safety; the staff actually kept the bed out of the seclusion room, except for brief intervals, during the first three days of the plaintiff's hospitalization. It was returned on the fourth day without any order from her own or any other physician. Even though the plaintiff's situation deteriorated, a condition which one of the defendant's experts admitted would have required the removal of the bed for safety reasons, the bed nevertheless was permitted to remain in the seclusion room. . . . The failure of the defendant to have a written policy on seclusion and the failure to break the plaintiff's seclusion were clear violations of the applicable standard of care, as was the design and location of the seclusion room so that the inside was not clearly visible from the nursing station. Finally, the failure to notify Dr. Sullivan . . . of significant changes in the plaintiff's condition was also improper. . . .

In addition to all the other evidence in the case, the significance of the revised hospital record should not be overlooked. Although the defendant understandably attempts to minimize what was done by characterizing the action as merely one of ordering expanded notes and by attributing it to poor judgment, the trier was not required to be so charitable. An allowable inference from the bungled attempt to cover up the staff inadequacies . . . was that the revision indicated a consciousness of negligence. . . .[81]

In Illinois, a patient alleged that the hospital was liable for the malpractice of physicians in the administration of ECT. The patient alleged that the hospital permitted ECT to be administered in violation of hospital policies in that the physician failed to examine the patient physically prior to treatment and failed to administer a muscle relaxant. In addition, it was alleged that the hospital breached its duty "to inform the plaintiff of the risks that attend the administration of electroconvulsive therapy in order to obtain his consent to it."[82]

The duty allegedly breached by the hospital was the duty to use reasonable care to discern the medical qualifications of persons who perform medical services in the hospital and to review treatment rendered by such persons. . . . A hospital has the duty to know the qualifications and the standard of performance of the physicians who practice on its premises. To permit a physician on its staff whom the hospital knows or should have known is unqualified or negligent is a breach of the hospital's duty of due care to its patients. To fail to periodically review physicians to determine whether they follow hospital procedures and render proper care would be a breach of a hospital's duty to its patients.[83]

The court noted that the patient did not allege that the physicians were unqualified or that the hospital failed to review the performance of its staff physicians, by which reviews it would have known the treating physician would not follow its policies with regard to the patient.

The court stated that there is no "duty on the part of the hospital's administration to insure that each of its staff physicians will always perform his duty of due care to his patient."[84] While a hospital may be held liable for malpractice committed on its premises with its knowledge or under circumstances putting it on notice of the performance of wrongful acts, a hospital will not be held liable for an act of malpractice performed by an independently retained physician unless it has reason to know the act of malpractice would take place. The court dismissed the complaint because it did not allege that the hospital knew or should have known the physician would violate its policies and because a hospital has no duty to inform the patient of risks associated with the treatment performed by the physician.

As with suits against practitioners, once the standard of care has been established, a patient must prove a deviation from the standard and that the deviation was the proximate cause of injury to recover damages.

A South Dakota court[85] also found grounds for liability. In this case the defendant, a Veterans' Administration hospital, negligently released a patient who had a history of violent behavior. The day after his release the patient shot and killed a man. The man's death was caused by the negligent release in the sense that he would not have been shot had the defendant hospital staff not improperly released the patient. Cause in fact is not enough, however, to find the defendant liable: ". . . [T]he defendant's negligent act must be the proximate cause of the plaintiff's injury. That is, the harm suffered must be found to be a foreseeable consequence of the act complained of. This does not mean, of course, that the precise events which occurred could, themselves, have been foreseen as they actually occurred; only that the events were within the scope of foreseeable risk."[86] It was not necessary that the defendant foresee the precise harm that occurred; rather, it was sufficient that the harm was of a type that could naturally be expected. The court also required that the negligent act be a substantial factor in bringing about the harm. Applying this standard of proximate cause, the court decided that given the patient's history of hostile behavior, the hospital's negligence in releasing the patient was a proximate cause of the harm to the man. The court consequently held the hospital liable for the wrongful death of the third party.

Other Legal Requirements for Malpractice and Negligence Actions

Additional legal requirements apply to malpractice and negligence actions against either practitioners or hospitals. Common law sometimes proves inadequate to meet the needs of the times. Because it is based on the accumulation of judicial precedent, the common law takes time to adapt and adjust to changing conditions and new technologies. This hiatus may leave parties without adequate legal remedies. Legislators, both federal and state, occasionally act to override or supplement common law to meet changing conditions.

Statutes of Limitations

All states have "statutes of limitations" that limit the time within which a plaintiff must file a legal action. Some states have statutes that set specific time limitations for malpractice actions. State laws vary on when the statutory period of time begins to run. In some states time begins to run when the act of malpractice or negligence occurs. In others it begins to run when the patient knew or reasonably should have known of both the existence of an injury and the possibility of its wrongful causation by someone else.[87] In determining the period of limitations, courts confront two basic policies, which sometimes are in conflict. One policy is to protect the practitioner from stale lawsuits with the danger of missing witnesses and errors in memory. The other policy is the protection of patients against malpractice by practitioners, which is often difficult to discover within the statutory period.[88]

Ascertaining when the patient knew or should have known of the injury can be complex. A Pennsylvania case[89] illustrates this complexity. The statute of limitations was two years, but in Pennsylvania the running of the statute in malpractice cases begins at the time the plaintiff discovers or reasonably should discover the injury and its cause. The jury was allowed to consider the influence of drugs on the patient in ascertaining when the statute of limitations began to run.

The defendant psychiatrist contended that the statute of limitations cannot be stopped from running by the patient's diminished mental capacities. The court agreed but stated that, "the general rule is that in determining the reasonableness of a person's conduct, his or her illness or physical disability can be considered in defining the standard which he or she must meet, but that a mental deficiency cannot be taken into account."[90] The instruction to the jury was not aimed at a consideration of the intelligence or general mental characteristics of the patient in making a determination of when she should have discovered the injury and cause. In effect, the law does not give a person with a mental deficiency a longer period of time in which to file a lawsuit. Rather, it was "aimed at permitting the jury to take into account mental disabilities caused by the drugs which were prescribed and/or administered to the . . . [patient] by the . . . [psychiatrist] as part of the therapy which the . . . [patient] proved was negligent."[91] The testimony of a psychiatrist called as an expert witness established that the psychiatrist's therapy had impaired the judgment and mental processes of the patient. In effect, the conduct of the psychiatrist brought about the patient's failure to discover the injury and cause.

Finally, the court stated that three factors were significiant in the analysis. First, the patient was dependent on the psychiatrist. The expert witness explained this "as a consequence of . . . [the psychiatrist's] mishandling of the psychoanalytic phenomenon known as transference." Second, the psychiatrist reassured the patient that their sexual relationship and the administration of drugs were proper therapy. Third, the continuing relationship of the psychiatrist and the patient impacted on the court's analysis. All of these factors were relevant to a determination of when the patient knew of the injury and its cause. The court refused to set aside the verdict on the grounds that the patient did not file the action within the statutory time period because the jury, considering all the factors, could have reasonably concluded that the action was filed in time.[92]

If the time of discovery of the injury is clear on the face of the legal complaint filed, the court will determine whether the action has been filed in a timely manner. If the time of discovery is a question of fact, a jury may make the determination. In a Kansas case,[93] a patient alleged that a general physician had failed to diagnose a mental illness and manipulated the transference phenomenon to assault her sexually. The patient had been treated for almost three years. She then was hospitalized and treated by another psychiatrist for two more years. She filed legal action one year and three weeks after her discharge.

The patient argued that she was not able to ascertain the fact of her injury until her release. The court considered various provisions of the statute of limitations and concluded that the lawsuit had not been filed on time. If the patient was alleging sexual assault, the statutory period for filing of one year ended one year after her discharge. If the time was calculated from the time of the injury which was no later than termination of treatment (the day she entered the hospital), the two-year period would bar the action as of 11 months prior to the actual filing date. If the patient were to argue that the fact of injury was not ascertainable until some time after the initial act, she would have two years from the time the injury was ascertained. The court said that the injury was ascertained "no later than April 25, 1967, by her family, her psychiatrist, and herself, when, having changed doctors, she began a new course of treatment." This would bar the action on April 26, 1969 (11 months prior to filing). Finally, the last possibility was that the patient was under a legal disability by reason of incapacity. Assuming she was, the statute provides that a person may file an action one year after the disability is removed. The disability was removed when she was discharged from the hospital. Applying the one-year statute, the action was barred 19 days prior to the filing of the action.[94]

Some states have a specific time limitation on medical malpractice actions, which is generally a shorter time period than that for a negligence action. These statutes do not apply to psychologists and may not apply to nurses. Case law may mandate that actions against nurses be filed as negligence actions rather than as malpractice actions.[95] The result is that the defense of failure to timely file an action may not be available. In Ohio, a court determined that the statute of limitations on malpractice, which was one year, did not apply to nurses and that the two-year statute of limitations on negligence applied.[96]

Notice of Claim

The federal government and some states require that a notice of claim be filed as a condition precedent to the filing of a legal action against a state or federal entity. For example, in Illinois a notice of claim must be filed within six months of the incident if the action is to be filed against a government entity.[97] Notices generally require that the essential facts underlying the claim be included.[98] In effect, two time requirements must be met: The notice of claim must be filed within six months, and the legal action generally must be filed within two years.

Limitations on Medical Malpractice Liability

Some states have enacted statutory limits on tort liability for medical malpractice. Sharply increased malpractice insurance rates accompanied the increase in malpractice litigation. Reacting to these rising rates, health care providers threatened to withdraw services unless state legislatures provided a solution.[99] The states have taken two approaches in responding to the malpractice problem. One approach is to limit the total amount of damages recoverable by setting ceilings on the liability of physicians and hospitals.[100] Illinois held this approach unconstitutional because it sets an arbitrary limit on a patient's malpractice remedy without setting such limits on other types of injuries.[101] It has been argued that such legislation constitutes special privilege legislation. These statutes seemingly discriminate against seriously injured patients while favoring those with small or moderate claims.[102]

Another approach has been the formation of arbitration panels to prescreen claims.[103] These statutes require that a complaint be submitted to a panel, usually made up of attorneys and physicians, for review. The goal is to encourage the parties to settle their grievances through arbitration. This approach has been criticized for denying a party equal access to a jury trial.[104]

Actions against State and Federal Agencies

Tort claims acts expand the liability of the government for torts committed by public employees and public agencies. For reasons of public policy, it has long been established that a person cannot sue the sovereign (the government) without the sovereign's consent. This sovereign immunity extended to public servants and agents who committed tortious acts in the conduct of their duties. Because many mental institutions are state-run, sovereign immunity prevented patients from bringing malpractice actions against the government. Legislators, recognizing the injustice of precluding victims from a remedy because they received treatment from a public servant rather than from a private person, passed various statutes that limit or abolish sovereign immunity.[105] The federal and state tort claims acts and the federal Civil Rights Act are examples.

The Federal Tort Claims Act (FTCA)[106] makes the federal government responsible for the consequences of actions taken by its officers, employees, or representatives in certain situations. The act, ". . . declares that the United States shall be liable, respecting the provisions of the United States Code relating to tort claims, in the same manner and to the same extent as a private individual under like circumstances."[107] "Under like circumstances" includes "under the law of the place where the tortious acts or omissions occurred."[108] The FTCA erodes the protective shield of governmental immunity, and under the act the tort liability of the United States now extends to cases involving allegations of medical negligence or malpractice in Veterans' Administration and military hospitals.[109]

Before suing the federal government for medical malpractice under the FTCA, a plaintiff must establish the elements necessary for any malpractice or negligence action.[110] In addition, the plaintiff must initially determine that the alleged tort-feasor (the person charged with committing the tort) was an employee, agent, or representative of the government "acting within the scope of his or her office or employment" or, if the alleged tort-feasor served as a member of the armed forces, that he or she was "acting in the line of duty." Both phrases refer ". . . to those acts which are so closely connected with what the . . . [person] is employed to do, and so fairly and reasonably incidental to it, that they may be regarded as methods, even though quite improper ones, of carrying out the objectives of the employment."[111]

While the FTCA obliterates the government's immunity from tort liability in many instances, it does contain exclusions or exceptions that maintain immunity in other cases. For example, the act specifically excludes from its coverage claims based on the government's exercise or performance of, or its failure to exercise or to perform, discretionary functions.[112] However, federal courts have held that diagnosis and treatment of patients is beyond the discretionary function, exclusion, or exception to the act.[113] The FTCA also exempts charges alleging assault, battery, or misrepresentation, as well as those alleging false arrest and false imprisonment. These exclusions or exemptions may restrict a patient's claim brought under the FTCA.[114]

Finally, a patient must first present a claim under the FTCA to the "appropriate" federal agency. The agency must take written action on the claim within six months; failure to do so implies denial and permits a plaintiff to institute suit against the agency in federal district court.[115]

CONSTITUTIONAL CLAIMS

Public hospitals and the mental health professionals who provide services in them may be held liable for violation of rights guaranteed patients by the United States Constitution or by federal statutes under the federal Civil Rights Act. During the past ten years patients have filed numerous lawsuits, many of them class actions, under the Civil Rights Act alleging a lack of fairness—in violation of the due process clause of the Fourteenth Amendment—in state admission standards and procedures,[116] and a constitutional right to treatment,[117] to refuse treatment,[118] and to protection and safety. Patients have recovered damages,[119] and classes of patients have been granted broad injunctive relief, such as smaller staff-patient ratios.[120] Additionally, institutions have been ordered to pay attorney's fees.

Federal Civil Rights Act

The Civil Rights Act, at section 1983 of the United States Code, provides:

> Every person who, under color of any statute, ordinance, regulation, custom, or usage, of any state or territory subjects or causes to be subjected, any citizen of the United States or other person within the jurisdiction thereof to the deprivation of any rights, privileges, or immunities secured by the Constitution and laws, shall be liable to the party injured in an action at law, a suit in equity, or other proper proceeding for redress.[121]

To maintain an action under section 1983, a patient must establish two essential elements.[122] First, the patient must establish that the conduct complained of was committed by a person acting "under color" of state or territorial law (statute, ordinance, regulation), custom, or usage. A state official acts "under color" of state law, custom, or usage when he or she ". . . [misuses] power, possessed by virtue of state law and made possible only because the wrongdoer is clothed with the authority of state law."[123] Because the under-color-of-state-law element depends largely upon the appearance of the official's authority, an official acts under color of state law when he or she takes unconstitutional action with or without state authority.

While section 1983 does not extend to purely private conduct, private, individual conduct may constitute state action. The courts regard such action as analogous to action "under color of law," where (1) state courts enforce an agreement affecting private parties; (2) the state is "significantly" involved with a private party; or (3) there is private performance of a government function.

Recognizing that a private person may act under color of state law, a New Hampshire court held that a private physician employed by a private hospital could incur section 1983 liability even though the hospital itself could not.[124] The court reasoned that the two New Hampshire statutes that gave the physician the power to place a rehabilitative patient into emergency diagnostic detention at a state mental health institution constitute delegation by the New Hampshire legislature to a private individual of the power to detain a person against that person's wishes, a power normally and historically exercised by sovereign states and other governmental entities. These statutes clothed the defendant physician with state authority so substantial as to render his actions (which he took against the plaintiff patient's desire) ". . . virtually identical to actions traditionally taken by a state."[125]

Second, the patient must show that the conduct complained of deprived him or her of rights, privileges, or immunities secured by the Constitution or laws of the United States. An allegation of mere negligence is not enough.[126] As one court noted, the rights protected by section 1983 ". . . are public ones, created or adopted by the Federal Constitution or by Congress. These federal rights entail a person's civil rights and personal liberties, including nondiscrimination, voting, free speech and freedom of assembly, equal protection and due process in safeguarding proprietary rights, as well as personal liberties."[127]

If a patient successfully establishes the two elements essential to a section 1983 cause of action, he or she need not allege that the defendant mental health professional or institution acted in bad faith to claim relief. If a plaintiff brings an action against a public official whose position might entitle him or her to immunity when acting in good faith, the official must plead qualified immunity as a defense.[128] Whether a defendant may assert "good faith" as a defense depends on facts peculiarly within the defendant's knowledge and control, for "[it] is the existence of reasonable grounds for the belief formed at the time and in light of all the circumstances, coupled with good faith belief, that affords a basis for qualified immunity of executive officers for acts performed in the course of official conduct."[129] The immunity's availability hinges on both objective and subjective beliefs; the official must have acted sincerely and with the belief that he or she acted rightly under the circumstances.[130]

In some instances, medical defendants have successfully invoked "good faith" to avoid liability under section 1983. For example, state mental health officials in Colorado denied liability for allegedly failing to protect a female patient from an unconsented touching by a male patient. Although the officials had responsible positions in the hospital, they could invoke their qualified immunity because they had acted in a reasonable manner to prevent any harm to the patient.[131] Similarly, in Maryland, medical defendants sued in an action challenging a city police department's involuntary commitment procedures, which admitted arrested individuals suspected of mental illness to the psychiatric screening and evaluation unit of a hospital. City officials claimed immunity for their activities because they lacked any reason to suspect that the department's procedures had deprived the plaintiff of her constitutional rights.[132]

As a remedial device to discourage violations of federal constitutional and statutory rights, the Civil Rights Act empowers a court, in its discretion, to allow a prevailing party other than the United States a reasonable attorney's fee as part of the trial costs.[133] Such awards can substantially increase the financial cost of liability under the act as the following case illustrates.

A federal district court in Pennsylvania awarded Community Legal Services of Philadelphia and a private public interest attorney more than $200,000 in attorney's fees and costs under section 1988 for their roles in litigating a case concerning the right of patients confined in Pennsylvania state mental hospitals to control and manage their own property.[134] The court awarded hourly rates comparable to fees charged by attorneys in private practice and then doubled the award to account for the importance of the litigation in furthering the underlying policies of the Civil Rights Act, the quality of the attorneys' work, the bad faith exhibited by the defendants, and the delay in recovering the fees.[135]

LICENSING AND CERTIFICATION

The justification for licensing legislation is that it is necessary to protect the pubic from incompetent and unethical practitioners.[136] To accomplish this goal, the states require most practitioners to obtain licenses before providing mental health services. Psychiatrists and nurses are subject to licensure in all states. Psychologists are covered in most states. The states have statutes that require a certain level of experience and education before the practitioner receives a license. The statutes also provide grounds for license renewal, suspension, revocation, and reinstatement. In addition, various duties, including ethical ones, are sometimes imposed upon the licensed practitioner. Violation of these duties could result in disciplinary action, suspension, or revocation of the license.

The grounds for suspension or revocation fall into several broad categories that involve personal disqualifications, criminal acts, and unprofessional conduct. Personal disqualifications include mental or physical illness, alcoholism, narcotics addiction, and gross immorality. Criminal acts include conviction of a felony or misdemeanor involving moral turpitude and aiding or abetting an unlicensed person to practice medicine. Some examples of unprofessional conduct are fee splitting, improper advertising, violation of confidentiality, gross malpractice, and fraud.

The procedure for suspension or revocation of a license in Illinois[137] involves the following:

1. A complaint is filed with the Department of Registration and Education setting forth the alleged misconduct against the named party.

2. The practitioner charged is served with a copy of the complaint and a summons to appear before a committee and file a sworn, written answer to the charge.
3. A hearing takes place within 30 days. The practitioner charged is given an opportunity to present a defense in person, with the assistance of legal counsel. Testimony, tangible evidence, written statements, and oral argument may be presented on the practitioner's behalf. A written record is made of the proceeding.
4. The hearing committee makes a written report and recommendation to the department director, who makes the decision, which is subject to judicial review by the courts. In most states, the courts will affirm the decision if substantial evidence supports it.

To protect consumers, some other states rely on certification statutes. These statutes are a weaker form of regulation and merely require that the practitioner register with the state. These certification statutes govern only the use of a title or designation; unregistered practitioners can still render services without using a particular label.[138]

ETHICAL RESPONSIBILITIES

In addition to legal standards governing their professional conduct, mental health professionals are subject to ethical standards proscribing certain activities. Various professional associations promulgate canons of ethics,[139] which define unethical practices. They uniformly proscribe sexual contact between patient and professional,[140] indiscriminate release of confidential patient information,[141] and exploitation of the patient by the professional.[142] The canons generally include potential sanctions for unethical conduct.

Violation of an ethical canon may result in a reprimand or censure.[143] In more severe cases the practitioner may be suspended or expelled from the professional association that issued the canons.[144] Before being sanctioned, the practitioner learns the complainant's identity and the charges levied. Complaints are made by aggrieved patients, fellow mental health professionals, and third parties. The complaints cannot be anonymous.[145] The practitioner may be given the right to counsel[146] and the right to appeal an adverse determination to the association's general membership.[147] Most professional associations have special ethics committees that investigate all charges of unethical behavior and recommend appropriate sanctions.[148]

An association member may violate an ethical canon and be severely sanctioned without violating the law.[149] Sexual activity between nonmarried, consenting adults is not proscribed in many states, but such activity between patient and professional violates one of the most fundamental ethical canons. Conversely, a member "could violate the law without being guilty of professionally unethical behavior."[150]

Nevertheless, some overlap exists between legal sanctions and unethical behavior. Some state licensing boards have incorporated the corresponding professional association's code of ethics into the state's licensing requirements.[151] Others have more generally proscribed unprofessional or unethical behavior without referring to a specific code of ethics.[152] Courts cite the professional codes of ethics to support appropriate standards of care in negligence cases or legal obligations inherent in physician-patient contractual relationships.[153]

INSURANCE

Mental health professionals should carry insurance that provides coverage by occurrence and not for a time period. In a Florida case, an outpatient clinic and a psychiatrist were held liable for "the sexual abuse and exploitation of the patient, negligent administration of drugs on numerous occasions and failure to prescribe proper drugs and treatment."[154] The expert psychiatric witnesses testified that it was medically impossible to allocate any of the damages suffered by the patient to any time period during which she saw the psychiatrist. The insurance company was held responsible for all damages, even for those suffered during the period after the psychiatrist left the employ of the clinic. The court stated:

> Vigilant Insurance Company's responsibility for paying damages is derivative of . . . [the psychiatrist's] liability. The policy in issue is an occurrence policy, that is, Vigilant agrees to pay "all damages because of . . . [i]njury arising out of the rendering of or failure to render, professional services . . .," during the policy period. As in all such liability policies, the insurer's obligation is not simply limited to damages which occur during the policy period. Rather, as stated in the policy, it is obligated to pay "all damages" which arise out of injuries caused by the defendant's negligence during the policy period.[155]

Nurses should carry their own liability insurance. While hospitals carry general liability policies, such policies contain exclusionary provisions in which the insurance company disclaims any liability for malpractice actions brought against the insured. If the action is for acts of malpractice rather than negligence, the insurance company has no obligation to defend either the nurse or the hospital. A Louisiana suit alleged that nurses failed to observe that a patient's condition was deteriorating and failed to notify the patient's physician. The court held that the nurses had acted in their professional capacity and therefore fell within the exclusion.[156]

A nonprofessional act does not fall within the exclusionary provision. In another Louisiana case, where a nurse incorrectly counted sponges in surgery, it was held that the act of counting was an "administrative" act and not a professional act. Therefore, the conduct did not fall within the exclusion.[157]

SUMMARY

Practitioners must be able and careful. They must use their best judgment in caring for patients to avoid malpractice liability. This, of course, does not indemnify a practitioner against legal actions. Good therapist-patient relations are important. According to a Chicago physician who gives expert testimony and evaluates potential malpractice incidents for lawyers, many patients file legal actions against physicians because they are angry at what they perceive as a lack of communication and sensitivity.[158]

In the hospital environment, participation on credentialing committees, on peer review committees, and in other quality assurance/risk management activities[159] is important if quality care is to be maintained.

NOTES

1. Duty is "an expression of the sum total of those considerations of policy which lead the law to say that the particular plaintiff is entitled to protection." Elam v. College Park Hospital, 183 Cal. Rptr. 156, 160 (1982). "Any number of considerations may justify the imposition of a duty in particular circumstances, including the guidance of history, our continually refined concepts of morals and justice, the convenience of the rule, and social judgment as to where the loss should fall." *Id.* at 161, n. 9.

2. Thomas Shea, "Legal Standards of Care for Psychiatrists and Psychologists," 6 *Western State U.L. Rev.* 71, 74 (1962) (citing Barbine v. Wrey, 75 N.J. Super. 327, 183 A.2d 142 (1962)) [hereinafter cited as Shea].

3. Henry Black, *Black's Law Dictionary* (5th ed.) (St. Paul, Minn.: West Publishing Co., 1979), pp. 250–251.

4. *Id.* at 930–931.

5. Pamela D. Andrade and John C. Andrade, "Malpractice of Psychiatric Nurses," 26 POF2d 363, 373 (1981).

6. Matthews v. Walker, 34 Ohio App. 2d 128, 130, 296 N.E.2d 569, 570 (1973).

7. Comment, "The Liability of Psychiatrists for Malpractice," 36 *U. Pitt. L. Rev.* 108, 114–118 (1974); Comment, "Tort Liability of the Psychotherapist," 8 *U. San Francisco L. Rev.* 405, 408 (1973); Note, "The Liability of Psychiatrists," 48 *Notre Dame Law* 693 (1973).

8. Comment, 8 *U. San Francisco L. Rev.*, *supra* note 7, at 408–409.

9. Harvey Sarner, *The Nurse and the Law* (Philadelphia: W.B. Saunders Co., 1968), p. 34.

10. *See, e.g.*, Hill v. Leigh Memorial Hospital, 204 Va. 501, 132 S.E.2d 411, 416 (1963), where the court declined to impose liability because the record did not indicate the kind of nurses involved in the incident, and therefore the standard of care could not be ascertained.

11. In some states, whether an action is characterized as malpractice or negligence may determine whether the statute of limitations for medical malpractice or the regular negligence statute of limitations, which is longer, applies to actions against nurses. *See* section on statute of limitations, this chapter.

12. Chatman v. Millis, 517 S.W.2d 504, 509 (Ark. 1975) (dissenting opinion) (psychologist); Giovanni v. Pessel, 109 N.J. Super. 550, 250 A.2d 756, 762–763 (App. Ct. 1969) (physician); Williams v. United States, 450 F. Supp. 1040, 1045–46 (D.S.D. 1978); Farrow v. Health Services Corporation, 604 P.2d 474 (Utah 1979) (nurse, psychiatrist).

13. Shea, *supra* note 2, at 74.

14. Note, 36 A.L.R.3d 440 (1971).

15. Speer v. United States, 512 F. Supp. 670 (N.D. Tex. 1981).

16. 61 Am.Jur.2d §§ 218, 219.

17. *Id.* Nevertheless, it has also been argued that "widespread availability of medicines and 'miracle drugs' . . . has had the effect of 'equalizing' the kinds of treatments (and diseases) found from locality to locality." Ronald J. Cohen, *Malpractice—A Guide for Mental Health Professionals* (New York: Free Press, 1979).

18. Farrow v. Health Services Corporation, *supra* note 12, at 477.

19. Pisel v. Stamford Hospital, 180 Conn. 314, 430 A.2d 1, 12 (1980).

20. Rogers v. Okin, 478 F. Supp. 1342, 1384–1385 (D.C. Mass. 1979).

21. Scarano v. Schnoor, 158 Cal. App. 2d 612, 323 P.2d 178, 181–182 (1958).

22. 61 Am.Jur.2d §§ 205, 206 (1982).

23. Ralph Slovenko, "Malpractice in Psychiatry and Related Fields," *J. Psychiatry & Law* 9, no. 2 (Spring 1981): 5, 11 [hereinafter cited as Slovenko].

24. Hood v. Phillips, 537 S.W.2d 291, *aff'd*, 554 S.W.2d 160 (Tex. 1977).

25. 61 Am.Jur.2d § 214 (1982).

26. Physician-Patient Relationship, 17 A.L.R. 4th 132 (1982) and 61 Am. Jur. 2d §§ 158–160 and cases collected therein.

27. Oliver v. Brock, 342 So. 2d 1 (Ala. 1976).

28. Davis v. Tirrell, 110 Misc. 2d 889, 443 NYS 2d 136 (1981).

29. Hiser v. Randolph, 126 Ariz 608, 617 P.2d 774 (App. Ct. 1980).

30. Giallanza v. Sands, 316 So. 2d 77 (Fla. App. 1975).

31. Keene v. Wiggins, 69 Cal. App. 3d 308, 138 Cal. Reptr. 3 (1977).

32. Hoover v. Williamson, 236 Md. 250, 203 A. 2d 861 (1964).

33. *Id.*

34. *Id.*

35. Dunbar v. Greenlaw, 152 Me. 270, 128 A.2d 218 (1956).

36. James v. Brown, 637 S.W. 2d 914 (Sup. Ct. Tex. 1982).

37. Clark v. Grigson, 579 S.W. 2d 263 (Tex Ct. App. 1979).

38. Chatman v. Millis, *supra* note 12.

39. *See* Pisel v. Stamford Hospital, *supra* note 19, at 12–14; Slovenko, *supra* note 23, at 15.

40. Crawford v. Anagnostopoulos, 69 Ill. App. 3d 954, 387 N.E.2d 1064, 1069 (1979).

41. Slovenko, *supra* note 23, at 16.

42. Hammer v. Rosen, 7 N.Y.2d 376, 165 N.E.2d 756, 757 (1960).

43. Slovenko, *supra* note 23, at 16–18; Shea, *supra* note 2, at 76.

44. Pisel v. Stamford Hospital, *supra* note 19, at 12, 13.

45. *Id.* at 13.

46. Bylaws and regulations have been allowed into evidence to establish the standard of care. Darling v. Charleston Community Memorial Hospital, 33 Ill. 2d 326, 211 N.E.2d 253, 256–257 (1965), *cert. denied*, 383 U.S. 946 (1966).

47. *See, e.g.*, American Psychiatric Association, *Principles of Medical Ethics with Annotations Especially Applicable to Psychiatry* (Washington, D.C., 1981); American Psychological Association, *Ethical Principles of Psychologists* (Washington, D.C., 1981); National Association of Social Workers, *Code of Ethics* (Washington, D.C., 1980). The standards of the American Psychiatric Association on ECT were allowed into evidence in a negligence action. Stone v. Proctor, 259 N.C. 633, 131 S.E.2d 297, 299–300 (1963). Joint Commission on Accreditation of Hospitals (JCAH), *Consolidated Standards Manual for Child, Adolescent, and Adult Psychiatric, Alcoholism, and Drug Abuse Facilities* (Chicago, 1981). JCAH standards have been admitted as evidence of the standard of care. Darling v. Charleston Community Memorial Hospital, *supra* note 46.

48. Edward Cleary, ed., *McCormick's Handbook of the Law of Evidence* (2d ed.) (St. Paul, Minn.: West Publishing Co., 1972), pp. 743–745.

49. John H. Wigmore, *Evidence* (Boston: Little, Brown and Co., 1976), §§ 1690–1700; Symposium, "Substantive Admissibility of Learned Treatises and the Medical Malpractice Plaintiff," 71 *N.W.L. Rev.* 678 (1976).

50. Plost v. Louis A. Weiss Hospital, 62 Ill. App. 3d 253, 378 N.E.2d 1176, 1180 (1978).

51. Graham v. St. Luke's Hospital, 46 Ill. App. 2d 147, 196 N.E.2d 355, 360 (1964), and authorities cited from other jurisdictions.

52. 61 Am.Jur.2d § 208 (1981), and collected cases.

53. *Id.* at § 209 and collected cases therein.

54. Walski v. Tiesenga, 72 Ill. 2d 249, 381 N.E.2d 279, 285 (1978).

55. Slovenko, *supra* note 23, at 29–30.

56. *See* section on confidentiality, Chapter 10.

57. 61 Am.Jur.2d § 359 (1981).

58. Runyon v. Reid, 510 P.2d 943 (Sup. Ct. Okla. 1973).

59. Watkins v. United States, 589 F.2d 214, 219 (5th Cir. 1979).

60. Giovanni v. Pessel, *supra* note 12, at 762–763.

61. Wilson v. Clark, 84 Ill. 2d 186, 417 N.E.2d 1322, 1325 (1981), *cert. denied*, 102 Sup. Ct. 140 (1981).

62. McDonald v. Moore, 323 So.2d 635 (Fla. App. 1975).

63. Greenberg v. McCabe, 453 F. Supp. 765 (E.D. Pa. 1978).

64. *Id.* at 766, 773.

65. Elam v. College Park Hospital, *supra* note 1; Pickle v. Curns, 106 Ill. App. 3d 734, 435 N.E.2d 877 (1982) (allegations of failure to administer muscle relaxant for ECT treatment).

66. JCAH, *supra* note 47.

67. *See, e.g.*, Lucy Webb Hayes National Training School for Deaconesses and Missionaries v. Perotti, 419 F.2d 704 (D.C. Cir. 1969).

68. Pisel v. Stamford Hospital, *supra* note 19, at 13–14.

69. On absence of equipment, *see* Annot., 50 A.L.R.3d 1141 (1973); on defective equipment, *see* Annot., 14 A.L.R.3d 1254 (1967).

70. On assault by one patient upon another, *see* Annot. 48 A.L.R.3d 1288 (1973); on suicide, *see* Chapter 11.

71. Black, *supra* note 3, at 1179. "Under this doctrine the master is responsible for want of care on servant's part toward those to whom master owes duty to use care, provided failure of servant to use such care occurred in course of his employment." *Id.*

72. Bing v. Thunig, 2 N.Y.2d 656, 143 N.E.2d 3 (1957).

73. Capasso v. Square Sanitorium, 3 Misc.2d 173, 155 N.Y.S.2d 313, 315 (1956).

74. *Id.*

75. Davis v. Wilson, 265 N.C. 139, 143 S.E.2d 107 (1965).

76. Arthur Southwick, "The Hospital as an Institution: Expanding Responsibilities Change Its Relationship with the Staff Physician," 9 *Cal. W. L. Rev.* 429 (1973).

77. Elam v.College Park Hospital, *supra* note 1.

78. Pickle v. Curns, *supra* note 65, at 881.

79. Arthur Bernstein, "Darling is Alive and Well in California," *Hospitals* 56, no. 10 (October 1, 1982); Elam v. College Park Hospital, *supra* note 1.

80. Elam v. College Park Hospital, *supra* note 1; Pickle v. Curns, *supra* note 65.

81. Pisel v. Stamford Hospital, *supra* note 19, at 14–15.

82. Pickle v. Curns, *supra* note 65, at 880–881.

83. *Id.* at 881.

84. *Id.* at 882.

85. Williams v. United States, *supra* note 12.

86. *Id.* at 1045–1046.

87. Quick v. Aetna Casualty & Surety Company, 347 So. 2d 59 (La. Ct. of App. 1977).

88. 61 Am.Jur.2d § 318 (1981).

89. Greenberg v. McCabe, *supra* note 63.

90. *Id.* at 768.

91. *Id.*

92. *Id.* at 771–772.

93. Seymour v. Lofgreen, 209 Kan. 72, 495 P.2d 969 (1972).

94. *Id.* at 974.

95. Note, "A Revolution in White—New Approaches to Treating Nurses as Professionals," 30 *Vand. L. Rev.* 839 (1977).

96. Richardson v. Doe, 176 Ohio St. 370, 199 N.E.2d 878 (1964).

97. Ill. Rev. Stat., ch. 37, § 439, 22–1 (1980).

98. 61 Am.Jur.2d § 315 (1982).

99. *See* Annot., 80 A.L.R.3d 583 (1977); 84 A.L.R.3d 375, § 2(a) (1978); *see generally* Comment, "An Analysis of State Legislative Responses to the Medical Malpractice Crisis," *Duke L. J.* 1975:1417.

100. Annot., 80 A.L.R.3d, *supra* note 99, at §§ 2, 3; 61 Am.Jur.2d § 218 (1981).

101. *See* Wright v. Central Du Page Hospital Association, 63 Ill. 2d 313, 347 N.E.2d 736 (1976); Jones v. State Board of Medicine, 97 Idaho 859, 555 P.2d 399 (1976); 80 A.L.R.3d, *supra* note 99 at § 3.

102. *Id.*

103. 80 A.L.R. 3d *supra* note 99, at §§ 2, 8–12; Comiskey v. Arlen, 55 A.D.2d 304, 390 N.Y.S.2d 122 (1976).

104. *See generally* 80 A.L.R.3d *supra* note 99. Arbitration panels were held to be constitutional in Halpern v. Gozan, 85 Misc.2d 753, 381 N.Y.S.2d 744 (1976), and Carter v. Sparkman, 335

So.2d 802 (Fla. 1976); such panels were held unconstitutional in Jones v. State Board of Medicine, 97 Idaho 859, 555 P.2d 399 (1976).

105. *See* 35 Am.Jur.2d *Federal Tort Claims Act* (1967 and Supp. 1982).

106. 28 U.S.C. § 1346, 2671–2680 (1970 & Supp. IV 1980).

107. Annot., 9 A.L.R. Fed. 16 (1971 and Supp. 1982).

108. Lipari v. Sears, Roebuck & Co., 497 F. Supp. 185, 188 (D. Neb. 1980).

109. Rosario v. American Export-Isbrandtsen Lines, Inc., 395 F. Supp. 1192 (E.D. Pa. 1975), *rev'd on other grounds*, 531 F.2d 1227 (3d Cir. 1976).

110. *See* discussion, Chapter 1.

111. Annot., 6 A.L.R. Fed. 373, 384 (1971) (citing William Prosser, *Law of Torts* (3d ed.) (St. Paul, Minn.: West Publishing Co., 1964), § 69.

112. 28 U.S.C. § 2680(a).

113. *See* Moon v. United States, 512 F. Supp. 140, 144 (D. Nev. 1981), and cases cited therein.

114. 28 U.S.C. § 2680(h).

115. *Id.* at § 2675(a).

116. *See* Chapter 7.

117. *See* Chapter 8.

118. *Id.*

119. O'Connor v. Donaldson, 422 U.S. 563 (1975).

120. Wyatt v. Stickrey, 344 F. Supp. 387 (M.D. Ala. 1972), *modified sub. nom.* Wyatt v. Aderholt, 503 F.2d 1305 (5th Cir. 1974).

121. 42 U.S.C. § 1983; *See* Annot., 42 A.L.R. Fed. 463 (1979 and Supp. 1982), with respect to private hospitals.

122. Parratt v. Taylor, 451 U.S. 527, 531–535 (1981).

123. United States v. Classic, 313 U.S. 299, 325–326 (1941).

124. Kay v. Benson, 472 F. Supp. 850 (D.N.H. 1979).

125. *Id.* at 851.

126. Patton v. Dumpon, 425 F. Supp. 621 (S.D.N.Y. 1977).

127. Dorak v. Schapp, 403 F. Supp. 863, 866 (D.C. Pa. 1975).

128. Gomez v. Toledo, 446 U.S. 635 (1980).

129. *Id.* at 641 (quoting Scheuer v. Rhodes, 416 U.S. 232 (1974)).

130. Wood v. Strickland, 420 U.S. 308, 321–322 (1975).

131. Knight v. People of State of Colorado, 496 F. Supp. 779 (D. Colo. 1980).

132. Gross v. Pomerleau, 465 F. Supp. 1167, 1174 (D. Md. 1979).

133. 42 U.S.C. § 1988.

134. Vecchione v. Wohlgemuth, 481 F. Supp 776 (E.D. Pa. 1979).

135. *Id.*

136. Jeanne Fischer, "State Regulation of Psychologists," 58 *Wash. U.L.Q.* 639, 639 n. 4 (1980).

137. Ill. Anno. Stat., ch. 127, ¶ 60 (1982).

138. Judy Freiberg, "The Song is Ended but the Malady Lingers On: Legal Regulation of Psychotherapy," 22 *St. Louis U.L.J.* 519, 530 (1978).

139. *E.g.*, American Psychological Association, *Ethical Principles of Psychologists*, *supra* note 47; American Psychiatric Association, *Principles of Medical Ethics with Annotations Especially Appli-*

cable to Psychiatry, supra note 47 [hereinafter cited as *Principles of Medical Ethics*]; National Association of Social Workers, *Code of Ethics, supra* note 47.

140. *Id.*

141. *E.g., Principles of Medical Ethics, supra* note 139 at § 4 at pp. 5–7.

142. *E.g., Id.* at § 1 at p. 3.

143. Hare-Mustin and Hall, "Procedures for Responding to Ethics Complaints Against Psychologists," 36 *Amer. Psychologist* 1494, 1502 (Dec. 1981); *Principles of Medical Ethics, supra* note 139, at 11, 14.

144. Hare-Mustin and Hall, *supra* note 143, at 1504; *Principles of Medical Ethics, supra* note 139, at 12, 14.

145. Hare-Mustin and Hall, *supra* note 143, at 1495–1496; *Principles of Medical Ethics, supra* note 139, at 10–13.

146. *E.g., Principles of Medical Ethics, supra* note 139, at 11, 13.

147. *E.g., Id.* at 16.

148. *Principles of Medical Ethics, supra* note 139, at 11–14; Hare-Mustin and Hall, *supra* note 143, at 1501, 1504.

149. Hare-Mustin and Hall, *supra* note 143, at 1495.

150. *Principles of Medical Ethics, supra* note 139, at 5.

151. *See* Morra v. State Board of Examiners of Psychologists, 212 Kan. 103, 510 P.2d 614 (1973).

152. *See* Clark v. Michigan State Board of Registration in Medicine, 367 Mich. 343, 116 N.W.2d 797 (1962).

153. *Cf.* Horne v. Patton, 291 Ala. 701, 287 So.2d 824 (Ala. 1974).

154. Vigilant Insurance Company v. Keiser, 391 So.2d 706, 714 (Fla. App. 1981).

155. *Id.* at 710.

156. Tankersly v. Insurance Company of North America, 216 So.2d 333, 335–336 (La. Ct. of App. 1968); *see also* Ratliff v. Employers' Liability Assurance Corporation, Ltd., 515 S.W.2d 225 (Ky. 1974), where a nurse's determination that a patient was capable of safely walking unassisted was held a professional judgment.

157. Grant v. Touro Infirmary, 254 La. 204, 223 So.2d 148 (1969).

158. Gardner, "An Inside Look at Malpractice by Expert Witness William B. Buckingham, M.D.," 8 *Q.R.B.* 7, 9 (1982).

159. *See* Chapter 6.

Part III

Outpatient Setting

Chapter 4

Treatment in the Community

Therapists have a duty not to abuse their relationships with patients for personal gratification or gain, not to abandon their patients during treatment, not to violate their patients' rights to confidentiality and privacy, to protect their patients from themselves, and to protect third parties threatened with harm by their patients. Psychiatrists must be able and careful; they must use their best judgment in the administration of medication.

Traditionally, litigation has involved failure to protect patients from themselves, improper administration of medication, and violations of the confidentiality and privacy rights of patients,[1] but in recent years the bases for suits have grown. There has been an increase in the number of reported cases alleging malpractice based on sexual relations between therapist and patient (no statistics are available on the number of such cases settled). Gradually, courts around the country are imposing the therapist's duty to take steps to protect a third party threatened with harm by a patient. Finally, it is being advocated that patients discharged from a public hospital have a constitutional right to appropriate outpatient treatment in the community.

Few reported cases of malpractice involve psychotherapy because of imprecise standards of care and difficulties of proof where verbal therapies are involved, reluctance of patients to expose their personal problems in court, and the diffusion of anger by the therapist. Those that have been reported involve abuse of the therapist-patient relationship by the therapist's manipulation of the patient's conduct for personal gratification or economic gain. Such conduct by therapists falls below the standard of care and exposes them to liability for malpractice, criminal prosecution, license revocation, and loss of membership in professional organizations.

The standard of care in the field of psychotherapy is imprecise because several theories of psychotherapy exist. Even with traditional psychotherapy, it is difficult to prove that transference has been mishandled. A therapist fails to recognize the positive feelings of a patient and interprets only the anger and hostility. A therapist allows a positive transference to continue without analysis because of gratification from the patient's idealization and makes no attempt to work through to the point where the patient becomes more independent and idealizes the therapist less. A therapist "may advise psychoanalysis for a patient too close to decompensation to tolerate this kind of treatment, and a psychosis may develop." A therapist may make untimely or incorrect interpretations followed by a rejection of the patient, who becomes depressed and suicidal. These are all examples of inappropriate treatment that are not provable as malpractice, deviations from professional standards that are proximate causes of injury.[2]

In traditional psychotherapy the basis of the treatment process is verbal and nonverbal interchange between therapist and patient. To benefit from psychotherapy patients must learn to trust their therapists. A therapist encounters not only a patients' conscious resistance, but, due to transference, the patients' deeper inability to distinguish feelings for the therapist from feelings for other significant persons in his or her life. As the relationship between psychotherapist and patient develops, it is foreseeable that the patient will develop toward the therapist intense feelings of affection, anger, sexual arousal, dependency, rejection, or a mixture of these. The therapist, in turn, may develop similar feelings about a patient but presumably is prepared by training and experience to keep the patient's interests paramount. The psychotherapist is also trained to avoid exploiting the patient's "acting out" of this transference, and is obligated by the canons of the profession to withdraw from treating a patient when unable to control the relationship.[3]

Nontraditional psychotherapy involves many treatment modes, including behavior therapy, direct decision therapy, existential therapy, art therapy, music therapy, and dance therapy. Many of these approaches go far beyond verbal exchanges. They call for touching, confrontation, exposure to probic objects, electric shock, and adversive stimulation; they may encourage screaming, pounding, etc. Some schools of treatment advocate touching and massaging a patient as a routine part of therapeutic treatment. Forms of group therapy involving nudity are intended to facilitate self-disclosure and acceptance of one's physical attributes. Such encouragement may lead to the advocacy of sexual intimacy between patient and therapist.[4]

SEXUAL INTIMACY

Sexual intimacy between therapists and patients is not uncommon. More than 5 percent of male therapists responding to recent surveys stated that they were sexually intimate with patients during treatment.[5] Such sexual activity with a patient is a breach of the therapist's duty. As with all abuses of the therapist-patient relationship, a variety of sanctions against sexual relations exists. Courts in New York, Michigan, Missouri, Pennsylvania, and Texas have held that a therapist who engages in sexual intercourse with a patient has committed malpractice. A Florida court held such conduct to be a breach of the contract between the therapist and the patient. Michigan and New Hampshire make such conduct a crime. New York revoked the license of a psychiatrist for such conduct. The American Psychiatric Association condemns sexual activity with a patient as unethical, and has expelled members for such conduct. The American Psychological Association and the National Association of Social Workers also consider it unethical.

While the actual number of civil actions, criminal prosecutions, and complaints to professional organizations based on sexual activity between therapist and patient continues to increase, the overall number filed still is a very small percentage of those patients who have engaged in such activity with their therapists. Patients are reluctant to file lawsuits or to complain to professional organizations for many reasons. Some do not feel such activity is wrong; others are embarrassed, ashamed, or feel guilty about it. Other patients fear they will not be believed, or that their complaint will be made public.[6] Officers of state psychological associations and regulatory agencies say reported cases of therapist-patient sexual abuse represent only "the very tip of the top of the iceberg."[7]

Ethical Sanctions

In the late 1960s, one psychiatrist openly advocated sexual intimacy as a form of therapy consistent with the required standard of treatment.[8] Other psychiatrists have concluded that such therapy sometimes is helpful.[9] In general, however, the medical profession rejects sexual intimacy as appropriate therapy. In 1973, a survey of the attitudes and practices of physicians regarding erotic contact with patients revealed that only 20 percent of the psychiatrists responding thought that such contact might benefit a patient.[10]

In the same year, the American Psychiatric Association adopted the position that sexual activity with a client is unethical.[11] The American Psychological Association,[12] the American Psychoanalytical Association,[13] the Association of Sex Educators, Counselors & Therapists,[14] and the National Association of Social Workers[15] concurred.

While professional organizations consider sexual activity with patients unethical and officially impose strong sanctions in some cases, they receive few complaints. Even if a complaint is filed, a professional organization may not deal adequately with it. Many organizations have neither the resources nor the inclination to pursue such complaints.[16] The district branches of the American Psychiatric Association have trouble finding members who will accept appointments to the Ethics Committee, and they often do not have funds for legal representation or formal hearing procedures.[17]

State licensing bodies receive few complaints,[18] but occasionally they have revoked licenses.[19] In California, the license of a psychologist who attempted to justify sexual intercourse with a patient as a form of therapy was revoked.[20]

Malpractice Actions

To recover damages in a civil action for a therapist's sexual activity, the patient must prove that the activity was the proximate cause of injury. Proving harm and causation can be difficult, and a number of factors may affect a patient's recovery of damages.[21] If the patient knowingly encouraged the conduct of the therapist, the jury may not sympathize with the patient. Another important factor is the mental disorder being treated. For example, because a neurosis does not involve the loss of contact with reality to the same extent as a psychosis, it is difficult for a neurotic patient to persuade a jury that a psychiatrist mishandled the transference phenomenon. If the patient is severely disturbed, convincing a jury that the therapist's conduct was malpractice is much easier. The age of the patient is also significant. If the patient is youthful, the situation will be viewed as more serious than if the patient is 30 or 40 years old. With older patients the distinction between an "affair" and malpractice may be blurred. Also, while of doubtful relevance, a patient's past sexual history may become an issue.[22]

Notwithstanding these possible difficulties, patients have prevailed in civil action damage suits against their therapists.[23] In New York,[24] a psychiatrist engaged in sexual intercourse with a patient over a 13-month period as a prescribed form of therapy for her lesbianism. The patient's mental illness was aggravated, and as a result she was hospitalized twice. The psychiatrist was held negligent for failure to treat the patient "with professionally acceptable procedures" and for engaging in acts of sexual intercourse with her. The trial court awarded the patient $50,000 in compensatory damages and $104,679 in punitive damages. On review, the award was reduced to $25,000 compensatory damages and no punitive damages.

In 1982, a California patient recovered $4.6 million from her psychiatrist for sexual and mental abuse. The complaint alleged that the psychiatrist had sexual intercourse with the patient, advised her to commit suicide, and gave her the drugs to do so. In addition to money damages, the psychiatrist lost his license for one year and was placed on probation for ten years. Upon his return to practice, the California Board of Medical Quality Assurance prohibits him during the probationary period from treating female patients, working alone, or prescribing drugs that have potential for abuse.[25]

In 1983, an Illinois patient recovered $81,250 from a therapist for sexual abuse. The jury indicated that it would have awarded more in damages, but it did not because the patient bore some of the responsibility for the "affair."[26]

A South Carolina federal district court awarded $70,000 in damages against the United States for a case involving a physician's assistant who made improper sexual advances, causing the patient to believe that the best course of treatment was to engage in sexual relations with him. The attending physicians were found negligent for failure to supervise treatment. The court also awarded damages to the plaintiff's husband for grief, past and present, and for the loss of companionship.[27]

In Michigan, a patient's claim that she suffered mental and emotional damages when her psychiatrist induced her to engage in sexual intercourse with him "during the course of or under the guise of psychiatric treatment" was held to be malpractice, no different from improper administration of a drug or a defective operation.[28] The court rejected the argument that this was actually an action for seduction of a person 18 years of age or older, a cause of action that had been abolished in Michigan. The court did not consider the fact that the psychiatrist could also be subjected to criminal and professional sanctions for his conduct a reason to deny the patient's claim for malpractice.[29]

Mental health practitioners have also been found liable to third parties related to their patients. In Florida, the former husband of a patient recovered in an action against a psychiatrist and the psychiatrist's employer for breach of contract by failing to treat his former wife within the standard of care.[30] The psychiatrist had acted out his feelings toward the patient, conduct that fell below the standard of care.

Because the abuse of the transference phenomenon for sexual, economic, or other gratification is malpractice or negligence, such activity is covered by professional liability insurance, unless expressly excluded from coverage.[31] Some of the newer policies issued to psychiatrists do expressly exclude damages arising out of sexual activity with patients.[32]

Generally, a therapist will deny any sexual activity with the patient. An admission almost always results in the malpractice insurance carrier refusing to provide legal representation. The malpractice insurance carrier for the American Psychological Association will not pay damages assessed against an insured psychologist based upon sexual contact with a patient.[33]

Some carriers have refused to provide legal representation even when the accused therapist denies sexual activity. A New York court denied a psychiatrist's claim for costs and expenses incurred because of a carrier's refusal to defend.[34] Additionally, if the action is based not on negligence but rather on a contract theory, there may be no professional liability insurance. In Florida, a husband filed an action against a hospital where a psychiatrist acted out his feelings toward the wife-patient. He recovered from the hospital the amount paid for his wife's therapy. In an action by the hospital against the insurance company, the court held that the husband's recovery was based on a contract. Therefore, the hospital's professional liability insurance carrier did not have to indemnify the hospital.[35]

Criminal Prosecution

While it has been suggested that sexual intercourse by a therapist with a patient should be prosecuted as rape,[36] such prosecutions would not succeed in most jurisdictions because many rape statutes apply only if the act is committed with force and against the will of the victim. Prosecutions have been successful, however, in particularly offensive situations, for example, where a psychiatrist had sexual intercourse with a 16-year-old girl he was treating for promiscuity.[37]

Criminal statutes in several states provide that any person having sexual intercourse with another who is under the influence of a drug is guilty of rape.[38] Michigan and New Hampshire criminal laws provide that a therapist who has sex with any patient commits a crime. The New Hampshire criminal statute prohibits "sexual penetration . . . [w]hen the actor engages in the medical treatment or examination of the victim in a manner or for purposes which are not recognized as ethical or acceptable."[39] Michigan's statute[40] goes further; it punishes as a felony a therapist who represents to a patient that sexual intercourse with anyone except her husband "is, or will be, necessary or beneficial to her health."[41] The Gross Sexual Imposition section of the Model Penal Code provides that, "a male who has sexual intercourse with a female not his wife commits a felony of the third degree if: . . . he knows that she suffers from a mental disease or defect which renders her incapable of appraising the nature of her conduct."[42]

OTHER INAPPROPRIATE CONDUCT

A Missouri case provides an extreme example of unprofessional conduct and control by a psychiatrist.[43] A psychiatrist was found negligent where he entered into a social relationship with his patient as part of her therapy. The patient, with the doctor's approval, became his lover. She left her family and moved into an apartment over his office. She went on trips and to nude swimming parties with him and other patients and their families. She invested money in his business ventures. With the encouragement of the psychiatrist, she broke into her husband's house and took some of his clothes, broke into her brother's office to find evidence for use in a lawsuit, and filed lawsuits against various members of the family. The patient moved to the psychiatrist's farm, which was financed in part by $14,000 that the doctor had induced her to invest from her personal funds.[44]

A psychiatrist testified as an expert witness and gave the opinion that the defendant psychiatrist's conduct fell below the standard of care. In particular, the testifying psychiatrist said that the things that took place outside the office were not proper treatment for neurosis; that while group therapy is an accepted form of psychiatric treatment, the nude parties described were not group therapy; and that it was unacceptable treatment for the patient and the doctor to take overnight trips together. He also stated that a social relationship between psychiatrist and patient distorts the transference situation, inhibiting the patient's improvement. Thus, treatment should have taken place in the office.[45]

Another extreme example of improper conduct comes from New York, where a psychiatrist had beaten his young female patient several times during the course of psychotherapy. The psychiatrist argued that the patient failed to establish through expert testimony that the treatment fell below the required standard. The court held that "the very nature of the act complained of bespeaks improper treatment and malpractice."[46]

A California court imposed judgments of $304,000 and $89,000 against a psychiatrist who had engaged in conduct that departed from the accepted standard of care in the treatment of two patients. Both patients attended group therapy sessions during which the psychiatrist and the patients smoked marijuana and discussed the sexual relationships of other patients and the sexual relationships the psychiatrist had with other patients. One patient lent the psychiatrist thousands of dollars to remodel a house and pay off old debts. With one patient, the psychiatrist engaged in sexual relations for four months in the patient's apartment and in the office. The psychiatrist testified that he went to that patient's apartment two or three times "just to keep her alive" because she was suicidal. The progress notes did not refer to suicide ideations or attempts. The court found that the treatment was not properly documented and that the manner of sex treatment fell "outside the standard of care." The court also found that borrowing money from and smoking marijuana with patients was improper.[47]

PROTECTION OF PATIENT FROM SELF

In a clinic, a psychiatrist may be held liable as the supervisor of other professionals treating patients,[48] and psychologists and social workers may be liable for the suicide of a patient when they fail to refer, but psychiatrists are rarely held liable for patient suicides in outpatient settings.[49] Nevertheless, a number of situations expose a therapist to liability in an outpatient setting.

> (1) Where . . . [a therapist] makes a gross error in judgment with respect to whether a patient should be confined; (2) Where in situations where the risks of suicide are great, . . . [a psychiatrist] writes a prescription ordering a number of pills which could be fatal if taken in one dose, and the patient uses the pills to commit suicide; and (3) Where a . . . [therapist] negligently or intentionally discloses confidential communications made to him by the patient in situations where it is foreseeable that the disclosure may cause the patient to harm himself, and the disclosure is a decisive factor in the decedent's decision to commit suicide.[50]

Liability for "therapist induced suicide" has also been suggested. In this situation, a therapist triggers a suicide by dwelling on a subject "in a way that upsets the patient and he is unable to deal with it, and becomes increasingly depressed."[51]

Failure to provide a suicidal patient with appropriate treatment (medication or ECT) may expose a therapist to liability. One psychiatrist stated:

> Those who treat severe depression should have the broadest possible knowledge of the limitations of various psychotherapeutic techniques. Similarly, they should have an intimate knowledge of the benefits and limitations of the antidepressant drugs. . . . Finally, the therapist who does not have facilities for emergency hospitalization at his disposal, should this become necessary, should not treat severely depressed patients, let alone suicidal patients.[52]

This position has led some to conclude that psychologists, psychiatric nurses, and social workers who practice independently should not treat severely depressed or suicidal patients without a consulting psychiatrist.[53]

TREATMENT BY ADMINISTRATION OF MEDICATION

Prescriptions written by psychiatrists in their private offices or in public clinics involve the same basic issues as medication administered in an institutional setting except that patients must be informed of possible side effects and given access to medical assistance if a problem should arise. Issues raised with regard to administration of medication are discussed in Chapter 8.

A psychiatrist who prescribes medication to a nonhospitalized patient must take a medical history, conduct a physical examination, and provide any special instructions necessary to educate the patient and the patient's family as to possible side effects. The psychiatrist must also provide referral services in the event that a problem should arise.

In Alabama, an airman had been diagnosed and treated for "acute and chronic and situational reaction manifested by hysteria, anxiety, and depression" at a military psychiatric clinic for several days. A month after his release, he went to an outpatient clinic, where a physician prescribed an "extreme" amount of Valium (enough for 50 days) on the basis of an "inadequate" medical history and without a check of the clinic's records.[54]

Several days later the airman, after ingesting Valium and alcohol, drove his automobile head-on into the plaintiffs' automobile at 50 to 60 miles per hour, causing injuries. The plaintiffs filed suit in federal court under the FTCA. The defendant/physician testified that, had he known that the airman "was suffering from depression and recently had been treated for psychiatric problems," he would not have prescribed Valium because the effect would be to increase the depression.

An expert witness testified that "prescribing a large amount of Valium to an unknown patient without asking the patient if he had a history of mental problems and without checking for records with a psychiatric clinic on the same military installation fell below the standard of care in the medical community."[55]

Private therapists and those employed by community mental health centers have a duty to supervise the dispensation and use of medication properly. In California a court determined the death of an outpatient following her treatment for depression with Sinequan and Benedrye to be grounds for an action against the treating clinic. The patient's mother had advised clinic personnel that the patient was taking six pills at one time and was sleeping for long periods during the day; the center not only continued to provide the medication, but also increased the dosage. Two weeks later, the patient was dead.[56]

Inadequate follow-up on treatment may constitute abandonment. In Minnesota, a patient was treated with ECT and sleep-inducing medication after having been admitted to the hospital for postoperative depression. The patient had a history of mixing alcohol and medications. A psychiatrist discharged the patient by telephone, without evaluation, after prescribing Paraldehyde to be taken at home. The family received no instructions. The patient took an excessive amount of Paraldehyde, became groggy, and severely burned himself, causing permanent injury to his right elbow and necessitating skin grafts. The physician was held liable for "failure to warn against excessive use of drugs used by the patient at home."[57] The Supreme Court of Minnesota stated:

> [I]t is the duty of the physician or surgeon, in dealing with a case, to give the patient or his family or attendants all necessary and proper instructions as to the care and attention to be given to the patient and the cautions to be observed, and a failure to give such instructions is negligence which will render him liable for resulting injury.[58]

Education of the patient can promote compliance with a prescribed medication regimen as well as possibly avoid serious problems. Family members or other significant people in the life of the patient should participate in the education process as well, for any positive support that the patient receives will foster the patient's understanding and compliance. A family member or close friend may be the best person to notice a side effect or change in behavior that would necessitate intervention by a nurse or a physician. An outpatient taking medication and being monitored professionally only at prescribed intervals should be given appropriate referral sources, such as telephone numbers, in the event that a problem should arise during these intervals. Without this valuable information, a patient could be in serious trouble.[59]

ABANDONMENT

While a therapist need not agree to treat a prospective patient, once treatment begins a therapist has a duty to continue treatment until proper withdrawal. A therapist must exercise reasonable and ordinary care and skill in determining when treatment may be properly terminated. For example, treatment may be terminated when the patient no longer needs treatment or when the patient no longer wishes the therapist to continue treatment.

A therapist has a right to terminate treatment, but if it is discontinued while a need still exists, due notice and an opportunity to obtain another therapist must be given.[60] A therapist must also properly provide for a competent substitute therapist when treatment is temporarily interrupted for vacations, conferences, etc. The patient must be informed that the therapist will be unavailable and that a substitute therapist will be covering the case, and treatment may not be interrupted if the patient is in a critical situation.[61] There may be a very thin line between being in a very critical situation and being in need of hospitalization.

While no reported cases specifically address a psychiatrist's or psychologist's duty to continue therapy, a New Jersey case involved abandonment of a mentally ill patient by a general practitioner. In that suit, which alleged both abandonment and negligence, a general physician was alleged to have abandoned an anxious, depressed man by referring him for a psychiatric evaluation after administering 10 milligrams of Thorazine. The man went to a psychiatric clinic in a general hospital, where he was advised to seek psychiatric assistance. One month after his contact with the general physician he was admitted to the psychiatric ward of a general hospital where he committed suicide. An expert witness testified that the general physician deviated from "accepted standards of practice in not adequately assessing the seriousness of the situation. . . ." The expert witness stated in his report that "[s]imply to give the patient a small dose of Thorazine and tell the patient to get psychiatric help was clearly inadequate for the needs of the situation."[62] The trial court found the physician liable, but the appellate court reversed, stating:

> A physician who upon initial examination determines that he is incapable of helping his patient, and who refers that patient to a source of competent medical assistance, should be held liable neither for the actions of subsequent treating professionals nor for his refusal to become further involved with the case.[63]

There is a strong argument that the courts will treat therapists as they do physicians,[64] who cannot abandon a patient once therapy has begun.[65]

The following precedents cite a number of instances in which a therapist breached the required standard of care by terminating a doctor-patient relationship:

- A therapist abruptly discontinued treatment without giving the patient sufficient time to find another therapist.[66]
- A therapist interrupted a treatment program for a vacation or for other reasons, without making arrangements for the care and treatment of the patient during the interim period.[67]
- A therapist failed to respond to a patient's expressed or implied need for emergency care.[68] This applies especially where the patient is psychotic, homicidal, or suicidal.

As with all malpractice claims, the patient must prove that the physician's conduct caused actual harm. A therapist-patient relationship is not perpetual. The patient may terminate the arrangement at will. The therapist may terminate the relationship at will if the patient receives adequate notice and an opportunity to secure another therapist or if the patient fails to cooperate.[69]

INTERRUPTION OF TREATMENT

Many therapists are concerned about the interruption of a patient's treatment when a therapist dies. One solution is a "professional will." Such a will would include the following provisions:

- Colleagues should be designated to inform patients of the death by telephone so that appointments can be canceled.
- The designated colleagues are asked to make themselves or other therapists available for prompt consultation regarding interim therapy, resumption of therapy, or referral.
- Appointment books, diaries, and ledgers and other financial records should be retained in the event patients need substantiation of visits for insurance claims.
- Clinical records, initial interviews, and summaries should be retained; a copy may be forwarded to a successor therapist.
- Progress notes are designated for destruction at the end of three months. These are records that only the treating therapist can interpret and evaluate.
- For good reason, the therapist may include a request that certain patients not attend his or her funeral.
- A designated therapist should inform the family of the deceased therapist that, should patients contact them beyond extending condolences, the family should discuss the matter with the designated therapist.[70]

CONSTITUTIONAL RIGHT TO TREATMENT IN THE COMMUNITY

One of the most significant legal issues of the 1980s is whether an outpatient of a public hospital has a constitutional right to treatment. The shift since 1955 from inpatient to outpatient treatment in state mental health systems has been dramatic. While three-fourths of all patients were being treated in hospitals in 1955, by 1979 three-fourths were receiving outpatient treatment.[71] This shift, characterized as deinstitutionalization, is based on a number of assumptions:

- Persons in need of mental health services should be treated in an environment less restrictive than a state hospital.
- Treatment in the community will facilitate the adjustment of the patient to a normal life.
- High-quality treatment in the hospital should be provided for those for whom treatment in the community would be inappropriate.[72]

While treatment in the community has succeeded in some places, it has failed with respect to substantial numbers of patients. Patients placed in the community have often lacked support services such as continuing psychiatric care, training in basic living skills, and preparation for work.[73] In some major urban areas, these problems have been intensified by placing large numbers of patients in one neighborhood, creating what has been referred to as a psychiatric ghetto where patients live in substandard housing and lack adequate food and clothing. One example is the Uptown Community in Chicago, which is saturated with halfway houses. Another example is Queens in New York City, where former patients live in run-down hotels.[74] The opposition to such facilities in most communities contributes to the creation of ghettos.

Most former patients have meager welfare allowances on which to live. Treatment consists of a prescription for medication. The result is that the patient often is readmitted to the hospital and released again into the community only to repeat the cycle.

This movement toward deinstitutionalization was fostered in part by litigation challenging various state policies such as hospitalization without consideration of other, less restrictive alternatives,[75] refusal to release patients capable of functioning in the community,[76] and confinement where patients received no treatment to improve their disability.[77]

Public interest and mental health lawyers have litigated the issue of whether a mentally ill person who was an inpatient in a state hospital has a constitutional right to receive appropriate treatment in a community setting.[78] In Maine, a case involved allegations that mentally retarded persons in Pineland Center were not receiving adequate care and that those persons placed in the community were not receiving services tailored to meet their needs. The case was settled with a consent order that set standards governing food and nutrition, staffing, education and training, therapy, and medical services.[79]

NOTES

1. Confidentiality is discussed in Chapter 10.

2. Jonas Robitscher, *The Power of Psychiatry* (Boston: Houghton Mifflin Company, 1980), pp. 409–412 [hereinafter cited as Robitscher].

3. Richard Beresford, "Professional Liability of Psychiatrists," *Defense L. J.* 21 (1972):123, 142.

4. Ronald J. Cohen, *Malpractice* (New York: The Free Press, 1979), pp. 17–20.

5. California State Psychological Association, "Task Force Study, 1982," reported in *Chicago Tribune* (May 1, 1983), pp. 1, 14. Holroyd and Brodksy, "Psychologist's Attitudes and Practices Regarding Erotic and Nonerotic Physical Contact with Patients," *Am. Psychologist* 32 (1977):843. Kardener, Fuller, and Mensch, "A Survey of Physicians' Attitudes and Practices Regarding Erotic and Nonerotic Physical Contact with Patients," *Am. J. Psychiatry* 130 (1973):1077, 1080 [hereinafter cited as Kardener, Fuller, and Mensch].

6. Leonard L. Riskin, "Sexual Relations Between Psychotherapists and Their Patients: Toward Research or Restraint," 67 *Calif. L. Rev.* 67 (1979):1000, 1006–1007.

7. *Chicago Tribune*, May 1, 1983, sec. 1, pp. 1–14.

8. J. McCartney, "Overt Transference," *J. Sex Research* 2 (1966):227.

9. M. Shepard, *The Love Treatment* (New York: P.H. Wyden, 1971), p. 207. Taylor and Wagner, "Sex Between Therapists and Clients: A Review and Analysis," *Prof. Psychiatry* 7 (1976):593, 594.

10. Kardener, Fuller and Mensch, *supra* note 5, at 1077.

11. American Psychiatric Association, *The Principles of Medical Ethics with Annotations Especially Applicable to Psychiatry* (Washington, D.C.: The American Psychiatric Association, 1981), ¶ 2.1.

12. American Psychological Association, *Ethical Standards of Psychologists* (1977 Rev.), Principle 62. In *American Psychologist* 36, 6 (June 1981):633–638.

13. American Psychoanalytic Association, *Principles of Ethics for Psychoanalysts and Provisions for Implementation of the Principles of Ethics for Psychoanalysts* (1975), § 10.

14. American Association of Sex Educators, Counselors & Therapists, *Code of Ethics for Sex Therapists* (1975), Ethical Standard 4.

15. National Association of Social Workers, *Code of Ethics* (Washington, D.C.: National Association of Social Workers, 1980), § II 5.

16. Riskin, *supra* note 6, at 1006.

17. *Id.* at 1007.

18. Daniel B. Hogan, *The Regulation of Psychotherapists,* Vol. 1 (Cambridge, Mass.: Ballinger Publishing Co., 1979), p. 260. For a thorough discussion, *see* Hogan, *supra* Volumes 1–4.

19. Shepard v. Ambach, 68 App. Div. 2d 984, 414 N.Y.S.2d 817 (1979) (psychiatrist); Bernstein v. Board of Medical Examiners, 204 Cal. App. 2d 378 (1962) (psychiatrist); Morra v. State Board of Examiners of Psychologists, 212 Kan. 103, 510 P.2d 614 (1973) (psychologist).

20. Cooper v. State Board of Medical Examiners, D–1329 (Cal., Jan. 24, 1972) (before the Psychology Examining Committee), *discussed in* Note, "Standard of Care in Administering Non-Traditional Psychotherapy," *U. Cal. Davis L. Rev.* 7 (1974):56, 60–66.

21. W.C. Gentry, "Abuse of the Therapist-Patient Relationship," *Trial* 16 (May 1980):26, 27 [hereinafter cited as Gentry].

22. *Id.*

23. *E.g.*, Greenberg v. McCabe, 453 F. Supp. 765 (E.D. Pa. 1978).

24. Roy v. Hartogs, 85 Misc.2d 891, 381 N.Y.S.2d 587 (Sup. Ct. App. Term 1976).

25. *Chicago Tribune, supra* note 7.

26. *Id.*

27. Andrews v. United States, 548 F. Supp. 603 (D.S.C. 1982).

28. Cotton v. Kambly, 101 Mich. App. 537, 300 N.W.2d 627 (1981).

29. *Id.*

30. Anclote Manor Foundation v. Wilkinson, 263 So. 2d 256 (Fla. 1972).

31. Zipkin v. Freeman, 436 S.W.2d 753 (Sup. Ct. Mo. 1968).

32. Gentry, *supra* note 21, at 28.

33. Richard Imbert, President of American Professional Agency Insurance, quoted in *Chicago Tribune, supra* note 7. However, legal fees will be paid if the psychologist wins the case. *Id.*

34. Hartogs v. Employers Mut. Ins. Co. of Wis., 89 Misc. 2d 468, 391 N.Y.S.2d 962 (Sup. Ct. 1977).

35. Anclote Manor Foundation v. Wilkinson, *supra* note 30.

36. Masters and Johnson, "Principles of the New Sex Therapy," *Am. J. Psychiatry* 133 (1976):548, 553.

37. People v. Bernstein, 171 Cal. App. 2d 279, 340 P.2d 299 (Cal. App. 1969).

38. *See, e.g.*, Miss. Code Ann. § 97–3–65 (1982 Supp.); N.J. Stat. Ann. § 2A:138–1 (1970); Ala. Code Tit., 13A, §§ 13A–6–60(b), 13A–6–66 (1982); Tenn. Code Ann. §§ 39–2–602(7), 39–2–603 (1982).

39. N.H. Rev. Stat. Ann. § 632–A: 2 VII (Supp. 1979).

40. Mich. Comp. Laws § 750.90 (1968).

41. *Id.*

42. *Model Penal Code* § 213.1(2) (b) (1974).

43. Zipkin v. Freeman, *supra* note 31.

44. *Id.*

45. *Id.*

46. Hammer v. Rosen, 198 N.Y.S.2d 65 (1960).

47. Robitscher, *supra* note 2, at 427–429.

48. Ralph Slovenko, "Malpractice in Psychiatry and Related Fields," *The Journal of Psychiatry and Law*, 5 (Spring 1981):20 [hereinafter cited as Slovenko].

49. See Chapter 11 for a discussion of suicide in an inpatient setting.

50. Runyon v. Reid, 510 P.2d 943, 950–951 (Sup. Ct. Okla. 1973).

51. Slovenko, *supra* note 48, at 20.

52. *Id.* at 21, quoting Dr. Stanley Lesse.

53. *Id.*

54. Watkins v. United States, 589 F.2d 214 (5th Cir. 1979).

55. *Id.* at 217.

56. Bohrer v. County of San Diego, 104 Cal. App. 3d 155, 163 Cal. Rptr. 419 (1980).

57. Christy v. Saliterman, 38 Minn. 144, 179 N.W.2d 288 (1970).

58. *Id.* at 303.

59. *Id.* at 307. Pamela D. and John C. Andrade, "Malpractice of Psychiatric Nurse," 26 POF 2d 363, 387 (1981).

60. 61 Am. Jur. 2d, *Physicians and Surgeons*, §§ 234–237 (1982).

61. *Id.* at § 243.

62. Brandt v. Grubin, 131 N.J. Super, 182, 329 A.2d 82 (1974).

63. *Id.* at 89.

64. *See* Annot., 57 A.L.R.2d 432 § 1(c) (1958).

65. *Id.* § 1 at 434.

66. *Id.* § 8(a) at 445 (citing Norton v. Hamilton, 92 Ga. App. 727, 89 S.E.2d 809 (1955)).

67. *Id.* § 9 at 447 (citing Vann v. Harden, 187 Va. 555, 47 S.E.2d 314 (1948)).

68. *Id.* § 10 at 446 (citing Burnett v. Layman, 133 Tenn. 323, 181 S.W. 157 (1915)).

69. Tancredi, Lieb, and Slaby, *Legal Issues in Psychiatric Care* (Hagerstown, Md.: Harper & Row, Inc., 1975), 118–122; Annot., 57 A.L.R.2d 434, § 21.

70. A draft professional will by Irvin A. Kraft, M.D., P.A., July 9, 1980.

71. Richard Rapson, "The Right of the Mentally Ill to Receive Treatment in the Community," *Colum. L.J.* 16 (1980):193, 194 [hereinafter cited as Rapson].

72. *Id.* at 195.

73. *Id.* at 208.

74. *Id.* at 208, n. 62.

75. Covington v. Harris, 419 F.2d 617 (D.C. Cir. 1969); Lake v. Cameron, 364 F.2d 657 (D.C. Cir. 1966), *cert. denied*, 382 U.S. 863 (1965); Lessard v. Schmidt, 394 F. Supp. 1078 (E.D. Wis. 1972).

76. O'Connor v. Donaldson, 422 U.S. 563 (1975).

77. *E.g.*, Wyatt v. Stickney, 325 F. Supp. 781 (M.D. Ala.), *enforced*, 334 F. Supp. 1341 (M.D. Ala. 1971), *orders entered*, 344 F. Supp. 373 (M.D. Ala. 1971), 344 F. Supp. 387 (M.D. Ala. 1972), *aff'd. in part, rev'd. and remanded in part sub nom.*, Wyatt v. Aderholt, 503 F.2d 1305 (5th Cir. 1974).

78. Rapson, *supra* note 71, at 218.

79. Wuori v. Zitnay, No. 75–80–SD (D. Me. July 14, 1978) *reported in Mental Disability L. Rep.* 2 (1978):729.

Chapter 5

Duty to Third Parties

Courts in a growing number of states have imposed an affirmative duty on therapists treating mentally ill individuals to protect nonpatient third parties from foreseeable harm caused by their patients.[1] Traditionally, the law did not recognize a practitioner's duty toward individuals with whom no formal relationship existed, but by analogizing the practitioner's duty to use his or her best professional judgment to diagnose and predict a patient's potential for violent behavior as found in malpractice law to third-party situations, courts have established a basis for holding a practitioner liable for harm caused to a third party by a patient. In *Tarasoff v. Regents of University of California*, the landmark case in this area, the California Supreme Court held:

> [O]nce a therapist does in fact determine, or under applicable professional standards reasonably should have determined, that a patient poses a serious danger of violence to others, he bears a duty to exercise reasonable care to protect the foreseeable victim of that danger. While the discharge of this duty of due care will necessarily vary with the facts of each case, in each instance the adequacy of the therapist's conduct must be measured against the traditional negligence standard of reasonable care under the circumstances.[2]

Under the *Tarasoff* formulation therapists are not liable unless they have made or should have made a determination, applying professional standards, that a patient is dangerous to a third party, and failed to take steps to protect the third party. Note that the court did not frame the duty in terms of a warning to third parties, a misleading and inaccurate characterization some authors use. The court said that a therapist "bears a duty to exercise reasonable care to protect the foreseeable victim of that danger."[3] The discharge of this duty depends upon the specific facts in an individual case.

In addition, therapists need only exercise their best judgment to discharge the duty:

Within the broad range of reasonable practice and treatment in which professional opinion and judgment may differ, the therapist is free to exercise his or her own best judgment without liability; proof, aided by hindsight, that he or she judged wrongly is insufficient to establish negligence.[4]

The duty to protect third parties from harm by the patient applies to those professionals licensed for independent practice: psychiatrists, psychologists, psychiatric social workers, and psychiatric nurses. This duty does not require a therapist to warn the parents of a patient that their child is suicidal.[5]

Therapists must be aware of their duty toward third parties, be able to recognize situations in which that duty calls for protective action, and decide which course of action best meets the demands of the situation without breaching their patients' privacy or trust. This requires consideration of alternative means of fulfilling the responsibility.

Most courts define the duty in terms of exercising reasonable care to protect potential victims when, in the professional judgment of the therapist, it is foreseeable that a patient may harm a third party. The crucial element is the foreseeability of harm. Therapists are not liable for errors in judgment; rather, they must exercise the same degree of skill and knowledge used by other members of their profession under similar circumstances to determine whether a particular patient presents a serious danger to others.

This duty may arise in a number of circumstances. For instance, in *Tarasoff*, the patient had revealed during therapy sessions his intention to kill a girl. At the psychologist's request, the police briefly detained the patient but released him when he appeared rational. Although two psychiatrists concurred with the psychologist that the patient should be involuntarily admitted to a psychiatric hospital, the chief of the psychiatry department directed that no further action be taken to detain the patient. No one even attempted to warn the girl or her family or friends.

The patient did murder the girl, and her parents sued the killer's psychologist and three psychiatrists. The trial court dismissed the complaint as not stating a cause of action. In other words, even if the facts alleged in the complaint were true, there was no liability on the part of the therapists and the state as a matter of law. The state supreme court reversed, stating that if the facts alleged in the complaint were proved, the defendants could be held liable for failure to take steps to protect a third party threatened with harm by the patient.

In a New Jersey case involving a wrongful death, *McIntosh v. Milano*,[6] the court refused to enter a summary judgment against the patient's psychiatrist. The psychiatrist had counseled a 17-year-old boy for two years for what was initially diagnosed as "an adjustment reaction of adolescence." Among other matters, the patient related his sexual and emotional involvements with a 21-year-old woman who lived next door. According to the psychiatrist, the patient had never exhibited any violent feelings toward the victim, nor had he ever threatened to harm her even though the patient admitted firing a BB gun at her car and her house windows.

On the day of the murder, the patient had stolen a prescription form from the psychiatrist's office. He attempted to obtain 30 Seconal tablets, but the pharmacist became suspicious and called the psychiatrist who instructed him not to fill the prescription. The psychiatrist tried to contact the patient at home, but did not warn the woman. The patient obtained a pistol and fatally shot the woman in a park near her parents' home.

The parents had filed an affidavit of a psychiatrist, which stated that the defendant's failure to warn constituted a "gross deviation" from accepted medical practices. The court rejected the defendant's arguments that a psychiatrist cannot accurately predict dangerousness, noting that psychiatrists routinely give such professional opinions in litigation concerning criminal insanity, mental illness, and civil commitments. The court found that the prediction in this case did not call for a judgment beyond the psychiatrist's expertise. The court also rejected as factually unproven the defendant's contentions that a duty to warn would interfere with treatment of a violent patient and would unduly increase the number of involuntary admissions to psychiatric treatment facilities. The court ordered the matter to proceed to trial.

Both *Tarasoff* and *McIntosh* dealt with clearly identifiable potential victims. In situations where the potential victim cannot be readily identified, most courts refuse to hold a therapist liable. For instance, the same court that wrote the *Tarasoff* opinion refused to find a county juvenile detention facility liable for releasing a known child molester with violent tendencies into the community. The former patient sexually assaulted and murdered a young boy; yet the court reasoned the tragedy was not foreseeable merely because the victim lived in the neighborhood.[7]

Similarly, a Pennsylvania federal district court refused to extend the duty to warn to "unidentifiable" third parties.[8] In this instance, therapists at the Veterans' Administration treated a voluntary patient for paranoid schizophrenia and chronic alcoholism. During a ten-year course of treatment, the patient displayed violent outbursts and other aggressive, impulsive, and unstable behavior due to alcoholism, but he continued drinking.

The patient finally discharged himself, informing hospital personnel that he would be staying with friends. One evening, the former patient and his friends went to a club where the patient drank nearly a case of beer. Later, at the friends' home, he drank more beer and took 400 milligrams of Thorazine. During that night, the friends were beaten by an unseen assailant.

The friends sued the Veterans' Administration. The court, however, found the plaintiffs were not foreseeable victims as the patient did not pose any greater danger to them than he did to anyone else he was likely to meet in a violent state. The fact that the therapists knew the patient was staying with his friends did not make them identifiable victims.

Yet a Nebraska federal district court has found that a practitioner's duty extends to any potential victim.[9] After release from a Veterans' Hospital, a man entered a nightclub and fired into a crowded dining room, wounding the plaintiff and killing her husband. The plaintiff claimed that the Veterans' Administration personnel who treated the assailant negligently failed to detain him or to initiate involuntary admission proceedings. The court held that, under Nebraska law, the psychotherapist-patient relationship gives rise to a duty to initiate "whatever precautions are reasonably necessary to protect potential victims of the patient. This duty arises only when in accordance with standards of the profession the therapist knows or should know that the patient's dangerous propensities present an unreasonable risk of harm to others." Thus, in Nebraska the patient's dangerous propensities must be foreseeable, but the patient's victim need not be identifiable. However, while this opinion is phrased in terms of the therapist's duty to take steps to protect a third party from a patient, it seems more like a negligent discharge of a patient from an institution.[10]

A therapist should be alerted any time a situation arises where the potential victim of a dangerous patient can be clearly identified. The absence of an identifiable victim, however, should not necessarily cause a therapist to assume he or she has no further duty in regard to third persons. Rather, the therapist should carefully evaluate the foreseeability of potential harm the patient might cause. Where, in the therapist's judgment, the patient will resort to violence, the practitioner should consider possible steps to prevent a mishap.

The necessary actions of the practitioner will depend on the entire situation. Unfortunately, no absolute guidelines can be given. The practitioner must balance a number of factors in deciding whether protective steps are necessary and what those steps should be. In situations involving identifiable victims, such as *Tarasoff* and *McIntosh*, one solution may be to warn the third party of the danger. A warning should not be undertaken, however, until the practitioner has fully considered the effects of the revelations of a patient's privileged confidences to a third party.[11] In both *Tarasoff* and *McIntosh*, the defendants argued that warnings would have violated the patient's confidence and breached professional ethics; yet the respective courts reached different balances among the competing interests. The *Tarasoff* court determined that "protective privilege ends where public peril begins."[12] Nevertheless, the court cautioned that even in life-threatening situations, disclosures must be made only when necessary to avert danger and must be made discreetly and in a fashion that will preserve the patient's privacy to the fullest extent possible.

A Maryland court held that the patient's right to confidentiality outweighs the therapist's duty to take steps to protect a third party. However, the circumstances were peculiar. The plaintiff and a couple were being treated by the same defendant psychiatric team, consisting of a psychiatrist, a psychologist and a psychiatric nurse. The plaintiff engaged in an affair with the wife. While the plaintiff and the wife were in bed nude at the plaintiff's apartment, the husband entered the bedroom and shot the plaintiff five times. The husband never indicated to the psychiatric team that he planned to harm the plaintiff. [13]

The court distinguished the case from *Tarasoff* by stating that there was no showing that the psychiatric team had any knowledge of a threat to the plaintiff. The court could have held that no liability existed based on this ground alone. However, the court added gratuitously that members of the psychiatric team could not lawfully disclose, had they known, that the husband threatened harm to the plaintiff because such disclosure would violate the state confidentiality act.

A therapist first must determine whether his or her patient poses a serious danger to an identifiable third party or parties. If such a danger is posed, the therapist then must determine what protective action must be taken. Several factors are relevant to these determinations, among them the seriousness of the threatened harm, the likelihood that the patient will harm the third party, the standards in the therapeutic community for assessing the danger and its likelihood, and the impact of protective action on the third party and the patient.

The more serious the threatened harm, the more likely it is that some action is necessary to protect the third party. [14] A wide difference exists between harm threatened with a dangerous weapon—such as a knife, a revolver, or poison— and a threatened punch in the mouth or slap across the face.

The likelihood of the patient carrying out the threatened harm may require consideration of many factors. Were similar threats of serious harm made in the past carried out? Is there any other history of threats or overt acts of harm? Is the likelihood of harm based solely on the prediction of dangerousness without any recent overt threat or harm as a basis? Is the patient suffering from a delusion involving the third party, upon which he or she may act in a violent way? Other factors that may be relevant are the degree of psychotic manifestations, the patient's cultural background, and whether the patient has a history of being physically assaulted as a child. The more likely the harm, the more likely it is that some protective action will be necessary. [15]

The danger posed must be upon a specific individual or some group of persons who are identifiable, except in Nebraska. Mere propensity toward violence is not enough. For example, a California court stated that a police officer's alleged propensity toward unnecessarily violent acts to particular racial or ethnic groups was insufficient impetus for a psychotherapist to take protective steps. The court apparently based its reasoning on the fact that the standard of an identifiable victim was not met. [16] If the potential victim is not sufficiently identified, the protective action possible obviously is limited, but, while no victim can be warned, a therapist may have a responsibility to initiate involuntary hospitalization if the patient's condition meets the standard for such an admission.

Another significant factor is the third party's knowledge of the potential harm. If the victim already knows of the threatened harm, protective action such as a warning may have no value. Nevertheless, a warning may confirm to the third party that the threatened harm should be taken seriously. A court in the state of Washington held that a lawyer had no duty to warn a potential victim of his client's intent to do harm where the victim knew of the danger.[17] If the victim has no knowledge of the threatened harm, however, a warning may be necessary. The third party may be harassing the patient and, as a result, may expect retaliation.[18] In the Pennsylvania case, mentioned earlier, the court said that whether the victim knowingly and voluntarily assumed the risk of being assaulted is a relevant factor in establishing whether a therapist is liable for failure to take protective action.[19] Other considerations may be whether the potential victim is a minor or mentally retarded and thus incapable of self-protection. The third party's geographic proximity to the patient is also a factor.[20]

Will a warning to the potential victim cause harm to the victim or invite an attack upon the patient? It has been suggested that a warning to the potential victim may result in an action for mental distress against the therapist for the fear and anxiety caused by the warning or that the potential victim may confront the patient and one or the other may be injured.[21] An action for mental distress by the third party based on fear and anxiety caused by a warning seems a bit farfetched. The possibility of the patient being injured because of a warning does exist, depending on the third person. Nevertheless, in some situations it may be difficult to avoid injury to one or the other.

Aside from warning the potential victim, the major alternatives are the initiation of involuntary admission proceedings and notification of law enforcement authorities. Both of these alternatives were initiated but aborted in *Tarasoff*. Taking action that results in the patient's disposing of a weapon may discharge the duty.[22] In other cases, continuation, intensification, or modification of the patient's therapy may eliminate the danger.[23]

Finally, a major consideration is the standard applied in the therapeutic community for a determination of whether the threatened harm is serious and likely to happen and, if so, the standards for determination of the nature of the protective action to be taken.

LIABILITY OF PSYCHIATRIC NURSES

In those states where they are licensed to practice independently, psychiatric nurses would be held to the same duty as other therapists.[24] The American Nurses' Association has recommended state legislation that would allow diagnosis, counseling, intervention, and the management of illness within the definition of nursing.[25] A few states have adopted such legislation.[26]

A psychiatric nurse who is not acting independently, but rather under the supervision of a psychiatrist, nevertheless may have a responsibility to take steps to protect a third party threatened by a patient. When a patient confides in the nurse, but not the psychiatrist, the nurse should contact the psychiatrist instead of taking personal action to protect the intended victim, assuming there is time to do so. There is no breach of confidentiality when the nurse contacts the psychiatrist. In fact, a nurse who concludes that a patient presents a serious danger of violence to another may have a duty to take protective action and could be liable for the breach of that duty. The standard that should apply is whether a reasonable psychiatric nurse exercising a reasonable duty of skill, knowledge, and care ordinarily possessed and exercised by psychiatric nurses would determine that the patient presents a serious danger of violence to a specific person or persons. If the nurse contacts the psychiatrist and conveys the patient's intentions and the psychiatrist decides not to take any protective action, it is doubtful whether the nurse could ever be held liable. The treating physician is responsible for the patient; hence, his or her decisions should govern as long as the nurse presents all the facts to the psychiatrist.[27]

NOTES

1. Lipari v. Sears, Roebuck and Co., 497 F. Supp. 185 (D. Neb. 1980); Leedy v. Hartnett, 510 F. Supp. 1125 (M.D. Pa. 1981); Tarasoff v. Regents of University of California, 131 Cal. Rptr. 14, 551 P.2d 334 (1976); Department of Health and Rehabilitative Services v. McDougall, 359 So. 2d 528 (Fla. 1978); McIntosh v. Milano, 168 N.J. Super. 466, 403 A.2d 500 (1979).

2. Tarasoff v. Regents of University of California, *supra* note 1, at 551 P.2d 345.

3. *Id.*

4. *Id.*

5. Bellah v. Greenson, 141 Cal. Rptr. 92 (Cal. App. 1977).

6. McIntosh v. Milano, *supra* note 1.

7. Thompson v. County of Alameda, 167 Cal. Rptr. 70, 614 P.2d 728 (1980). *See also*, Mavroudis v. Superior Court, 102 Cal. App. 3d 594, 162 Cal. Rptr. 724 (1980).

8. Leedy v. Hartnett, *supra* note 1.

9. Lipari v. Sears, Roebuck and Co., *supra* note 1.

10. See Chapter 11.

11. See Chapter 9.

12. Tarasoff v. Regents of University of California, *supra* note 1, at 554 P.2d 347.

13. Shaw v. Glickman, 45 Md. App. 718, 415 A.2d 625 (1980).

14. George E. Dix, "Tarasoff And The Duty to Warn Potential Victims," *Law and Ethics in the Practice of Psychiatry* (New York: Brunner & Mazel, Publishers, 1981), pp. 118, 125 [hereinafter cited as Dix].

15. *Id.* Diane K. Kjervik, "The Psychiatric Nurse's Duty to Warn Potential Victims of Homicidal Psychotherapy Outpatients," *Law, Medicine & Health Care* (Dec. 1981):11, 13 [hereinafter cited as Kjervik].

16. Lemelle v. Superior Court for the County of Orange, 143 Cal. Rptr. 450, 457 (Cal. App. 1978).

17. Hawkins v. King County Department of Rehabilitative Services, 602 P.2d 361, 365–366 (Wash. App. 1979).

18. Kjervik, *supra* note 15, at 13.

19. Leedy v. Hartnett, *supra* note 1, at 1131.

20. Kjervik, *supra* note 15, at 13; *See also* Dix, *supra* note 14, at 128, 129.

21. E.J. Griffith and E.E.H. Griffith, "Duty to Third Parties, Dangerousness, and the Right to Refuse Treatment: Problematic Concepts for Psychiatrist and Lawyer," *Calif. L. Rev.* 14 (1978):241, 274.

22. L.H. Roth and A. Meisel, "Dangerousness, Confidentiality and the Duty to Warn," *Am. J. Psychiatry* 134 (1977):508–511.

23. Dix, *supra* note 14, at 130.

24. Kjervik, *supra* note 15, at 11.

25. American Nurses' Association, *The Nursing Practice Act: Suggested State Legislation* 6 (ANA Publication Code #G–1421M, Feb. 1980).

26. Kjervik, *supra* note 15, at n. 4.

27. Pamela D. Andrade and John C. Andrade, "Malpractice of Psychiatric Nurse," 26 POF 363, 393.

Part IV

Inpatient Setting

Responsibilities of Governing Boards, Chief Executive Officers, and Medical Staffs

GOVERNING BOARDS

Governing boards have the primary responsibility for the quality of health care provided in inpatient and outpatient programs and for the competency of those appointed to the medical staff or employed by the hospital.[1] A governing board's responsibility for the operation of a psychiatric program is similar to its responsibility for other hospital programs. Nevertheless, psychiatric programs are subject to far more legal regulation than other hospital programs. State mental health codes not only govern admission to and discharge from psychiatric programs, but also generally regulate in some detail the treatment and rights of patients. Confidentiality acts also regulate the flow of information concerning patients. These statutes and regulations set out numerous standards with which mental health professionals must comply. Thus the governing board and, in state institutions, the director of the mental health agency are ultimately responsible for the operation of the psychiatric program.[2]

Governing boards carry out the responsibility for the quality of mental health care provided to patients by ensuring that: (a) the appointments and reappointments to the medical staff are based on current demonstrated competence and delineations of privileges are based on individual ability to perform competently; (b) performance of the professional staff is periodically reviewed; and (c) an effective quality assurance/risk management program exists.

The JCAH has promulgated specific standards for psychiatric programs, which provide that the governing board, through the hospital's chief executive officer, must adopt "a written statement of the goals and objectives of the program" as well as written procedures for implementing these goals and objectives.[3] Bylaw provisions must give the professional staff the authority necessary to encourage high-quality patient care and must require the establishment of controls to encourage the staff to observe professional standards of care and carry out its functions in accordance with local, state, and federal laws.[4]

While the governing board retains ultimate authority, it delegates to the medical staff or professional staff organization "the overall responsibility for the quality of all clinical care provided to patients, and for the ethical conduct and professional practices of its members."[5] When the psychiatric program is a component of a larger hospital, its staff must be given the authority necessary to plan, organize, and operate the program, subject to the overall responsibility of the governing board.[6]

Finally, the governing board must establish, maintain, and support through the hospital's administration and professional staff "an ongoing quality assurance program that includes effective mechanisms for reviewing and evaluating patient care, and that includes an appropriate response to findings."[7]

The governing board has the legal responsibility to adopt general policies and procedures to ensure that the care and treatment provided in a psychiatric program meet legally acceptable standards. Such policies must take into consideration the obligation to comply with state law and to provide for the safety and protection of patients, staff, and visitors. In addition, the governing board has a moral and professional responsibility to ensure that the optimal level of care is provided, given the resources available.

While governing boards are ultimately responsible for medical appointments and retention, no opinions have been reported in which board members were held liable for the failure of the administration or medical staff to evaluate staff qualifications adequately, but courts have imposed legal liability on the hospital corporation. Individual board members are not held liable for the negligence of the professional staff or the administration unless they participate directly in the incident.

In general, governing board members will not be exposed to any personal liability for any injury to patients because they are not directly involved in diagnosis or treatment. While the famous *Darling v. Charleston Community Memorial Hospital*[8] opinion is sometimes cited as authority for governing board liability for negligent injury to patients, in fact, it was the hospital corporation that faced liability for not having limited the privileges of a physician who was unqualified to treat the patient.

In South Carolina, the trustees of a hospital were sued for the death of a patient caused by the crossing of gas lines—oxygen and nitrous oxide—in the operating room. The court dismissed the lawsuit because the trustees did not participate in the installation of the pipeline system and thus could not be held personally liable.[9]

In New Jersey, a trial court held that where a patient was injured because of the malpractice of the treating physician, the governing board as a group could be sued if they knew, or ought to have known, that the physician was incompetent.[10] Trial court opinions generally are not reported and have little value as precedent. Thus, other courts have not followed the opinion. Nevertheless, the possibility always exists that some court may cite the case for authority.

An Illinois court awarded $10.2 million to the family of a patient who was to have surgery for the removal of a small tumor between her toes. She had been diagnosed as having high blood pressure and an abnormal electrocardiogram, so a local anesthetic was scheduled. Nevertheless, a general anesthetic was administered because, the judge stated, employees of the financially strapped hospital were under pressure from the hospital's governing board to use general rather than local anesthetics, which provided a greater source of income for the hospital.[11] There have been assertions that some small psychiatric hospitals administer ECT extensively because it makes the difference between a profit and a loss for the year. If a governing board should set a policy requiring such action, exposure to liability would result.

While the possibility is remote that governing board members would be held liable for acting in that role, they may be subjected to annoying lawsuits. Thus, governing board members should be protected by Directors and Officers insurance (D and O) and indemnification.[12]

In many states, hospitals agree to indemnify governing board members for the cost of defending lawsuits, judgments, and any settlements that arise out of their activities as members of the board. The indemnification provision is usually included in the hospital's corporate bylaws. In some states, a governing board member may be reimbursed even when found liable for breach of responsibility. D and O may be purchased to cover the indemnification agreement or to cover only liability not covered by the indemnification provision.[13]

California permits a not-for-profit hospital to indemnify governing board members for expenses in defending against a lawsuit charging corporate wrongdoing. If the defense fails, the governing board member may still be indemnified if the action taken was in good faith and believed to be in the hospital's best interest and if the board approves the payment. If the board member has been found liable, the court must approve reimbursement. If a settlement occurs, the attorney general or the appropriate court must approve the payment. The statute prohibits the purchase of D and O to cover trustees found liable.[14]

CHIEF EXECUTIVE OFFICERS

The chief executive officer (CEO) is responsible to the governing board "for the overall operation of the facility, including the control, utilization, and conservation of its physical and financial assets and the recruitment and direction of staff."[15] The CEO of a proprietary hospital may also be a part owner. In that case CEO will function as a superior and as an owner. As part owner the CEO will have a voice in determining hospital policy. In public hospitals, the CEO is usually an appointed official.[16] The CEO assists the governing board in formulating policy by presenting to the board recommendations and reports on short- and long-term plans, available resources, operations, efficiency and effectiveness of the program, and financial reports.[17]

The CEO must ensure that the rules of the hospital are complied with by patients, visitors, employees, and all members of the medical staff. The CEO must take disciplinary action when there is noncompliance with the rules unless such authority has been retained by the governing board or delegated to the medical staff.[18] The CEO coordinates the activities of the medical staff with the board by working with the executive committee and with other committees of the medical staff and the board. The CEO is responsible for the overall administration and coordination of all hospital activities. Because CEOs have this broad responsibility, they often are named as defendants in lawsuits filed by individual members of the medical staff against the hospital for suspension or retention of privileges.

The CEO is liable only for his or her own negligence or the intentional invasion of another person's rights. Liability may also be imposed where the CEO failed to carry out supervisory duties and this failure results in the proximate cause of injury to another. The negligent or intentional act of the CEO, while acting as an agent or employee of the hospital, may result in liability for the hospital. If liability is imposed on the hospital, it has the right to be indemnified by the CEO for the amount of damages paid to the injured person.

MEDICAL STAFFS

The medical staff "has the overall responsibility for the quality of all clinical care provided to patients, and for the ethical conduct and professional practices of its members. . . ."[19] The medical staff is accountable to the board for this responsibility. The manner in which this responsibility is carried out is described in the bylaws of the medical staff, which must be approved by the governing board.[20]

A licensed physician must be responsible for diagnosis and all medical care and treatment unless otherwise provided by law.[21] "The professional staff shall strive to assure that each member is qualified for membership and shall encourage the optimal level of professional performance of its members through the appointment/reappointment procedures, the specific delineation of clinical privileges, and the periodic reappraisal of each staff member. . . ."[22] The privileges of each member of the professional staff must be delineated based upon all information available concerning the professional competence of the individual.[23] Reappointment is based on "the individual's past and current and professional competence as well as his or her adherence" to the governing board and professional staff bylaws.

The responsibility for the quality of mental health care provided to patients includes the selection and maintenance of qualified medical staff and clinical psychologists.[24] In a 1976 survey conducted by the American Hospital Association on the subject of clinical privileges for nonphysician groups, "1,209 hospitals out of 5,734 reporting indicated that clinical psychologists held some level of clinical privileges.''[25] JCAH standards on privilege delineations do not include clinical psychologists.[26] While the governing board may delegate the credentialing responsibility to the medical staff, such delegation does not relieve the trustees or officials of the ultimate responsibility for ensuring that the credentialing process is carried out properly. The credentialing process exists for the purpose of preventing an incompetent physician or clinical psychologist from achieving staff membership.[27] Privileges must be delineated for each member of the professional staff, and must be based on all verified information available in the applicant's or staff member's credentials file. Whatever method is used to delineate clinical privileges for a professional staff applicant, evidence must exist that the granting of such privileges is based on the member's demonstrated current competence.[28] The bylaws describe the procedure for conferring clinical privileges on all professional staff.[29]

If a psychiatrist (or clinical psychologist) who is not currently competent is granted privileges and a patient is injured because treatment fell below the required standard of care, the hospital may be liable to the patient for negligently granting privileges to an incompetent practitioner. The duty to ensure that practitioners granted privileges are competent began with *Darling*[30] and has been adopted by courts in 14 states.

Members of the credentialing committee should be conservative and look for any facts that would justify denial of privileges. Application form information should be verified. References should be carefully checked. An applicant should be asked to disclose any physical or mental problem that might impair performance and any action taken by a state licensing authority, professional society, or medical facility to suspend, limit, or revoke the applicant's license, membership, or clinical privileges. In addition, the review should include a discussion of the privileges sought and relevant methods of treatment in order to judge current competence on diagnosing and treating various mental illnesses. The information gathered in this process, along with the recommendation of the reviewing physician, should be provided to members of the credentialing committee to review and prepare for questions to be asked of the applicant. The committee then makes a recommendation to the governing board.[31]

In a Wisconsin case, the hospital did not investigate the credentials of a physician who applied for staff privileges. A patient sued the physician for malpractice and the hospital for failure to investigate the physician's credentials before granting him staff privileges. The court held the hospital liable, finding that a cursory check of the physician's credentials and references would have indicated that he had staff privileges denied and curtailed at other hospitals because of malpractice problems. The court, therefore, felt that the hospital had breached its duty to appoint only qualified physicians and surgeons to staff.[32]

The duty to ensure that mental health professionals are competent is not restricted to the credentialing process. Whenever the members of the medical staff or the administration learn that a practitioner is or may be providing care below the required standard, the peer review committee should investigate such allegations. How serious must an allegation be to avoid negligence for failure to conduct a peer review of the care provided by the practitioner? In a California case, a patient who had surgery sued a podiatrist for malpractice and the hospital for negligence in failing to conduct an investigation of the quality of care by the podiatrist. The hospital knew that a malpractice action had been filed against the podiatrist four and one-half months prior to the surgery performed on the patient. The court held that this was sufficient to state a cause of action against the hospital.[33]

Often physicians refuse to appear before a peer review committee and state facts known to them concerning another physician's incompetence. They may complain to the CEO that a particular physician is incompetent and that they do not want the physician near their patients. Yet when it comes to making statements before a peer review committee, they simply refuse. Such an attitude results in lower-quality care and may expose the hospital to liability.

In New Jersey, a hospital medical staff was sued as a group on the theory that its members knew that a surgeon was incompetent to perform the scheduled surgery and that it failed to investigate the surgeon when he applied for privileges. The court held that the medical staff could be held liable if the plaintiff could show that it permitted an operation by a surgeon known to be incompetent and the patient suffered injury as a result.[34]

No case has been found holding a hospital liable for granting privileges to a psychiatrist or clinical psychologist who had not demonstrated his or her current competence to practice or for failure to revoke medical staff membership and privileges for incompetence. There are situations, particularly in state institutions, where staff physicians or psychiatrists who clearly have not demonstrated their competence are granted privileges or employed as staff members, exposing the institution to liability. Such psychiatrists often do not have a command of the English language and/or do not understand the cultural background of the patients and hence find it very difficult to conduct a psychiatric evaluation or treat by psychotherapy a young black patient from the south side of Chicago.

As for the competence of current staff, effective quality assurance and risk management activities will identify practitioners who improperly administer medication or ECT or engage in other activities that fall below the required standard of care.

When privileges are denied, a physician may ask the courts to review the action. If the hospital is a public hospital, the courts will review the matter to ensure that the decision was fair.[35] If the hospital is a private, nonprofit institution, the majority rule is that the courts will not review the matter on the theory that they will not substitute their judgment for that of private hospital authorities. Nevertheless, some courts are agreeing to review such actions.[36] Practitioners should read their medical staff bylaws and be familiar with their rights. Requests for hearing or a governing board review are subject to time limitations.

Where privileges are suspended or revoked, the general rule is that courts will conduct a limited review to determine whether the bylaws were followed. Those courts that review the initial denial of privilege would also conduct a review of whether the process was fair and the decision supported by substantial evidence and not merely whether the bylaws were enforced.[37]

The medical staff executive committee acts for the staff. It is responsible for recommendations to the governing board on all matters related to appointments, reappointments, clinical privileges, and corrective actions; and accountable to the governing board "for the quality of the overall clinical care rendered to patients . . .," for initiating and implementing corrective action where warranted in accordance with the bylaws,[38] for certain record requirements,[39] and for quality assurance and risk management activities.[40]

QUALITY ASSURANCE AND RISK MANAGEMENT

All psychiatric programs, including outpatient programs,[41] should have quality assurance/risk management programs to: ensure and improve the quality of care and treatment provided patients; protect the assets of the hospital and mental health professionals from any legal liability arising from the care and treatment provided; retain JCAH accreditation;[42] and qualify for participation in Medicare[43] and Medicaid programs.[44]

Quality Assurance and Risk Management Defined

A quality assurance program is "a well-defined, organized program designed to enhance patient care through the ongoing assessment of important aspects of patient care and the correction of identified problems."[45] The goal is to provide optimal care and treatment given available resources. It is an objective hospital self-analysis of the quality of care and treatment provided. It seeks to measure and evaluate levels of service in light of prevailing standards of professional conduct and to change the behavior of mental health personnel to meet these standards. Quality assurance includes the credentialing process, which ensures that practitioners appointed and reappointed to the medical staff and granted clinical privileges are competent to provide appropriate care and treatment. It also includes the employment of practitioners and other mental health personnel to ensure that the staff is highly qualified.

Risk management has been defined as "the science of detecting, evaluating, financing, and reducing risk of financial loss."[46] The purposes of such a program are to (1) avoid the causes of losses, (2) lessen the operational and financial effects created by unavoidable losses, and (3) provide for inevitable losses at the lowest practical cost.[47] Risk management includes ensuring that the medical staff is competent to provide appropriate care and treatment.

One commentator states:

> There is often a tendency to look at new programs such as this only
> in terms of their financial appropriateness. Risk management in a health
> care institutional setting should primarily be considered a means of
> improving and maintaining quality patient care. The area of loss control
> should be viewed first from the humanitarian standpoint and second
> from the financial standpoint. [48]

While quality assurance is directed at meeting high standards of care and
treatment given available resources, risk management is directed at ensuring that
the standards required by law are met to protect the hospital and health professionals from any liability arising from the care and treatment provided.

State mental health codes and regulations govern admission, discharge, rights
while hospitalized, and even, to some extent, treatment. Violation of such codes
may render a hospital civilly liable for damages. In Illinois,[49] a patient can
maintain a civil action for damages against a hospital and its medical director
who supervises and controls admission and discharge procedures for violation
of the code. For example, in one case a patient was voluntarily admitted and
subsequently signed a request to leave. Under the code, he had a right to discharge
within five working days, unless a petition and two certificates for involuntary
admission were filed. The patient was not discharged, nor were the requisite
petition and certificates filed. He alleged that he had been held against his will
for approximately four months after his request to leave. The court found that
the public's interest in individual liberty and the Illinois Mental Health Code
supported an individual's right to damages for violation of the code.[50] "To hold
otherwise would ignore the underlying public policy, disregard the clear legislative interest, facilitate questionable hospitalizations of those unable to assert
for themselves their statutory and constitutional rights to liberty, and advise the
putative voluntary patient that the statutory assurance of release is transient, if
not evanescent."[51]

Some patients are dangerous to themselves and must be deprived of the opportunity and means to harm themselves. For example, they must not have access
to windows through which they may jump or to physical objects like razors or
linen with which they may be able to harm themselves. Patients also may be
dangerous to others. Staff, other patients, and visitors must be protected. Generally, hospitals have policies to provide this protection.

The role of the administration, attending psychiatrists, and other mental health
professionals is to propose a quality assurance/risk management program to the
governing board for its approval. The professional staff is responsible for implementing the program and accountable to the governing board for its operation.
Reports are submitted to the governing board that summarize the studies conducted, the problems and risks identified, and the corrective action taken.[52]

Quality assurance and risk management should, it has been argued, be integrated into one program because both are concerned with the quality of care and treatment provided to patients. Quality assurance focuses on optimal care and treatment while risk management focuses on an acceptable level of care from a legal perspective. The same sources of data are often used to identify problems and risks, and an integrated program will maximize the use and benefit of limited resources available for such activities. As health care resources become increasingly limited, need for cost-effective strategies[53] grows greater.

Components

The components of a quality assurance program are:

1. identification of important or potential problems, or related concerns, in the care of patients;
2. objective assessment of the cause and scope of problems or concerns, including the determination of priorities for both investigating and resolving problems (ordinarily, priorities should be related to the degree of impact on patient care that can be expected if the problem remains unsolved);
3. implementation, by appropriate individuals or through designated mechanisms, of decisions or actions that are designed to eliminate, insofar as possible, identified problems;
4. monitoring activities designed to assure that the desired result has been achieved and sustained; and
5. documentation that reasonably substantiates the effectiveness of the overall program to enhance care and to assure sound clinical performance.[54]

The components of risk management are risk identification, risk control, and risk financing.[55]

This is a description of an integrated quality assurance/risk management process. The actual structure of a program depends on the size, environment, and other factors unique to an individual hospital.[56]

Problem and Risk Identification

The problems to be identified are treatment and care that fall below professional standards. The risks to be identified are treatment and care that fall below the required legal standards; they are discussed throughout this book.

The major sources of data on problems and risks are patient records and incident reports[57] relating to both clinical care and individual safety. Other important sources of information include the monitoring activities of the professional staff (for example, review of the use of restraints, seclusion, and special treatment procedures); findings of the facility's committees (for example, safety and prescriptions reviews); financial data (for example, liability claim resolutions); utilization review findings; data obtained from staff interviews and from observations of patient services; and patient surveys or comments.[58]

Data analysis should include the determination of priorities for both investigating and resolving problems and risks. Priorities should be related to the degree of impact on patient care that can be expected if the problem remains unresolved. Obviously risks that expose the professional staff and the hospital to liability should receive a high priority.[59]

A patient record is a continuing history of the care and treatment provided to a patient. If the patient records do not contain the required information in an appropriate form, identification and correction of the problem, which is also a serious risk, must be one of the highest priorities.

An incident report is a primary tool for collecting data about an incident, analyzing the data, and translating the information into a strategy for change. Past incident reports should be analyzed to determine whether problems and risks uncovered have been corrected or at least contained.

An incident report should be completed for any unusual occurrence involving persons or property. Unusual occurrences include, but are not limited to: (a) physical harm to patients, staff, or third parties (visitors, workers, students, etc.); (b) unauthorized leave by patients; (c) accidents in which patients, staff, or third parties are injured or die; (d) drug or alcohol use or traffic from the outside; and (e) damage to property.

Incident reports should be abstracted for problem patterns—types of incident, date, time, location, extent of injury, primary and secondary types of persons involved, diagnosis, length of hospitalization, age, disposition and admission status. Abstracted data can be analyzed and compared with other analyses and national studies, for example, *Malpractice Claims*, published by the National Association of Insurance Commissioners. Comparison of data for different periods is useful for evaluating the impact of policy changes over time and identifying existing problems that may require new policy formulation.[60]

Problem and Risk Assessment

There must be an objective assessment of the problem or risk and its cause and scope. This assessment may be prospective, concurrent, or retrospective. Whatever time frames and quality assessment processes are used, the assessment must represent an adequate sampling of all the disciplines. All individual clinicians must be evaluated. The assessment of risks and situations that expose the hospital to liability must be in terms of the cost/risk benefit of alternative changes necessary to reduce or avoid the risk.[61]

Correction of Deficiencies

Corrective action must be taken to eliminate, insofar as possible, the identified problem or risk. Such action may include a broad range of remedies, among them reminders to record more fully in physician and nurse notes the procedures followed; new or revised policies or procedures and educational programs; equipment or facility changes; motivation of personnel; additional personnel; adjustment in clinical privileges; and staffing changes. Risks may be controlled through prevention, containment efforts, or transfer of the risk to another party. The risk may be financed through insurance, pooling, self-funding trusts, or a combination of these devices.[62]

Once a corrective action decision is made, a committee or an individual must assume the responsibility for implementation. If the corrective action involves staff education, it is referred to the education committee. If it involves a change in a policy or procedure, it is referred to the committee that regularly implements such changes. In most cases, it is appropriate to give the responsibility to an existing committee.

Is the deficiency sufficiently serious to require corrective action? Balance the effect on patient care with available resources. Corrective action is inappropriate if extensive resources are required for minimal improvement. This is especially true if resources are needed for more serious problems.

The psychiatric program chair or department head should recommend appropriate corrective measures. Most problems can be solved in a one-time corrective action. However, problems or risks that tend to recur should be closely monitored to ensure that they are corrected or at least contained.

Monitoring of Problem and Risk Correction

Periodic monitoring of the results of corrective action taken must be conducted to assure that the identified problem or risk has been eliminated or satisfactorily reduced or contained. The attainment of a suitable solution to the problem must be a function and responsibility of the quality assurance/risk management committee. A second survey, conducted on a reduced scale, or the collection of additional data may affect the initial interpretation. Changes in responsibilities or advances in knowledge and techniques in a specific area subsequent to initial survey may require revision of the initial study for follow-up.[63]

Program Monitoring

The quality assurance program should include documentation that reasonably substantiates the effectiveness of the overall program in enhancing patient care, in striving to assure sound clinical performance, and in eliminating, reducing, or containing risks.[64]

Patient Care Evaluation

Patient care evaluation studies are the basic tools for the identification and assessment of problems and risks. Study components are: selection of a topic for study; development of a specific criterion statement; collection of data; and the analysis of the data to determine the existence of any significant deviations from the standard.

Selection of a Topic for Study

The psychiatric program chair or department head, with staff participation, selects a topic for study. Personnel working in the psychiatric department are the most knowledgeable and aware of actual or potential problems. While a topic for study may come from any number of sources, it is essential that psychiatric department personnel actively participate in developing and carrying out all phases of the study.

Criteria to Measure the Quality of Care and Treatment

Sources of standards to develop the criteria for studies include accepted standards of professional practice, JCAH standards, mental health codes, confidentiality acts, and hospital licensing acts and regulations. The standards should be significant and lend themselves to measurement.[65] Violation of medical staff rules designed to influence positively the quality of care is not conclusive on the question of negligence, but simply evidence of negligence.[66] JCAH standards have been admitted into evidence to establish the standard of care.[67]

The criteria must:

- relate to essential or critical aspects of patient care or be an activity required by law;
- be generally acceptable to the medical staff as clinically valid in that when applied to actual practice, they can be expected to result in improved patient care and clinical performance;
- be specific and include all the necessary conditions;
- include a practical level of achievement; and
- be capable of measurement in a reasonable period of time and be within the resources of the hospital.

The criteria should be restated as questions. For example, a criterion that "all activities which are required to be documented in the medical record by the Mental Health Code must be entered into the patient's medical record when the activity is completed" can be rephrased into the following questions:

- How many medical records did not contain the required entries?
- What required activities were not documented in the records?
- What categories of staff failed to make the necessary entries (psychiatrists, psychologists, psychiatric social workers, nurses, technicians, etc.)?

The questions should:

- elicit the specific information needed to determine the magnitude of the problem or risk;
- isolate possible sources of the problem or risk; and
- define the problem or risk accurately.

Collection and Analysis of Data

The data are collected from a review of medical charts and analyzed to determine whether the criteria were met.[68] A written report is prepared; it contains:

- the criteria and any necessary explanation;
- whether the criteria were met (include numbers and percentages);
- if the criteria were not met, an assessment of whether the deviation significantly affected the quality of care or resulted in any risk of exposure to liability;
- if there was a significant effect, an assessment of the responsible agents or conditions;
- any factors that are inhibiting the achievement of the criteria. (For example, why is an important form not completed? Is it physician indolence, lack of orientation, inappropriate location in the chart, or awkwardness or lack of clarity of the form itself? This may necessitate the gathering of more information.)

The patient care evaluation study is an excellent tool to measure compliance with state mental health codes and confidentiality acts. An illustration of a patient care evaluation study follows.

Topic. A particular topic is chosen because there are indications of a problem or risk. It may be a clinical topic, such as administration of medication or ECT, or a legal requirement found in the mental health code. For example: In Missouri, within three hours of the time at which a respondent (person subject to involuntary admission) arrives at a mental health facility he or she must be seen by a mental health professional or a registered nurse. The respondent must receive a copy of the application for initial detention and evaluation, a notice of rights, a notice giving the name, business address, and telephone number of the attorney appointed to represent him or her, and assistance in contacting the appointed attorney or an attorney of choice, if so requested. Within 18 hours after arrival at the facility, a licensed physician must examine the respondent.[69]

Criteria for Study. The statutory requirements are the criteria.

Time Period and Data Collection. Data will be collected from all records of persons admitted over a six-month period beginning May 1 and ending November 30. A medical records staff person reviews all records and collects the data.

Survey Questions.

- How many persons were admitted during the time frame?
- How many persons were not seen by a mental health professional or registered nurse within three hours of arrival?
- In how many cases was the record unclear as to whether the person was seen by a mental health professional or registered nurse within three hours?
- How many persons were not given a copy of the application, a notice of rights, or a notice of the attorney appointed?
- In how many cases was the record unclear as to whether such documents were given to the person?
- In how many cases did the record contain no entries on whether the documents were given to the individual?
- How many persons were not examined by a licensed physician within 18 hours?
- On what shifts were the criteria not met?

File Search. There is a search of the files for all records of persons admitted for the survey period.

Review of Records. A staff person reads the selected records and records the data to answer the survey questions.

Summary Report. A record technician or other assigned person prepares a summary report based on the data collected. For example:

- There were 120 admissions during the survey period.
- Mental health professionals and registered nurses failed to see 27 persons within three hours of their arrival. Twenty of the 27 were on the second (evening) shift.
- In 16 cases the records were unclear as to whether the person was seen within three hours. Ten of the 16 were on the second shift.

- In six cases there were no entries that the person was given a copy of the application, a notice of rights, or a notice of the attorney appointed to represent him or her. Two of the six were on each shift.
- Sixteen persons were not examined by a physician within 18 hours.

Corrective Action. A meeting is held with the mental health professionals and registered nurses of the second shift to stress the importance of meeting with the persons within three hours as required by statute. A memorandum is sent to all examining physicians stressing the importance of meeting the 18-hour requirement. A policy is adopted whereby the department chair or the chair's designee assigns examinations. This policy is included in the memorandum.

Final Report. This report summarizes the findings and corrective actions taken. It also includes the time (three months) for a follow-up study to verify that the action taken corrected the problem.

Confidentiality of Quality Assurance/Risk Management Data

Care must be taken to ensure the confidentiality of the minutes of quality assurance/risk management committee meetings and peer review records. Such documents may contain valuable information for a patient's attorney in a malpractice action.

States give varying degrees of protection of such documents from discovery and admissibility into evidence.[70] For example, an Illinois court held that while such documents are by statute not admissible into evidence, they were still discoverable in a lawsuit.[71] The state legislature amended the statute to provide that such documents "shall not be admissible as evidence, nor discoverable in any action of any kind in any court or before any tribunal, board, agency or person."[72] Your state statute should be reviewed to determine the extent of confidentiality.[73] Incident reports are discoverable in malpractice or negligence actions in state court.

In federal courts, incident reports and other hospital documents prepared outside of quality assurance/risk management committee deliberations are discoverable under the Federal Rules of Civil Procedure. Incident reports will quite likely be admissible in evidence as a record of a regularly conducted activity under the Federal Rules of Evidence. One author states that this need not be "a devastating blow to any case" because incident reports should report facts only and not speculations, conclusions, or opinions relating to cause or fault. Such speculations, etc., are topics more properly discussed within the quality assurance/risk management committee itself where the discussions are confidential and protected from discovery.[74]

Because incident reports are discoverable, they should be timely, accurate, objective, complete, and factual. They should not be altered or rewritten. If a correction is necessary, the same policy that applies to the correction of medical records should be used. Altered incident reports raise an inference of wrongdoing, just as altered medical records do. Similarly, critical comments or comments blaming others for incidents should not be included in incident reports. Basically, the same principles that apply to medical records apply to incident reports.[75]

PATIENT MEDICAL RECORDS

Medical records are absolutely necessary to ensure the delivery of appropriate care and treatment to patients, for effective quality assurance and risk management programs, and to defend against malpractice and negligence actions. Where patient records are incomplete, altered, inadequate, untimely, and improperly corrected, the hospital and mental health professionals are exposed to liability and other negative consequences. These possible consequences include loss of JCAH accreditation, difficulties with state health agencies, refusal of third-party payers to reimburse because the records do not adequately reflect the services provided, suspension of physician privileges, and malpractice claims.

Records Are Required by Law

State and federal law require medical records for all patients. Most state licensing agencies require records. For example, the Hospital Licensing Requirements of the Illinois Department of Public Health require that "for each patient there shall be an adequate, accurate, timely and complete medical record."[76] The Illinois Mental Health and Developmental Disabilities Code provides that hospital psychiatric programs must "maintain adequate records which shall include . . . [the statutory section] under which the patient was admitted, any subsequent change in the patient's status, and the requisite documentation for such admission and status."[77] Medicare regulations require that "the medical records contain sufficient information to justify the diagnosis and warrant the treatment and end results."[78] Medicaid regulations mandate that patient records include certain information for utilization reviews.[79]

Finally, the JCAH standard for medical records requires that, "The hospital shall maintain medical records that are documented accurately and in a timely manner, that are readily accessible, and that permit prompt retrieval of confirmation, including statistical data."[80]

While a number of laws require the maintenance of patient records, it is more important that the hospital and staff meet the current standards of professional practice that courts will apply. These standards are found in the JCAH standards, professional literature, and reports of the various professional organizations.

Record Content

State and federal laws specify the general categories of information that must be included in patient records. Such laws also contain specific record requirements for certain kinds of patients. For example, the Illinois Mental Health and Developmental Disability Code contains numerous provisions for mentally ill and developmentally disabled patients. In addition, Medicare and Medicaid regulations contain special provisions for records of psychiatric patients. Medicaid regulations require specific kinds of information for utilization review. Of course, JCAH standards contain general and specific requirements for psychiatric patient records.

The state hospital licensing authority may have specific record requirements. For example, the Illinois Department of Public Health has set minimum requirements for record content. They are:

> patient identification and admission information; history of patient as to chief complaints, present illness and pertinent past history, family history and social history; diagnostic and therapeutic reports on laboratory test results, x-ray findings and surgical procedure performed, any pathological examination, any consultation, and any other diagnostic or therapeutic procedure performed; orders and progress notes made by the attending physician and when applicable by other members of the medical staff and allied health personnel; observation notes and vital sign charting made by nursing personnel; and conclusions as to the primary and any associated diagnoses; brief clinical resume, disposition at discharge to include instructions and/or medications and any autopsy findings on a hospital death.[81]

The state mental health code also may set record requirements. In Illinois the Mental Health and Developmental Disabilities Code requires that a substantial number of activities or events be documented. For example, a record of a patient in a psychiatric program must specifically contain:

1. copies of all legal documents, including petitions, certificates, and notices of hearings;[82]
2. entries concerning required explanation of rights and, if the patient's major language is other than English, noting whether the rights were explained in a language the patient understands;[83]
3. if the patient was admitted on a voluntary basis, entry indicating why it was not suitable to admit the patient on an informal basis;[84]
4. treatment plan;[85]
5. copies of all consent forms for treatment (for example, ECT);[86]
6. court order for ECT for a minor or person under guardianship;[87]

7. an entry indicating restrictions (for example, on telephone calls, letters, visits) that are placed on a patient's rights with the clinical or other reason included;[88] and
8. written orders for restraints and seclusion.[89]

In addition, where the staff members carry out activities required by statute, they should be documented in patient records to establish compliance if the need arises. For example:

- entries that copies of documents such as petition, notice of hearing, and written statement of rights were given to the patient and other required parties;[90]
- entry that the patient was informed of the right not to speak to the mental health professional conducting the examination for certificate and that any statements made could be repeated in an involuntary admission proceeding;[91]
- entries of all required reviews and results of the patient's clinical condition;
- entry that the patient was informed of the right to refuse treatment, including but not limited to medication. (If treatment was not administered because the patient refused, an entry to this effect must be made in the record. If treatment was administered over the patient's objection, an entry to this effect also should be made.)

State confidentiality acts also may set record requirements. For example, Illinois requires that when there is written consent for disclosure of records or communications, "[a] copy of the consent and a notation as to any action taken thereof shall be entered in the recipient's record."[92]

Medicare regulations require specific information to be recorded in the records of psychiatric patients.[93] See Appendix B.

Professional Standards

In addition to the records requirements of various state and federal laws, the JCAH has standards on records and professional groups such as the American Psychiatric Association. JCAH standards require: (a) that personal information, including legal documents, be recorded for each patient;[94] (b) that unusual occurrences such as treatment complications, accidents, or injuries to the patient, morbidity, death of the patient and procedures that place the patient at risk or that cause unusual pain be recorded; (c) necessary consent of the patient, appropriate family members, or guardian for admission, treatment, evaluation, aftercare, or research; (d) physical and emotional diagnoses, laboratory, roentgenographic, or other diagnostic procedures; (e) correspondence and notations of telephone calls regarding the patient's treatment; (f) a discharge summary; and (g) an aftercare plan.[95]

All entries must be signed and dated.[96] The medical staff bylaws must require: (a) that professional staff approve the symbols and the explanatory legend; (b) that the categories of personnel who are qualified to accept and transcribe verbal orders be identified; (c) that the period of time within which history and physical examination entries must be made in the medical record be specified; (d) that the time limit within which patient records must be completed after discharge of a patient with a limit of 15 days be specified;[97] and (e) that the entries be dated and authenticated by the responsible practitioner.[98]

The American Psychiatric Association report on ECT recommends that records include:

(a) the nature and history of the clinical condition leading to the consideration of ECT;
(b) the details of previous treatments including therapeutic response and adverse reactions;
(c) the reasons for selecting ECT;
(d) the details of all discussions relevant to consent to treatment;
(e) the signed consent form, with the signatures of the patient and/or the relatives, or guardian when appropriate;
(f) the signed concurring and contradictory professional opinions where they exist; and
(g) specifics of the treatment, e.g., unilateral or bilateral electrode placement, dates of treatment, characteristics of the current, drugs administered, etc.[99]

While much information is required by the law or by professional standards to be included in a patient record, some documents should never be included. First, quality assurance and risk management documents should not be placed in a patient record. See the section on Confidentiality of Quality Assurance/Risk Management Data in this chapter.

Some states have laws that deem certain records absolutely confidential unless revealed to unauthorized persons. For example, Illinois has a special provision for "personal notes," which should not be entered into the patient's records. However, once such personal notes are disclosed to anyone except the therapist's supervisor, consulting therapist, or attorney, they are then considered "part of the recipient's record for the purpose of the Act."[100]

Legal Standards for Medical Records

The Hospital Licensing Requirements of the Illinois Department of Public Health require that a committee of the medical staff "be responsible for reviewing the medical records to ensure adequate documentation, completeness, promptness, and clinical pertinence."[101] JCAH standards require that "medical records shall be confidential, secure, current, authenticated, legible and complete."[102] What do all of these requirements mean?

Timely Records

JCAH standards require that:

> Each clinical event, including the history and physical examination, shall be documented as soon as possible after its occurrence. Records of discharged patients shall be completed following discharge, within a reasonable period of time to be specified in the medical staff rules and regulations.[103]

Medicare regulations require that current records be completed within 24 to 48 hours following admission and records of patients discharged be completed within 15 days following discharge.[104]

Making timely entries into the record is important for several reasons. The sooner an entry is made after the event, the more accurate it is likely to be. Some reports or entries convey crucial information upon which other mental health professionals will rely to make specific treatment decisions or to release a patient. If a transfer of physician responsibility occurs and important information has been left out of the record, or if EKG results are not available, the result may be injury to the patient or to a third party, followed by a malpractice action.

Adequate Documentation

All entries in the record must be dated and authenticated, and a method must be established to identify the authors of entries. JCAH standards mandate that identification be made by signature, initials, or computer key. The physician must authenticate the parts of the record that are his or her responsibility.

Medicare regulations provide that only members of the medical staff and the house staff are competent to write or dictate histories and physical examinations. They also require that each physician sign every entry he or she makes, and that, in hospitals with house staff, the attending physician countersign at least the history and physical examination and summary written by the house staff. A single signature on the face sheet of the record, Medicare says, does not suffice to authenticate the entire record.[105]

Completeness of the Record

If important entries, reports, or other documents are missing from the medical record, a malpractice action involving the faulty record will be very difficult, if not impossible, to defend.

In one case, a patient filed a malpractice action after a visit to the emergency room. At the trial, the evidence indicated that the records had been destroyed. The jury was allowed to infer that had the record been retained, "it would have shown that a medical emergency existed and that a doctor should have been called and that more attention should have been given him than was given."[106]

One physician who gives opinions for both sides on whether there was malpractice in a particular course of treatment commented:

> [The doctor's] opinion of the facts is based almost entirely on the medical record. As he says, "If the record isn't good or doesn't reflect what actually happened, it's almost impossible to defend a case. When information is missing from the record, the case has to be settled; one cannot over emphasize the importance of the record. I remember one surgical case where the operative report as well as the postoperative progress notes were missing from the record. That's indefensible.[107]

In a California case involving a military hospital, the physician ordered that the patient not be allowed to leave the ward without a staff escort. By the fourth day after admission, the nurses began to let him go to specific places unescorted. On the fifth day he went to breakfast by himself and subsequently was found dead below the window of a seventh-floor lounge. After the patient's death, a note was added to the medical record indicating that, two days earlier, the physician had authorized the patient to leave the ward unescorted. The physician testified that he had changed the status of the patient. The court found that the patient's status had not been changed. The inserted note was held not to be a proper medical order. The court stated that even if the physician had changed the status, the hospital would still be liable because the physician's "failure to maintain contemporary notes, orders or other records adequately recording and explaining his action in reclassifying [the patient] . . . fell below the applicable standard of care."[108] The court awarded $184,000 in damages.

In Illinois, if a mental patient is in a psychiatric hospital and there is no voluntary admission form signed by the patient and no court order for involuntary admission, then the hospital and the medical director may be held liable.[109]

Incomplete records make it very difficult to prove the diagnosis and nature of treatment provided to a patient. In a New York case where physicians in a state hospital were found negligent in providing psychiatric and medical care to a patient, the court stated:

> The hospital record maintained by the State . . . was about as inadequate a record as we have ever examined. We find that said record did not conform to the standards in the community; and that the inadequacies in this record mitigated against proper and competent psychiatric and ordinary medical care being given this claimant during his stay at Matteawan State Hospital. We further find that the lack of psychiatric care was the primary reason for the inordinate length of this incarceration, with the concomitant side effects of physical injury,

moral degradation, and mental anguish. Therefore, to the extent that a hospital record develops information for subsequent treatment, it contributed to the inadequate treatment this claimant received. . . . [T]his record . . . was so inadequate that even a layman could determine that fact.[110]

The absence of entries in the record substantiated a lack of treatment in this case. Testimony indicated that a physician had examined the patient during a particular period of time, but the lack of any notation to this effect in the record led the court to find that no examination had taken place.[111]

The court reproduced one note in full in the opinion because it was so "illustrative of the inadequacies of the hospital treatment":

November 2, 1955: He was sent visiting to Ward 2 at 6:30 A.M. because he was found unconscious in his bed. Physical examination showed T. 99.2, P. regular and strong B.P. 70/50, both pupils regular and contracted, left knee plantar reflexes decreased. Blood sugar 99.3 percent. Blood RBC 3,700,000. Hge: 78 percent. S. R. 18. Hem. 38. Patient remained unconscious until noon. His pupils then showed reaction to light and the sluggish left side reflexes disappeared. On November 3rd this patient *apparently* regained consciousness but he did not react to questioning. On November 7th, patient remained very uncooperative, used profane language to the doctors and attendants and he claimed he was poisoned and physically abused.[112]

The court commented on this entry:

One might fairly ask, what treatment? Were x-rays taken, were fluids induced, how often were pulse and respiration taken, were drugs given, how long was this patient unconscious, 5–½ hours or 24 hours, what was done for him on the 2d, 3d, 4th, 5th, 6th, 7th, and 8th days of November, 1955? Such a record substantiates claimant's position that he was not given adequate medical care. . . . We might state here that Exhibit "15," the prescription record . . . during his stay in the hospital sets forth the fact that he received vaseline and rectal suppositories during his 14–½ hours. There was no indication of medication from November 2–8, 1955.[113]

Courts have specified minimum standards for patient medical records in class-action lawsuits on the right to treatment. For example, one court has required that records include "a detailed summary of each significant contact by a Qualified Mental Health Professional with the patient," "a detailed summary on at least a weekly basis by a Qualified Mental Health Professional involved in the patient's treatment of the patient's progress along the treatment plan," and "a weekly summary of the extent and nature of the patient's work activities . . . and the effect of such activity upon the patient's progress along the treatment plan."[114]

Psychiatrists frequently state in commitment proceedings that the patient has been restless and unable to sleep over a certain time span or that the patient has not eaten during a certain time span, only to be confronted on cross-examination with the fact that there are no entries in the medical record to support these statements. Sometimes the record is accurate, and the psychiatrist has overdrawn conclusions from the facts. In one such case a young patient with a broken finger saved up three Darvon pills and took them all at once to "get a high." The only effect was that the young woman threw up. The psychiatrist testified that in his opinion this was a suicide attempt. No entry in the record characterized the incident as a suicide attempt, and no entry ordered special precautions to prevent any such future attempt.

Alteration of Records

The alteration of patient records is not uncommon. Sometimes it is done to cover up a negligent act. At other times it is done to cover up a mistake in judgment, the person making the change not realizing that such a mistake is not a basis for liability. Whatever the reason, such alterations are often discovered, resulting in a litigation settlement favorable to the patient, the alteration itself raising such a strong inference of wrongdoing that it overshadows the actual act of wrongdoing, if indeed, there was one.

A Kansas case involved a nurse who made a false entry in the patient's medical records to indicate that appropriate care had been given, when in fact the nurse had ignored a maternity patient's request for her physician. The patient delivered her child with the assistance of the nurse and suffered torn vaginal tissue. The court indicated that once the jury was aware that an entry in the chart was purposefully incorrect, it might assume that other entries in the chart that were favorable to the hospital might also be untrue and could give them little credence.[115]

In a Connecticut hospital, a director of nursing ordered every staff member who had charted a patient's care to change the hospital's records. The nurse substituted the revised record without the knowledge of the hospital administration and in violation of explicit hospital policy. The revised record was false and conflicted with other records and the testimony of staff members. The Connecticut Supreme Court held it "[a]n allowable inference" from the falsified records that the staff acted with knowledge that they were at fault.[116]

Correction of Records

It is important to correct patient medical records in the right way to avoid suspicion of tampering, which could be fatal in a malpractice action. The preferred method is to line out the incorrect data with a single line in ink, leaving the original legible. The reason for the change should be noted, the date of the striking should be indicated, and the persons making the change should initial or sign it. Corrected material should never be obliterated or erased.[117] To do so raises the question of whether the entry contained damaging information.

Good Medical Records

For the protection of both medical professionals and hospitals, medical records must be complete, objective, consistent, and accurate. Entries should be made promptly while the mental health professional's memory of the subject is fresh. They should be relevant. Argumentative notes or statements critical of others or blaming others should not be placed in the record. Such entries can only harm a hospital and staff if a malpractice action is filed. Medical records are not the proper forum for dealing with such problems anyway. Time should be taken to write complete records. This will be the only accurate record of what happened long after everyone's memory, including the patient's, has faded.[118]

Preservation of Records

How long should a patient's medical records be preserved? State law often does not specify any particular length of time. Sometimes, state law dictates that records be preserved in accordance with a hospital policy based on American Hospital Association recommendations and legal opinion.[119]

The American Hospital Association recommends that complete patient records be retained for ten years "after the most recent patient care usage." After ten years they may be destroyed, provided that the hospital:

1. Retains basic information such as dates of admission and discharge, names of responsible physicians, records of diagnoses and operations, surgical procedure reports, pathology reports, and discharge resumes for all records so destroyed.
2. Retains complete medical records of minors for the period of minority plus the applicable period of statute of limitations as prescribed by statute in the state in which the health care institution is located.
3. Retains complete medical records of patients under mental disability in like manner as those under disability of minority.
4. Retains complete patient medical records for longer periods when requested in writing by one of the following:
   a. An attending or consultant physician of the patient.
   b. The patient or someone acting legally in his behalf.
   c. Legal counsel for a party having an interest affected by the patient medical records.[120]

Medicare regulations provide that patient records be preserved "for a period of time not less than that determined by the statute of limitations in the respective state."[121]

The question is, when does the statute of limitations begin to run? Generally, the rule is that the statute begins to run when the final event creating the cause of action occurs. In malpractice actions, the running of the statute depends on the patient's discovery of his or her injury and its cause. See Chapter 1.

NOTES

1. The overall responsibilities for governing board members are beyond the scope of this book. The authority and responsibilities of governing board members are found in state statutes and court decisions. Investor-owned hospitals are subject to state business corporation acts. Not-for-profit hospitals are subject to the state not-for-profit corporation acts and, to some extent, by charitable trusts acts. Public hospitals are subject to specific federal and state statutes. Governing board members have a fiduciary responsibility to the hospital. Stern v. Lucy Webb Hayes National Training School for Deaconesses and Missionaries, 381 F. Supp. 1003 (D.C. 1974) (where some governing board members invested funds in noninterest-bearing accounts in banks to which they were connected). Governing board members have been held liable for failure to invest funds in income-producing accounts. Lynch v. John M. Redfield Foundation, 88 Cal. Rptr. 86 (1970).

2. In Veterans' Administration (VA) institutions, the VA Administrator and the administrators of individual institutions have this responsibility; in military institutions, the secretary of the particular service and the officer in charge of the individual institution have this responsibility.

3. JCAH, *Consolidated Standards Manual for Child, Adolescent and Adult Psychiatric, Alcoholism and Drug Abuse Facilities*, (Chicago: JCAH, 1981), § 1.5 [hereinafter cited as JCAH].

4. *Id.* at ¶ 1.10.3.8.

5. *Id.* at ¶ 3.1.

6. *Id.* at ¶ 1.7.

7. *Id.* at ¶ 9.2.

8. Darling v. Charleston Community Memorial Hospital, 211 N.E.2d 253 (Ill. 1965), *cert. denied*, 383 U.S. 946 (1966). For a discussion of the misapplication of the Darling doctrine, *see* Thomas R. Mulroy, "Hospital Liability Revisited: How Governing Boards Can Protect Themselves And Improve Patient Care," *Inquiry Book* (Chicago: Blue Cross Association, Chicago 1980), pp. 9–10; Moore v. Board of Trustees of Carson-Tahoe Hospital, 495 P.2d 605, 608 (Sup. Ct. Nev. 1972), *cert. denied*, 409 U.S. 879 (1972); Tucson Medical Center, Inc. v. Misevch, 545 P.2d 958, 960 (Sup. Ct. Ariz. 1976), citing *Moore, supra.*

9. Hunt v. Rabon, 272 S.E.2d 643 (Sup. Ct. S.C. 1980).

10. Corleto v. Shore Memorial Hospital, 350 A.2d 534 (N.J. Super. Ct. 1975).

11. *Chicago Sun Times* (Nov. 17, 1982), p. 20.

12. Care should be taken to ensure that the policy protects governing board members against suits for decisions they have made and for failure to oversee the administration of the hospital and its medical staff properly. Limitations on scope of coverage and imposition of deductibles are not uncommon.

13. Arthur H. Bernstein, "Hospital Trusteeship: Liability and Protection," *Hospitals* 56, 1 (Jan. 1, 1982), p. 50.

14. Calif. Corp. Code § 5238.

15. JCAH, *supra* note 3, at ¶ 2.5.

16. David G. Warren, *Problems in Hospital Law* (Germantown, Md.: Aspen Systems Corp., 1978), pp. 15–16 [hereinafter cited as Warren].

17. JCAH, *supra* note 3, at ¶ 2.6.

18. Warren, *supra* note 16, at 17.

19. JCAH, *supra* note 3, at ¶ 3.1.

20. *Id.*

21. *Id.*

22. *Id.* at ¶ 3.1.1.

23. *Id.* at ¶ 3.4.

24. Emily Friedman, "Staff Privileges For Non-Physicians—Part I: How Clinical Psychologists and Podiatrists are Fitting In," *The Hospital Medical Staff* 7, 2 (Feb. 1978), p. 16.

25. *Id.* at 17.

26. JCAH, *supra* note 3, at ¶ 3.4. The 1984 standards are expected to include nonphysicians such as psychologists.

27. Thomas C. Shields, "Guidelines For Reviewing Applications For Privileges," *The Hospital Medical Staff* 9, 9 (Sept. 1980), p. 11 [hereinafter cited as Shields].

28. JCAH, *supra* note 3, at ¶ 3.4.

29. *Id.* at ¶ 1.10.3.12.

30. Darling v. Charleston Community Memorial Hospital, *supra* note 8.

31. Shields, *supra* note 27.

32. Johnson v. Misericordia Community Hospital, 301 N.W.2d 156 (Sup. Ct. Wisc. 1981); *see also* Darling v. Charleston Community Memorial Hospital, *supra* note 8.

33. Elam v. College Park Hospital, 183 Cal. Rptr. 156 (1982). Fourteen states impose a duty on the hospital to ensure that the practitioners with privileges are competent: Arizona, California, Colorado, Georgia, Michigan, Missouri, Montana, Nebraska, New Jersey, New York, Nevada, Washington, West Virginia, and Wisconsin. Arthur H. Bernstein, "Darling is Alive and Well in California," *Hospitals* 56, 10 (Oct. 1, 1982), p. 114.

34. Corleto v. Shore Memorial Hospital, *supra* note 10.

35. Groseclose, "Hospital Privilege Cases: Braving the Dismal Swamp," *So. Dakota L. Rev.* 26 (1981):1, 4.

36. *Id.* at 10.

37. *Id.*

38. JCAH, *supra* note 3, at ¶ 3.7.

39. *Id.* at ¶ 3.8.5.

40. *Id.* at ¶ 3.8.8.

41. Richard L. Grant, M.D., "Quality Assurance in Community Mental Health Centers: Why It May Not Be Working," *QRB* 8 (Sept. 1982):3; Paul S. Sherman and Madeleine Gomez, "Quality Assurance Uses of Level of Functioning Ratings, Applications in a Community Mental Health Center," *QRB* 8 (July 1982):22.

42. JCAH, *supra* note 3, at ¶ 9.0.

43. Utilization Review, 42 C.F.R. § 1035.

44. "The plans must include a description of methods and standards used to assure that services are of high quality." 42 C.F.R. § 440.2601.

45. JCAH, *supra* note 3, at ¶ 9.1.

46. Bernard L. Brown, Jr. *Risk Management For Hospitals* (Germantown, Md.: Aspen Systems Corp., 1979), p. 1 [hereinafter cited as Brown].

47. *Id.* at 1, 2.

48. *Id.* at 2.

49. Montague v. George J. London Memorial Hospital, 78 Ill. App. 3d 298, 396 N.E.2d 1289 (1979).

50. *Id.*

51. *Id.* at 396 N.E.2d at 1293.

52. JCAH, *supra* note 3, at ¶ 9.2.

53. James E. Orlikoff and Gary B. Lanham, "Why Risk Management and Quality Assurance Should be Integrated," *Hospitals* 55, no. 6 (June 1, 1981), p. 54.

54. JCAH, *supra* note 3, at ¶ 9.7.

55. Brown, *supra* note 46, at 2.

56. *See* JCAH, *supra* note 3.

57. Huber & Walford, "Investigative Reporting Cuts Risk at Psychiatric Facility," *Hospitals* 55, no. 5 (May 1, 1981), p. 73.

58. JCAH, *supra* note 3, at ¶ 9.7.1.

59. JCAH, *supra* note 3, at ¶ 9.7.1.2.

60. Andrew J. Korsak, "How to Use Malpractice Data in Quality Assessment," *The Hospital Medical Staff* 9, no. 2 (Feb. 1980), p. 28.

61. JCAH, *supra* note 3, at ¶ 9.7.2.

62. *Id.* at ¶ 4.7.3.

63. *Id.* at ¶ 9.7.4.

64. *Id.* at ¶ 9.7.5.

65. Frederick L. Newman, "Outcome Evaluation and Quality Assurance in Mental Health," *QRB* 8 (Apr. 1982):27; Mary Ellen Guy and Linda S. Moore, "The Goal Attainment Scale for Psychiatric Inpatients," *QRB* 8 (June 1982):19.

66. Foley v. Bishop Clarkson Memorial Hospital, 173 N.W.2d 881 (Sup. Ct. Neb. 1970) (failure to document admission history; no record of an admission physical examination). *But see* Pickle v. Curns, 106 Ill. App. 3d 734, 435 N.E.2d 877 (1982), where it was held that the hospital was not liable where a physician violated a hospital rule because the hospital had no knowledge that the physician would violate the rule. It was alleged that the physician failed to conduct a physician examination and administer muscle relaxant prior to ECT treatment.

67. Darling v. Charleston Community Memorial Hospital, *supra* note 8.

68. Richard H. Allen, "Use of the Problem-Oriented Record to Evaluate Treatment in a Chronic Psychiatric Population," *QRB* 8 (Mar. 1982):13.

69. Mo. Rev. Stat. § 632.320.

70. Daniel G. Suber, *AMA Peer Review: A Legal Update* (Chicago: American Medical Association, 1981) [hereinafter cited as Suber].

71. Walker v. Alton Memorial Hospital Ass'n., 91 Ill. App. 3d 310, 414 N.E.2d 850 (1980).

72. Ill. Code of Civil Procedure, Ch. 110, § 8–2102 (1982).

73. *See* Suber, *supra* note 70, for a review of statutes by state.

74. *See* Spencer, USAF, "The Hospital Incident Report: Asset or Liability," *The Air Force L. Rev.* (1980–1981):148.

75. *See* Kay Laboratories Inc. v. District Court in and for Pueblo County, 653 P.2d 721 (Sup. Ct. Colo. 1982).

76. Section 12–1.2(b).

77. Ill. Ann. Stat. Ch. 91½, ¶ 3–202.

78. 42 C.F.R. § 405.1026.

79. 42 C.F.R. § 456.111.

80. JCAH, *Accreditation Manual for Hospitals* 83 (1981).

81. Ill. Hospital Licensing Requirements, § 12–1.2(b).

82. Ill. Ann. Stat., Ch. 91½, ¶¶ 3–205, 3–611 (Smith-Hurd Supp. 1982–1983).

83. *Id.* at ¶ 3–204.

84. *Id.* at ¶ 3–300(c).

85. *Id.* at ¶ 3–209.

86. *Id.* at ¶ 2–110.

87. *Id.* at ¶ 2–110.

88. *Id.* at ¶ 2–108(a); 2–109(a).

89. *Id.* at ¶ 2–201.

90. *Id.* at ¶ 3–205.

91. *Id.* at ¶ 3–208.

92. *Id.* at ¶ 805(b).

93. 42 C.F.R. ¶ 405.1026.

94. JCAH, *supra* note 3, at ¶ 15.1.6.

95. *Id.* at ¶ 15.1.5, ¶ 15.1.13.

96. *Id.* at ¶ 15.1.14.

97. Medical Staff Bylaws generally provide for the automatic suspension of a physician who fails to complete patient records in a timely manner.

98. JCAH, *supra* note 3, at ¶ 3.8.5.

99. American Psychiatric Association, Electroconvulsive Therapy 163, *Task Force Report 14* (September 1978), p. 163.

100. Ill. Ann. Stat., ch. 91–½ § 810(7) (Smith-Hurd Supp. 1982–1983).

101. Section 12–1.2(d).

102. JCAH, *Accreditation Manual for Hospitals* 88 (1981).

103. *Id.* at 89.

104. 42 C.F.R. § 405.1026.

105. *Id.*

106. Carr v. St. Paul Fire and Marine Insurance Co., 384 F. Supp. 821, 831 (W.D. Ark. 1974).

107. Gardner, "An Inside Look at Malpractice by Expert Witness William B. Buckingham, M.D.," *QRB* 8 (1982):7.

108. Abille v. United States, 482 F. Supp. 703, 708 (N.D. Cal. 1980).

109. Montague v. George J. London Memorial Hospital, *supra* note 49.

110. Whitree v. State of New York, 56 Misc.2d 693, 290 N.Y.S.2d 486, 495–496 (1968).

111. *Id.* 290 N.Y.S. 2d at 498–499.

112. *Id.* at 449.

113. *Id.*

114. Wyatt v. Stickney, 344 F. Supp. 373, 385 (M.D. Ala. 1972).

115. Hiatt v. Groce, 215 Kan. 14, 523 P.2d 320 (1974).

116. Pisel v. Stamford Hospital, 180 Conn. 314, 430 A.2d 1, 15 (1980).

117. Karen K. Kaunitz, "Point of Law," *The Hospital Medical Staff* 10, no. 6 (June 1981), p. 24.

118. *Id.*

119. Section 12–1.2(d).

120. 42 C.F.R. § 405.1026(c).

121. American Hospital Association, "Preservation of Medical Records in Health Care Institutions," *Technical Advisory Bulletin* (1981).

Chapter 7

Admission to Inpatient Programs

Increasingly, courts and legislatures are emphasizing the procedural protection of individuals who are candidates for admission to inpatient programs. No longer do courts, lawyers, psychiatrists, and psychologists meet informally to decide what is in the best interests of the individual. The involuntary admission proceeding has become adversarial. Petitions and certifications must contain more specific information to inform individuals adequately of the facts supporting allegations that they meet the standard for involuntary hospitalization. Some states require those conducting evaluations to inform patients undergoing psychiatric interviews that they need not talk, and that if they do, their conversations may be repeated in court proceedings. Patients must be informed of their rights, including their rights to a lawyer, a hearing, and an independent expert examination. An attorney advocates a patient's position, not the best interest of the patient as viewed by the attorney. The time periods for hearings have been shortened to reduce periods of detention. The standard of proof has been changed from "preponderance of evidence" to "clear and convincing evidence," a higher standard. Generally, hospitalization is ordered only when it is shown to be the least restrictive alternative. In short, the law dominates the admission process. Mental health professionals often view this shift in the system as an interference that can only result in delay in treatment and harm to patients.

Admission to an inpatient psychiatric program is governed by state statutory law that prescribes standards and procedures. Most admissions are voluntary. For example, in Illinois more than 70 percent of admissions are voluntary.[1] Even where involuntary proceedings are initiated, a high percentage of patients are admitted as voluntary patients.

Generally, the statutory standard or criterion for voluntary admission is whether a person is mentally ill and suitable for treatment. The standard for involuntary admission is generally whether a person has a mental illness that causes the person to be dangerous or unable to care for his or her own physical needs.[2]

Minors, younger than 16 or 18 years of age, are sometimes admitted by a different procedure and under a different statutory standard. For example, in

Illinois, the statutory standard for admission of a minor is "a mental illness or emotional disturbance of such severity that hospitalization is necessary and that the minor is likely to benefit from such inpatient treatment."[3]

VOLUNTARY ADMISSIONS

A voluntary admission is far more beneficial to a patient than an involuntary admission because it is an acknowledgment of a need for help, which is the first step toward effective treatment. Almost all admissions to private hospitals and a very high percentage of public hospital admissions are voluntary.

All states except Alabama provide for voluntary admission to inpatient programs.[4] Generally, if an individual is younger than 18, states require the consent of a parent or guardian. Some states allow individuals 15 years of age or older to apply for voluntary admission. The ages vary to some extent from state to state.[5]

The standard for a voluntary admission generally is whether an individual is mentally ill and would benefit from treatment. The standard in Georgia is whether there is "evidence of mental illness" that is "suitable for treatment."[6] South Dakota provides for admission where "clinically suitable,"[7] and Tennessee provides for the admission of a mentally ill person for "diagnosis, observation and treatment."[8]

To be admitted voluntarily, a patient simply signs an application that contains the conditions of the admission. Generally, a mental health professional witnesses the signing. In a few states, persons denied a voluntary admission to a public hospital have a right to an administrative review, but of particular importance to the patient is the release provision. Most states provide for the release of a patient within three to five days unless involuntary admission procedures are initiated.[9] Some provide for immediate release unless involuntary admission procedures are initiated. Generally, a patient may retract a request to leave.

Five states provide for two types of voluntary admissions: formal and informal.[10] Under formal admission, a patient who requests release will be released within a certain number of days unless the involuntary admission procedure is initiated. Under informal admission, a patient is released upon request.

Persons who admit themselves voluntarily are presumed as a matter of law to understand the conditions of the admission. In fact, such persons often do not understand.[11] Patients too ill to understand the conditions at the time of admission often believe they are entitled to immediate release or that they admitted themselves for a specific number of days, generally the number of days provided for a determination of whether to discharge them after a request to leave is made. In Illinois, hospital personnel must orally inform patients of their right to discharge in a language they understand and give them a copy of the Application For Voluntary Admission that they signed. The application contains a statement of rights.[12]

Patients and their attorneys complain that voluntary admissions and retractions of requests to leave are often coerced. Persons may be told that the court will involuntarily admit them anyway so they might just as well admit themselves voluntarily. Others who may have criminal charges pending are told that if they do not admit themselves on a voluntary basis, they will be sent back to the local jail.

Psychiatrists and other mental health professionals have a responsibility to recommend and encourage their patients to admit themselves or remain in the hospital if they need treatment. A therapist may also advise a patient that he or she meets the standard for involuntary admission. It is not appropriate, however, for a therapist to coerce a patient into submitting to voluntary hospitalization by telling the patient that he or she will surely be involuntarily admitted when, in fact, the therapist has no intention of initiating involuntary admission proceedings.

Colorado provides the following statement to candidates for voluntary admission:

> The decision to sign in voluntarily should be made by you alone and should be free from any force or pressure implied or otherwise. If you do not feel that you are able to make a truly voluntary decision, you may continue to be held at the hospital involuntarily. As an involuntary patient, you will have the right to protest your confinement and request a hearing before a judge.[13]

Illinois prohibits physicians, qualified examiners, or clinical psychologists from informing any person that involuntary admission may result should he or she refuse voluntary admission to a mental health facility, unless (a) the practitioner who examined the person is prepared to execute a certificate under the involuntary procedure, and (b) the person is advised that, following admission upon certification, he or she will be entitled to a court hearing—with counsel—at which the state will have to prove the person is subject to involuntary admission.[14]

Some tension exists between mental health professionals and patients' lawyers on the persuasion of persons to become or remain voluntary patients. Mental health professionals feel it is their responsibility to encourage patients in need of treatment to remain. An involuntary admission proceeding is considered destructive to the treatment process. In addition, involuntary proceedings are a resource drain in terms of time—they call for paper work, additional evaluations, travel to court, and a hearing. Many private psychiatrists and hospitals simply do not accept involuntary patients for treatment because of the time factor.

The lawyers answer that if the patient does not understand the situation or is coerced, the admission is not voluntary and violates the statute. Under these circumstances the therapeutic value is questionable. Finally, if persons are to be hospitalized over their objections, then they have a constitutional right to a hearing to establish that the statutory standard is met.

INVOLUNTARY ADMISSION OF ADULTS

The state extends its *parens patriae* ("parent of the country") power to involuntarily hospitalized mentally ill persons who are unable to care for their own physical needs. It exercises its police power to hospitalize involuntarily mentally ill persons who are dangerous to themselves or to others. It has been argued that the *parens patriae* power should be used to hospitalize only those persons who are incompetent to make a decision whether to seek treatment. It also has been argued that the police power should be used to hospitalize only those persons who are dangerous to others. If these arguments were accepted, the state would not have the power to hospitalize involuntarily mentally ill, nondangerous individuals unless they had been found incompetent to make a treatment decision. Neither could it hospitalize mentally ill individuals who are dangerous only to themselves. Courts have ignored both arguments.[15]

Because involuntary hospitalization results in substantial restrictions of the rights of an individual, the admission process is subject to the guarantee of the Fourteenth Amendment to the United States Constitution that no state may "deprive any person of life, liberty, or property, without due process of law; nor deny to any person within its jurisdiction the equal protection of the laws."[16] This means that while a state may, in the exercise of its *parens patriae* power or its police power, involuntarily hospitalize individuals, the standards and procedures used must be fair (due process) and applied evenhandedly (equal protection).

Standards for Involuntary Admission

There is some confusion regarding the difference between a clinical finding that a person needs inpatient treatment and statutory standards for involuntary hospitalization. Many individuals clinically diagnosed as in need of inpatient treatment do not meet the statutory standard for involuntary hospitalization. This results in some friction between mental health professionals and the legal system.

Mental Illness Defined

All state standards for involuntary hospitalization require the existence of a mental illness or disorder. Some states do not define the term. In the Illinois code, for example, the term "mental illness" is undefined "because any definition which could be made legally explicit would necessarily be so broad or circular as to preclude accurate application. By not providing an explicit statutory definition, a common-law definition fashioned by the courts on a case-by-case basis is deemed to be preferable. . . ."[17]

An example of a circular definition is found in Oregon where:

"Mentally ill person" means a person who, because of a mental disorder, is either:

(a) dangerous to himself or others; or
(b) unable to provide for his basic personal needs and is not receiving such care as is necessary for his health and safety.[18]

Maryland and Utah simply incorporate by reference the American Psychiatric Association's *Diagnostic and Statistical Manual of Mental Disorders* (DSM-III);[19] but at least one court has held these manuals (DSM-II, DSM-III) to be "simply outlines of diagnostic categories. Their purpose is to achieve a uniform nomenclature in psychiatry to facilitate statistic gathering and information exchange."[20] Another court has criticized the use of DSM manuals:

Obviously, the description of mental illness is left largely to the user and is dependent upon the norms of adjustment that he employs. Usually the use of the phrase "mental illness" effectively masks the actual norms applied. And, because of the unavoidably ambiguous generalities in which the American Psychiatric Association describes its diagnostic categories, the diagnostician has the ability to shoehorn into the mentally diseased class almost any person he wishes, for whatever reason, to put there.[21]

The term "mental illness" has been interpreted to be broader than the term "mental disorder," used in DSM-III.[22]

The Minnesota statute defines a "mentally ill person" as an individual with a "substantial psychiatric disorder of mood, perception, orientation or memory which grossly impairs judgment, behavior, capacity to recognize reality, or to reason or understand" that results in dangerousness or an inability to care for oneself.[23]

A court is not so much interested in labels as it is in a description of the conduct of an individual that substantiates that he or she is suffering from a mental illness. If substantial evidence of abnormal conduct exists—evidence that cannot be explained as the result of a physical cause—a mental illness or disorder will be found by the court.

A mental health professional testifying as an expert witness in an involuntary admission proceeding must be prepared to testify to the underlying facts establishing a mental disorder. These facts include references to statements made in the psychiatric or psychological interview, psychological test results, and entries in the medical chart. Too often in state hospital settings, the mental health professional testifies in generalities, having conducted an inadequate interview (ten minutes or less) and being unfamiliar with the information in the medical chart. A good defense attorney can sometimes raise substantial doubt under these circumstances.

The U.S. Supreme Court in *O'Connor v. Donaldson*[24] held that the existence of mental illness alone does not justify involuntary hospitalization. State standards require a specific impact or consequence to flow from the mental illness that involves dangerousness or an inability to care for one's own needs.[25]

Dangerousness

In addition to proving mental illness before involuntarily hospitalizing an individual, the state also must establish that the individual is dangerous or unable to care for himself. State statutes generally are framed in terms of a mental illness or disorder causing an individual to pose a "significant risk," an "imminent threat," or a "substantial risk" of physical harm to himself or herself or to others.[26] The Iowa statute includes one who "is likely to inflict serious emotional harm on members of his or her family or others who lack reasonable opportunity to avoid contact with the afflicted person if the afflicted person is allowed to remain at liberty."[27] Some states include harm to property.

Many statutes include a general description of the kinds of facts that must support a finding of dangerousness. For example, Arkansas provides that the individual must pose "a significant risk of physical harm to others as manifested by recent overt behavior evidencing homicidal or other assaultive tendencies toward others."[28] Florida requires evidence of at least one dangerous incident "within the 20 days prior to initiation of proceedings."[29] The Pennsylvania standard states that the individual must pose "a clear and present danger of harm," which must "be shown by establishing that within the past 30 days the person has inflicted or attempted to inflict serious bodily harm on another and that there is a reasonable probability that such conduct will be repeated."[30]

Where the standard has been framed in general terms, it has been argued that it is unconstitutional for a court to find that an individual is dangerous based solely on the expert opinion of a mental health professional predicting dangerousness, without any evidence of incidents or threats of dangerousness.

A few federal courts have held that evidence of a recent overt act or threat must support a finding of dangerousness.[31] One court rejected this position, stating:

> [T]he state must balance the curtailment of liberty against the danger of harm to the individual or others. The paramount factor is the interest of society which naturally includes the interest of the patient in not being subjected to unjustified confinement. We agree with respondent that the "science of predicting future dangerous behavior is inexact,

and certainly is not infallible.'' We also agree that the mere establishment of a mental problem is not an adequate basis upon which to confine a person who has never harmed or attempted to harm either himself or another. However, we are of the opinion that a decision to commit based upon a medical opinion which clearly states that a person is reasonably expected to engage in dangerous conduct, and which is based upon the experience and studies of qualified psychiatrists is a determination which properly can be made by the State.[32]

The difficulty with an expert opinion based "upon the experience and studies of qualified psychiatrists" is that they generally do not exist. Psychiatrists and psychologists who render opinions based on their experience generally have not performed any follow-up studies on whether their past opinions were accurate. Similarly, few studies have been performed that can form the basis of such an opinion. This problem does not exist in those states where evidence of a recent, overt act or threat is required by statute.

Courts have held that the danger of harm posed must be imminent and substantial,[33] a standard either found in the state statute or required by judicial opinion.

Ability To Care for One's Self

An individual who is mentally ill and who, as a result, cannot care for his or her own physical needs may be involuntarily hospitalized. The failure to care for one's self is established by showing that an individual is incapable of providing for his or her own food, clothing, shelter, medical care, and personal safety. Vermont requires a showing that an individual has

behaved in such a manner as to indicate that he is unable, without supervision and the assistance of others, to satisfy his need for nourishment, personal or medical care, shelter, or self protection and safety, so that it is probable that death, substantial physical bodily injury, serious mental deterioration or serious physical debilitation or disease will ensue unless adequate treatment is afforded.[34]

Inability to care for oneself cannot be established by a showing that an individual lacks the resources to provide the necessities of life.[35] Rather, it is the inability to make use of available resources.

Preparation of Testimony

Some state statutes have been revised to permit psychiatric nurses and social workers to conduct evaluations, sign certificates, and appear in court to give expert opinions on whether an individual is mentally ill, dangerous, and able to take care of personal needs. Most statutes require social workers to have a master's degree; registered nurses must have a master's in psychiatric nursing. In addition, state statutes often require up to three years of clinical training and experience. Most states still require testimony of a least one physician to support a finding of need for involuntary hospitalization.

Psychiatrists, psychologists, psychiatric nurses, and social workers who testify that a person meets the statutory standard for involuntary hospitalization should have a working knowledge of the standard in their state. In most cases attorneys for the state will be happy to make a nuts-and-bolts presentation on the requirements of the state standard and the views of the judge presiding at the proceedings. For example, it is important to know that a particular judge is cautious where alcohol is involved and requires a very strong showing of mental illness.

Preparation should be thorough to ensure that all the significant facts are presented and to withstand cross-examination by the patient's attorney. The psychiatrist or psychologist should be prepared to testify to the underlying facts that support the existence of all the elements found in DSM-III for a particular diagnosis. An adequate psychiatric interview should be conducted. Most courts would consider one ten-minute interview inadequate. Defense counsel would closely question the ability to make a diagnosis in such a short interview.

The facts should be documented in the patient's record. A defense attorney will question significant facts in testimony that are not documented in the record. All significant facts involving a patient are generally required to be noted in the record. In an Illinois case:

> [t]he psychiatrist diagnosed respondent's mental disorder as paranoia schizophrenia. He was able to clearly indicate the basis for his diagnosis, having observed respondent and interviewed her several times. He pointed to respondent's behavior in continuously having her face covered, her inappropriate and irrational responses to questions and her delusions about hearing voices and being in danger from snakes and devils.[36]

The court stated that a mental disorder was established by clear and convincing evidence. In another case, a psychiatrist:

> stated that he interviewed the respondent, that she was silent for the most part, although she answered some of his questions. He further testified that he did not know how her memory or thinking process was, but that they appeared to be coherent and relevant to his questions. Although diagnosing that respondent had a depressive neurosis, he explained that he could not give the specific underlying cause precipitating her disease.[37]

The court held that a mental disorder was not established by clear and convincing evidence.

With regard to predictions that a person is dangerous, where there is no history of dangerous acts, the witness should be prepared to explain on cross-examination the basis for the prediction. Undoubtedly, the witness will be asked such questions as: Have you made predictions in other cases? How do you know your past predictions were accurate? Have you conducted follow-up studies of past patients you predicted to be dangerous? These questions can be difficult because most testifying psychiatrists have not conducted any follow-up studies. If the person was admitted to the hospital, the likelihood of dangerous acts decreases. If the person was released, there was no opportunity for follow-up studies. One approach is to be thoroughly familiar with existing studies and the factors that increase the certainty of predictions of dangerousness.

Finally, the testifying psychiatrist should be prepared to inform the attorney for the state of the significant facts, particularly necessary witnesses. Because hearsay is not admissible, witnesses to dangerous acts and to conduct that indicates a person cannot care for himself or herself should testify. Pertinent record entries should be shown to the attorneys for the state. All this is helpful, particularly in those situations where the attorney for the state sees the court file for the first time on the morning of the hearing. There is often insufficient time to review the whole record and conduct lengthy witness interviews.

Procedure for Involuntary Admission

The following summary illustrates the general characteristics of the procedures for emergency involuntary admission. This summary is followed by a comparison of procedures in Maine,[38] Illinois,[39] and Pennsylvania[40] to illustrate differences in various states.

In general, individuals may be detained for an emergency evaluation if, based on their actions, it is believed they meet the statutory standard for admission requiring that a person be dangerous to self or others. The petitioner, a law enforcement officer, or other responsible person, asserts in a petition that the individual meets the statutory standard.

A physician or clinical psychologist conducts an evaluation of the individual and executes a certificate stating that the individual meets the standard. An individual who does not meet the standard is released. Generally, a second evaluation by a physician or clinical psychologist other than the person who executed the first certificate is required. If the individual is found to meet the standard, a second certificate is executed. An individual who is found not to meet the standard is released.

The petition and certificates are filed with the court, although they may be filed at different times. The individual alleged to meet the standard is generally characterized as a "respondent" in the legal proceeding. Upon the filing, the court sets a hearing date. Notice is given to the respondent, relatives, and others. Counsel is appointed if the respondent cannot afford to retain private counsel. Similarly, a respondent generally is entitled to an expert, independent evaluation by a psychiatrist or clinical psychologist, and in some states a psychiatric social worker or nurse whose fee is paid by the state.

Hearings are informal, but the rules of evidence apply (hearsay evidence, for example, is not admissible). The respondent has a right to a jury trial in most states, to be present at the hearing, to present evidence, and to confront and cross-examine witnesses for the state (through counsel). Generally, the testimony of a physician or clinical psychologist is necessary to support the finding of need for involuntary admission. In most states, the respondent may be called to testify. A small number of states allow the respondent to refuse to answer questions that call for an answer that would tend to incriminate (form the basis for criminal charges).

The judge or jury determines whether the respondent meets the standard for admission. If the respondent meets the standard, there may be a requirement that the placement be the least restrictive alternative. The respondent may be placed with a family member or relative, ordered to undergo outpatient treatment, or hospitalized. The length of involuntary hospitalization varies from state to state.

The order may be appealed to a higher court, but this is generally an inadequate remedy for a patient's release because a decision on appeal usually takes more than a year. Such decisions are appealed to clarify the law and to relieve the respondent of the costs of treatment. To obtain a speedy release, a patient may file a petition for a writ of *habeas corpus*.

The following comparison of procedures in Maine, Illinois, and Pennsylvania illustrates the differences from state to state.

Initiation of Proceedings

All three states provide that a law enforcement officer may detain an individual for examination without a warrant or writ if, based upon personal observation, it is reasonable to believe that the individual meets the standard for emergency involuntary admission. In Pennsylvania, a physician or person authorized by the county administrator also may take such an individual to a facility for an emergency examination without warrant. In Illinois, a judge may enter an order for emergency detention of an individual for up to 24 hours based on personal observation and testimony in open court.

In all three states a responsible person may sign a petition or application setting forth facts based on personal observation that constitute reasonable grounds for belief that the individual meets the standard. In Illinois, the petitioner must be 18 years of age or older, and the petition must include the petitioner's relationship to the respondent and a statement as to whether the petitioner has a legal or financial interest in the matter or is involved in litigation with the respondent. This requirement is intended to prevent persons with ulterior motives from filing petitions, for example, one party to a divorce filing a petititon to hospitalize the other party involuntarily. In Illinois, the petition must include the names and addresses of the spouse, parent, guardian, and close relative, or, if none, the name and address of a known friend. If such information is unknown, the petitioner must state that a diligent inquiry was made to learn this information and specify the steps taken. The names, addresses, and telephone numbers of witnesses who may be able to prove the facts asserted must be included in the petition.

Pennsylvania allows the county administrator to issue a warrant based upon the application. Illinois requires that the petition be accompanied by a certificate executed by a physician, clinical psychologist, or qualified examiner (certified social worker or registered psychiatric nurse). The certificate states that the individual meets the standard and requires immediate hospitalization. The certificate must contain the observations and other factual information relied upon to make the diagnosis. If an appropriate person is not available to execute a certificate and a diligent effort has been made to obtain a certificate, a writ may be issued to detain the individual based upon the petition alone. The petition must state that a diligent effort was made to obtain the certificate and that no appropriate person could be found to execute it.

In Maine, the application must be accompanied by a certificate executed by a physician or clinical psychologist. The judge endorses the application and certificate and authorizes a health officer, peace officer, or other person to take the individual into custody and transport him or her to a hospital. In both Maine and Illinois the examination must take place within 72 hours of admission of the individual to the hospital. In Maine, an individual may be held up to 18 hours pending endorsement of the application and certificate.

Examination upon Admission to Hospital

In Pennsylvania, a physician must examine the individual within two hours of arrival to determine whether he or she meets the standard. An individual who does not meet the standard is discharged. One who does meet the standard begins treatment immediately.

In Maine, if the head of the hospital determines a person is suitable for voluntary admission and the individual agrees, the individual is admitted on a voluntary basis. If it is determined that the person is not suitable for voluntary admission, an Application for an Order for Hospitalization may be filed with the court within five business days from the date of admission, excluding the day of admission. Upon filing of the application, the court will order examinations by two examiners—either physicians or clinical psychologists. One of the examiners, if reasonably available, must be chosen by the respondent or by his or her counsel. This is intended to provide the respondent with an independent evaluation early in the proceeding. Neither examiner may be the initial certifying examiner. If the examiners determine that the respondent does not meet the standard, the respondent must be released "forthwith." If the examiners find that the respondent meets the standard, a hearing date is set.

In Illinois, a psychiatrist must conduct a second examination as soon as possible but no later than 24 hours after admission to the hospital. The psychiatrist may not be the person who executed the first certificate. If the respondent is not examined or the psychiatrist does not execute a certificate, the respondent must be released immediately.

When respondents are examined in Illinois for the execution of a certificate, they must be informed that they are not obligated to speak to the examiner and that any statements made may be repeated in an involuntary admission proceeding. Failure to warn will result in the examiner's testimony being excluded.

Notice of Rights

In Pennsylvania, an individual must be informed of the reasons for the emergency examination and of the right to communicate with others and be given reasonable use of the telephone. The respondent must be asked for the names of parties to notify of his or her custody and to be kept informed of his or her status.

In Illinois, treatment of the respondent may begin upon completion of one certificate, provided that the respondent has been informed of the right to refuse medication. Medication refused by the respondent must not be administered unless it is necessary to prevent the respondent from causing serious harm.

The respondent must be given a copy of the petition and statement within 12 hours of admission "explaining the person's legal status and his right to counsel and a court hearing in a language he or she understands." In addition, the facility director shall provide the address and telephone number of the guardianship and advocacy commission within 24 hours of admission, excluding Saturdays, Sundays, and holidays. The petition and statement must be sent to the respondent's attorney and guardian, if any, and, if the respondent so desires, copies must be sent to any two additional persons the respondent designates. The respondent must be allowed to complete no less than two telephone calls at the time of admission to anyone he or she chooses.

Court Hearing or Review

In Pennsylvania, an individual detained for emergency examination and treatment must be discharged upon a determination that the individual no longer needs treatment and in any event within 20 hours, unless within that period the individual agrees to a voluntary admission or an application for extended involuntary emergency treatment is filed.

The application must state the grounds for the belief that extended emergency treatment is necessary. It must contain the name of any examining physician and the substance of the opinion regarding the mental condition of the individual. Upon the filing of the application with the court of common pleas, the court must appoint counsel unless the person can afford and desires private counsel.

Within 24 hours of the filing, a judge or mental health review officer holds an informal hearing. If practical, the hearing is held at the facility. The judge or review officer informs the respondent of the nature of the proceedings. A physician gives reasons why the respondent meets the standard and explains the need for extended emergency treatment. The judge or review officer may consider any relevant information believed to be reliable, even if it would normally be excluded under the rules of evidence. The respondent or respondent's counsel may question the witnesses and present any relevant information. If at the conclusion of the review, the individual is found to meet the standard, the judge or review officer will certify the need for extended emergency treatment. If the respondent is found not to meet the standard, the facility director will be instructed to release the respondent. A certification by a review officer of the need for extended treatment is not a final, appealable order. The extended treatment may not exceed 20 days.

The respondent certified by a review officer to be in need of extended treatment may petition the court of common pleas for a review of the certification. The review must be conducted within 72 hours. The court reviews the certification and "such evidence as the court may receive or require." If the court finds extended treatment necessary, the petition is denied. If such treatment is found unnecessary, the respondent is released.

If the facility staff feels the respondent needs care in addition to the 20 days allowed, a petition for court-ordered involuntary treatment (not to exceed 90 days) may be filed.

Where a petition is filed for a person already subject to involuntary treatment, it is sufficient to represent and upon hearing to reestablish that the conduct originally required in fact occurred and that the respondent's condition continues to evidence a clear and present danger. In such event it is not necessary for the state to show reoccurrences of dangerous conduct, either harmful or debilitating, within the last 30 days.

The petition must include a statement of facts constituting reasonable grounds to believe that the person is severely disabled and in need of treatment. The petition must state the name of an examining physician and the substance of his or her opinion regarding the person's mental condition. It must also state that the person has received information concerning need for treatment and a copy of the petition. The administrator shall also serve a copy of the petition on the respondent's attorney and those designated to be kept informed, including an explanation of the nature of the proceedings, the person's right to an attorney, and the services of an expert in the field of mental health. A hearing on the petition must be held within five days after the filing of the petition, and treatment is permitted pending determination of the petition.

The person has the right to employ a physician, clinical psychologist, or other expert in mental health to assist in connection with the hearing and to testify on the person's behalf. If the person cannot afford to engage such a professional, the court shall on application allow a reasonable fee for such purpose.

The respondent has the right to counsel and to the assistance of an expert in mental health and may not be called as a witness involuntarily. The respondent has the right to confront and cross-examine all the witnesses and to present evidence. The hearing must be public unless the respondent or respondent's counsel requests that it be private. A record must be made of the hearing. The court will impound the record; it may be obtained or examined only upon the request of the respondent or respondent's counsel by order of the court on good cause shown. The hearing will be conducted by a judge or by a mental health review officer and may be held at a location other than the courthouse when doing so appears to be in the best interest of the respondent. A decision will be rendered within 48 hours after the close of the evidence.

Upon a finding by clear and convincing evidence that the respondent meets the standard, an order will be entered directing treatment in an approved facility as an inpatient or as an outpatient, or in a combination of such treatment, as the director of the facility from time to time shall determine. Inpatient treatment must be deemed appropriate only after a less restrictive alternative has been fully considered. Investigation of treatment alternatives shall include consideration of the person's relationship to his or her community and family, the person's employment possibilities, all available community resources, and guardianship services. An order for inpatient treatment must include findings on this issue.

In Maine, a court hearing must be held within 15 days of the filing of the application for an order for hospitalization. The hearing may be delayed for ten days upon request of either party. In Illinois the respondent has a right to a hearing in five days, excluding Saturdays, Sundays, and holidays, from the time of the filing of the petition and first certificate. The court on its own motion or the state may request a hearing delay for up to 15 days. The respondent is not limited in the time delay that may be requested. In Maine, if the hearing is not held within the specified time, the application must be dismissed and the respondent discharged.

While Illinois provides that a respondent may request a jury trial, neither the Maine nor the Pennsylvania statutes make such a provision.

As to the hearing itself, in both Maine and Illinois, the rules of evidence apply. In Pennsylvania, the rules of evidence apply to court ordered extended treatment. The respondent has a right to counsel, to present evidence, and to cross-examine witnesses. In Maine, the hearing is "confidential" but may be public at the request of the respondent or respondent's counsel. In Illinois, the hearing is public but may be closed at the respondent's request. In Maine and Illinois, the respondent has a right to be present, although in Illinois this right may be waived by respondent's attorney if the court is satisfied that the respondent's attendance "would subject him to substantial risk of serious physical or emotional harm."

In Pennsylvania, the state may not call the respondent as a witness, but Illinois law allows the state to call the respondent and ask any question as long as it does not tend to incriminate (that is, require an answer that may form the basis for a criminal prosecution). Maine makes no provision that the respondent may not be called.

Both Pennsylvania and Illinois provide that a respondent is entitled to an expert witness, to be provided at the state's expense. Maine provides that the respondent or counsel may choose one of the two examiners ordered by the court, contingent upon availability. In effect, the result is the same.

Upon a finding that the respondent meets the standard, Maine, Pennsylvania, and Illinois all require that the respondent be treated in the least restrictive setting. Maine also requires "testimony indicating the individual treatment plan to be followed by the hospital staff in the event of commitment. . . ." The court must be satisfied with the treatment plan and, if not, may continue the case for ten days pending resubmission of a treatment plan by the hospital.

Length of Disposition

Pennsylvania uses a tier approach. A respondent may be detained up to five days for emergency examination and treatment. Extended emergency treatment may be ordered for up to 20 days. Court-ordered involuntary treatment may be ordered for up to 90 days (up to one year if dangerous acts give rise to certain specified criminal charges). Finally, an additional period of 180 days of treatment may be ordered.

In Maine, the length of the initial disposition is four months; thereafter a respondent may be treated for a period of up to one year. In Illinois, the initial disposition is 60 days. Additional periods of 180 days may be sought by petition to the court. The respondent has a right to a hearing upon requests for additional treatment.

Notice

Notice to a respondent of an involuntary admission proceeding is a fundamental element of due process. Most state statutes require that notice be given to the respondent, although some require that only minimal amounts of information be included. Most states also provide that notice be given to relatives and other parties designated by the respondent. It has been held that due process requires:

Notice must be given sufficiently in advance of scheduled court proceedings so that reasonable opportunity to prepare will be afforded, and it must set forth with particularity the alleged conduct or condition upon which the proposed detention is based. . . . Besides date, time and place of hearing, the notice should include a clear statement of the purpose of the proceeding and of the possible consequences to the subject thereof, a statement of the legal standard upon which commitment is authorized, the names of examining physicians and others who may testify in favor of detention and the substance of their proposed testimony.[41]

The court rejected the argument that serving legal papers on a mentally ill person would cause unnecessary agitation, which is contrary to good medical practice, stating that such an argument presupposed that the individual was mentally ill, the issue in question. Further, it is more traumatic to have a hearing without notice.

However, a federal court in New Jersey held that, constitutionally, notice need not include the factual basis, names of examining physicians, other witnesses, and a summary of the proposed testimony because counsel for the respondent has access to such information. Presumably, counsel will review all evidence with the respondent.[42]

Right to Counsel

The right to effective assistance of counsel is a required element of due process. All states provide counsel for individuals in involuntary admission proceedings. The individual should be informed that he or she has a right to counsel and that such counsel will be appointed if the individual cannot afford retained counsel. Counsel must be made available far enough in advance to provide sufficient time for preparation.[43]

There is some question as to whether a respondent can waive the right to counsel. In Nebraska, it was held that ". . . the right to counsel may be waived by an intelligent, knowing, voluntary waiver." This would require an initial inquiry to determine the competency of the respondent.[44] In Illinois, a court allowed a person to decline the representation of a public defender but ordered the public defender to remain at the hearing as an adviser to assist the person.[45] Other courts have held that a mentally ill person cannot validly waive the right to counsel.[46] A federal court in Alabama held that a knowing and intelligent waiver of constitutional rights ". . . is acceptable, provided that that waiver is made by counsel with the informed consent of the subject and with the approval of the court."[47] Where a waiver is allowed the burden is on the state to establish that it is valid. In Ohio, the court stated:

The record in the probate court hearing must show with clarity that the petitioner (the alleged mentally ill individual) knew of his right to counsel, or to appointed counsel at state expense if unable to afford counsel, and that he knew of the allowable commitment which would result from the hearing; in short, that he was apprised of all the facts essential to a broad understanding of the whole matter.[48]

Some older court decisions have approved the concept that a patient's lawyer should act as a *guardian ad litem*, that is, the lawyer should determine the client's best interest independent of the client's wishes, and represent the client from that perspective.[49] The respondent has a right to effective assistance of counsel. Older cases have held that if counsel's representation was based on the best interest of the client as counsel perceives those interests, then even though the client's expressed interests were not advocated, there was no denial of effective assistance of counsel.[50] In one case the court determined there was no denial of effective assistance of counsel even though counsel had never met the client, the client was not present at the hearing, and the client was committed.[51]

More recent cases have taken the contrary position. The Wisconsin Supreme Court held that the right to counsel means the right to a lawyer "who has the same function, duties and responsibilities as he would have if he were retained by the person involved as his or her own attorney" and that the attorney's responsibilities included "representing the client competently and zealously within the bounds of law."[52] Several federal courts have held that the attorney must serve as an advocate for the client's position.[53] Most state statutes simply require that a person be represented by counsel; they do not specify the role counsel should perform.

In the past a Colorado statute required the *guardian ad litem* to perform certain responsibilities concerning the acquisition of information about the client's particular case; now an attorney is appointed.[54] The Michigan Supreme Court rules require that the attorney "consult with the respondent about alternatives to hospitalization, and serve as an advocate for the respondent's preferred disposition."[55]

The American Bar Association Code of Professional Responsibility (Code) supports the position that the attorney should advocate the client's interest as the client defines those interests. The Code requires that the attorney "represent his client zealously, protect the client's legal interest and present every legally possible defense."[56] The Code also provides that "the professional judgment of a lawyer should be exercised within the bounds of the law, solely for the benefit of his client and free of compromising influences and loyalties. Neither his personal interest, the interest of other clients, nor the desires of third parties should be permitted to dilute his loyalty to his client."[57] The Code provides that the client has the exclusive authority to make decisions affecting the merits of the case, and they are binding on counsel.[58] Of course, the attorney must apprise the client of all the relevant considerations and alternatives so that the client can make an informed decision. This includes a recommendation to seek treatment if it appears from all the facts that the client needs it. The decision to oppose commitment is the client's and not the attorney's.

Where it is unclear that the client has the capacity to make decisions or to communicate such decisions to counsel, the Code states that "where the mental or physical condition of a client renders him incapable of making a considered judgment on his own behalf the attorney has additional responsibilities."[59] First, the attorney should look to the client's guardian or legal representative to make those decisions the client would normally make. If the client is unrepresented by such a person, then "his lawyer may be compelled in court proceedings to make decisions on behalf of the client."[60] The attorney must consider all the circumstances then prevailing and act carefully to safeguard and advocate the client's interests.[61]

Counsel does not have the right to be present while the respondent's psychiatric interview is conducted. A Wisconsin federal court held that "the benefit to counsel's presence at the interview does not outweigh the interests of the state in meaningful consultation."[62] Other courts have reached the same conclusion.[63]

Sometimes tension and friction develop between mental health professionals and lawyers defending patients. This is largely attributable to the unfamiliarity of mental health professionals with the role of attorneys in the process. Lawyers view themselves as problem solvers; their goal is to work out the best solution possible under the circumstances for each client. Nevertheless, once a client considers all the options available and decides to oppose hospitalization, the process becomes adversarial. The lawyer is obligated to raise all reasonable defenses on behalf of the client. Lawyers cannot defend fully those they perceive as mentally healthy or at least not meeting the statutory standard, and simply go through the motions for those who are obviously seriously mentally ill. Such action is unethical.

The adversary process depends on both sides bringing out all of the facts and each making its best arguments. If all the facts are exposed, then those who meet the statutory standard for admission will be hospitalized. Facts are developed and credibility of witnesses tested by cross-examination of witnesses by both sides. Questions are sometimes sharp and perceptive, and sometimes the credibility of witnesses is questioned. As a result, mental health professionals sometimes view cross-examination as a personal attack. Normally, this is a misperception.

Sometimes all the facts do not come out at the hearing because the defense counsel objected to certain evidence on hearsay grounds, or the testimony of a psychiatrist is stricken, or the psychiatrist is not allowed to testify because of a failure to inform the respondent that what was said in the psychiatric interview may be repeated in an involuntry proceeding (as required in Illinois). Good reasons exist for not allowing hearsay testimony, the credibility of which cannot be tested by cross-examination. As to the failure to inform a person with respect to a psychiatric interview, this is a policy decision upon which there is disagreement. Nevertheless, it is part of the process, and the disagreement with the policy should not be translated into anger at defense counsel.

Finally, some lawyers appear rude and intimidating. While some may view intimidation as a legitimate weapon in dealing with the system they feel oppresses their clients, often they are young, inexperienced, and lack confidence. Generally, good communication can resolve this problem. Once mental health professionals and defense lawyers realize that, even while they play different roles in the system, they share a common goal—helping the respondent—then hostility changes to respect.

Duty To Warn

During a psychiatric interview to determine whether a person is subject to involuntary admission,[64] a few courts have held that a person has a right to remain silent. Other courts have held that the right to remain silent does not apply during the psychiatric interview because it would place an undue burden on those attempting to make an objective evaluation of an individual's mental condition.[65]

A Wisconsin federal district court held that a patient should be told by counsel and a psychiatrist that he or she is going to be examined with regard to his or her mental condition, that any statements made by the patient during the exam may be used as a basis for commitment, and that the patient does not have to speak to the psychiatrist. If the patient agrees to the examination with "knowledge" that he or she does not have to speak, the patient's statements are admissible at the commitment hearing.[66] The court defined "knowledge" in a footnote as follows:

> We use the term knowledge advisedly. The presumption in a civil commitment proceeding must be that the individual is indeed competent. If his rights are explained to him in simple terms it may be assumed that he has the requisite knowledge. If the individual, in fact, does not have the requisite knowledge because of mental illness, a subsequent finding of mental illness or mental incapacity on the basis of the statements cannot be said to violate due process. The state will be obliged to prove that he is dangerous in order to sustain a recommendation of commitment.[67]

A Hawaii statute provides that, should a person refuse to be examined by a physician and there is sufficient evidence that the allegations in a petition are true, the individual may be detained for up to five days for diagnosis and evaluation. A federal district court held the statute unconstitutional because it denies a patient the right to remain silent.[68] The appeals court reversed, stating "that the state statute was constitutional. . . . [I]f such a holding were allowed to stand it would contravene public policy by allowing individuals to secure their releases simply by refusing to participate in a psychiatric interview."[69]

An Alabama court interpreted this right as "protect[ing] any disclosures which the subject may reasonably believe could be used in a criminal prosecution or which could lead to other evidence that might be so used."[70]

An Illinois code provision requires that whenever a person 12 years of age or older is being examined for the purpose of certification in an involuntary admission proceeding:

> [T]he person conducting this examination shall inform the person being examined in a simple comprehensive manner of the purpose of the examination; that he does not have to talk to the examiner; and that any statement he makes may be disclosed at a court hearing on the issue of whether he is subject to involuntary admission.[71]

Failure to warn bars the testimony of the examiner at a subsequent court hearing. This is significant because the testimony of a psychiatrist or a clinical psychologist who has examined the respondent is a prerequisite to a finding that a person is subject to involuntary admission.[72] The failure to warn may result in insufficient evidence to admit the person to the hospital involuntarily.

The Report of the Governor's Commission for Revision of the Mental Health Code of Illinois explained the rationale of this requirement:

> Many of the examiners in the private sector inform respondents of the purpose of the mental examination and that their verbal participation is not required. Experience in the public and private sectors has shown that application of the privilege against self-incrimination does not seriously impair the State's ability to achieve the valid objectives of civil commitment. It should be stressed that this section will not nullify the legality of a certificate executed by an examiner who has not given the required warning, but only prevents his testifying in court.[73]

The commission report stated that the psychiatric examination is highly intrusive. It seeks to obtain information concerning the respondent's innermost thought processes and emotions and to elicit accounts of personal conduct in order to ameliorate the patient's condition, but it also may cause the loss of a respondent's freedom in a civil commitment proceeding. According to the commission, "these disclosure requirements apply solely to instances where the immediate purpose of the examination is certification; they do not apply to the traditional therapist-patient relationship nor do they preclude the therapist's testimony if the disclosure is made when the issue of involuntary admission becomes apparent.'' Thus, information revealed by a patient in the normal course of therapy may be included in the testimony of a therapist,[74] but the therapist has a duty, upon becoming an examiner for purposes of involuntarily committing the patient, to inform the patient of the patient's right to remain silent and that any statements the patient makes may be revealed at a hearing. The commission concluded that the provisions "will satisfy due process yet not unduly intrude upon the therapist-patient relationship.''[75]

Courts have interpreted this provision to mean that the examining psychologist or psychiatrist must personally and clearly inform the respondent of this right. A "vague statement that he does not have to talk to the doctors'' is not sufficient. Nor is it sufficient for the admitting nurse to recite the respondent's rights.[76] In Illinois, the duty to inform applies to examinations for both certificates necessary for admission in that state.[77] Nevertheless, where both examiners are present when the first examiner informs the respondent of this right and the two interviews occur in immediate succession, it is unnecessary for the second examiner to repeat the information to the respondent.[78]

While one court reprimanded personnel of the Illinois Department of Mental Health and Developmental Disabilities for failure to inform a respondent of his rights and reversed the finding that the respondent was subject to involuntary admission, it also questioned whether informing an individual of the right to remain silent is an appropriate way to assure protection of fundamental liberties.[79] The court, in apparent disagreement with the Governor's commission, reasoned that psychiatric examinations, as opposed to police interrogations, were not inherently prejudicial. Rather, they were purely investigative, and would lose their value if the free exchange of views were inhibited. Also, a candidate for involuntary commitment would, by definition, be incapable of a rational or "voluntary'' decision to remain silent. The warning, therefore, would not ensure that the respondent's decision to participate was voluntary, as the legislature intended. Moreover, a person's right to avoid self-incrimination as to criminal matters is already protected by statute. The court found it contradictory that a person can avoid psychiatric examination, and yet be forced to testify in court before doctors sitting in the gallery, who would later testify in the hearing based, in part, on the testimony of the respondent.[80]

Access to Hospital Records

Most state statutes provide for access to the medical records by the defense attorney upon the client's consent.[81] If the hospital refuses to grant access to the records the respondent may apply for a court order to force access to the information. A Wisconsin court held that "counsel must also have access to all reports psychiatric and otherwise which will be introduced at the hearing on commitment."[82] Another court held that counsel's access to medical and psychiatric records was essential to effective representation by counsel.[83]

While most mental health codes provide patients with access to records when litigation is involved,[84] one federal court has held that there is "no basis for the proposition that mental patients have a constitutionally protected property interest in the direct and unrestricted access to their records. . . ."[85] The case involved a former mental patient seeking access to her hospital records for purposes of writing a book on her hospitalization. Nevertheless, by statute many states give patients access to their own records.[86]

Probable Cause Hearing

State statutes set the length of time a person may be detained without a hearing. It has been held that "no significant deprivation of liberty can be justified without a prior hearing on the necessity of detention."[87] Another court stated: "Where a person said to be mentally ill and dangerous is involuntarily detained, he must be given a hearing within a reasonable time to test whether the detention is based upon probable cause to believe that confinement is necessary under constitutionally proper standards for commitment."[88] The courts justified detention prior to a hearing on probable cause on the basis of the states' compelling interest in emergency detention of persons who threaten violence to themselves or others for purposes of protecting society and the individual.[89]

In the state of Washington, a statute that authorized a mental health professional, after investigation of a complaint, to issue a summons requiring an individual to report to a hospital within 24 hours for evaluation was held to violate due process. The court based its holding on the failure to require a judicial finding that the individual probably presents a danger to his or her own person or to others and that involuntary hospitalization is the least restrictive alternative.[90]

Courts have held that a hearing must be provided within 48 hours,[91] 72 hours,[92] five days,[93] seven days,[94] and "promptly."[95] One court held that a full hearing within 20 days is sufficient.[96] Finally, a Connecticut court held that an individual may be detained up to 45 days before being given a formal hearing. This length of time was constitutionally justified because of the "compensating advantage to the committed person. . . ." During that period the "medical staff of the hospital can adequately alleviate his mental illness by use of non-emergency diagnostic procedures to determine that he is not a danger to himself or others."[97] Such a rationale is questionable because it assumes the person is mentally ill.

Right to Independent Expert Examination

Some state statutes provide for a right to an independent expert witness, such as a psychiatrist or psychologist to be paid for by the state if the person is indigent.[98] It is not clear whether a respondent has a constitutional right to an independent expert witness. There are few cases on the issue.[99] In many cases, however, a respondent's chances of being found not in need of hospitalization are greatly diminished when no expert witness is available to testify on his or her behalf.

Effect of Medication

Under some circumstances a person may have a right not to be under the influence of medication during a hearing. One court barred prehearing treatment including medication on the theory that involuntary drug treatment would "delude or destroy his ability to assist in the presentation of his defense."[100] Another court prohibited prehearing treatment including medication unless absolutely necessary to prevent physical injury.[101] Other courts have banned all involuntary medication that affects meaningful participation because such medication interferes with the client's right to be present at hearings.[102]

Right to a Hearing

A Wisconsin case held that a full hearing must be held within 14 days of a probable cause hearing.[103] Two weeks would seem to be adequate time to diagnose most individuals. If additional time is needed for evaluation, most courts will allow a limited period. In Illinois, the state may request a continuance of the hearing for up to 15 days.[104]

Several federal courts have held that the right to a jury in civil commitment proceedings is not guaranteed by the Constitution. One court stated that if the state used civil commitment to detain persons who would otherwise be charged with criminal conduct the right to a jury trial would be arguably stronger. However, where civil commitment for mental illness "is limited to time and treatment oriented the pressure for the right to a jury trial is less forceful."[105] Two other courts have held that a jury trial is not required.[106]

Other courts disagree. Two courts have held that because the state provided jury trials in related types of cases, it would be a violation of equal protection not to provide a jury trial in a commitment proceeding. Alabama, by statute, provides jury trials when an individual raises the issue of sanity in a *habeas corpus* proceeding. The court held that because jury trials were available in that proceeding they must be made available in commitment proceedings.[107] In some states, Illinois for example, this right is statutory rather than constitutional,[108] and, if not requested, it is waived.[109] Denial of a jury trial upon request is reversible error.[110]

Right To Be Physically Present

While the fear of trauma has led many states to excuse an individual from attending his or her own hearing when attendance would be detrimental to the respondent's health, there are good reasons for requiring the individual's presence at both the preliminary and the full hearing. First, by participating in the proceedings the individual might be assured that his or her interests are being protected. The individual might be able to point out errors in factual testimony regarding his or her behavior, which would otherwise go unnoticed by the attorney. Second, the fact finder has an opportunity to speak to the individual and to observe the individual's demeanor. Where the psychiatric reports are sparse and characterized by medical terminology that is unrelated to standards of commitment, the individual's presence will make it possible for the fact finder to test the individual's observations and also the psychiatrist's.

Courts have held that a person has a right to be present at an involuntary admission proceeding to which the person is subjected.[111] A Hawaiian court held that ". . . due process requires the presence of the person supposed to be committed at all judicial proceedings conducted for that purpose. . . ."[112] A Kentucky case has held "[t]he minimum requirements of due process for involuntary commitment of mentally ill persons includes the right of the patient to be present at all hearings. . . ."[113] Of course, an individual whose behavior is found by the court to be too disruptive may be excluded from the hearing.[114] One court in Michigan held that even if the individual's behavior or physical condition precludes his or her attendance, the court should consider the alternative of conducting the proceedings at the mental health facility rather than totally excluding the individual from the hearing. The court based this conclusion on a least-restrictive alternative theory.[115]

Many state statutes provide that the respondent is entitled to be physically present at the hearing.[116] Illinois provides that the respondent is entitled to be present at the hearing unless the respondent's attorney waives the right to be present and the court "is satisfied by a clear showing that the respondent's attendance would subject him to substantial risk of serious physical or emotional harm."[117]

Two courts have prohibited waiver of the right to be present.[118] Most courts have allowed the waiver standards described in an Alabama case. Those standards allow a waiver only upon ". . . acceptance by the court following a judicial determination that he understands his rights and is competent to waive them."[119] The Alabama court also felt that counsel may not waive his or her client's personal appearance at the hearing except with the approval of the court. That approval can be given only after an adversary hearing in which it is determined whether the individual is mentally or physically incapable of attending the hearing.[120]

Standard of Proof

The U.S. Supreme Court held that a state must prove by "clear and convincing evidence" that the statutory standard for involuntary admission has been met.[121]

This is a higher standard than "preponderance of the evidence," which is used in negligence cases, but a lower standard than "beyond a reasonable doubt," which is used in criminal cases. In rejecting the standard of "beyond a reasonable doubt" the court stated: "Given the lack of certainty and the fallibility of psychiatric diagnosis, there is a serious question as to whether a state could ever prove beyond a reasonable doubt that an individual is both mentally ill and likely to be dangerous."[122] The court concluded that the clear and convincing evidence standard was a "middle level of burden of proof that strikes a fair balance between the rights of the individual and the legitimate concerns of the state."[123] Nevertheless, a state may adopt the higher standard if it so chooses.[124]

Length of Disposition

The lengths of disposition vary from 45 days in Arkansas to three years in Idaho. The length in Alaska, the District of Columbia, and Texas is indeterminate, and in Connecticut and Rhode Island it is for the period of the duration of the mental illness. Arizona ranges from 60 days to one year. In general, the spread is three months (eight states), six months (eight states), one year (five states), and three years (two states).[125]

Appeal

All states provide that a patient has the right to appeal an order of involuntary hospitalization. This is not a means to a speedy release in most states because generally an opinion on appeal takes considerable time. Nevertheless, a reversal of the order on appeal will relieve a patient of the responsibility for paying for the care and treatment provided. Mental health attorneys appeal cases to change the law to benefit patients.

A patient will sometimes pursue a writ of *habeas corpus* if the attorney concludes that a good argument can be made that the admission is illegal, that is, the hearing procedure violated the statute or the constitutional rights of the patient.

ADMISSION OF MINORS

In most states, a child may be admitted voluntarily to an inpatient psychiatric program by a parent or guardian.[126] A psychiatrist makes a determination that the standard for admission is met. This authority or power of parents to admit minors has been under attack. In 1972, an Illinois court held that a child 12 years of age or older is entitled to a hearing similar to that provided adults.[127] The standard considered in this case was whether the person had a mental disorder causing the person to be dangerous or unable to care for himself or herself, the same standard that applied to adults.

In 1975, a North Carolina court held that while no preadmission hearing was necessary, a postadmission hearing is required. The court stated:

> The judicial deference afforded to parental authority along with the parent's interest in being able to seek immediate treatment and the policy of encouraging voluntary admissions outweigh any interest the minor may have in pre-admission hearings. However, the continued confinement of a minor based on that procedure requires procedural safeguards consistent with the Due Process Clause. Such procedural due process should be afforded at the earliest possible time after admission.[128]

The court left it up to the legislature to provide a postadmission procedure. The legislature passed a procedure similar to its adult involuntary admissions procedure, which included an initial hearing and a series of rehearings as well.[129]

In 1977, the California Supreme Court held in *In re Roger S.*[130] that a minor younger than age 14 possesses rights that the parent or guardian may not waive. Among these rights guaranteed by the Fourteenth Amendment to the U.S. Constitution and by the California Constitution is the right "to procedural due process in determining whether the minor is mentally ill or disordered, and whether, if the minor is not gravely disabled or dangerous to himself or others as a result of mental illness or disorder, the admission sought is likely to benefit him."[131]

This procedural due process includes an opportunity for a precommitment hearing before a neutral fact finder. "Clearly, post admission procedures would be inadequate to avoid the trauma of removal of the child from the home and unnecessary placement in a mental hospital."[132] An administrative hearing satisfies this right, and a judicial hearing is not required.[133]

Finally, in 1979, the U.S. Supreme Court considered the issue when it reviewed *Parham v. J.R.*[134] Chief Justice Burger considered the child's interests in liberty, the parent's interest in the welfare and health of the child, and the interest of the state in proper utilization of its mental health facilities. Balancing these competing interests, the court concluded:

> [T]he risk of error inherent in the parental decision to have a child institutionalized for mental health care is sufficiently great that some kind of inquiry should be made by a "neutral factfinder" to determine whether the statutory requirements for admission are satisfied. That inquiry must carefully probe the child's background using all available resources, including but not limited to, parents, schools, and other social agencies. Of course, the review must also include an interview with the child. It is necessary that the decisionmaker have the authority to refuse to admit any child who does not satisfy the medical standards

for admission. Finally, it is necessary that the child's continuing need for commitment be reviewed periodically by a similarly independent procedure.[135]

Following this decision, many states continued to apply, as they did before *Parham*, due process standards based on their state statutes and constitutions. These standards tend to be more stringent than those required by *Parham*.[136] California[137] and Massachusetts[138] are among the states applying those standards.

In 1979 Illinois revised its code and changed not only the procedure, but also the standard for the admission of children. Any minor 16 years of age or older may be voluntarily admitted if the minor personally executes the application. A minor so admitted shall be treated as an adult and shall be subject to all of the provisions of the voluntary admission procedure for adults. The parent, guardian, or person *in loco parentis* of the minor shall be immediately informed of the admission.[139]

Any minor may be admitted for inpatient treatment upon application "if the facility director finds that the minor has a mental illness or emotional disturbance of such severity that hospitalization is necessary and that the minor is likely to benefit from inpatient treatment."[140]

Before admission, a psychiatrist or clinical psychologist must state in writing after a personal examination that the condition of the minor meets this standard. The statement must set out in detail the reasons supporting this conclusion and "indicate what alternatives to hospitalization have been explored."[141] Because the admission process has been solely in the control of facility psychiatrists who, it has been asserted, often defer to the wishes of parents rather than exercising independent judgment, this section "requires that a rigorous clinical determination be made that the disturbance is of such severity as to produce maladjustment or disturbances in peer, family, school, or social behavior, functioning, or relationships which can be treated, changed, or ameliorated only by psychiatric hospitalization and that this hospitalization is likely to benefit the minor."[142]

The application may be executed by a parent, a guardian, or, in the absence of a parent or guardian, a person *in loco parentis*. The Department of Corrections or the Department of Children and Family Services may make application for wards of the state.[143] However, a minor whose condition meets the above standard and who is in immediate need of hospitalization may be admitted upon the application of a person 18 years or older if the parent, guardian, or person *in loco parentis* cannot be located after a diligent search is made. If the parent, guardian, or person *in loco parentis* is located and consents to the admission, the minor may continue to be hospitalized. However, such a person may request the minor's discharge.[144] If no parent, guardian, or person *in loco parentis* is found within three days, or if such person is found and refuses to consent or to request a discharge, a petition is filed under the Juvenile Court Act to ensure that appropriate guardianship is provided.[145]

The facility director must review the patient's record 20 days after admission and assess the continuing need for hospitalization. If continued hospitalization is indicated, the director must consult the person who executed the application for admission and request authorization to continue treatment. A review must be conducted every 60 days, and, if continued treatment is necessary, authorization must be obtained. Failure to obtain or refusal to give authorization for treatment constitutes a request for discharge.[146]

A minor who is 12 years of age or older may object to admission, and any interested person 18 years of age or older may also object on the minor's behalf. Such objection will be noted in the minor's record.[147] When an objection is made the minor will be discharged at the earliest appropriate time, not to exceed five days, excluding Saturdays, Sundays, and holidays, unless the objection is withdrawn in writing or unless within that time, a petition for review of the admission and two certificates are filed with the court.[148] The application for admission must contain—in large, boldface type—a statement, in simple, non-technical terms, of the objection and hearing rights of the minor. The rights must be explained to the minor in an understandable manner. Copies of the application must be given to the minor, the person who executed it, the minor's parent, guardian, or person *in loco parentis*, and attorney, if any, and two other persons whom the minor may designate.[149]

A petition for review and two certificates must be executed, which state that "the minor has a mental illness or an emotional disturbance of such severity that hospitalization is necessary, that he can benefit from inpatient treatment, and that a less restrictive alternative is not appropriate."[150] The certificates must meet the requirements, and notices must be given, except that a minor who is younger than 12 need not be informed of the right not to speak to the examiner.[151]

The court shall appoint counsel for the minor upon receipt of the petition and set a hearing within five business days. Notice must be given to the minor, the minor's attorney, the person who executed the application, the objector, and the facility director. The minor may be kept in the facility pending further order of the court.[152]

The minor must be discharged if the court determines that the minor "does not have a mental illness or an emotional disturbance of such severity that hospitalization is necessary, that he cannot benefit from inpatient treatment, or that a less restrictive alternative is appropriate." Otherwise, the court shall authorize the continued hospitalization of the minor for the remainder of the admission period or may make such order as it deems appropriate.[153] However,

> [u]nwillingness or inability of the minor's parent, guardian, or person in loco parentis to provide for his care or residence shall not be grounds for the court's refusing to order the discharge of the minor. In that case, a petition may be filed under the Juvenile Court Act to ensure that appropriate care or residence is provided.[154]

Illinois revised its statute without the guidance of *Parham*. The procedural requirements are stricter than those required in *Parham*, providing for either a discharge or a court review upon an objection to the hospitalization. Nevertheless, there is no preadmission hearing. The standard for admission is broader than that required for adults. Proof of dangerousness or the inability to care for one's own needs is not necessary. Primarily, admission is based on the testimony of a psychiatrist that the mental disability is severe, that hospitalization is necessary, and that the minor will benefit from such treatment. From this perspective, it is in line with *Parham*, which places the decision primarily in the hands of the psychiatrist.

In Maryland, a federal court held after *Parham* that the state's exercise of its *parens patriae* power "must bear some relationship to actual need or realistic goals."[155] A standard that permits hospitalization where it "is in the best interests of the child" is unconstitutionally vague. The state cannot confine a nondangerous child who is capable of surviving safely either independently or with the help of willing and responsible family members or friends.[156] The court also required mandatory periodic review,[157] appointment of counsel[158] and treatment in the least restrictive setting.[159]

LIABILITY FOR CERTIFICATION IN INVOLUNTARY ADMISSION PROCEEDINGS

Generally, the physicians, clinical psychologists, social workers, and psychiatric nurses who conduct court-ordered evaluations and certify under oath that an individual, in their opinion, should be involuntarily hospitalized are not liable for performing this function so long as they acted in good faith. Such examiners are immune because they are performing a quasi-judicial function.[160] Some courts have gone further, holding that the initiation of commitment hearings cannot create liability for denial of due process because the certification is not the proximate cause of the actual confinement. The actual hearing and decision of the court is an intervening cause. An exception is liability for malicious prosecution.[161]

Most state statutes provide immunity to mental health professionals in connection with certification in involuntary admission proceedings. For example, Georgia provides:

> Any physician, psychologist, peace officer, attorney or health official or any hospital official, agent or any person employed by a private hospital or facility operated by the State . . . who acts in good faith in compliance with the admission and discharge provisions . . . shall be immune from civil or criminal liability for his actions in connection with the admission of a patient to a facility or the discharge of a patient from a facility.[162]

Other states, such as Illinois, provide exemption from liability for persons preparing applications, petitions, or other documents if they are "acting in good faith and without negligence."[163] Often a state attorney general must defend state personnel against such actions.[164]

Nevertheless, where there is a lack of good faith, psychiatrists and psychologists conducting evaluations and preparing certificates may be found liable for malpractice,[165] malicious prosecution,[166] false imprisonment,[167] or libel.[168]

In a shift from the trend, the Texas Supreme Court reinstated a dismissed malpractice action alleging misdiagnosis by psychiatrists. The psychiatrist filed reports with the probate court stating that a woman was likely to cause injury to herself or others if not immediately restrained and that she was not of sound mind and was incompetent to manage her financial affairs. The woman was released by a writ of *habeas corpus* and filed suit against the psychiatrist. The state high court held that the filing of the reports with the court was privileged and no damages for defamation could be recovered. Nevertheless, the court stated that the psychiatrists may be liable for malpractice for misdiagnosis. The court remanded the case for trial on the merits.[169]

In a North Carolina case,[170] a physician certified that he had examined an individual and recommended her admission to the hospital where she remained for four days. In fact, the physician had not examined her. The woman filed a damage action for wrongful commitment, which the trial court dismissed. The decision was reversed. The appellate court stated that a cause of action for false imprisonment was stated because the plaintiff was deprived of her liberty without due process. The court stated:

> It is the purpose of the statute that only mentally ill persons in need of restraint be deprived of their liberty. This can only be assured by the doctor making the required examination before executing the certificate. An intentional or negligent violation of this duty cannot be the subject of immunity. The physician is not communicating when he fails to make the examination. Plaintiff's action is not one for libel.[171]

An Illinois court held that where physicians falsely certified on two occasions that they had examined the plaintiff within 72 hours of his admission to the hospital as required by statute, there should be a trial on the issue of malicious prosecution.[172] The plaintiff's wife, a physician, had signed the petition and asked the defendant physicians to sign the certificates (she was also a defendant). The elements necessary for malicious prosecution are:

1. commencement of civil proceeding (petition and certificates initiate involuntary admission proceeding);

2. termination of proceeding in favor of the plaintiff (plaintiff was released prior to a hearing);
3. absence of probable cause for such proceeding (false certification that the defendants had examined the plaintiff);
4. presence of malice (false certification); and
5. damages.[173]

False imprisonment and false arrest were rejected because the hospitalization was pursuant to legal process.[174]

Finally, some states make it a violation of criminal law for "any person who conspires unlawfully to cause, or unlawfully causes, any person to be adjudicated" as subject to involuntary admission "or to be detained at or admitted to a mental health facility contrary to the" mental health code.[175]

NOTES

1. Department of Mental Health and Developmental Disabilities, *Illinois Mental Health Statistics, Fiscal Year 1982* (1983): p. 51. Statistics indicate two-thirds of admissions are voluntary. When one considers that a substantial number of admissions that begin as involuntary are converted to voluntary, the total is over 70 percent.

2. *See* Appendix A, "State Involuntary Admission Statutes."

3. Ill. Ann. Stat. ch. 91–½, § 3–503 (Smith-Hurd Supp. 1982–1983).

4. *See* Appendix C, "State Voluntary Admission Statutes."

5. *Id.*

6. Ga. Ann. Stat. § 37–3–20.

7. So. Dak. Ann. Stat. § 27A–8–1.

8. Tenn. Ann. Stat. § 33–601a.

9. *See* Appendix C, *supra* note 4.

10. *Id.*

11. P.S. Appelbaum, S.A. Mirkin, A.L. Bateman, "Empirical Assessment of Competency to Consent to Psychiatric Hospitalization," *Amer. Jur. of Psychiatry* 138, no. 9 (Sept. 1981):1170–1176.

12. Ill. Ann. Stat. ch. 91–½, § 3–204 (Smith-Hurd Supp. 1982–1983).

13. Colo. Ann. Stat. § 27–10–103.

14. Ill. Rev. Stat., ch. 91–½, § 3–204 (Smith-Hurd Supp. 1982–1983).

15. For a full discussion of the powers of the state to involuntarily hospitalize individuals, *see* "Civil Commitment of the Mentally Ill," *Harv. L. Rev.* 87 (1974):1191, 1207–1222.

16. In re Ballay, 482 F.2d 648, 655 (D.C. Cir. 1973), *quoting* Morrissey v. Brewer, 408 U.S. 471, 481 (1972).

17. Governor's Commission to Revise the Mental Health Code of Illinois, Report 14 (1976) [hereinafter cited as Report].

18. Ore. Ann. Stat. § 426.005.

19. Md. Ann. Stat. § 10–620; Utah Code Ann. § 64–7–28(1).

20. In the Matter of Marquardt, 100 Ill. App. 3d 741, 427 N.E.2d 411, 414 (1981).

21. Lessard v. Schmidt, 349 F. Supp. 1078, 1094 (E.D. Wis. 1972).

22. In re Janovitz, 82 Ill. App. 3d 916, 920 (1980).

23. Minn. Ann. Stat. § 253B.02(13).

24. O'Connor v. Donaldson, 422 U.S. 563 (1975).

25. *See* Appendix A, *supra* note 2.

26. *Id.*

27. Iowa Ann. Stat. § 229.11(b).

28. Ark. Ann. Stat. § 59–1401 (1981 Cum. Supp.).

29. Fla. Ann. Stat. § 94.467.

30. Pa. Ann. Stat. ch. 50, § 7301.

31. Lessard v. Schmidt, *supra* note 21; Lynch v. Baxley, 386 F. Supp. 378 (M.D. Ala. 1974); Suzuki v. Alba, 438 F. Supp. 1106, 1110 (D. Hawaii 1976), *rev'd., on other grounds*, Suzuki v. Yuen, 617 F.2d 173, 178 (9th Cir. 1980).

32. People v. Sansone, 18 Ill. App. 3d 315, 309 N.E.2d 733, 739 (1974), *leave to appeal denied*, 56 Ill. 2d 584 (1974), United States ex rel Mathew v. Nelson, 461 F. Supp. 707 (N.D. Ill. 1978).

33. Appendix A, *supra* note 2.

34. Vt. Ann. Stat. tit. 18, ch. 1701(17)(B)(ii).

35. In re Doe, 56 Ill. App. 3d 1052, 372 N.E.2d 866, 870 (1978).

36. *Id.*

37. In re Dieter, 55 Ill. App. 3d 7, 370 N.E.2d 84 (1977).

38. Maine Ann. Stat. Tit. 34, § 2332–A, *et seq.*

39. Ill. Ann. Stat. ch. 91–½, § 3–800, *et seq* (Smith-Hurd Supp. 1982–1983).

40. Pa. Ann. Stat. ch. 50, § 7301, *et seq.*

41. Suzuki v. Quisenberry, 411 F. Supp. 1113, 1127 (D. Hawaii 1976), and authorities cited therein.

42. Coll v. Hyland, 411 F. Supp. 905, 911 (D. N.J. 1976).

43. Suzuki v. Quisenberry, *supra* note 41, at 1129.

44. Doremus v. Farrell, 407 F. Supp. 509, 516 (D. Neb. 1975).

45. In re Tuntland, 390 N.E.2d 11 (Ill. App. Ct. 1979); *see also* In re Hop, 623 P.2d 282 (Sup. Ct. Cal. 1981).

46. Dooling v. Overholser, 243 F.2d 825, 829 (D.C. Cir. 1957).

47. Lynch v. Baxley, *supra* note 31, at 396.

48. McDuffie v. Berzzarins, 43 Ohio St. 2d 23, 330, N.E.2d 667 (1975).

49. Prochaska v. Brinegar, 102 N.W.2d 870 (Sup. Ct. Iowa 1960); In re Basso, 299 F.2d 933 (D.C. Cir. 1962).

50. *Id.*

51. Prochaska v. Brinegar, *supra* note 49, at 872.

52. State ex rel Memmel v. Mundy, 249 N.W.2d 573, 577 (1977), Lynch v. Baxley, *supra* note 31.

53. Suzuki v. Quisenberry, *supra* note 41, at 1129, and cited authorities.

54. Colo. Rev. Stat. Ann. § 27–9–109(2), (3); § 27–10–107(5) (1975).

55. Michigan Probate Court Rules, 732.2(1) (2) (1981).

56. American Bar Association Code of Professional Responsibility EC 7–1.

57. *Id.* at EC 5–1.

58. *Id* at EC 7–8, 7–7.

59. *Id.* at EC 7–12.

60. *Id.*

61. *Id.*

62. Lessard v. Schmidt, *supra* note 21.

63. Hawks v. Lazaro, 203 S.E.2d 109 (W.Va. 1974); Finken v. Roop, 339 A.2d 764 (Pa. Super. Ct. 1975), *cert. denied*, 424 U.S. 960 (1976).

64. Lessard v. Schmidt, *supra* note 21, at 1078; Lynch v. Baxley, *supra* note 31.

65. Hawks v. Lazaro, *supra* note 63; *See also* Tippett v. Maryland, 436 F.2d 1153 (4th Cir. 1971), *cert. dismissed as improvidently granted sub. nom.*, Murel v. Baltimore City Criminal Court, 407 U.S. 355 (1972).

66. Lessard v. Schmidt, *supra* note 21, at 1101.

67. *Id.* at 1101 n. 33.

68. Suzuki v. Alba, *supra* note 31, at 1111–1112 (D. Hawaii 1977).

69. Suzuki v. Yuen, 617 F.2d 173, 176–178 (9th Cir. 1980).

70. Lynch v. Baxley, *supra* note 31, at 394.

71. Ill. Ann. Stat., ch. 91–½, § 3–208 (Smith-Hurd Supp. 1982–1983).

72. Ill. Ann. Stat., ch. 91–½, § 3–807 (Smith-Hurd Supp. 1982–1983).

73. Report, *supra* note 17, at 38, 39.

74. *Id*; In the Matter of Germich, 431 N.E.2d 1092 (Ill. App. 1981).

75. Report, *supra* note 17, at 38, 39.

76. Matter of Collins, 429 N.E.2d 531 (Ill. Ct. App. 1981).

77. In re Rizer, 409 N.E.2d 383 (Ill. App. Ct. 1980).

78. In the Matter of Porter, 424 N.E.2d 952 (Ill. App. Ct. 1981).

79. Matter of Collins, *supra* note 76, at 538.

80. *Id.*

81. *See, e.g.*, N.Y. Mental Hyg. Law § 33.13(c) (3) (McKinney 1978); Ohio Rev. Code, § 5123.60(E) (Pages 1981).

82. Lessard v. Schmidt, *supra* note 21, at 1099–1100.

83. Lynch v. Baxley, *supra* note 31, at 89.

84. N.Y. Mental Hyg. Law and Ohio Rev. Code, *supra* note 81.

85. Gotkin v. Miller, 514 F.2d 125 (2d Cir. 1975).

86. *See* Appendix G, "Information and Record Rights."

87. Lessard v. Schmidt, *supra* note 21, at 1091.

88. Lynch v. Baxley, *supra* note 31, at 388.

89. *Id.* Lessard v. Schmidt, *supra* note 21, at 1091; *accord,* Lynch v. Baxley, *supra* note 31, at 387–388; Bell v. Wayne County General Hospital, *infra* note 95, at 1098; Doremus v. Farrell, *infra* note 93, at 515; Stamus v. Leonhart, *infra* note 93, at 446.

90. In re Detention of Harris, 51 U.S.L.W. 2346 (Dec. 14, 1982).

91. Lessard v. Schmidt, *supra* note 21, at 1091; In re Barnard, 455 F.2d 1370, 1375–1376 (D.C. Cir. 1971).

92. Luna v. Van Zandt, 51 U.S.L.W. 2347 (Dec. 14, 1982).

93. Stamus v. Leonhart, 414 F. Supp. 439, 446 (S.D. Iowa 1976); Doremus v. Farrell, 407 F. Supp. 509, 515 (D. Neb. 1975).

94. Lynch v. Baxley, *supra* note 31, at 388.

95. Bell v. Wayne County General Hospital, 384 F. Supp. 1085, 1098 (E.D. Mich. 1974).

96. Coll v. Hyland, 411 F. Supp. 905, 911 (D. N.J. 1976).

97. Logan v. Arafeh, 346 F. Supp. 1265, 1269 (D. Conn. 1972), *aff'd. mem. sub. nom*, Briggs v. Arafeh, 411 U.S. 911 (1973).

98. Ill. Ann. Stat. ch. 91–½, § 3–804 (Smith-Hurd Supp. 1982–1983); Ohio Rev. Code, § 5122.05 (Page's 1981); Rev. Code Wash. § 71.05.300(C) (2)). In Illinois, another psychiatrist from a state hospital is appointed to satisfy this requirement. Because the patient is being held in a state hospital, the independence of such witnesses is questionable, according to defense attorneys for patients.

99. *See* Dixon v. Attorney General of Pennsylvania, 325 F. Supp. 966, 974 (M.D. Pa. 1971) (consent order).

100. Doremus v. Farrell, *supra* note 93, at 515.

101. Bell v. Wayne County General Hospital, *supra* note 95, at 1099, 1100.

102. Lessard v. Schmidt, *supra* note 21, at 1092; Lynch v. Baxley, *supra* note 31, at 389; Suzuki v. Quisenberry, *supra* note 41, at 1129.

103. Lessard v. Schmidt, *supra* note 21, at 1092.

104. Ill. Rev. Stat., ch. 91–½, ¶ 3–800(b) (Smith-Hurd Supp. 1982–1983).

105. Suzuki v. Yuen, *supra* note 69, at 1128.

106. Doremus v. Farrell, *supra* note 93; Markey v. Wachtel, 264 S.E.2d 437 (Sup. Ct. App., W.Va. 1979).

107. Lynch v. Baxley, 386 F. Supp. at 394. *See also* Gomez v. Miller, 337 F. Supp. 386 (S.D. N.Y. 1971); In re Hop, 623 P.2d 282 (Cal. Sup. Ct. 1981); B.J.B. v. District Court of Oklahoma County, 611 P.2d 249 (Okla. Sup. Ct. 1980); In re Wagstaff, 287 N.W.2d 339 (Mich. Ct. App. 1979).

108. Ill. Ann. Stat., ch. 91–½, § 3–802 (Smith-Hurd Supp. 1982–1983).

109. People v. Bradley, 22 Ill. App. 3d 1076, 318 N.E.2d 267 (1974).

110. In re James, 67 Ill. App. 3d 49, 384 N.E.2d 573, 547 (1978).

111. Stamus v. Leonhart, *supra* note 93; Lessard v. Schmidt, *supra* note 21; Doremus v. Farrell, *supra* note 93.

112. Suzuki v. Quisenberry, *supra* note 41, at 1129.

113. Kendall v. True, 391 F. Supp. 413, 419 (W.D. Ky. 1975).

114. *Id.*

115. Bell v. Wayne County General Hospital, *supra* note 95, at 1094; *See also* Suzuki v. Alba, *supra* note 31.

116. Ill. Rev. Stat. ch. 91–½, § 3–806 (Smith-Hurd Supp. 1982–1983).

117. *Id.* In re James, 67 Ill. App. 3d 49, 384 N.E.2d 573 (1978).

118. Lessard v. Schmidt, *supra* note 21, at 1091; Hawks v. Lazaro, *supra* note 63.

119. Lynch v. Baxley, *supra* note 31, at 388–389.

120. *Id.*

121. Addington v. Texas, 441 U.S. 418 (1979).

122. *Id.* at 429.

123. *Id.* at 431.

124. In California, the standard is "beyond a reasonable doubt." In re Hop, *supra* note 107.

125. *See* Appendix A, *supra* note 2.

126. Elliot M. Silverstein, "Civil Commitment of Minors: Due and Undue Process," *W.C.L. Rev.* 58 (1980):1133, 1139.

127. In re Lee, Nos. 68 J(D) 1362, 66 J(D) 1383, Cir. Ct. Cook Cty., Ill. Order of Feb. 20, 1972 (unpublished).

128. In re Long, 25 N.C. App. 702, 214 S.E.2d 626, *cert. denied*, 217 S.E.2d 665 (1975).

129. N.C. Gen. Stat. § 122–56.7(e) (1981).

130. In re Roger S., 569 P.2d 1286 (Sup. Ct. Cal. 1977).

131. *Id.* at 1289.

132. *Id.* at 1296.

133. *Id.* at 1297.

134. Parham v. J.R., 442 U.S. 584 (1979).

135. *Id.* at 606, 607.

136. Glaessner, "Due Process in the 'Voluntary' Civil Commitment of Juvenile Wards," *Jour. of Legal Med.* 2 (1981):169.

137. In re Long, *supra* note 128.

138. Doe v. Doe, 385 N.E.2d 995 (Sup. Ct. Mass. 1979).

139. Ill. Ann. Stat., ch. 91–½, § 3–502.

140. *Id.* at § 3–503(a).

141. *Id.*

142. Report, *supra* note 17, at 46.

143. Ill. Ann. Stat, ch. 91–½, § 3–503(b) (Smith-Hurd Supp. 1982–1983).

144. *Id.* at § 3–504(a).

145. *Id.* at § 3–504(b).

146. *Id.* at § 3–506.

147. *Id.* at § 3–507(b).

148. *Id.* at § 3–507(a).

149. *Id.* at § 3–505.

150. *Id.* at § 3–507(c).

151. *Id.*

152. *Id.* at § 3–509.

153. *Id.* at § 3–510.

154. *Id.* at § 3–511.

155. Johnson v. Solomon, 484 F. Supp. 278, 289 (D. Md. 1979).

156. *Id.*

157. *Id.* at 290.

158. *Id.* at 294.

159. *Id.* at 300.

160. *See, e.g.*, Byrne v. Kysar, 347 F.2d 734 (7th Cir. 1965), *cert. denied*, 389 U.S. 913, *reh. denied*, 384 U.S. 914, *motion to file second petition for reh. denied*, 384 U.S. 994 (1965).

161. *See, e.g.*, Whittington v. Johnson, 201 F.2d 810 (5th Cir. 1953), *cert. denied*, 346 U.S. 867 (1953).

162. Ga. Ann. Stat., § 37–3–4. *See also* Md. Ann. Stat. § 10–618.

163. Ill. Ann. Stat., ch. 91–½, § 6–103 (Smith-Hurd Supp. 1982–1983).

164. Ill. Ann. Stat., ch. 91–½, § 5–117 (Smith-Hurd Supp. 1982–1983).

165. Daniels v. Finney, 262 S.W.2d 431 (Tex. Civ. App. 1953); Dunbar v. Greenlaw, 128 A.2d 218 (Sup. Ct. Maine 1956).

166. Daniels v. Finney, *supra* note 165; Lowen v. Hilton, 351 P.2d 881 (Sup. Ct. Colo. 1960).

167. Stowers v. Ardmore Acres Hospital, 172 N.W.2d 497 (Mich. Ct. of App. 1969); Giovanni v. Pessel, 250 A.2d 756 (N.J. App. Ct. 1969).

168. Dunbar v. Greenlaw, *supra* note 165; Fowle v. Fowle, 122 S.E.2d 722 (Sup. Ct. N.C. 1961).

169. James v. Brown, 637 S.W.2d 914 (Tex. Sup. Ct. 1982).

170. McLean v. Sale, 38 N.C. App. 520, 248 S.E.2d 372 (1978).

171. *Id.* at 375.

172. Olsen v. Karwoski, 25 Ill. Dec. 173, 386 N.E.2d 444 (1979).

173. *Id.* at 178, 179.

174. *Id.* at 180.

175. Ill. Rev. Stat., ch. 91–½, § 6–102 (Smith-Hurd Supp. 1982–1983).

Chapter 8

Diagnosis and Treatment

ASSESSMENT AND DIAGNOSIS

JCAH standards require that each patient receive a complete assessment, including but not limited to "physical, emotional, behavioral, social, recreational, and, when appropriate, legal, vocational, and nutritional needs."[1] A physical examination must be completed within 24 hours after admission.[2] In programs serving children the physical examination must include evaluations of motor development and functioning, sensorimotor functioning, speech, hearing, and language functioning, visual functioning, and immunization status.[3] In addition, such programs must have "all the necessary diagnostic tools and personnel available to perform physical health assessments, including electroencephalographic equipment, a qualified technician trained in dealing with children and adolescents and a properly qualified physician to interpret electroencephalographic tracing of children and adolescents."[4]

The emotional and behavioral assessment of each patient, child or adult, must include, but not be limited to, a history of previous problems, current emotional and behavioral functioning, and, when indicated, "a mental status examination appropriate to the age of the patient, a psychological assessment, including intellectual, projective and personality testing and functional evaluations of language, self care and social-affective and visualmotor functioning."[5]

Finally, a legal assessment, which includes a legal history and "a preliminary discussion to determine the extent to which the individual's legal situation will influence his or her progress in treatment and the urgency of the legal situation,"[6] is required.

Therapists have a duty to possess the degree of skill and learning ordinarily possessed and used by members of their profession in making diagnoses, and to apply that skill with reasonable care, using their best judgment. What is reasonable care in the diagnosis of mental illness? In contrast to physical illness and injuries, the classifications of mental illness are imprecise and uncertain and not agreed upon by members of the profession. Hence, it is difficult to establish the standard of care. "[W]hen the entity called a disease is manifested entirely by a behavioral disturbance, then there is a great subjective element in the decision that a disease is present."[7]

The U.S. Supreme Court has stated that "the subtleties and nuances of psychiatric diagnosis render certainties virtually beyond reach. . . . Psychiatric diagnosis . . . is to a large extent based on medical 'impressions' drawn from subjective analysis and filtered through the experience of the diagnostician. This process often makes it very difficult for the expert physician to offer definite conclusions. . . ."[8] While still an appeals court judge, Chief Justice Warren Burger stated:

> Not being judicially defined, these terms mean in any given case whatever the expert witnesses say they mean. We know also that psychiatrists are in disagreement on what is a "mental disease" and even whether there exists such a definable and classifiable condition. . . . No rule of law can possibly be sound or workable which is dependent upon the terms of another discipline whose members are in profound disagreement about what those terms mean.[9]

The descriptions of mental illness found in the DSM III are compromises of the membership of the American Psychiatric Association, and are influenced significantly by politics and social attitudes.[10] "Psychiatrists have not agreed to the clinical features of the DSM III classifications of mental illness, do not know what dynamics produce these features and have not disclosed the causes that trigger those dynamics in action."[11] "[I]n some situations, 'you have no way of knowing whether your diagnosis is better than anyone else's . . . until you see if the treatment works.' "[12]

Thus, it is not surprising that there are no known malpractice cases involving the misdiagnosis of mental illness, for example, a diagnosis of depression where the patient was actually suffering from schizophrenia. Failure to diagnose a physical cause of a patient's symptoms may be malpractice. While no reported cases were found, "failure to distinguish, diagnose and treat both psychiatric and medical symptoms of patients can be costly. For example, one hospital paid $900,000 in 1978 to settle two suits that were brought because the neurological disorders of two persons who came to the ED [Emergency Department] in psychological distress were overlooked by the examining psychiatrist."[13] Other cases involve the failure to diagnose a patient as suicidal.[14] (Suicidal tendencies are more properly characterized as caused by a mental illness.) Finally, wrongful diagnosis has arisen in the context of court-ordered evaluations.[15]

In a Kansas case, a patient alleged that a general practitioner "failed to diagnose that she was mentally ill, when she was in fact suffering from a mental illness of schizophrenic disorder and paranoid trends of depression." The case was dismissed on an unrelated issue and never went to trial.[16] One commentator cites a case where a patient filed an action against several defendants, including a psychologist, for failure to diagnose the existence of a brain tumor. The psychologist had administered a Wechsler Adult Intelligence Scale test. The outcome of this action is unknown.[17]

A difficult problem of diagnosis and treatment in state institutions is the difference of opinion as to whether a patient is a "burned out" schizophrenic or suffers from mental retardation. The issue is significant in terms of whether the individual receives treatment or habilitation or both. If both, in what sequence? The mental health staff argues that the individual is mentally retarded or suffers from some other developmental disability and that they have neither the time nor the training required to deal with the problem. The developmental disability staff argues that the individual is actually a difficult-to-deal-with "burned out" schizophrenic that the mental health staff would like to transfer. In any event, even if the individual is suffering from borderline retardation, the acting out caused by the mental illness must be treated first. The result is that such disagreements often are not resolved and the patient receives little treatment or habilitation. One solution is to create a separate treatment unit for the diagnosis, treatment, and habilitation of such persons. State mental health agencies may be unwilling to implement this solution for financial reasons.

RIGHT TO TREATMENT

Mentally disabled persons have no right to treatment, or, more accurately, no general common law mandates that physicians treat mentally disabled persons. Of course, a physician who has begun to treat a patient may be liable for providing inadequate treatment and in some instances may even be liable for discontinuing treatment.[18] Nevertheless, initially the physician has no common law duty to treat.

Many states have given patients a statutory right to treatment in public hospitals.[19] Most statutes frame the right to treatment in general terms. For example, the District of Columbia Code simply provides that "a person hospitalized in a public hospital for a mental illness shall, during his hospitalization, be entitled to medical and psychiatric care and treatment."[20] Illinois provides that patients have a right to "adequate and humane care and services in the least restrictive environment."[21]

In the absence of a statutory right to treatment, plaintiff patients must rely on their constitutional right to treatment. The exact parameters of this constitutional right are unclear because this is a recent and still-developing area of constitutional law. Courts have based the constitutional right to treatment on the Fourteenth Amendment right to due process and the Eighth Amendment prohibition against cruel and unusual punishment.

The first significant judicial recognition of a constitutional right to treatment came in 1966 in Chief Judge Bazelon's opinion in *Rouse v. Cameron*.[22] *Rouse* involved the right of a patient who was involuntarily committed in a criminal (as opposed to civil) proceeding. While Judge Bazelon based the decision on Rouse's statutory right to treatment, he suggested that there might be a constitutional right to treatment based upon the Fourteenth Amendment requirement of due process of law or possibly the Eighth Amendment prohibition of cruel and unusual punishment.[23]

A federal court in Alabama squarely faced the issue of a constitutional right to treatment in the case of *Wyatt v. Stickney*.[24] *Wyatt* was a class action on behalf of mental patients; it challenged the constitutionality of conditions at Alabama mental institutions.[25] The court expressly decided that patients involuntarily committed through civil proceedings had a constitutional right to treatment. The court reasoned, "Adequate and effective treatment is constitutionally required because, absent treatment, the hospital is transformed into a penitentiary where one could be held indefinitely for no convicted offense."[26] The court explained that the very purpose of involuntary hospitalization of mentally ill patients is treatment and not mere custodial care or punishment. In fact, treatment is the only justification that allows civil commitment to mental institutions. In other words, the *quid pro quo* for involuntary commitment is the provision of adequate treatment.[27] The Constitution requires, at a minimum, "such individual treatment as will give each [patient] a realistic opportunity to be cured or to improve his or her condition."[28] Specifically, the *Wyatt* court decided there were three fundamental conditions for adequate and effective treatment programs: (1) a humane psychological and physical environment, (2) qualified staff in numbers sufficient to administer adequate treatment, and (3) individualized treatment plans.[29]

The Supreme Court has never explicitly endorsed this *quid pro quo* theory. In fact, Chief Justice Burger rejected it in his separate opinion in *O'Connor v. Donaldson*.[30] Nevertheless, many writers conclude that the theory remains forceful and vigorous. They point to the frequent use of the theory by lower federal courts, the absence of Supreme Court action striking down the theory, and the unanimity of favorable law review commentary.[31]

Many courts have equated civil commitment without treatment to punishing persons for their disabilities.[32] Punishment for mental disease is thought to be an infliction of cruel and unusual punishment.[33] Even if treatment is provided, administering such treatment in inadequate facilities may constitute cruel and unusual punishment.[34]

Stemming from the Eighth Amendment's proscription of cruel and unusual punishment is a person's right to freedom from harm.[35] This right is described in the leading case of *New York State Association for Retarded Children v. Rockefeller*.[36] Residents of a New York institution for mentally retarded persons brought suit to require New York state officials to raise the level of treatment and care conditions at the institution. The court based its decision for the residents on their right to freedom from harm.[37] The court analogized the rights of the mental institution residents to those of persons confined under criminal law, and stated that "a tolerable living environment is now guaranteed by law."[38] The court specified a number of rights that fall within the right to freedom from harm. For example, a confined person has a right to protection from assaults by fellow residents or by staff, to medical care, to adequate heat during cold weather, and to the necessary elements of basic hygiene.[39]

While a number of other lower federal courts have recognized a right to treatment,[40] until recently the Supreme Court never expressly ruled out the right to treatment. The Supreme Court did, however, recognize a limited right to treatment in *Youngberg v. Romeo*.[41] The patient Romeo had been civilly committed by his mother and had little or no possibility of being released. Doctors at his hospital often ordered physical restraints to protect Romeo and his fellow patients. The court decided that patients clearly have constitutionally protected interests in conditions of reasonable care and safety and freedom from undue bodily restraint. The court ruled that a "state is under a duty to provide [patients] with such training as an appropriate professional would consider reasonable to ensure his safety and to facilitate his ability to function free from bodily restraints."[42] Thus, while not recognizing a right to treatment that is designed to cure or improve a patient's condition, the Supreme Court did recognize a patient's constitutional right at least to treatment necessary to protect the liberty interests of the patient while in the mental institution.

CONSENT FOR TREATMENT

The psychiatrist-patient relationship is generally a consensual one; therefore, the practitioner generally must obtain consent of the patient (or the parent or guardian) prior to treatment. Failure to obtain consent constitutes battery. Every person, with some limited exceptions, has a right not to be touched or treated medically. The intentional touching of another person without consent is a legal wrong characterized as a "battery," an intentional tort rather than malpractice or negligence. The question is whether consent was given regardless of any injury or benefit from the treatment. Of course, if there was no injury, it will be reflected in the amount of damages recovered.[43]

Consent must be "informed." That is, the doctor must divulge "all facts which a reasonable medical practitioner [in the same or similar community] would divulge under the same or similar circumstances, including the general nature of the treatment, general risks and probable consequences, and the possibility that unforeseen conditions may necessitate a change in procedure."[44] Such consent should be clear and unequivocal; thus, submission to treatment will not be considered to be a means of consent.[45] However, exceptions to the rule requiring full and fair disclosure do exist, among them: an emergency where the patient is in no condition to exercise judgment; treatment that involves minimal risk and an explanation of all risks would alarm a patient who was already apprehensive and who might refuse to undergo the treatment as a result; or occasions where the patient's mental and emotional condition may be harmed, thus adversely affecting treatment.[46] Failure to obtain an *informed* consent may result in liability for malpractice or negligence.

In an Illinois case involving consent for the administration of ECT, the court said that the special relationship between a physician and a patient "vests the doctor with the responsibility of disclosure [of risks and] requires the doctor to exercise discretion in prudently disclosing information in accordance with his patient's best interests."[47] The hospital has no duty to obtain informed consent for treatment.[48] While a hospital has no duty to obtain informed consent where the treating physician is an independent member of the medical staff, the hospital may be liable where the physician is an employee or agent of the hospital or a respondent superior.[49] The hospital may also be liable where an independent physician with privileges has failed to obtain informed consent in the past, and the hospital administration and/or medical staff knew or should have known of this failure.[50]

The issue of informed consent arises in a number of areas. For example, patients administered medication should be informed of possible adverse effects resulting from use of a prescribed drug. One commentator suggests that whenever dealing with a potent psychotropic drug, the patient's consent should be received in writing; if it is not possible to obtain such consent because the patient is disabled, this same commentator advises the appointment of a temporary legal guardian to obtain such consent.[51]

An area of uncertainty regarding informed consent is where effective treatment of one psychiatric condition causes other, often unpleasant disorders. A warning about side effects may cause a patient to resist treatment necessary to prevent further decline. For example, a schizophrenic's disabling paranoia may be reduced with Chlorpromazine, but the medication may also cause a Parkinsonian-like movement disorder, which may persist after the drug is withdrawn. Is the psychiatrist required to inform the patient prior to initiating treatment that such a side effect may occur? The patient may argue that, having been so informed, he or she would not have consented to the administration of the drug. The psychiatrist may contend that at the time treatment began the patient could not have made a reasonable decision about treatment and that the patient urgently needed treatment to prevent serious deterioration. Courts have held that informed consent is unnecessary when divulging full information might worsen a patient's condition or cause the patient to reject clearly beneficial therapy.[52] Additionally, courts may be willing to find a patient's knowing acceptance of treatment sufficient to imply consent,[53] or they may find informed consent given by a member of the patient's immediate family sufficient.[54]

One psychiatrist/lawyer recommends telling the patient of all life-threatening or disabling side effects, no matter how uncommon, and all other side effects that are reasonably predictable. The only exceptions are occasions when the psychiatrist is convinced that full disclosure will cause the patient to refuse urgently needed therapy and when the patient has mental impairment or major psychiatric disease.[55]

RIGHT TO REFUSE TREATMENT

Closely related to the requirement of informed consent is a patient's right to refuse treatment. Not long ago, the involuntarily committed patient had no right to refuse. To the contrary, some courts concluded not only that forced medication was permissible treatment, but also that failure to medicate a mental patient forcibly, when it is the prescribed therapy, was mistreatment. In one case, the Massachusetts Supreme Judicial Court found it to be "inconsistent with good practice" that psychotropic drugs "were not . . . administered involuntarily where patients refused medication."[56] In another case, the New York Court of Claims found that "the reason for not using such drugs was that [the patient] refused them. We consider such reasons to be illogical, unprofessional and not consonant with prevailing medical standards."[57]

Since these two cases were decided, a near revolution has occurred in patients' rights to refuse treatment. The courts are beginning to recognize a constitutional right to refuse intrusive treatments. The American Hospital Association has formulated the right in this manner: "The patient has the right to refuse treatment *to the extent permitted by law*, and to be informed of the medical consequences of his action."[58] As this position reflects, it is standard medical practice that, before embarking on a treatment program with potentially harmful effects, the patient be given a chance to balance the possible benefits with the dangers involved. Even though statistically the likelihood of benefit might be very high with the possibility of harm very low, the decision to receive treatment is an inherently individual decision for the patient to make. It is not a medical determination.[59] "It is the individual making the decision, and no one else, who lives with the pain and disease, . . . who must undergo or forego the treatment [and] . . . live with the results of that decision."[60]

When a person's incompetence has not been established, that person retains the right to make treatment decisions. Commitment is not a determination of incompetence. The decision to label a person incompetent has important social and legal ramifications for that person; hence, it is a distinctly judicial question. Many mental patients are capable of functioning competently, and there is no reason why the competent patient should be presumed incapable of making rational treatment decisions. Indeed, the competent committed patient retains the right to endorse checks, file income tax returns, engage in correspondence, sell his or her house, write a will, and otherwise conduct his or her life autonomously in noncontroversial matters.[61] Hence, although committed, the adult mental patient retains all other legal rights. Also, as one court pointed out, the competent committed mental patient is uniquely capable of making self-determinate decisions in the treatment area:

> [A]lthough committed mental patients do suffer at least some impairment of their relationship to reality, most are able to appreciate the benefits, risks, and discomfort that may reasonably be expected from receiving psychotropic medication. This is particularly true for patients who have experienced such medication and, therefore, have some basis for assessing comparative advantages and disadvantages.[62]

Even in the event that a patient is declared to be incompetent, decisions regarding that patient's treatment are not entirely relegated to others. Many states require a determination of what that person would do if he or she were competent. Sometimes this decision is relatively easy, as in the case of a person with a religious conviction against organic therapies or one who has expressed a preference while competent. At other times, the court or a guardian must make a more subjective determination. While courts readily admit the difficulty of making such determinations, the general feeling is that some such attempt is better than none at all.

One court, in a case involving an incompetent but uncommitted ward, itemized the factors that it deemed should be taken into account in determining what an incompetent person would choose for himself or herself if competent:

1. the ward's expressed preferences regarding treatment;
2. the ward's religious beliefs;
3. the impact upon the ward's family;
4. the probability of adverse side effects;
5. the consequences if treatment is refused; and
6. the prognosis with treatment.[63]

In some states a court must make the substituted judgment decision; in others an appointed guardian may do so; still others allow the treating physician to make a judgment on what the patient would choose. Each must accord due respect to the interests of the incompetent patient.

The state, however, may have countervailing legal interests of its own, including some that may affect the treatment decisions of patients in its mental institutions. The legal rights of a committed patient must be weighed against the concurrent interests of the state. To understand when the rights of the patient may be compromised, it is crucial to understand what interest the state has in committing the patient.

Two justifications for involuntarily confining a mentally ill person are related to the validity of forcible treatment. The first justification is that the patient is a danger to self or others. The state has the authority under its police power to remove such individuals from society. Once that precaution has been taken, however, the authority to treat such individuals must come from another source because the police power does not extend beyond the safety of society or the individual to making such decisions for an individual as whether or not to undergo treatment for mental illness.

However, while committed, patients may become violent and pose dangers to themselves and others. In such instances the state may restrain such patients through means that may include forcible medication, which would in other contexts be considered treatment. Such emergencies must place hospital staff or patients in danger before the patient's right to refuse treatment is overridden. Therefore, once society is protected by the institutionalization of the individual, only the safety of those in the institution may justify the forcible treatment of a patient under police power. The involuntarily committed patient's liberty "is diminished only to the extent necessary to allow for confinement by the state so as to prevent him from being a danger to himself or to others."[64]

When police power is used to allow the exercise of medical restraints, these restraints must be "the least intrusive necessary."[65] One commentator has styled "instrusiveness" in the mental institution context as a continuum, beginning with verbal rehabilitative techniques, and moving successively to behavioral techniques, organic techniques (including psychotropic medication, ECT, and surgical intervention).[66] Presumably, physical restraint would fall between behavioral techniques and organic techniques. The basis of the order is the degree to which the patient may avoid the desired effects by withholding cooperation and the duration, nature, and extent of the intrusion. Another commentator has argued that even if the administration of drugs is justified, the choice of drugs is important because "barbiturates or benzodiazepines may be less overwhelming than psychotropic drugs and therefore ought to be used in their place when dealing with short-term emergency situations. These sedative-hypnotic drugs are arguably less intrusive than psychotropic drugs in terms of both intrusion and discomfort."[67]

The second justification for committing an individual is the state's *parens patriae* power. The *parens patriae* power (literally, "parent of the country") is exercised by the state as guardian of persons under legal disability.[68] However, at least with adults, "the *parens patriae* relationship does not materialize until a patient is declared judicially incompetent."[69] Merely because an individual is institutionalized does not mean that that patient is sufficiently incapacitated to awaken the *parens patriae* power of the state. Patients in mental hospitals who have not been adjudicated incompetent are presumed capable of making rational treatment decisions.

The exact nature of the balance between state interests and an individual's right to refuse treatment is still unclear. Courts and legislatures are currently making important decisions that will define the parameters of the right to refuse treatment. Meanwhile, some guidance is possible. An American Psychiatric Association task force report made the following recommendations:

> Except in emergencies, if a patient who is competent to participate in treatment decisions declines to accept treatment recommended by staff, we accept the patient's right to refuse. If the physician believes the patient is not competent to participate in treatment decisions, he should ask a court to rule on the patient's competency. If the patient is found not competent, an impartial third-party, designated by the court, should be given the authority of consent. . . .[70]

The task force statement represents a safe, conservative stance on the right to refuse treatment. In all likelihood, most states would not require an appointed guardian to give consent to treatment for an incompetent patient, but it is too early to tell. At the very least, the decision to treat a nonconsenting incompetent patient should be made in concurrence with a physician other than one treating the patient.

The nature of a patient's right to refuse treatment has been raised mainly with respect to treatment with antipsychotic drugs. Concerned practitioners can derive guidance from reviewing the current trends in rulings in cases involving the administration of these drugs.

Antipsychotic Drugs

Since the introduction of Thorazine in the United States, antipsychotic drugs have become the mainstay of treatment therapy for schizophrenia. Widespread use of these drugs has been cited as the major reason for the dramatic decrease of the population of mental hospitals,[71] and the National Committee on Brain Sciences has called the introduction of antipsychotic drugs "the outstanding single practical contribution to psychiatry over the last twenty years."[72] The administration of antipsychotic drugs, however, is an intrusion into the body and/or mind, which can have serious and possibly harmful results and effects. Avoidance of unpleasant primary and secondary effects may lead many patients to resist these therapies and to bear the consequences of letting their mental illnesses go untreated. Still others may view the application of medical science to their bodies as not consonant with their religious beliefs.

Patients have sometimes taken their objections to court. In one case, a federal district court concluded that no state interest could provide justification for the administration of psychotropic drugs without the consent of a competent patient, unless the patient presents a danger to self or to others in the institution.[73] Even if a competent patient is medicated because he or she presents a danger, the patient must be provided with a hearing as soon as possible. Furthermore, the decision to forcibly medicate may have to be reviewed periodically to comply with due process requirements. Interestingly, the court did not say that the decision maker may not be connected with the institution.

In *Rogers v. Okin*,[74] the U.S. Court of Appeals for the First Circuit recognized that competent patients could not be forcibly medicated for treatment purposes. However, patients who had been adjudicated incompetent may be forcibly medicated as a part of treatment therapy without a guardian's approval if other reasonable treatment alternatives have been ruled out. Both competent and incompetent mental patients may be forcibly medicated in emergencies, which the appeals court defined broadly to include situations where a patient might "slip into possibly chronic illness while awaiting an adjudication of incompetency." The *minimal* process due a patient is an individualized determination by a qualified physician that forced medication is necessary.

However, the U.S. Supreme Court vacated the *Rogers*[75] decision and remanded it for reconsideration by the court of appeals in light of a subsequent Massachusetts case,[76] in which the Supreme Court of Massachusetts stated that in the case of an uncommitted, incompetent ward, the guardian of that ward may not make the decision to allow treatment of the ward with antipsychotic drugs. The court said that in view of the fact that competent individuals could exercise the right to refuse such treatment themselves, denying this right to incompetent patients would be degrading and disrespectful of this "basic right."[77] Therefore, for noncommitted incompetent individuals, a court must determine what the individual would choose to do if he or she were not incompetent ("substituted judgment"). The court did not purport to be concerned with what is in a ward's best medical interest—an inherently professional decision to be made by those properly trained in medicine. Rather, it concerned itself with what the individual would choose when medically informed. Thus, the individual's values and preferences are sought and given appropriate weight and effect.

Given the tenor of the Massachusetts decision, it is likely that the court would give greater deference to the wishes of an institutionalized patient than the appeals court did in *Rogers*. In fact, the Massachusetts high court referred to the statement in the court of appeals decision that a physician need not stand by and watch a patient "slip into possibly chronic illness while awaiting an adjudication," and stated that because an expedited decision can be obtained in Massachusetts, no such case need ever arise in that jurisdiction. The Massachusetts court also elected to consider antipsychotic drugs as equivalent in terms of intrusiveness to psychosurgery or ECT. Given this approach to the determination of noncommitted individuals' rights to refuse treatment, the court of appeals will have difficulty on remand to state that Massachusetts law does not give greater rights to committed mental patients than it recognized in *Rogers*.

In the third federal case, *Rennie v. Klein*,[78] the U.S. Court of Appeals for the Third Circuit struck down the additional procedures the district court had placed upon New Jersey institutions wishing to medicate committed patients forcibly. The district court attempted to create greater independence in such decision making by setting up a comprehensive system involving patient consent forms outlining their rights, independent psychiatrists, "patient advocates," and an adversarial hearing. The appeals court ruled that, in view of the protections afforded by the New Jersey legislature, such additional procedures were not constitutionally necessary. The New Jersey administrative procedure calls for a meeting of the patient and the "treatment team" when the patient declines the recommended medication. If after that meeting an impasse remains, the medical director of the institution may concur with the treating physician and order administration of the medication. Otherwise, the individual has a right to refuse medication. In any event, the court put great weight on the requirement that hospitals use the least restrictive method available.[79]

In an Oklahoma case, the state supreme court ruled that a competent mental patient may not be forced to undergo electroshock, psychosurgery, or forced medication.[80] The court called such treatments "intrusive in nature and an invasion of the body." According to that decision, involuntarily committed but legally competent patients have a constitutional right to refuse psychotropic drugs in nonemergency situations. The court stated that, "It is time to recognize [that] liberty includes the freedom to decide about one's own health."[81] Involuntary treatment through organic techniques must be preceded by a judicial proceeding where the patient has been declared legally incompetent. An incompetent patient may have a guardian appointed to make an "informed decision" through the substituted-judgment approach.

Another court held that if a patient had a firm religious conviction, while competent, against medical treatment before being committed, then that conviction should be accorded effect, even after the patient has been adjudged incompetent and has been committed.[82]

Finally, a federal district court in Utah ruled that an involuntary patient in that state does not have a right to refuse medication, even in nonemergency situations. However, that decision was certainly prompted by the fact that the Utah commitment statute requires that it be shown prior to commitment that a person is unable to make rational treatment decisions.[83] Most states do not require such a showing, and even those that do might not make any further determination than that the mentally ill respondent's resistance to hospitalization is rational or irrational.[84] Despite such a determination, all treatment decisions are not automatically relegated to the patient's treating physician simply because the patient cannot make a rational decision with regard to treatment. At least, religious convictions held prior to commitment will probably override such an assignment of the treatment decision.

The Mental Health Systems Act of 1980 provides that a patient has the right not to receive treatment without informed, voluntary, written consent, except in a documented emergency or as permitted under applicable law for someone who has been committed.[85] In 17 states a patient has a right to refuse treatment.

Another 22 states provide for the right to refuse some treatment. Only 11 states fail to provide for the right of a patient to refuse treatment.[86]

The Mental Health Systems Act of 1980 recommends that patients have the right not to receive treatment without informed, voluntary, written consent, except in a documented emergency or as permitted under applicable law for someone who has been civilly committed.[87] The act also provides that patients do not have to participate in experimentation in the absence of informed, voluntary, written consent.[88]

In 19 states a patient has the right not to participate in experimental treatment. Two other states provide the right not to participate in some treatment. Another 27 states and the District of Columbia do not provide for such a right.[89]

TREATMENT

JCAH standards provide that each patient shall receive individualized treatment, which shall include at least the following:

a. the provision of adequate and humane services, regardless of source(s) of financial support;
b. the provision of services within the least restrictive environment possible;
c. the provision of an individualized treatment plan;
d. the periodic review of the patient's treatment plan;
e. the active participation of patients over 12 years of age and their responsible parents, relatives or guardians in planning for treatment; and
f. the provision of an adequate number of competent, qualified, and experienced professional clinical staff to supervise and implement the treatment planned.[90]

JCAH standards also require that a patient's family or legal guardian should be fully informed about the nature of the care, procedures, and treatment that the patient will receive; the risks, side effects, and benefits of all medication and treatment procedures used, especially those that are unusual or experimental; the alternate treatment procedures that are available; discharge plans; and the plans for meeting continuing mental and physical health requirements following discharge.[91]

The Mental Health Systems Act of 1980[92] is a congressional recommendation that states grant patients the following rights:

- the right to appropriate treatment and related services in a setting that is most supportive and least restrictive of the person's liberty;[93]
- the right to an individualized, written treatment or service plan;[94]

- the right, consistent with one's capabilities, to participate in and receive a reasonable explanation of the care and treatment process;[95]
- the right not to participate in experimentation in the absence of informed, voluntary, written consent;[96]
- the right to a humane treatment environment that affords reasonable protection from harm and appropriate privacy.[97]

The statutes in 43 states and the District of Columbia provide that patients are entitled to appropriate treatment and services. South Dakota provides some right to treatment. Only Alabama, Kentucky, Massachusetts, Mississippi, Oregon and Vermont have failed to provide that a patient has a right to appropriate treatment and services.[98] Patients in 25 states have a right to an individual treatment program. Another 7 states provide some right to an individual treatment plan, and 21 states make no provision regarding individual treatment plans. Only 10 states provide that treatment must be based on a plan. Nebraska makes some provision for treatment based on a plan.[99]

Laws in 31 states and the District of Columbia provide for the periodic review of treatment provided patients. Six states provide for some review of the treatment provided to patients. Only 13 states fail to provide for any review of the treatment provided to patients.[100] Thirty states provide that treatment must be provided in a humane environment. Iowa also provides a somewhat similar right. Another 21 states provide no such right.

In 22 states some after-care plan must be provided for patients, and an identical number of states provide that discharge referrals must be made for patients.[101]

Eight states provide that a patient has the right, consistent with one's capabilities, to participate in the care and treatment process. Four other states provide for some participation. Thirty-nine states make no provision for patient participation in the care and treatment process.[102]

Thirty-one states provide that a patient has the right to privacy for personal needs, and three others provide for some kind of privacy.[103]

Patients in 13 states have the right to be treated in a safe environment.[104]

Treatment by Administration of Medication

Physicians, nurses, and pharmacists[105] have a duty to possess the degree of skill and learning ordinarily possessed and used by members of their profession in good standing engaged in prescribing, dispensing, and administering medication in the same or a similar community in which they practice, and they must apply these skills with reasonable skill, using their best judgment. Such professionals may be liable for conduct that falls below the standard, which is the proximate cause of injury to a patient.[106]

As an employer, a hospital may be liable for acts of malpractice or negligence by pharmacists who dispense medication, by physicians who prescribe, and by nurses or others who administer medication in the hospital. A hospital also may be liable for failure to hire a qualified pharmacist as it would be liable for employing unqualified physicians and nurses who commit acts of malpractice or negligence.

Medication-related issues arising in the mental health context differ little from the drug liability issues in other medical areas. In both instances, the physician must use due care in prescribing the drug, considering all the surrounding circumstances. All physicians are held to a reasonable knowledge of drugs prescribed by them, and to a reasonable standard of care with respect to the conditions for which and the manner in which the drugs are prescribed. The standard of care and treatment must be established by an expert witness, often a forensic pharmacologist.

Nurses and others authorized to administer medication[107] may be held to different standards. In those states where nurses are recognized as professionals liable for malpractice, they are subject to the same standards of care and treatment as physicians.[108] An expert witness must establish the standard. Nonnurses who administer medication will be held to the negligence standard of what a reasonable and prudent person would do under similar circumstances. No expert witness is required to establish the standard of care in a negligence action.

Treatment by administration of medication by a physician has been found to fall below the required standard in numerous situations, including: (1) failure to administer a physical examination before prescribing medication; (2) prescribing a drug where it is not indicated; (3) prescribing the wrong dosage of a drug; (4) prescribing a drug to a patient allergic to such drugs; (5) failure to inquire about and take into account other medications the patient might be taking that may potentiate the toxic effects of the prescribed drug; (6) failure to warn about or monitor for side effects that may be caused by the prescribed drug; and (7) failure to obtain informed consent to use of the drug.

Failure To Administer a Physical Examination

A physician may be liable for injury that results from failure to administer a physical examination or to check the medical records of the patient. In Alabama, a military doctor was held liable where he wrote a prescription for 100 five-milligram tablets of Valium for an unknown airman who had mild anxiety. The doctor did not ask if the patient had a history of mental problems, and did not check the records of the base clinic. Had he checked, the physician would have found that the patient recently had been discharged from a clinic that had treated him for a psychotic episode. The doctor testified that he certainly would not have prescribed Valium had he known the patient was suffering from depression.

Two days after the defendant physician treated him the patient had an automobile accident that was proximately caused by his taking the Valium. The court held that the physician's conduct in prescribing the medication fell below the required standards of care in the military and in that part of Alabama. The physician at least should have checked the patient's record at the base clinic.[109]

In New York, a patient allegedly swallowed 100 aspirin at 10:00 a.m. At 2:00 p.m. he jumped in front of a bus in a suicide attempt. He was taken to a community hospital. Because no physicians were available, he was taken to the office of a psychiatrist at 3:40 p.m. A superficial examination revealed some symptomatology of aspirin toxicity, or salicylate poisoning. His pulse was rapid, and he complained of nausea and ringing in his ears. The psychiatrist did not believe the patient had taken the quantity of aspirin claimed.[110]

The community hospital sent the patient to a state hospital. He arrived between 4:30 and 5:00 p.m. He vomited on the way. The psychiatrist claimed that he reviewed the patient's history and symptomatology with the nursing supervisor upon the patient's admission and that he advised the nurse that the patient should receive only clear fluids.

The admitting physician at the state hospital did not conduct a physical examination because the patient arrived at the hospital after the normal time for such procedure. He testified that the doctor at the community hospital did not inform him of what had been done to "clear the patient at the hospital," and he did not ask. He placed the patient on suicide alert and prescribed 100 milligrams of Thorazine at 7:00 p.m. The patient vomited ten minutes after receiving the medication. The physician was not informed of this because he did not instruct the medical staff on duty to notify him of any irregular reaction to the medication or to observe for other signs of toxicity. The patient died at 11:00 p.m. from salicylate poisoning.

The court found malpractice in that (1) the physician was not licensed or certified and thus did not possess the skill or professional judgment to—essentially unsupervised—provide ordinary and reasonable psychiatric care and treatment; (2) no informed judgment was ever made after careful examination—the examination was cursory; (3) the physician took no steps to guard against the foreseeable risks and hazards of prescribing dangerous medication, those risks and hazards being shock and irregular heart beat; (4) the physician ignored the warning of available signs of toxicity; (5) no one was instructed to notify, and no one notified, the physician when the patient vomited after administration of the medication; (6) an internal medicine specialist should have been called; and (7) blood tests to determine the level of aspirin poisoning should have been conducted.[111]

Prescription of Medication Not Indicated

Liability may be imposed upon a physician for prescribing a medication considered inappropriate under the general standards of treatment for the diagnosed mental illness or mental disorder. For example, the drug Phenothiazine and related tranquilizers are considered appropriate for the treatment of many psychotic reactions. However, while such tranquilizers may be helpful in treating anxious patients who have some depressive features, they are inappropriate treatment for severe depression, and may even worsen it. A physician who prescribes tranquilizers for a severely depressed patient may be liable for any resulting adverse reaction on the grounds that such treatment falls below the required standard of care. Thus, the liability of the psychiatrist for an adverse reaction would depend upon the diagnosis of the patient and the reason for which the medication was prescribed. Where a physician prescribes such medication to an anxious patient who has some depressive symptoms, the reasons for the prescription should be clearly documented in medical records.[112]

An example of liability for improper prescription of tranquilizers for the diagnosis occurred in Iowa. There a state court awarded substantial damages to a young mentally retarded man who was found to suffer from tardive dyskinesia as a result of his prolonged exposure to tranquilizers. The condition had caused a major and permanent lessening of his ability to care for himself and to function as he had prior to the administration of the drugs. The court found that the use of tranquilizers for the young man's condition fell below the standard of medical care required for the institution.[113]

Failure to follow the instructions on the pharmaceutical package insert regarding proper application and dosage of a medication may render the physician liable for harm suffered by the patient.[114] In some states, a drug manufacturer's prescription brochure is evidence in support of a malpractice claim where a physician deviates from the instructions.[115] An appeals court held that the pharmaceutical package insert for the drug Phioridazine (Mellaril) should have been allowed into evidence in a suit that questioned whether such a drug should have been administered to a depressed patient.[116] The package indicated that such medication should not be given for depression.

Prescription of Improper Dosage

Drug dosage tolerance varies considerably from patient to patient. For example, a young psychotic may tolerate 1,000 milligrams of Chlorpromazine daily with no effect on alertness whereas the agitated senile patient may become quite somnolent on 150 milligrams per day. Consequently, it is difficult for a court to determine when a patient has received an incorrect dosage. Nonetheless, in certain cases a physician can be found liable for prescribing an improper dosage. For example, "[a] dosage of Chlorpromazine that causes a patient frequently to lose consciousness, because it lowers his blood pressure to the point where perfusion of the brain fails, is clearly too high for that patient and should be revised. A failure to change the dose would be a basis for liability if permanent brain damage resulted."[117]

In a Nevada case, the question was whether an improper dosage caused the death of a patient who drowned on an outing. The patient received more than 20 milligrams of Prolixin on numerous days during his stay at a Veterans' Administration hospital. A forensic pharmacologist testified that "Prolixin should be administered only in dosages of 2 to 10 milligrams per day and that dosages in excess of 20 milligrams should be prescribed only with precautionary measures."[118] This testimony was based upon the manufacturer's recommendations and the *Physicians' Desk Reference* (PDR).

A psychiatrist in private practice testified in the same case "that if more than 20 milligrams per day were prescribed the vital signs of a patient (blood pressure, pulse, etc.) should be frequently checked." The patient's vital signs were not checked. This psychiatrist also testified "that a patient receiving such large dosages of Prolixin should be examined daily to determine if side effects are developing and should be closely observed."[119]

The court acknowledged a serious dispute as to whether the dosages of Prolixin prescribed were in fact excessive. The Veterans' Administration doctors testified that such dosages were not excessive. Certain treatises read into the record indicated that the dosages were appropriate. "The limitations on Prolixin dosages set out by manufacturers and in the PDR appear to the Court to be merely cautionary for physicians and not to present any absolute limits for the amounts of such medication which may be safely prescribed."[120]

The court concluded that the administration of drugs "was reasonable, skillful and prudent, for the treatment of schizophrenia" and even "[t]hough there may be dispute as to how each physician might have treated . . . [the patient] for this disorder, the treatment given was within the standards allowable and not negligent."[121]

Allergic Reactions

Where a patient has an allergic reaction to a drug, only a physician who knew or should have known that such a reaction was likely to occur is ordinarily held liable. If the physician could have obtained knowledge of a previous reaction to such a drug by reading the patient's medical records or by asking the patient or family members, the physician may be liable.

Hospital administrators may also be liable if the improper prescription is due to negligent record keeping.[122] Administrators of mental health programs, however, are not liable for improper treatment involving administration of medication where they are not involved in the day-to-day administration of drugs and did not approve an unlawful medication policy that caused the harm. In Rhode Island, a juvenile who was moderately retarded and suffered from childhood schizophrenia received doses of Phenothiazine despite indications that he suffered an allergic reaction to that family of drugs. He was given the drugs several times because of poor record keeping. Yet the court held that the hospital staff involved in the plaintiff's treatment, and not the director, were the proper defendants. The court denied monetary damages and injunctive relief against the director because there was no showing that he was involved in the day-to-day care of the patient or the administration of drugs, or that he had approved an unlawful policy that had caused the harm.[123]

Mixed Medications Resulting in Adverse Effect

Physicians may also be held liable where they fail to inquire about other medications the patient is taking, and such medication, mixed with the prescribed medication, has an adverse effect on the patient.

A hypertensive patient was admitted to a Maryland hospital. Her family physician prescribed three ten-milligram doses of Librium daily for her nervousness and anxiety. Three days later she was found walking the hospital corridor with a sheet over her and waving a knife. She was subdued and the family physician ordered administration of five milligrams of Valium. Approximately three hours later a nurse called the family physician's answering service and reached a physician covering for him. She explained the patient had been given the Valium and was still restless. The physician prescribed 50 milligrams of Seconal. Less than an hour later the patient tried to escape through a window and was severely injured in a fall of several floors.[124]

The court held that the issue of liability should be submitted to the jury. An expert witness testified that the family physician should have determined whether the Librium was responsible for the patient's agitation and confusion. He should have personally examined her before prescribing the Valium. As to the second physician, the order was inadequate in that, if the Seconal did not contribute to her agitation, it did not relieve it.[125]

Adverse Effects

When powerful drugs are administered, the patient should be warned of possible side effects. Ideally, such a warning to the patient should be written and in easily comprehensible terms in order to avoid confusion and later disagreements about whether the warning ever was given.[126] Any oral warning given should be noted in the patient's medical records. The physician then should obtain the patient's consent, preferably in writing, to taking the potent psychotropic drugs. In a Virginia case, prisoners and other untrained personnel administered excessive doses of powerful psychotropic drugs to a fellow inmate without his consent and without proper supervision; this resulted in the virtual paralysis of his limbs. The prisoner "developed massive bedsores all over his body, which left untreated and neglected, became severely infected and infested with maggots, and threatened his life." While officials of the prison and hospital denied any liability, the state agreed to a settlement of $518,000. The officials would have been in a much stronger position had they obtained written consent from the prisoner.[127]

In warning a patient in writing of possible dangerous side effects of a drug, one should consider the psychological impact of the formal notice itself. A commentator recommends:

> Tell the patient of all life-threatening or disabling side effects, no matter how uncommon, and all other side effects which are reasonably predictable, unless the prescriber is convinced that the full disclosure will cause the patient to refuse urgently needed therapy and unless the patient has mental impairment or major psychiatric disease.[128]

Knowledge that a drug has predictable side effects also imposes a duty on a physician to monitor the patient's reaction to the drug and to take appropriate action when adverse reactions occur. Often simply discontinuing the drug will clear up the adverse reaction. Other effects may require more active treatment, such as prescribing anti-Parkinsonian drugs for movement disorders caused by Phenothiazine and related tranquilizers. Certain adverse reactions, such as severe bone marrow depression or acute liver damage, may require hospitalization and intensive management. The earlier the adverse reaction is detected, the better the chances are that it will be cleared up. Periodic physical examinations and laboratory tests such as blood cell counts and liver function tests are important.

Administration of Medication

Nurses are legally responsible for correct and effective drug administration, and a nurse who delegates drug administering duties to others can be held liable. A patient can sustain serious injury if a medication is administered intramuscularly at the incorrect site. Nurses are trained to search for the appropriate "landmarks" prior to administering the medication.[129] The danger in the hip region, for example, is hitting the sciatic nerve, which could result in great pain, loss of use of the leg, or even paralysis. If the patient is squirming or fighting, the nurse must be extra cautious in administering the injection.[130] A psychiatric nurse may have to administer medication to an unwilling patient, usually by intramuscular injection. It is important for the nurse to explain as clearly as possible what is happening and, after securing the needed assistance, give the medication as swiftly as can be tolerated by the patient. After the patient's condition has stabilized, it is recommended that the nurse return and discuss the situation with him or her, including any feelings that can be recalled during the incident.[131]

A psychiatric nurse should have sharp observational skills in the administration of drugs, primarily the phenothiazine derivatives, which induce extrapyramidal side effects that can be frightening to the patient. However, if properly educated, the patient could alert the staff to the outbreak of symptoms, and a trained psychiatric nurse can verify the condition and administer the appropriate antidote for the reaction. A nurse should stay with the patient during a drug reaction to offer reassurance that the symptoms will subside and to allow the nurse a good opportunity to closely observe the patient.

In New York, a patient in a state hospital awoke at approximately 7:00 A.M. and became violent and assaultive. He was administered 200 milligrams of Thorazine within the next 30 minutes. He was then moved to a seclusion room and left unattended until found dead. The trial court record supported the conclusion that:

> Thorazine should be administered while the patient is prone; but here all injections were administered while decedent was upright; that after injection the patient should be carefully observed for a period of one to one and one-half hours; that Thorazine has numerous side effects, including shock and irregularity of heart beat and that defendant [state hospital staff] had knowledge of these side effects.[132]

The court of claims held that failure to watch the patient carefully after administration of the drug fell below the standard of care and was the proximate cause of death.

The appellate court affirmed, although a dissenting opinion stated that the lack of supervision or the side effects of Thorazine were not established as the proximate cause of death.[133]

A nurse who is in doubt about an order for medication, and who would uphold the standard of care, should call the prescribing physician.[134]

> [A] psychiatric nurse should be familiar with all the psychotropic drugs being prescribed to her patients with their common dosages and their routes of administration, and if she is not familiar or comfortable with them she should always check with the physician for clarification. The psychiatric nurse should not take on the responsibility for adjusting dosages or discontinuing medication. Such changes should be recommended to the physician, who then makes the final decision.[135]

A Utah case involved nurse liability. In that case a psychiatrist ordered a dosage of 100 milligrams of Mellaril to be administered "stat." The order was made at 8:00 p.m. The psychiatrist then recorded in the patient record that:

> Present episode is either a dissociative reaction or a paranoid schizophrenic reaction. His tension is very high; his anxiety level very high; his distortion of reality may lead to acts of poor judgment.

*　　*　　*

If aud. hallucinations don't subside promptly, may have to move to 3
North for safety. [3 North is the psychiatric ward of the hospital.][136]

The nurse did not administer the medication until 10:00 p.m., and the dosage
administered may have been only 50 milligrams. At 2:40 a.m., the patient jumped
through a window from the sixth floor and landed on the roof of the first floor
entrance. As a result of his fall he is now quadriplegic.

The testimony of a registered nurse "showed that the physician's order for
medication to be administered stat means immediately, and that to administer
medication at 10:00 p.m. when a stat order is given at 8:00 p.m. is not compliance
with the physician's order."[137] The lower court had found for the defendant
hospital and physician on the theory that an intentional suicide attempt relieved
them of any liability. The decision was reversed and remanded for a new trial.[138]

A psychiatrist in Connecticut ordered antipsychotic medication for a psychiatric patient diagnosed as suffering from schizophrenia. "The nursing staff failed
to record the order until the following day, at which time the staff discovered
that the medication was out of stock." The psychiatrist was not notified, and
the nursing staff did not seek a substitute antipsychotic medication. As a result
the patient received no antipsychotic medication for three days, and her agitation
consequently increased. While liability was based on other acts of negligence,
this conduct clearly falls below the required standard of care and treatment.[139]

Cases alleging acts of malpractice or negligence in the use of hypodermic
needles by nurses are quite common.[140] In Illinois[141] and Nevada[142] courts have
held that expert witnesses must establish the standard of care. Liability has been
found for use of unsterilized instruments, for not scrubbing the skin with an
alcohol sponge,[143] for selecting the wrong size needle,[144] for injuring nerves,[145]
and for injecting the wrong solution.[146] In a Georgia case, a patient developed
a "staph" infection from a hypodermic needle. There was no evidence that the
nurse who administered the injection had deviated from the accepted standard
by using a prepackaged needle and syringe. The nurse did not touch the needle
with her hands. The nurse was not found liable.[147]

Where a patient is given oral medicine, the nurse or other person administering
the medication should take steps to ensure that the medicine is ingested. Patients
often "tongue" the medication and either throw it away or save it up to be taken
in a larger quantity.

Unforeseen or undesirable reactions from medication or from injections can
result in a number of cases where no physician or nurse has acted in a manner
that falls below the standard, the causes being beyond the control of the physician
and nurse.[148]

Electroconvulsive Therapy

Electroconvulsive therapy (ECT) is treatment consisting of passing a small,
carefully controlled electric current between electrodes applied to the head of

the patient. There are two treatment methods, bilateral and unilateral. Bilateral treatment consists of applying one electrode to each side of the head. With unilateral treatment both electrodes are applied to the same side of the head, usually the right. The patient is given an injection to reduce secretion in the mouth, general anesthesia, and a muscle relaxant.[149]

During treatment, the patient has "generalized muscular contractions of a convulsive nature"[150] that last approximately 60 seconds. Minutes later, "the patient slowly awakens and may experience temporary confusion similar to that seen in patients emerging from any type of brief anesthesia." A standard course of treatment is six to ten sessions involving three treatments per week.[151]

Memory loss is a major side effect, particularly with bilateral treatment. Some memory loss may be permanent. In young patients ECT may damage undeveloped nervous systems.

Since the late 1960s, the trend has been toward replacing ECT with medication, primarily the MAO inhibitors and tricyclic antidepressants for depression and neuroleptics for schizophrenia. A 1978 study by the American Psychiatric Association (APA) states that "there is evidence . . . which strongly suggests that some severe depressions which fail to respond to drugs will specifically respond to ECT, although a specific ECT response to schizophrenia is not clear."[152] The APA report recommends the type of mental illnesses for which ECT is indicated and those illnesses where it is "probably effective."[153] It also cautions that where the patient has "serious physical conditions such as space-occupying intracranial lesions and recent myocardial infarction, as well as advanced pregnancy, the administration of ECT should be in the hands of a team of physicians who collectively have had considerable experience both with the use of ECT and with these conditions."[154]

A recent report concludes that ECT is appropriate to treat:

1. severe depression, severe endogenous depression, delusional depression, or involutional depression;
2. manic-depressive syndromes;
3. catatonia; and
4. schizophrenia.[155]

The APA report contains a survey in which 25 percent of the psychiatrists surveyed were of the opinion that ECT was appropriate for treatment of schizophrenia while 59 percent believed that it was not appropriate.[156] The report also contains information that should be included in the patient's medical chart, the elements of informed consent, pretreatment evaluation, treatment considerations, and posttreatment considerations.[157]

Liability of physicians in the administration of ECT has revolved around lack of consent or informed consent; improper administration of the treatment, such as the use or failure to use muscle relaxants; and lack of supervision of the patient subsequent to treatment.[158] No cases could be found where the administration of ECT was held to fall below the standard because it was counterindicated for a particular diagnosis.

At the outset, the physician must advise the patient of the risks involved in the administration of ECT.[159] If a patient is not informed of the possible risks and is thereafter injured, the physician may be liable even though he or she used the requisite standard of care when administering ECT.[160] In a Missouri case, the court concluded that the psychiatrist followed the appropriate measures, procedures, restraints, and treatment standards, but failed to warn the patient of the possibility of vertebrae fractures; hence, he was held liable for those injuries.[161]

Once a patient has consented to ECT, it must be administered according to professional standards.[162] The psychiatrist must prepare the patient for treatment. In so doing, a psychiatrist is generally required to administer a muscle relaxant prior to treatment. In a Louisiana case, the court concluded that there was not an established community practice of administering muscle relaxants prior to ECT. The doctors who administered a relaxant to decrease the risk of fractures recognized that the drug increased respiratory failure and cardiac arrest. Because of these problems, the court decided that a physician who failed to administer a muscle relaxant prior to ECT was not negligent. By way of contrast, a Florida court found that a psychiatrist was negligent when he did not use a muscle relaxant before administering ECT.[163] The APA recommends the administration of a muscle relaxant.[164]

After a treatment session, the psychiatrist must respond to any of the patient's complaints that suggest that injury was incurred during therapy.[165] In North Carolina, the patient complained of severe lower back pains after he received his first treatment. The court found that the doctor was negligent because he continued further ECT treatment without taking x-rays of the lower back.[166] Under similar circumstances, a New York court held that a hospital must maintain x-ray equipment to examine patients.[167] In Louisiana, the patient complained of pain to the nurses, but not to the psychiatrist. The court said that a psychiatrist has an affirmative duty to ask patients if they feel pain after ECT.[168]

After administration of ECT, the physician may be liable if the patient who was improperly restrained in bed falls and is injured. A physician in Pennsylvania allowed a patient to walk around shortly after his treatment. The patient fell down a flight of stairs. The physician was found negligent because he did not confine the patient to bed.[169] In a Texas case, the doctor properly tied the patient into bed, but the patient still fell out of bed. The court held that the doctor was not negligent in failing to put rails on the bed.[170]

A hospital is not liable for the malpractice or negligence of the physician unless he or she is an employee or agent of the hospital. An exception to this rule is where the administration or medical staff knew or should have known that the physician was incompetent. In Illinois, a court held that a hospital was not liable for the failure of a physician to examine the patient physically and to administer a muscle relaxant as required by hospital policy because the hospital had no reason to believe the physician would violate the policy.[171]

The use of ECT is under attack within the profession and by patients. During the 1970s, opposition to ECT increased. Many psychiatrists do not consider it a viable treatment option. States began regulating ECT by giving patients the right to refuse treatment or by requiring informed consent prior to administration. Alaska, Arkansas, Iowa, Kentucky, Massachusetts, Missouri, and South Carolina provide for patient refusal of ECT.[172] California, Connecticut, Delaware, Illinois, Louisiana, Michigan, North Carolina, North Dakota, New Jersey, New York, Oregon, South Dakota, and Wisconsin require that a patient give informed consent prior to ECT.[173] Washington gives patients the right not to consent to ECT.[174] Many states give patients the right to refuse treatment in general.[175]

In 1975, a federal court in Alabama severely restricted its use in Alabama hospitals by requiring that it be administered to a consenting adult only after at least four psychiatrists and one neurologist, with at least two attorneys monitoring the process, deem it advisable.[176] This, however, must be viewed in the context of the inadequate conditions existing in the Alabama state system.

In 1976, the portion of the California law regulating ECT was held unconstitutional in *Aden v. Younger*.[177] California provided that informed consent was required prior to the use of ECT and that patients had the right to refuse such treatment. Physicians were required to explain the risks and benefits of ECT, while discussing the nature and seriousness of the patient's mental disorder with the patient and a responsible relative, guardian, or conservator. The patient then was required to sign a consent form. The physician was required to document in the patient's record that the requirements had been met and indicate the reasons for the therapy.[178] A medical committee then reviewed the physician's decision that the patient was competent to give informed consent and the prescribed treatment. The committee had to unanimously approve the physician's decision. The committee could override the patient's decision to refuse ECT if it found the individual incapable of giving informed consent. It could also override the consent of a patient whether or not the patient was capable of giving consent.[179]

The court held some of these provisions unconstitutional. The court ruled that the provision requiring a relative, guardian, or conservator to be informed of the treatment was a violation of the patient's right to privacy. The provision that the treatment must be "critically needed for the welfare of the patient" was unconstitutionally vague. Certain informed consent requirements for competent, voluntary patients were held unconstitutional. The law also violated due process, according to the court, because it failed to require an adequate hearing for patients on the issues of competency and voluntariness.[180]

By referendum the city of Berkeley, California has made administration of ECT a criminal offense punishable by a fine of up to $500 and six months in jail.[181] This is a dangerous precedent because the ordinance mandates that no patient may choose such treatment, and, while serious questions have been raised about side effects, the data are not conclusive.[182]

The controversy surrounding the use of ECT does not involve only psychiatrists disagreeing with lawyers on the issues. Many psychiatrists do not consider ECT a viable treatment option. Some lawyers argue for less regulation. A number of arguments have been advanced by both sides.

Some argue that ECT is experimental, involving high risks and uncertain benefits. The counter argument is that ECT has certain benefits and does not present high risks when used properly. It is argued that "the regulation of ECT parallels the regulatory history of other medical procedures such as abortions." The early regulation of abortion was due in part from an effort "to protect women from the hazard of artificial termination of pregnancies." As modern medical techniques developed making such procedures relatively safe, the need for regulation has largely disappeared. Those who disagree maintain that ECT is unsafe, irreversible, and that women who obtain abortions are able to give fully informed consent.[183]

The JCAH considers the administration of ECT a special treatment procedure. A hospital must have written policies governing the use of ECT and the written informed consent of the patient. It may not be administered to children or adolescents "unless prior to the initiation of treatment, two qualified psychiatrists who have training or experience in the treatment of children and adolescents and who are not affiliated with the treatment program have examined the patient, have consulted with the responsible psychiatrist, and have written and signed reports in the patient's record that concur with the decision to administer such therapy."[184]

Some therapists state that ECT results in serious side effects such as permanent memory loss, brain damage, bone fractures, and possible damage to the not fully developed nervous systems of young patients. The opposing argument is that memory loss is generally temporary, although there have been some cases of permanent loss of memory. It is difficult to establish the extent of such loss since it may have occurred prior to the administration of ECT. While further research is needed, a recent study "indicates that there is no evidence to support the allegations that brain damage follows administration of ECT." The same study maintains that fractures do not occur if ECT is properly administered.[185]

Another argument in favor of regulation is the intrusiveness of ECT; that is, the physical and psychological invasion of the individual. Others respond that ECT does interfere with a patient's thought or behavior process, causing temporary confusion and memory loss (temporary and permanent) in some patients, "but when ECT is given to a properly selected patient, the illness is even more intrusive than the treatment." In addition, alternative treatments are equally intrusive.[186]

ECT is mind altering and therefore interferes with the First Amendment rights of expression and privacy, according to some parties. The counter argument is that "any infringement of [f]irst [a]mendment rights . . . [is] counterbalanced by the patient's recovery from a severely debilitating and freedom restricting illness." The mental illness is viewed as the intruder, not ECT.[187]

ECT is viewed as the last treatment to be administered. If any other less restrictive treatment is available, it should be administered. ECT advocates answer that ECT is often the only effective treatment for severely depressed patients.[188]

Advocates of regulation argue that ECT's "usefulness, benefits, and indications have not been clearly demonstrated." Proponents of ECT state that the usefulness, benefits, and indications have been clearly demonstrated.[189]

Finally, it is argued that ECT must be regulated because it is subject to abuse. Proponents of ECT argue that facilities for administration of ECT should be improved, informed consent should be obtained, and legal remedies are available for abuse.[190]

It is likely that after the controversy settles, states will require, at a minimum, that the patient give informed consent for ECT and have the right to refuse treatment if the patient is competent.

NOTES

1. JCAH, *Consolidated Standards Manual for Child, Adolescent and Adult Psychiatric, Alcoholism, and Drug Abuse Facilities* (Chicago: JCAH, 1981 ed.), ¶ 17.1.1 [hereinafter cited as JCAH].

2. *Id.* at ¶ 17.2.1.

3. *Id.*

4. *Id.* at ¶ 17.2.1.3.2.

5. *Id.* at ¶ 17.4.

6. *Id.* at ¶ 17.9.

7. Jonas Robitscher, *The Power of Psychiatry* (Boston: Houghton Mifflin Company, 1980), pp. 163–164 [hereinafter cited as Robitscher].

8. Addington v. Texas, 99 S. Ct. 1804 (1979).

9. Blocker v. United States, 288 F.2d 853 (D.C. Cir. 1961).

10. Robitscher, *supra* note 7, at 166–183.

11. Robert Stoller, psychiatrist, quoted by Robitscher, *supra* note 7, at 181–182.

12. Victor Adebimpe, psychiatrist, quoted by Robitscher, *Id.* at 181.

13. Keeran, Jr., Posnan, and Richardson, "Medical Behavioral Explosion Affects Hospital Operation, Policy," *Hospitals* (May 1981):56, 57; *see* JoAnn Ellison Rogers, "Brain Triggers: Biochemistry and Behavior," *Science Digest* 91 (Jan. 1983):60, for a discussion of body chemicals and their effect on behavior.

14. Chapter 7.

15. Chapter 10.

16. Seymour v. Lofgren, 209 Kan. 72, 495 P.2d 969, 971 (1972).

17. Ronald Jay Cohen, *Malpractice* (New York: The Free Press, 1979), p. 167.

18. *See* Abandonment, Chapter 4.

19. *See* Appendix E, "Treatment Rights"; *see also* Deborah Hardwick, "Legal Rights of the Mentally Retarded: Pennhurst State School & Hospital v. Haldeman," *Sw. L.J.* 35 (1981):959–968 [hereinafter cited as Hardwick].

20. D.C. Code § 21–562 (1981); *See* Rouse v. Cameron, 373 F.2d 451, 455 n. 21 (D.C. Cir. 1966).

21. Ill. Rev. Stat., ch. 91½ ¶ 2–102(a) (Smith-Hurd Supp. 1982–1983).

22. Rouse v. Cameron, 373 F.2d 451 (D.C. Cir. 1966).

23. *Id.* at 453.

24. Wyatt v. Stickney, 344 F. Supp. 373 (M.D. Ala. 1972), *enforcing* 344 F. Supp. 387 (M.D. Ala. 1971), *enforcing* 325 F. Supp. 781 (M.D. Ala. 1971), *aff'd. in relevant part*, Wyatt v. Aderholt, 503 F.2d 1305 (5th Cir. 1974).

25. For a description of the shocking conditions at the Alabama institutions *see* Wyatt v. Aderholt, *id.* at 1310–1312.

26. Wyatt v. Stickney, *supra* note 24, at 325 F. Supp. 781.

27. *Id.*

28. *Id.*

29. Wyatt v. Stickney, *supra* note 24, at 344 F. Supp. 373, 379–386.

30. O'Connor v. Donaldson, 422 U.S. 563 (1975).

31. Richard Rapson, "The Right of the Mentally Ill To Receive Treatment in the Community," *Colum. L.J.* 16 (1980):193, 220 [hereinafter cited as Rapson].

32. Trap v. Dulles, 356 U.S. 86, 101 (1958); Cross v. Harris, 418 F.2d 1095, 1101 (D.C. Cir. 1969).

33. Robinson v. California, 370 U.S. 660 (1962).

34. Flakes v. Percy, 511 F. Supp. 1325 (W.D. Wisc. 1981).

35. Rapson, *supra* note 31.

36. New York State Association for Retarded Children v. Rockefeller, 357 F. Supp. 752 (E.D. N.Y. 1973).

37. *Id.* at 764.

38. *Id.*

39. *Id.* at 764, 765.

40. *See* Hardwick, *supra* note 19, at 963 n. 35.

41. Youngberg v. Romeo, 102 S. Ct. 2452 (1982).

42. *Id.* at 4685.

43. Arnold J. Rosoff, *Informed Consent* (Rockville, Md.: Aspen Systems Corporation, 1981), pp. 3–4 [hereinafter cited as Rosoff]. This book contains a state-by-state analysis of the law of informed consent.

44. *Pitt. L.R.* 36, § 108 (1974):117–118. Natanson v. Kline, 186 Kan. 393, 350 P.2d 1093 (1960).

45. Shea v. Board of Medical Examiners, 81 Cal. App. 3d 564, 146 Cal. Rptr. 653 (1978).

46. Woods v. Brumlop, 71 N.M. 221, 377 P.2d 520 (1962).

47. Pickle v. Curns, 106 Ill. App. 3d 734, 435 N.E.2d 877, 880–881 (1982).

48. *Id.*

49. Rosoff, *supra* note 43, at 65.

50. *See* Chapter 1.

51. William S. Appleton, "Psychotherapist Prescribes a Drug in His Office: Medical-Legal Risks," *Medical Trial Technique Quarterly* 16 (1970):207.

52. Woods v. Brumlop, *supra* note 46.

53. Wilson v. Lehman, 379 S.W.2d 478 (Ky. 1964).

54. Lester v. Aetna Casualty & Surety Company, 240 F.2d 676 (5th Cir. 1957); Farber v. Olkon, 40 Cal. 2d 503 (1953), 254 P.2d 520 (5th Cir. 1957).

55. Richard Beresford, "Professional Liability of Psychiatrist," *Defense L.J.* 21 (1972):123, 141 [hereinafter cited as Beresford].

56. Nason v. Superintendent of Bridgewater State Hospital, 353 Mass. 604 n. 7, 233 N.E.2d 908, 912 n. 7 (1968).

57. Whitree v. State, 56 Misc. 2d 693, 707, 200 N.Y.S.2d 486, 501 (N.Y. Ct. Cl. 1968).

58. Right 4, Patient's Bill of Rights (published by the American Hospital Association in 1972) (emphasis added). *See also* section on consent, *id.*

59. *See* section on informed consent, *id.*

60. Andrews v. Ballard, 498 F. Supp. 1038, 1047 (S.D. Tex. 1980).

61. T. Szasz, ed., *The Age of Madness* (Garden City, N.Y.: Anchor Press/Doubleday, 1973):237.

62. Rogers v. Okin, 478 F. Supp. 1342, 1361 (D. Mass. 1979), *aff'd in part. rev'd in part, vacated and remanded*, 634 F.2d 650 (1st Cir. 1980).

63. In re Roe, III, 421 N.E.2d 40, 57 (Mass. 1981).

64. Rennie v. Klein, 653 F.2d 836, 843 (3rd Cir. 1981).

65. *Id.* at 846–847. *See* section on least restrictive alternative, Chapter 7.

66. Bruce Winick, "Legal Limitations on Correctional Therapy and Research," *Minn. L. Rev.* 65 (1981):331, 368. *See also*, In re K.K.B., 609 P.2d 747, 751 (Okla. 1980).

67. Comment, "Madness and Medicine: The Forcible Administration of Psychotrophic Drugs," *Wis. L. Rev.* (1980):497, 564.

68. Traditionally, "infants, idiots, and lunatics." *Black's Law Dictionary*, rev. 5th ed. 1979, p. 1003.

69. In re K.K.B., *supra* note 66, at 747, 750.

70. American Psychiatric Association, Task Force on the Right to Treatment, the Right to Adequate Care and Treatment for the Mentally Ill and Mentally Retarded (Final Draft, May 8, 1975), p. 5.

71. Bassuk and Gerson, "Deinstitutionalization and Mental Health Services," *Scientific Am.* (Feb. 1978):46.

72. J. Swazey, *Chlorpromazine in Psychiatry* (1974), pp. xi–xii.

73. Davis v. Hubbard, 506 F. Supp. 915, 938 (N.D. Ohio 1980).

74. Rogers v. Okin, *supra* note 62, at 634 F.2d 650 (1st Cir. 1980).

75. Mills v. Rogers, 102 S.Ct., 2442 (1982).

76. In re Roe, III, *supra* note 63.

77. *Id.* at 51.

78. Rennie v. Klein, *supra* note 64, at 836.

79. *Id.* at 844–848.

80. In re K.K.B., *supra* note 69.

81. *Id.* at 749.

82. *See* In re Boyd, 403 A.2d 744 (D.C. 1979).

83. A.E. & R.R. v. Mitchell, No. C–78–466 (D. Utah, June 16, 1980).

84. A.D. Brooks, "The Constitutional Right to Refuse Antipsychotic Medications," *Bull. Am. Acad. Psychiatry & L.* 8 (1980):179.

85. Mental Health Systems Act of 1980, § 501(1)(D).

86. *See* Appendix F, "Consent and Communications Rights."

87. Mental Health Systems Act of 1980, *supra* note 85.

88. *Id.* at (1)(E).

89. *See* Appendix F, *supra* note 86.

90. JCAH, *supra* note 1, § 14.2.3.

91. *Id.* at § 14.4c, e, f, o, p.

92. Pub. L. No. 96–398, 94 Stat. 1564 (1980).

93. Mental Health Systems Act of 1980, *supra* note 85, at § 501(1)(A).

94. *Id.* at (1)(B).

95. *Id.* at (1)(C).

96. *Id.* at (1)(E).

97. *Id.* at (1)(G).

98. *See* Appendix E, *supra* note 19.

99. *Id.*

100. *Id.*

101. *Id.*

102. *Id.*

103. *Id.*

104. *Id.*

105. The liability of pharmacists is beyond the scope of this book. For a discussion of criminal and civil liability, *see* David G. Warran, *Problems in Hospital Law* (3d ed.) (Germantown, Md.: Aspen Systems Corporation, 1978); JCAH, *supra* note 1, at ¶ 29; and American Society of Hospital Pharmacists, "Minimum Standards for Pharmacies in Hospitals with Guide to Application."

106. Physicians, nurses, and pharmacists are subject to criminal penalties for violations of the Controlled Substances Act and state statute regulating the area. Conversion of drugs to personal use is a ground for revocation or suspension of a license.

107. JCAH, *supra* note 1, at ¶ 29.8.

108. Harris v. State, 371 So.2d 1221 (La. 1979); Lauro v. Travelers Ins. Co., 261 So.2d 261 (La. Ct. App. 1972); Helms v. Saint Paul Fire & Marine Ins. Co., 289 So.2d 288 (La. Ct. App. 1974).

109. Watkins v. United States, 589 F.2d 214 (5th Cir. 1979).

110. Hirschberg v. State, 91 Misc. 2d 590, 398 N.Y.S.2d 470 (1977).

111. *Id.*

112. Appleton, *supra* note 51.

113. Clites v. Iowa, No. 46274 (Dist. Ct. Pottawattamie Cty., Iowa, Aug. 7, 1980), 5 *Mental Disability L. Rep.* (ABA) (1980):110.

114. Mulder v. Parke, Davis & Co., 288 Minn. 332, 181 N.W.2d 882 (1970).

115. W.S. Appleton, "Legal Problems in Psychiatric Drug Prescription," *American Journal of Psychiatry* (1968) [hereinafter cited as Appleton].

116. Meier v. Ross General Hospital, 71 Cal. Rptr. 903, 445 P.2d 519 (1968).

117. Beresford, *supra* note 55, at 123.

118. Moon v. United States, 512 F. Supp. 140, 146 (D. Nev. 1981).

119. *Id.*

120. *Id.* at 146, 147.

121. *Id.* at 147.

122. For a discussion of a hospital's duty to maintain medical records *see* Chapter 4.

123. Naughton v. Bevilacqua, 605 F.2d 586 (1st Cir. 1979).

124. Fleming v. Prince George's County, 227 Md. 655, 358 A.2d 892 (1976).

125. *Id.*

126. Beresford, *supra* note 55, at 141.

127. Tucker v. Hutlo, No. 78–0161-R, filed Sept. 8, 1978, E.D. Va., 3 *Mental Disability L. Rept.* 189 (1979).

128. Beresford, *supra* note 55, at 141.

129. Pamela D. Andrade and John C. Andrade, "Malpractice of Psychiatric Nurse," P.O.F.2d 26 (1981):363, 385 [hereinafter cited as Andrade & Andrade].

130. Honeywell v. Rogers, 251 F. Supp. 841 (W.D. Pa. 1966).

131. *Id.* at 387.

132. Brown v. State, 56 A.D.2d 672, 391 N.Y.S.2d 204, 205 (1977).

133. *Id.*

134. Searcy v. Porter, 381 So. 2d 540 (1980).

135. Andrade & Andrade, *supra* note 129, at 381.

136. Farrow v. Health Services Corporation, 604 P.2d 474 (Sup. Ct. Utah 1979).

137. *Id.* at 478.

138. *Id.*

139. Pisel v. Stamford Hospital, 180 Conn. 314, 430 A.2d 1 (1980).

140. *See* William O. Morris, "The Negligent Nurse—The Physician and The Hospital," *Baylor L. Rev.* 33 (1981):109, 118 [hereinafter cited as Morris].

141. Graham v. St. Luke's Hospital, 46 Ill. App. 2d 147, 196 N.E.2d 355 (1964).

142. Bailer v. Saint Mary's Hospital, 83 Nev. 241, 427 P.2d 957 (1967).

143. Kalmus v. Cedars of Lebanon Hospital, 132 Cal. 2d 243, 182 P.2d 872 (1955).

144. Su v. Perkins, 133 Ga. App. 474, 211 S.E.2d 421 (1974).

145. Morris, *supra* note 140, at ¶ 19.

146. *Id.*

147. Cohran v. Harper, 115 Ga. App. 277, 154 S.E.2d 461 (1967).

148. Bailer v. Saint Mary's Hospital, *supra* note 142.

149. American Psychiatric Association, *Electroconvulsive Therapy* 174, Task Force Report, Sept. 1978 [hereinafter cited as APA].

150. *Id.* at 175.

151. *Id.* at 168, 175.

152. *Id.* at 13, 14.

153. *Id.* at 162.

154. *Id.*

155. A.W. Scovern, et al., "Status of Electroconvulsive Therapy: Review of the Outcome Literature," *Psychological Bulletin* 87, no. 2:26–303.

156. APA, *supra* note 149, at 4.

157. *Id.* at 163–170.

158. Beresford, *supra* note 55, at 126; Thomas Shea, "Legal Standards of Care for Psychiatrist and Psychologist," *Western State U.L. Rev.* 6 (1962):71, 82.

159. Woods v. Brumlop, 71 N.M. 221, 377 P.2d 520 (1922); McDonald v. Moore, 323 So. 2d 635 (Fla. Dist. Ct. App. 1975).

160. Mitchell v. Robinson, 334 S.W.2d 11 (Mo. 1960).

161. *Id.*

162. *See* APA, *supra* note 149, at 164.

163. McDonald v. Moore, *supra* note 159. Contra:Pettis v. State Department of Hospitals, 336 So. 2d 521 (La. Ct. App. 1976).

164. APA, *supra* note 149, at 164.

165. McDonald v. Moore, *supra* note 159; Pettis v. State Department of Hospitals, *supra* note 163; Eisele v. Malone, 157 N.Y.S.2d 155 (N.Y. App. Div. 1956), *reh. denied*, 158 N.Y.S.2d 761 (1957).

166. *Id.*; Stone v. Proctor, 259 N.C. 633, 131 S.E.2d 297 (1963).

167. Eisele v. Malone, *supra* note 165.

168. Pettis v. State Department of Hospitals, *supra* note 163.

169. Brown v. Moore, 247 F.2d 711 (3rd Cir. 1957).

170. *But see* Constant v. Howe, 436 S.W.2d 115 (Tex. 1968).

171. Pickle v. Curns, 106 Ill. App. 3d 734, 435 N.E.2d 877 (1982).

172. Judie Tenenbaum, "ECT Regulation Reconsidered," 7 *Mental Disability Law Reptr.* 148, 151 (1983).

173. *Id.*

174. *Id.*

175. *See* Appendix F, Consent and Communication Rights.

176. Wyatt v. Hardin, No. 3195–N (M.D. Ala. Feb. 28, 1975, *modified*, July 1, 1975), *reported*, 1 *Mental Disability Law Rept.* (1976):55.

177. 57 Cal. App. 3d 622 (1976), *modified*, 58 Cal. App. 3d 990(a) and 59 Cal. App. 3d 174(a).

178. *Id.* at 57 Cal. App. 3d 622.

179. *Id.*

180. *Id.*

181. *Mental Disability Law Reptr.* 6 (Nov.–Dec. 1982):366.

182. *Id.* at 366, 367.

183. Tenenbaum, *supra* note 172, at 153.

184. JCAH, *supra* note 1, at § 19.3.

185. Tenenbaum, *supra* note 172, at 153, 154.

186. *Id.* at 152.

187. *Id.* at 152, 153.

188. *Id.* at 154.

189. *Id.*

190. *Id.* at 154, 155.

Chapter 9

Rights of Inpatients and Their Implementation

While the rights of patients are found in state statutes,[1] they have also been mandated by judicial opinions.[2] In its standards for accreditation the JCAH specifies the rights of patients.[3] In the Mental Health Systems Act of 1980[4] (MHS Act) Congress recommended that states provide certain rights to patients, many of which have already been adopted by most states in whole or in part.

The JCAH standards require hospitals to "support and protect the fundamental human, civil, constitutional, and statutory rights of each patient."[5] "A written plan or policies and procedures that describe the rights of patients and the means by which these rights are protected and exercised is also required."[6] Further, patients must be informed of their rights in a language they understand and be given a written statement of their rights.[7]

Most states require that patients be given information about their rights and some require that a statement of rights be posted.[8] Connecticut and Minnesota prohibit by statute reprisals for the exercise of rights by patients.[9] California and West Virginia prohibit reprisals with regard to certain rights.[10]

JCAH standards require that a patient and the patient's family or legal guardian be informed of "[t]he right to initiate a complaint or grievance procedure and the appropriate means of requesting a hearing or review of the complaint."[11] Most states, however, do not grant patients the right to assert grievances, and fewer still have any grievance process.[12] Only California, Georgia, Hawaii, Maine, Minnesota, Virginia, and Wisconsin provide grievance procedures for patients.[13]

COMMUNICATION

JCAH standards require that a patient be allowed visits from family and "significant others" and to conduct telephone conversations with family and friends "unless such visits are clinically contradicted."[14] Suitable areas providing privacy should be made available unless "contradicted by the patient's treatment plan."[15] Patients are to be "allowed to send and receive mail without hindrance."[16]

If clinical restrictions are placed on the right to communicate, such "restrictions shall be evaluated for therapeutic effectiveness by the clinically responsible staff at least every seven days."[17] If the restrictions are for practical reasons, for example, the expense of travel or telephone calls, the limitations should be determined with the family's and the patient's participation. Such restrictions should be explained to the family and the patient.[18]

Most states guarantee patients the right to communicate with persons outside health-care facilities[19] as well as the right of access to a legal representative.[20] Denial of access to counsel or the courts violates due process. A patient must be accorded the opportunity to argue that his or her admission is unlawful.

States implement these rights in different ways. For example, California law requires that health facilities personnel post a list, in a prominent place and in the predominant languages of the community, delineating the rights of patients in health facilities.[21] These rights include the patients' right to see visitors each day; to have ready access to letter-writing materials and stamps, and to mail and receive unopened correspondence; to have reasonable access to telephones, and to make and receive confidential calls or to have such calls made for them; and to see and receive the services of a patient advocate.[22]

Massachusetts law distinguishes between mentally ill and mentally retarded persons. Mentally ill persons cared for by the state's mental health department have the right to use stationery and postage in reasonable amounts as well as the right to have their letters forwarded unopened to various parties, including the governor, any court, and immediate family members. The superintendent or other director of a mental health facility may open and restrict the forwarding of any other letters written by mentally ill patients if he or she believes it is in a patient's best interests to do so. The superintendent or other director may similarly restrict or deny a mentally ill patient's visiting rights.[23] Mentally retarded persons have unrestricted mailing rights, and only if they become ill or incapacitated will the superintendent or director limit their visitation rights.[24] Both mentally ill and mentally retarded persons have reasonable access to telephones to make and receive confidential calls, and both have access to their attorneys and to the courts.[25]

In Michigan, mental health facility residents are entitled to unimpeded, private, and uncensored communication with other persons by mail and telephone as well as to visits with persons of their choosing.[26] However, a facility's head or director may limit a resident's right to communicate by mail or telephone or to receive visitors if he or she determines that the limitation will prevent the resident from violating a law or will protect the resident from substantial and serious physical or mental harm.[27] A facility's head or director may also prohibit a resident from telephoning an individual who has complained to the facility of previous telephone harassment by the resident and has requested the prohibition of future calls.[28] No limitation upon those communicative rights may apply between a resident and an attorney or a court, or between a resident and other persons when the communication involves matters subject to legal inquiry.[29]

Texas law affords mentally retarded persons living in a state facility or receiving services from the Texas Department of Mental Health and Mental Retardation the right to communication and visitation.[30] It does not, however, afford the same rights to mentally ill persons.

In Wisconsin, persons receiving services for mental illness or developmental disabilities have an unrestricted right to send sealed mail to and receive sealed mail from legal counsel, the courts, governmental officials, private physicians, and licensed psychologists. They may also send sealed mail to and receive sealed mail from other persons, but such correspondence may undergo physical examination in a patient's presence if services personnel have reason to believe that it contains contraband materials or objects that threaten the security of patients, prisoners, or staff. A facility's officers and staff may not read any mail sent or received by persons in treatment.[31] Patients in Wisconsin facilities may make and receive telephone calls, within reasonable limits.[32]

In Illinois, the state legislature recognized that institutional residents' right to communicate with persons outside the institution was "subject to the wide and, in practice, virtually unreviewable discretion of employees of the facility," and changed Illinois law governing patient communication.[33] A person institutionalized in Illinois now enjoys "unimpeded, private and uncensored communication by mail, telephone, and visitation" unless the facility director restricts the communication to protect the person or others from harm, harassment, or intimidation.[34]

Several cases have pointed out the need for basic communication rights for patients. In one, a Michigan housewife, pursuant to a court order, was taken from her home to a private psychiatric hospital. There, she was allowed to see her husband and children, and a psychiatrist frequently visited her, but she was permitted no phone calls or letters in or out. In addition, she was placed in a barred, locked, and bare room for six days, which prevented her communication with the outside world.[35]

Upon her release, she brought suit against the psychiatrist and the private hospital, alleging, among other things, false imprisonment. The Michigan court determined that the actions of the psychiatrist and the hospital violated the plaintiff's inherent legal rights, in that the denial of basic communication rights prevented the plaintiff from contacting persons who could represent her rights, and thereby caused her to suffer damages.[36] The court premised liability on a denial of her right to representation.

In Wisconsin, several persons confined to a state mental hospital complained that they had been transferred from minimum to maximum security, which resulted in the loss of certain rights and liberties, including physical amenities and freedom of movement. The transfer, they said, occurred after they had mailed letters to a Madison, Wisconsin Urban League official and a Madison newspaper reporter.[37] The patients brought suit to enjoin the hospital personnel from persisting in their self-styled discipline of dissident patients. The district court granted their request on the grounds that the defendants' actions were taken to "punish the plaintiffs for writing the letters and were taken without any notice or hearing." Thus the court protected the plaintiffs' right to communicate freely with the outside world.[38]

In Alabama patients dissatisfied with conditions in the state's mental institutions filed a class action.[39] Pursuant to its order and decree adjudging conditions to be legally unacceptable, the court struggled to formulate "Minimum Constitutional Standards For Adequate Treatment of the Mentally Ill." Among other things the court laid down the requirements that:

> Patients shall have the same rights to visitation and telephone communications as patients at other public hospitals, except to the extent that the Qualified Mental Health Professional responsible for formulation of a particular patient's treatment plan writes an order imposing special restrictions. The written order must be renewed after each periodic review of the treatment plan if any restrictions are to be continued. Patients shall have an unrestricted right to visitation with attorneys and with private physicians and other health professionals.
>
> Patients shall have an unrestricted right to send sealed mail. Patients shall have an unrestricted right to receive sealed mail from their attorneys, private physicians, and other mental health professionals, from courts, and government officials. Patients shall have a right to receive sealed mail from others, except to the extent that the Qualified Mental Health Professional responsible for formulation of a particular patient's treatment plan writes an order imposing special restrictions on receipt of sealed mail. The written order must be renewed after each periodic review of the treatment plan if any restrictions are to be continued.[40]

Because mental health care personnel in most states may incur legal liability under state law for failing to protect a mentally disabled patient's right to communicate with persons outside institutions, they should become familiar with the laws and policies of their institutions. Restrictions of these rights, including the justification for such restrictions, should be carefully documented in patient records. Such documentation may provide valuable defenses should a patient allege that the staff denied him or her the right to communicate with outsiders.

PERSONAL PROPERTY AND MONEY

Most states allow the reasonable use of their money or personal property by patients. Some problems arise in determining reasonable use in specific circumstances. Most patients admitted to an inpatient program are competent. They retain most of their rights. Some advocates argue that as long as patients are competent, they have a right to use their funds or property as they see fit, and they do not have to use good judgment in so doing. While this sounds good in theory, in practice, patients, particularly those in state institutions, would exhaust their funds in a short time. Reasonable limitation on the amount of funds periodically made available seems appropriate.

A second problem is that patients' personal property is often stolen, damaged, or destroyed by other patients, particularly in state institutions. Patients' money, watches, rings, radios, false teeth, glasses, and other personal property simply disappear. In fact, the author's coat pockets have been relieved of all loose change while visiting clients. While it may be argued that the institution should prevent such theft, it is simply not practical, given staff ratios in state hospitals. Thus, restrictions upon the amount of money made available at one time and the use of property such as valuable jewelry seem reasonable.

Although few judicial decisions involve a patient's right to possess and to manage personal property and money, the statutory laws of many states grant this right. Illinois law, for example, permits patients residing in mental health or developmental disabilities facilities to receive, possess, and use personal property and requires facilities to provide patients with reasonable amounts of storage space for personal property.[41] The law also permits patients, other than minors or persons covered by a court-ordered guardianship, to use their money as they choose.[42] Because ". . . there are certain kinds of property which are inappropriate in any living facility, whether a rooming house, general hospital or mental health or developmental disabilities facility,"[43] Illinois law allows a mental health facility director to restrict a patient's possession and use of certain property when necessary to protect the patient or others from harm or when the professional responsible for overseeing the patient's treatment requests restriction. All patients must receive notice upon their admission that the facility director has the power to so restrict their property rights.[44]

In California, all persons involuntarily detained for evaluation or treatment, admitted as a voluntary patient for psychiatric evaluation or treatment, or committed to a state hospital for the mentally retarded have the right to keep and use their personal possessions, including toilet articles; to have access to individual storage space for these possessions; and to keep and spend reasonable sums of their own money for canteen expenses and small purchases.[45]

Massachusetts law contains language identical to that found in California's code, but provides that a state mental health facility superintendent may deny a patient these rights for good cause. The superintendent must enter a statement of the reasons for the denial into the patient's treatment record.[46]

Both Maine and Maryland have statutes that protect a mentally retarded person's right to use and possession of their own clothing and personal effects.[47] Maine's statutory scheme also grants retarded persons the right to use their own money.[48] Neither state has equivalent provisions for the mentally ill. Louisiana, too, restricts these provisions to mentally retarded residents of state facilities.[49]

Mentally disordered adult patients residing in North Carolina's state treatment facilities retain the right to keep and use their own clothing and personal possessions; to keep and spend reasonable sums of their own money; and to have access to individual storage space. Only mental health or mental retardation professionals responsible for formulating patient treatment or habilitation plans can restrict these rights, and the professionals must detail their reasons for restricting rights in patient treatment records. A professional who restricts a patient's rights must so notify the patient's next of kin or guardian.[50] Minor patients in treatment facilities may keep and use their own clothing and personal possessions, under appropriate supervision, and may have access to individual storage space for personal use.[51]

Michigan's laws entitle state facility residents to receive, possess, and use all personal property, including clothing, except where the person who has established a resident's services plan decides to limit the entitlement. The person must deem limitation necessary to prevent the property's theft, loss, or destruction; to prevent a resident from causing physical harm; to achieve a compelling treatment objective; or to assure a facility's effective functioning.[52]

Unlike most states, Michigan has an extensive law pertaining to mentally ill or retarded persons' right to possess and to use their own money, which the law defines ". . . as including any legal tender, note, draft, certificate of deposit, stock, bond, check, or credit card."[53] A Michigan mental health or mental retardation facility may require that all money ". . . which is on [the] person of a resident, which comes to a resident, or which the facility receives in place of the resident under a benefit arrangement or otherwise be turned over to the facility for safekeeping."[54] The facility shall then account for the money in the resident's name and shall note the balance periodically in the resident's records. A facility may, upon request, turn over any money accounted for in a resident's name to the resident's authorized legal guardian.[55]

Although Michigan's law allows state facility residents easy access to the money in their accounts to spend or to use otherwise, as they choose, a facility may deny a resident this access if its designated representative determines that denial will prevent the resident from unreasonably and significantly depleting his or her assets. Each facility must designate its representative in writing and must also promulgate in writing the policies, procedures, and evidence governing denial determinations. Denial does not limit a resident's ability to spend or otherwise use personal funds in ways that would not constitute significant and unreasonable asset dissipation.[56]

The judicial decisions that discuss a mentally ill or mentally retarded person's right to personal possessions and money generally focus on the constitutionality of state statutes that allow a treatment facility to use a person's assets to defray treatment costs. A leading decision arose from a case involving a 70-year-old woman confined to a Pennsylvania state hospital for almost two years. Social Security benefits and personal property worth approximately $500 constituted the woman's means of support. The commonwealth conceded that the woman was at all times during her confinement competent to manage her financial affairs; yet, by virtue of a Pennsylvania statute, the commonwealth's revenue agent applied half of the woman's money to a petty cash reserve fund. He then used the other half and any funds in excess of $500 to pay for the woman's assessed treatment costs. No adjudication of the woman's liability nor any attachment proceeding preceded the agent's actions.[57]

The woman brought a civil rights action. She contended that the Pennsylvania statute deprived her of procedural due process of law because it permitted the revenue agent to appropriate her funds without deciding whether she could manage them herself. The court supported the woman's contention and rejected any presumption that mental patients ". . . are less capable of handling their assets than the public at large."[58] It then held that the revenue agent's practice of taking custody and control of all the plaintiff's money deprived the woman of her constitutional right to use her property.[59]

Other courts have reached similar conclusions.[60] One court refused to hold a state's health department director liable for denying a mental health hospital patient his right to an interest in a patient deposit fund because the patient did not allege that the director personally participated in taking the patient's property.[61] The court did find, however, that the patient could maintain a suit under the Civil Rights Act.[62] The patient never received personal notice that the state sought an order requiring the patient to pay such expenses of his hospitalization and maintenance as he could afford. Rather, notice was delivered to the hospital as the patient's "custodian"; this denied the patient his constitutionally guaranteed right to due process of law.[63]

Reacting to these decisions, many state legislatures have enacted provisions prohibiting mental health personnel from applying funds to the costs of care absent the patients' consent. In Massachusetts, a mental health facility superintendent may not use dependent funds deposited with him or her to pay the costs of a patient's care.[64] Illinois law states that unless a patient has given informed consent, neither mental health facilities nor their employees may be made representative payees for patients' Social Security, pensions, annuities, trust funds, or any other forms of direct payment or assistance.[65] The Illinois General Assembly passed this law ". . . to ensure that the 'representative payee' system is not abused, and that monies intended for the benefit of a person actually accrue to the recipient. Charges levied by a service provider against these monies must be handled like any other debts; assets may not simply be confiscated."[66] As a general rule, a mental health facility director or other employee should not apply a patient's personal funds to cover treatment costs unless the patient, or a person responsible for the patient's financial affairs, so consents.

LABOR

In the past, many mentally disabled persons residing in public or private institutions performed, for little or no compensation, institution-maintaining tasks.[67] This institutional labor, which often entailed dishwashing, cooking, gardening, or clerical work, came under attack in the early 1970s and elicited strong sentiments from both advocates and assailants. Advocates of institutional labor believe that it provides valuable therapy to residents physically able to work.[68] They assert that, even though the residents' labor benefits institutions, the therapeutic value of productive work outweighs the importance of compensating patient-workers. They also contend that compensating patient-workers would present severe fiscal problems for the institutions and would ultimately result in the discontinuance of most work programs. Noncompensated work proponents voice another concern as well:

> The abolition of patients' jobs does not sit so well with many patients . . . whose work gave them purpose and satisfaction. . . . Many states report that patients are bored and disgruntled without their own jobs. The effect, they say, is the same as being fired from a job in the outside world.[69]

Critics of noncompensated work programs do not deny the programs' therapeutic value; rather, they aver that compensated programs have even greater therapeutic value.[70] They argue that noncompensated work often leads to patient exploitation because institutions tend to rely on the work performed by the more proficient patients and, not surprisingly, become reluctant to release productive residents who no longer require institutional services.[71]

A suit brought by a former patient-worker in 1973 highlighted the arguments posed by noncompensated patient work opponents.[72] Released from an Ohio state hospital after nearly 33 years, the patient sought a judicial determination that minimum wage and overtime compensation provisions delineated in the 1966 amendments to the Fair Labor Standards Act (FLSA)[73] applied to patient-workers residing in nonfederal hospitals, homes, and institutions for the mentally ill and the mentally retarded. He also sought to recover unpaid wages that he felt the state owed him. During the time he lived at the hospital, the patient-worker spent up to 12½ hours a day preparing food, washing dishes, and cleaning in the hospital's kitchen. For this work, he received $2 a day and two free days each month.

In deciding that the 1966 amendments to the FLSA applied to patient-workers in nonfederal hospitals, homes, and institutions, the court used an "economic reality" test:

[T]he reality is that many of the patient-workers perform work for which they are in no way handicapped and from which the institution derives full economic benefit. So long as the institution derives any consequential economic benefit the economic reality test would indicate an employment relationship rather than mere therapeutic exercise.[74]

Because the patient-worker had not asked the court to award him unpaid wages, he then had to bring suit against Ohio in state court. The state court disallowed an award, deciding that ". . . under the Eleventh Amendment . . . a state may not be sued for damages by an individual under federal law, without its consent, and that this principle applies equally to state as well as federal courts."[75]

Although the Ohio patient-worker did not succeed in recovering "back pay," he did compel the U.S. Secretary of Labor to implement a regulatory program that makes the FLSA applicable to hospitals, homes, and institutions.[76] This program guarantees that a patient-worker possessing an unimpaired earning or productive capacity shall receive at least the statutory minimum wage.[77] A patient-worker who has an impaired earning or productive capacity may receive a subminimum wage if the Labor Department's Wage and Hour Division issues a certificate authorizing the wage.[78] The regulations also provide that an institution may not deduct from a patient-worker's earnings the cost of room, board, or services, but it may assess and collect the reasonable cost of room, board, and other services actually provided to a patient-worker, to the extent permitted by federal or state law, after it has paid the patient-worker.[79]

Nearly one-half of the states statutorily provide for patient-worker compensation.[80] JCAH standards provide that a patient may be allowed to work for the hospital if the work is "part of the individual treatment plan," "performed voluntarily," "the patient receives wages commensurate with the economic value of the work," and "the work complies with local, state, and federal laws and regulations."[81]

While Georgia's statutory provision applies only to outside work performed by patient-workers,[82] the state statutes generally reflect the federal regulations and stress that patients must voluntarily agree to perform the labor for which they receive compensation. The federal and state regulations concur in disallowing compensation for performing personal housekeeping chores.[83]

These regulations have upset proponents of noncompensated work programs. Many believe that the regulations have caused institutions to phase out patient work, ". . . leaving former patient workers idle and pathetic victims of bureaucracy. . . ."[84] Naturally, opponents of noncompensated work programs favor the regulations. Their views have influenced legislators to adopt proposals favoring compensation for patient-workers.

In its 1976 report, the Governor's Commission for Revision of the Mental Health Code of Illinois noted that, "The use of free or extraordinarily cheap patient 'therapeutic' labor is extremely susceptible to abuse" and, "Compensation may promote therapeutic goals by giving a sense of dignity and purpose to the work, by substituting a mutual relation in which the patient may choose whether or not to perform such labor."[85] The Illinois General Assembly heeded the commission's recommendations, and enacted a law that allows a recipient of mental health care services to perform labor to which he or she consents for a services provider. The professional responsible for the recipient's care must approve the work plan, and a recipient whose work consequentially benefits the services provider shall receive wages "commensurate with the value of the work performed."[86]

Similarly, Wisconsin permits a patient-worker to receive payment for work that benefits his or her institution. A Wisconsin patient may refuse to perform the beneficial work, and an institution cannot condition a patient's release on nonrefusal. Wisconsin also allows a patient to work voluntarily for no compensation, but only if the institution first attempts to compensate the patient-worker; if the uncompensated work does not result in staff layoffs; and if the institution does not require the patient to perform the work. An institution in Wisconsin may not apply a patient-worker's payment to treatment costs absent the patient-worker's informed written consent.[87] Michigan law guarantees much the same rights, and provides that an institution cannot collect one-half the amount paid to a resident patient-worker as payment for services rendered.[88]

To avoid liability in this patients' rights area, mental health professionals and other institutional personnel should become familiar with the rights guaranteed institutional patient-workers by the laws of their state. Although a 1976 U.S. Supreme Court decision held that Congress cannot constitutionally apply federal minimum-wage-and-hour coverage to state and local employees, the decision did not prohibit state and local authorities from adopting federal minimum-wage standards and did not affect the applicability of the standards to privately operated facilities for the mentally disabled.[89]

Mental health personnel should also recognize that noncompensated patient-workers may assert other bases for liability in actions to recover unpaid wages. The Thirteenth Amendment, added to the Constitution to abolish slavery, "has been construed to encompass or maintain a system of free and voluntary labor throughout the United States."[90] This broad construction has enabled aggrieved patient-workers to invoke the amendment's protection. For example, two mentally handicapped persons brought an action under the Thirteenth Amendment and the FLSA for monetary and declaratory relief, alleging that staff at private mental institutions forced them to work without compensation.[91] They asserted that the tasks they had performed—mowing lawns, washing dishes, scrubbing floors, cleaning bathrooms—lacked therapeutic value and served only the institutions' economic interests.

Although the court did not determine whether the plaintiffs could recover unpaid wages from the institutions, it did discuss "two substantial hurdles" that persons wishing to establish a Thirteenth Amendment cause of action must surmount. First, they must allege (and, ultimately, prove on the merits) that they performed their labors involuntarily. Even if they can meet this requirement, a court may find that their labor did not violate the Thirteenth Amendment because it served a "compelling state interest." Second, patient-workers must assert that they performed nontherapeutic work. The court recognized that this requirement places a heavy burden on the patient-workers because an institution can cast practically every task in a therapeutic light.[92] Nevertheless, an institution may violate a patient-worker's Thirteenth Amendment rights if it "requires inmates to perform chores which have no therapeutic purpose or are not personally related, but are required to be performed solely in order to assist in the defraying of institutional costs."[93]

To avoid possible liability under the Thirteenth Amendment for violating patients' rights, mental health care personnel must comply with FLSA requirements. They must also recognize that merely offering compensation to a patient-worker may not relieve them of liability, "for the mere payment of a compensation, unless the receipt of the compensation induces consent to the performance of the work, cannot serve to justify forced labor."[94] A patient should not have to perform "repetitive, nonfunctional, degrading, and unnecessary tasks," nor should a patient have to work in conditions that render the work nontherapeutic.[95]

Mental health personnel must also be aware that Section 504 of the 1973 Rehabilitation Act[96] may possibly give patient-workers a third actionable ground. Section 504 prohibits any program or activity receiving federal financial assistance from discriminating against an otherwise qualified handicapped individual. The regulations that support Section 504 include mentally impaired persons within their definition of "handicapped persons," and a noncompensated patient-worker could argue that Section 504 requires an institution to pay him or her the same wages it would pay nonpatients for completing the same tasks.[97] Although it remains unclear whether institutionalized patients may use this legislation to their advantage, mental health personnel should know that it exists and that it may expose them to liability for violating a patient's right to receive compensation for institutional labor.

RESTRAINT AND SECLUSION

Restraint

JCAH standards provide that a hospital must have written policies and procedures to govern the use of restraints or seclusion. Further,

> The use of restraint or seclusion shall require clinical justification and shall be employed only to prevent a patient from injuring himself or

others, or to prevent serious disruption of the therapeutic environment. Restraint or seclusion shall not be employed as punishment or for the convenience of staff.[98]

In deciding to restrain or seclude a patient the "inadequacy of less restrictive intervention techniques must be addressed."[99]

To ascertain that restraint or seclusion is justified a physician must clinically assess the patient. A physician's order is necessary for restraint or seclusion in excess of one hour. Such orders must be time-limited and, where ordered for more than 24 hours, they must be approved by the department chair.[100] Psychiatrists may not leave PRN (as necessary) orders for patients to be restrained or placed in seclusion.

The use of restraint or seclusion must be reported daily to the department chair or to his or her designee. A daily review of all restraint or seclusion must be conducted, as must an investigation of "unusual or possibly unwarranted utilization patterns. . . ."[101]

Staff who implement written orders for restraint or seclusion must have documented training in the use of such procedures. The procedures "shall not be used in a manner that causes undue physical discomfort, harm, or pain in the patient." Patients in restraint or seclusion shall be paid "appropriate attention . . . every 15 minutes . . . especially in regard to regular meals, bathing, and the use of the toilet." Such attention must be documented in the patient records.[102]

In an emergency, restraint or seclusion may be implemented without a written order if:

1. A member of the professional staff who is qualified by experience and training in the proper use of the applicable procedure gives the written order.
2. The professional staff member writing the order has observed and assessed the patient before writing the order.
3. The written order of the physician who is responsible for the patient's medical care is obtained no more than eight hours after initial employment of the restraint or seclusion.[103]

Most states prohibit the use of restraint or seclusion except in an emergency where a patient threatens harm to self or to others. Recent judicial and legislative decisions establish guidelines mental health personnel must follow in deciding whether a patient's behavior warrants restraint.[104]

In the early 1970s, judicial attention focused on whether involuntarily committed persons had a right under the Eighth and Fourteenth Amendments to freedom from bodily restraint. Several courts decided that these persons did have this right, that some restraints could constitute "cruel and unusual punishment" prohibited by the Eighth Amendment.[105] However, courts no longer regard the Eighth Amendment as an appropriate standard for determining the constitutionality of civil commitment. They believe that the Eighth Amendment limits the scope of judicial review of incarceration conditions to the criminal context, and have turned their attention to the Fourteenth Amendment when determining whether mental health personnel have violated the rights of committed patients.[106]

The Fourteenth Amendment protects an involuntarily committed mentally retarded person's right to freedom from unreasonable bodily restraints.[107] This right is not absolute; "there are occasions in which it is necessary for the State to restrain the movement of residents—for example, to protect them as well as others from violence."[108] A court's greatest concern, and a constitutional imperative, is that "professional judgment was in fact exercised in deciding to restrain a patient."[109] Decisions made by the appropriate professional are "presumptively valid,"[110] and only "if the professional's conduct . . . departed so substantially from accepted professional judgment, practice, or standards in the care and treatment of a patient that it demonstrates that the professional did not base [his or her] conduct or professional judgment" will a professional incur legal liability for violating an involuntarily committed mentally retarded person's rights.[111] This standard, designed to ensure ". . . that the choice in question was not a sham or otherwise illegitimate," will govern the behavior and establish the liability of all mental health professionals.[112]

Although most "freedom from restraint" cases have involved involuntarily admitted mentally retarded persons, the principles enunciated in the decisions seemingly apply to voluntarily and involuntarily admitted mentally ill persons as well. State statutes concerning restraint generally do not distinguish among the three groups. Indeed, Illinois abolished existing distinctions when it revised its mental health code; the Commission for Revision deemed the distinctions "unwarranted."[113] Illinois law now provides: "Restraint may be used only as a therapeutic measure to prevent a recipient [of habilitation or treatment] from causing physical harm to himself or others. In no event shall restraint be utilized to punish or discipline a recipient, nor is restraint to be used as a convenience for the staff."[114] Unless an emergency exists, only a physician, a clinical psychologist, or a registered nurse with supervisory responsibilities may write a restraint order.[115] In Illinois a restraint order remains valid for just 16 hours, and a restrained recipient may not be rerestrained during the two calendar days following his or her release without the facility director's prior written authorization.[116] Finally, the law requires a qualified person to observe the restrained person at least once every 15 minutes.[117]

Many state statutes limit the use of mechanical or other restraints to situations in which a patient is likely to cause harm, or in which such restraints are necessary for the patient's medical needs. For example, Massachusetts allows mental health personnel to restrain inpatients or residents of state facilities only in cases of emergency ". . . such as the occurrence or, serious threat of, extreme violence, personal injury, or attempted suicide."[118] Massachusetts law also allows any person who transports a mentally ill or mentally retarded person to or from a facility to use any restraint necessary for the safety of either the patient or persons likely to come into contact with the person being transported.[119]

In North Carolina, mental health personnel can physically restrain a patient only when necessary to prevent danger of abuse or injury to the patient or to others, or as a measure of therapeutic treatment.[120] Georgia's code, which prohibits "mistreatment, neglect, or abuse in any form of any client," states that medical personnel may not physically restrain a patient unless an emergency arises or a physician determines that restraints will prevent a client from causing injury.[121] California guarantees mentally ill persons the same legal rights guaranteed all other persons by the U.S. Constitution and federal laws and by the Constitution and laws of the state of California, including the right to freedom from unnecessary or excessive physical restraint.[122] Connecticut law protects mentally retarded persons from unnecessary restraint, but does not mention similar protection for the mentally ill.[123]

As in all patients' rights areas, mental health personnel and professionals must learn the law of their state concerning physical restraint of patients. Many states require personnel to record the reasons for restraining a patient, and mental health personnel in all states would do well to follow a similar procedure. Because courts want assurances that professional judgment "in fact was exercised," noting that judgment and its reasoning makes good sense.

When patients are placed in restraints and seclusion, care must be taken to ensure that no harm comes to them. For example, a Connecticut court held a hospital staff liable for brain damage suffered by a patient who was left in seclusion in a steel-frame bed without supervision. The patient wedged her neck between one raised side rail and the small mattress, decreasing the blood flow, and causing brain damage. The hospital was negligent, said the court, in leaving such furniture in the room, for failure to supervise the patient constantly, for having no written policy on seclusion, for not breaking the patient's seclusion at regular short intervals, and for the design and location of the seclusion room, which prevented it from being clearly visible from the nursing station.[124]

Seclusion or Isolation

Mental health personnel who seclude or isolate institutionalized patients to maintain order may incur legal liability for their actions. Because institutions often lack the staffing necessary to supervise patients adequately, personnel may have to seclude certain patients to keep them from harming themselves or others. Even so, "Inadequate resources can never be an adequate justification for the state's depriving any person of his constitutional rights."[125] Unless it proves the least restrictive alternative for treating an institutionalized patient, mental health personnel should not use seclusion.

Several judicial rulings have barred seclusion of mentally retarded patients except where personnel follow rigid guidelines.[126] In formulating its ruling, one court remarked:

> Patients have a right to be free from physical restraint and isolation. Except for emergency situations, in which it is likely that patients could harm themselves or others and in which less restrictive means of restraint are not feasible, patients may be physically restrained or placed in isolation only on a Qualified Mental Health Professional's written order which explains the rationale for such action. . . . Emergency use of restraints or isolation shall be for no more than one hour. . . .[127]

Many states have statutes that impose similar limitations on the use of seclusion in treating committed mental health patients. Georgia law mandates that mental health personnel use seclusion solely to provide effective habilitation and to protect the safety of the patient and other persons.[128] North Carolina, too, prohibits mental health personnel from secluding patients unless the patients threaten harm to themselves or to others.[129] California's statute guarantees mental patients the same right to freedom from seclusion or isolation that other persons enjoy.[130]

In states where no such law exists, mental health personnel should not isolate or seclude patients unless either an emergency arises or a physician, a supervising nurse, or another trained person has examined the patient and has determined that seclusion or isolation provides the best treatment for the patient. Personnel should document the reasons for secluding a patient and should monitor the patient at least once every 15 minutes. Patients should not remain secluded for more than several hours if they can function in a group environment without endangering their own safety or the safety of others.

LEAST RESTRICTIVE ALTERNATIVE

In the mental health area, the doctrine of least restrictive alternative is a major factor in the decision of where a patient should be treated as an alternative to hospitalization. Alternatives include outpatient clinics, day treatment programs in hospitals, nursing homes, the custody of friends or relatives, or home health aide services. It has also been applied to the decision of whether a patient should be treated in a maximum security hospital or in a less restrictive hospital or treated on a maximum security ward or on a less restrictive ward.

The doctrine ". . . requires the government to pursue its ends by means narrowly tailored so as not to encroach unnecessarily on important competing interests."[131] The landmark decision that articulated this constitutional principle involved a policy adopted by an Arkansas school district. It required teachers to list the names of organizations to which they belonged as a prerequisite to contract renewals. Ostensibly, the policy was to enable the school district to evaluate the qualifications of the teachers. In fact, it is suspected that the real purpose was to determine if the teachers belonged to the NAACP. The U.S. Supreme Court held that the school could utilize a less drastic means of evaluating the qualifications of the teachers than to abridge their First Amendment right of association.[132] As Justice Stewart remarked:

> [E]ven though the governmental purpose be legitimate and substantial, that purpose cannot be pursued by means that broadly stifle fundamental personal liberties when the end can be more narrowly pursued. The breadth of legislative abridgement must be viewed in the light of less drastic means for achieving the same basic purpose.[133]

By focusing on means rather than on ends, the least restrictive alternative doctrine seeks to reconcile the conflict between a committed person's protected liberty interest and a state's interest in protecting all its citizens.[134]

An early case that involved just such a conflict concerned a *habeas corpus* petition filed by a somewhat senile elderly woman found wandering about Washington, D.C.[135] The police officer who found the woman took her to a local hospital; she was later transferred, under district court order, to St. Elizabeth's Hospital for observation pending a commitment hearing. At the hearing, two psychiatrists testified that the woman was mentally ill and that she could not care for herself adequately. Based on this testimony, the district court ordered the woman committed to the state hospital. The court noted that the woman might be released from the hospital if other facilities were available for her care, but it required the woman to show the facilities' availability.[136] Because the woman failed to meet the requirement and because she endangered herself by wandering, the court upheld her commitment.

The court of appeals reversed the district court's requirement, noting that "[p]roceedings involving the care and treatment of the mentally ill are not strictly adversary proceedings" and that the woman did not know of and did not have the means to ascertain any available alternatives to her hospitalization.[137] Reviewing the newly promulgated District of Columbia Hospitalization of the Mentally Ill Act, which allows a court to order alternatives to hospitalization, the court of appeals decided that the district court, assisted by the government, should explore these alternatives for the woman. According to the court:

> The alternative course of treatment or care should be fashioned as the interests of the person and of the public require in the particular case. Deprivations of liberty solely because of dangers to the ill persons themselves should not go beyond what is necessary for their protection.[138]

The District of Columbia Court of Appeals reiterated this pronouncement in a later *habeas corpus* proceeding brought by a committed person who wanted to move from a maximum security state hospital pavilion to a less restricted ward.[139] In remanding the person's petition to the district court, the appeals court held that ". . . the principle of the least restrictive alternative consistent with the legitimate purposes of a commitment inheres in the very nature of civil commitment."[140] More importantly for the petitioner, the court found:

> The principle of the least restrictive alternative is equally applicable to alternate dispositions *within* a mental hospital. It makes little sense to guard zealously against the possibility of unwarranted deprivations prior to hospitalization, only to abandon the watch once the patient disappears behind hospital doors.[141]

Before it could determine whether the hospital's decision to confine the petitioner to a maximum security ward was within the hospital's broad discretion, "permissible and reasonable . . . in view of the relevant information," the court had to conclude that the hospital had considered and found inadequate all relevant alternative in-hospital dispositions.[142]

Since the late 1960s, other courts have followed the District of Columbia Court of Appeals' lead and applied least restrictive alternative analysis to commitment cases. Despite Justice Stewart's pithy definition of "least restrictive alternative," as well as the appeals court's application of the doctrine, these courts have differed as to the doctrine's characterization and contours. One commentator has stated that courts have used the doctrine in four different contexts: (1) in determining whether a person requires commitment; (2) in regulating commitment conditions; (3) in defining the parameters of treatment within the institution; and (4) in supporting the concept of a committed person's right to receive treatment.[143] An examination of illustrative judicial decisions should aid mental health care personnel in understanding the doctrine's increased importance in the mental health care area.

A leading decision invoking least restrictive alternative analysis in determining whether a person required commitment involved an action brought on behalf of a class composed of persons who had been or who might be involuntarily civilly committed.[144] The plaintiff class asked the court to review the constitutionality of Wisconsin's civil commitment procedures. This review resulted in a ruling that a person recommending full-time involuntary hospitalization for another— a "last resort"—must bear the burden of proving:

> (1) what alternatives are available; (2) what alternatives were investigated; and (3) why the investigated alternatives were not deemed suitable. These alternatives include voluntary or court-ordered outpatient treatment, day treatment in a hospital, night treatment in a

hospital, placement in the custody of a friend or relative, placement in a nursing home, referral to a community mental health clinic, and home health aide services.[145]

As a result of this ruling, the Wisconsin legislature revised its involuntary admission procedures.[146]

Judicial analysis in cases addressing commitment condition questions has proceeded along similar lines. In an action brought by a patient who had been involuntarily confined to a psychiatric hospital's maximum security section for nearly 25 years and who had endured "subhuman living conditions," the court decided that all courts ". . . have a duty to guard against unnecessary restraints not only at the confinement stage."[147] Relying on an earlier decision, the court held that due process considerations entitled the patient to a hearing at which the hospital would have to demonstrate that it had considered alternative security accommodations for the patient. It would also have to explain why it had found them inadequate.[148] The court's decision received further support from a New Jersey statute that mandates periodic review of civilly committed patients. Under the statute, the state's failure to justify a patient's status quo results in judicial "molding" of a new order providing for "the least restrictive restraints . . . consistent with the well-being of the community and the individual."[149]

Assuring "the well-being of the community and the individual" is also the end sought by courts using least restrictive alternative analysis to delineate the parameters of treatment within institutions. For example, a Louisiana court applied the doctrine in shaping a treatment order for mentally retarded, physically handicapped, and delinquent children from Louisiana who resided in out-of-state institutions.[150] While recognizing that the state must consider "the least drastic means" when it offers or requires institutional confinement, the court realistically asserted that

> the constitutional right to some [therapeutic] quid pro quo does not imply a right to the *best* treatment available, any more than the right to counsel means the right to the nation's foremost trial lawyers. Logic, economics, and the scarcity of human resources make it impossible to supply the finest to everyone. . . . The quid pro quo the state must provide is treatment based on expert advice reasonably designed to affect the purposes of state action.[151]

The court ordered the persons preparing the treatment plans for each child to consider the least restrictive alternative for each child, so as to afford each child ". . . a reasonable chance to acquire and maintain those life skills that enable him to cope as effectively as his own capacities permit with the demands of his own person and of his own environment and to raise the level of his physical, mental and social efficiency."[152]

The Supreme Court, too, has shaped a "realistic" treatment standard. The court recently deferred to the judgment of mental health care professionals, ". . . person[s] competent, whether by education, training or experience, to make the particular decision at issue" in the least restrictive treatment area.[153] To decide whether Pennsylvania had violated a mentally retarded, involuntarily committed person's constitutional rights, the U.S. high court adopted a test that balanced the person's liberty interests against relevant state interests.[154] The weight of the state's interest would increase if ". . . professional judgment in fact was exercised" in formulating the person's treatment plan:[155]

> In determining whether the state has met its obligations . . . [to provide reasonable care and safety, reasonably nonrestrictive confinement conditions, and some training], decisions made by the appropriate professional are entitled to a presumption of correctness. Such a presumption is necessary to enable institutions of this type—often, unfortunately, overcrowded and understaffed—to continue to function.[156]

Thus, the court indicated that professionals responsible for patient care are not susceptible to damage actions brought by patients as long as they exercise their best judgment, in good faith, in creating a patient program that they believe provides the least restrictive treatment alternative. This indication supports the conclusion reached by the Louisiana court, which also sought a pragmatic solution to a difficult problem.

The Supreme Court's decision also impacts on least restrictive alternative analysis in right-to-treatment cases. Apparently, a professional's treatment diagnosis deserves a presumption of correctness as well. This area may prove murky for professionals, who want to avoid liability for alleged patient mistreatment. Indeed, a New York court voiced its confusion and frustration in attempting to define a "least restrictive alternative" for patients asserting a right to receive treatment:

> Not only do courts differ with respect to the characterization of the least restrictive alternative requirement, they also do not share a uniform view of what such a requirement entails. One court has written in terms of subjective "good faith attempts" to place persons in appropriate settings. . . . Another court has described a duty to "explore and provide . . . practicable alternatives to confinement." Still another court has asked whether a mode of treatment is "overly restrictive on a comparative basis". . . . Finally, a more recent statement of the requirement, which takes into account a deference toward medical judgments in individual cases, probes into "which of two or more major treatment approaches is to be adopted" in regard to "initial

environmental disposition, not to ongoing therapeutic regimes or medical prescriptions."[157]

The court ultimately decided that, "under whatever version a court might adopt," involuntarily committed persons enjoy a right to treatment in settings "that pass muster under an appropriate least restrictive alternative inquiry."[158] The court also decided that voluntarily admitted persons have the same right, thus ensuring "that continued physical custody by the State does not wrongfully, or permanently, interfere with fundamental liberty interests like personal autonomy and bodily integrity."[159]

What do these decisions portend for mental health care personnel? Recent judicial decisions acknowledge that courts will not apply the least restrictive alternative doctrine in blanket fashion, forcing personnel to examine and discard or retain every possible alternative for every patient. As the Supreme Court noted, "[a] single professional may have to make decisions with respect to a number of residents with widely varying needs and problems in the course of a normal day. . . . Personnel should not be required to make each decision in the shadow of an action for damages."[160] Courts will examine the efforts made by personnel to treat each patient, whether admitted voluntarily or involuntarily, in a manner least restrictive of that patient's needs and abilities in a given context. Undoubtedly, good faith exercise of judgment will play a crucial role in a least restrictive alternative case. The judiciary and the public have become more aware of the rights of the mentally ill or retarded, and mental health care personnel should recognize that their actions may be subject to scrutiny. Although least restrictive alternative standards are hazy, the concept at their core seems clear: Personnel must attempt to provide treatment in a manner that least restricts the freedom of patients. Most states provide that the patient has a right to be treated in the least restrictive setting.[161]

OTHER RIGHTS

The states guarantee a number of other rights to patients by statute: the right to practice religion;[162] the right to physical exercise and outdoor recreation;[163] the right to spiritual treatment;[164] the right to a choice of physician;[165] the right to a nourishing diet;[166] the right to conjugal visits or contact with the opposite sex;[167] and the right not to be fingerprinted or photographed.[168]

NOTES

1. *See* Appendixes E–I.
2. *See, e.g.,* Wyatt v. Stickney, 344 F. Supp. 373, 379 (N.D. Ala. 1972); Pisel v. Stamford Hospital, 180 Conn. 314, 430 A.2d 1 (1980).

3. JCAH, *Consolidated Standards Manual for Child, Adolescent, and Adult Psychiatric, Alcoholism, and Drug Abuse Facilities* (Chicago: JCAH, 1981 ed.) [hereinafter cited as JCAH].

4. 94 Stat. 1564. *See* Appendix D, "Mental Health Rights and Advocacy."

5. JCAH, *supra* note 3, at ¶ 14.1.

6. *Id*. at ¶ 14.2.

7. *Id*. at ¶ 14.3.

8. *See* Appendixes D, *supra* note 4, and G, "Information and Record Rights."

9. Conn. Gen. Stat, § 19–575e(7); Minn. Stat. Ann. § 253A.16. Subd. (3). *See* Appendix D, *supra* note 4, at § 9501(N).

10. Cal. Welf. & Inst. Code, § 5326.5(b); W. Va. Code Ann. § 27-3-2.

11. JCAH, *supra* note 3, at ¶ 14.4n. See Appendix A, 9501(1)(L).

12. *See* Appendix H, "Grievance and Access Rights."

13. *Id*.

14. JCAH, *supra* note 3, at ¶ 14.2.4.1–4. *See* Appendix D, *supra* note 4, § 9501(1)(J).

15. *Id*. at ¶ 14.2.4.2.

16. *Id*. at ¶ 14.2.4.3.

17. *Id*. at ¶ 14.2.4.5.

18. *Id*. at ¶ 14.2.4.6.

19. *See* Appendix F, "Consent and Communications Rights."

20. *Id*.

21. Cal. Welf. & Inst. Code § 5325 (West Supp.).

22. Cal. Welf. & Inst. Code § 5325(c)-(e), (h) (West Supp.).

23. Mass. Gen. Laws Ann. ch. 123, § 23 (West Supp. 1982).

24. *Id*.

25. *Id*.

26. Mich. Comp. Laws Ann. § 330.1726(1) (1980).

27. *Id*. at § 330.1726(4).

28. *Id*. at § 330.1726(5).

29. *Id*. at § 330.1726(F).

30. Tex. Rev. Civ. Stat. Ann., tit. 92, art. 5547-300.25 (Vernon Supp. 1982).

31. Wis. Stats. Ann. § 51.61(1)(c) (West Supp. 1982).

32. *Id*. at § 51.61(1)(p).

33. "Report-Governor's Commission for Revision of the Mental Health Code in Illinois," (1976), p. 24 [hereinafter cited as Report].

34. Ill. Ann. Stat. ch. 91½, § 2–103 (Smith-Hurd Supp. 1982–1983).

35. Stowers v. Ardmore Acres Hospital, 91 Mich. App. 115, 172 N.W.2d 497 (1969).

36. *Id*. at 502.

37. Brown v. Schubert, 347 F. Supp. 1232, 1233 (E.D. Wis. 1972).

38. *Id*. at 1233.

39. Wyatt v. Stickney, *supra* note 2.

40. *Id*. at 379.

41. Ill. Ann. Stat. ch. 91½, § 2–104 (Smith-Hurd Supp. 1982–1983).

42. *Id*. at § 2–105.

43. Report, *supra* note 33, at 25.

44. Ill. Ann. Stat. ch. 91½, § 2–104 (Smith-Hurd Supp. 1982–1983).

45. Cal. Welf. & Inst. Code § 5325(a), (b) (West Supp. 1981).

46. Mass. Gen. Laws Ann. ch. 123, § 23 (West Supp. 1982).

47. Me. Rev. Stat. Ann. tit. 34, § 2143 (West 1978); Md. Ann. Code art. 59A, § 34 (Supp. 1981).

48. Me. Rev. Stat. Ann. tit. 34, § 2143 (West 1978).

49. La. Rev. Stat. Ann. § 28–391(c)(3) (West Supp. 1982).

50. N.C. Gen. Stat. § 122–55.2(b)(5), (8), (10); (d) (1981).

51. *Id.* at § 122–55.14(b)(3), (7).

52. Mich. Comp. Laws Ann. § 330.1728(1), (4)(a)–(d) (1980).

53. *Id.* at § 330.1730(1) (1980).

54. *Id.* at § 330.1730(2) (1980).

55. *Id.* at § 330.1730(2) (1980).

56. *Id.* at § 330.1730(3), (4) (1980).

57. Vecchione v. Wohlgmuth, 377 F. Supp. 1361 (E.D. Pa. 1974).

58. *Id.* at 1368.

59. *Id.* at 1370; *See* Dale v. Hahn, 486 F.2d 76 (2d Cir. 1973).

60. McAuliffe v. Carlson, 377 F. Supp. 896 (D. Conn. 1974), *supplemented*, 386 F. Supp. 1245 (D. Conn.), *rev'd.*, 520 F.2d 1305 (2d Cir.), *cert. denied*, 427 U.S. 911 (1975); Fayle v. Stapley, 607 F.2d 858 (9th Cir. 1979).

61. 607 F.2d at 862.

62. *See* Chapter 1 for a discussion of the elements of the Civil Rights Act.

63. Fayle v. Stapley, *supra* note 60, at 861.

64. Mass. Gen. Laws Ann. ch. 123, § 32 (West Supp. 1982).

65. Ill. Ann. Stat., ch. 91½, § 2–105 (Smith-Hurd Supp. 1982–1983).

66. Report, *surpa* note 33, at 26.

67. Paul Friedman, "The Mentally Handicapped Citizen and Institutional Labor," *Harv. L. Rev.* 87 (1974):567.

68. Peter Gelhaar, "Institutionalized Patient Workers and Their Right to Compensation in the Aftermath of *National League of Cities v. Usery*," *B.C.L. Rev.* 22 (1980):511 [hereinafter cited as Gelhaar].

69. Alvin Lebar, "Worker-Patients: Receiving Therapy or Suffering Peonage?," *A.B.A.J.* 62 (1976):219 (citing "American Psychologist Newsletter," April 2, 1975) [hereinafter cited as Lebar].

70. Gelhaar, *supra* note 68, at 511.

71. *Id.*

72. Souder v. Brennan, 367 F. Supp. 808 (D. D.C. 1973).

73. 29 U.S.C. §§ 201–219.

74. Souder v. Brennan, *supra* note 72, at 813.

75. Mossman v. Donahey, 46 Ohio St.2d 1 (1976).

76. 29 C.F.R. § 529.1–17 (1981).

77. 29 C.F.R. § 529.4(a) (1981).

78. 29 C.F.R. § 529.4(a) (1981).

79. 29 C.F.R. § 529.4(i) (1981).

80. Ariz. Rev. Stat. Ann. § 36–510; Colo. Rev. Stat. § 27–10–118; Conn. Gen. Stat. § 19–575(e)(9); Ga. Code Ann. § 88–502.11; Hawaii Rev. Stat. § 334E–2(16); Kan. Stat. § 59–2929(a)(5); Ky. Rev. Stat. § 202A.180(6); La. Rev. Stat. Ann. § 28:171H; Mo. Ann. Stat. § 630.115.1(4); Mont. Code Ann. § 53–21–167(1); Neb. Rev. Stat. § 83–1066(7); Nev. Rev. Stat. § 433.524; N.Y. Mental Hygiene Law § 33.09(b); Ohio Rev. Code Ann. § 5122.28; Okla. Stat. Ann. 43A § 191.1; Ore. Rev. Stat. §§ 426.385(1)–(j)(k); Pa. Stat. Ann. 50 § 4423(3); R.I. Gen. Laws § 40.1–5–5(6)(i); S.C. Code § 44–23–1060; S.D. Codified Laws § 27A–12–2–(1); Wis. Stat. Ann. § 51.61(1)(b).

81. JCAH, *supra* note 3, at ¶ 14.6.

82. Ga. Code Ann. § 88–2503.10 (1979).

83. *See* 29 C.F.R. § 529.2(d) (1981).

84. Lebar, *supra* note 69, at 219.

85. Report, *supra* note 33, at 27.

86. Ill. Ann. Stat., ch. 91½, § 2–106 (Smith-Hurd Supp. 1982–1983).

87. Wis. Stat. Ann. § 51.61(1)(b) (West Supp. 1981).

88. Mich. Comp. Laws Ann. § 330.1736(6) (Supp. 1981).

89. National League of Cities v. Usery, 426 U.S. 833 (1976); Report, *supra* note 33, at 27; Gelhaar, *supra* note 68, at 516–517.

90. Weidenfeller v. Kidulis, 380 F. Supp. 445, 450 (E.D. Wis. 1974).

91. *Id.*

92. *Id.* at 451; Report, *supra* note 33, at 27.

93. *Id.* at 450, citing Jobson v. Henne, 355 F.2d 129, 132 n. 3 (2d Cir. 1966).

94. *Id.* at 355 F.2d at 132, n. 3.

95. Davis v. Balson, 461 F. Supp. 842 (N.D. Ohio 1978); Gelhaar, *supra* note 68, at 521.

96. 29 U.S.C. § 794 (1976).

97. Gelhaar, *supra* note 68, at 530.

98. JCAH, *supra* note 3, at ¶ 19.2.1.

99. *Id.* at ¶ 19.2.1.1.

100. *Id.* at ¶ 19.2.

101. *Id.* at ¶ 19.2.7–8.

102. *Id.* at ¶ 19.2.9.–19.2.11.1.

103. *Id.* at ¶ 19.1.12.

104. *See* Appendix I, "Other Rights." *See also* Appendix D, *supra* note 4, at § 9501(1)(F).

105. *See* Wyatt v. Stickney, *supra* note 2, at 373, *aff'd. sub nom*, Wyatt v. Aderholdt, 503 F.2d 1305 (5th Cir. 1974); Wheeler v. Glass, 473 F.2d 983 (7th Cir. 1973); Welsch v. Likins, 373 F. Supp. 487 (D. Minn. 1974).

106. Romeo v. Youngberg, 644 F.2d 147 (3d Cir. 1982).

107. Youngberg v. Romeo, 102 S.Ct. 2452 (1982).

108. *Id.* at 2460.

109. *Id.* at 2457, citing Romeo v. Youngberg, *supra* note 106, at 178.

110. Youngberg v. Romeo, *supra* note 107, at 2462.

111. Romeo v. Youngberg, *supra* note 106, at 178, *accord* 102 S.Ct. 2462.

112. *Id.* at 644 F.2d at 178.

113. Report, *supra* note 33, at 29.

114. Ill. Ann. Stat., ch. 91–½, § 2–108 (Smith-Hurd Supp. 1982–1983).

115. Ill. Ann. Stat., ch. 91–½, § 2–108(a) (Smith-Hurd Supp. 1982–1983).

116. Ill. Ann. Stat., ch. 91–½, § 2–108(2), (e) (Smith-Hurd Supp. 1982–1983).

117. Ill. Ann. Stat., ch. 91–½, § 2–108(f) (Smith-Hurd Supp. 1982–1983).

118. Mass. Gen. Laws Ann., ch. 123, § 21 (West Supp. 1982).

119. Mass. Gen. Laws Ann., ch. 123, § 21 (West Supp. 1982).

120. N.C. Gen. Stat., § 122–55.2 (1981).

121. Ga. Code Ann. § 88–2503.5(a), (b) (Supp. 1981).

122. Cal. Welf. & Inst. Code § 5325.1(c) (West Supp. 1982).

123. Conn. Gen. Stat. § 19–575a(a) (1979).

124. Pisel v. Stamford Hospital, *supra* note 2.

125. Inmates of Suffolk County Jail v. Eisenstadt, 360 F. Supp. 676, 687 (D. Mass. 1973).

126. Welsch v. Likins, 373 F. Supp. 487, 503 (D. Minn. 1974); Wyatt v. Stickney, *supra* note 2, at 380 (M.D. Ala. 1972), *aff'd. sub. nom* Wyatt v. Aderholt, *supra* note 105; New York State Assoc. for Retarded Children, Inc. v. Rockefeller, 357 F. Supp. 752, 769 (E.D. N.Y. 1973).

127. Wyatt v. Stickney, *supra* note 2, at 380.

128. Ga. Code Ann. § 88–2503.5(a) (Supp. 1981).

129. N.C. Gen. Stat. § 12255.3 (1981).

130. Cal. Welf. & Inst. Code, § 5325.1(c) (West Supp. 1982).

131. David Zlotnick, "First Do No Harm: Least Restrictive Alternative Analysis and the Right of Mental Patients to Refuse Treatment," *W. Va. L. Rev.* 83 (1981):375, 381 [hereinafter cited as Zlotnick].

132. Shelton v. Tucker, 364 U.S. 479 (1960).

133. *Id.* at 488.

134. Zlotnick, *supra* note 131, at 381.

135. Lake v.Cameron, 364 F.2d 657 (D.C. Cir. 1966).

136. *Id.* at 659.

137. *Id.* at 661.

138. *Id.* at 660.

139. Covington v. Harris, 419 F.2d 617 (D.C. Cir. 1969).

140. *Id.* at 623.

141. *Id.* at 623–624 (court's emphasis).

142. *Id.* at 624 (citing Tribby v. Cameron, 379 F.2d 104, 105 (D.C. Cir. 1967)).

143. Zlotnick, *supra* note 131, at 401.

144. Lessard v. Schmidt, 349 F. Supp. 1078 (E.D. Wis. 1972), *vacated on procedural grounds*, 414 U.S. 473 (1974), *vacated on procedural grounds*, 421 U.S. 957 (1975), *reinstated*, 413 F. Supp. 1318 (E.D. Wis. 1976).

145. *Id.* at 1096; *see* Lynch v. Baxley, 386 F. Supp. 378 (M.D. Ala. 1974).

146. *See* Wis. Stat. Ann. §§ 51.1051.20 (Supp. 1981).

147. Scott v. Plante, 641 F.2d 117 (3d Cir. 1981), *vacated*, 102 S.Ct. 3474 (1982).

148. *Id.* at 641 F.2d 129 (citing Eubanks v. Clarke, 434 F. Supp. 1022 (E.D. Pa. 1977)).

149. *Id.* 641 F.2d at 129, n. 11 (citing State v. Fields, 77 N.J. 282, 390 A.2d 574, 584 (1978)); *see* N.J. Ct. Rules 4:74–7(f) (1980).

150. Gary W. v. State of Louisiana, 437 F. Supp. 1209 (E.D. La. 1976).

151. *Id.* at 1217–1218 (emphasis in original).

152. *Id.* at 1219.

153. Youngberg v. Romeo, *supra* note 107, at 2461, 2462, n. 30.

154. *Id.* at 2462.

155. *Id.*

156. *Id.* at 2463.

157. Philipp v. Carey, 517 F. Supp. 513, 518 (N.D. N.Y. 1981).

158. *Id.* at 518.

159. *Id.* at 519.

160. Youngberg v. Romeo, *supra* note 107, at 2462.

161. *See* Appendix I, *supra* note 104.

162. Alaska Stat. § 47.30.835(a); Ariz. Rev. Stat. Ann. § 36–514(4); Ark. Stat. Ann. § 59–1416(25); Ind. Code Ann. § 16–14–1.6–2; Mo. Ann. Stat. § 630.115.1(5); Mont. Code Ann. § 53–21–142(8); Neb. Rev. Stat. § 83–1066(6); N.J. Stat. Ann. § 43–1–6c, § 30:4–24.2(e)(11); N.M. Stat. Ann. § 43–1–6c; N.C. Gen. Stat. § 122–55.2(b)(7); N.D. Cent. Code § 25–03.1–40.8; Ohio Rev. Code Ann. § 5122–29(H); Ore. Rev. Stat. § 426.385(1)(d); Pa. Stat. Ann. 50 § 4423(2); R.I. Gen Laws § 40.1.5.5.6(d); S.D. Codified Laws, § 2714–12–9; Tex. Mental Health Code Ann. § 5547–86(a)(2); Wis. Stat. Ann. § 51.61(e).

163. Ark. Stat. Ann. § 59–1416(26); Haw. Rev. Stat. § 334E–2(13); Mo. Ann. Stat. § 630.110.1(7); Mont. Code Ann. § 53–21–142(9); N.J. Stat. Ann. §§ 30:4–24.2(e)(8), (9); N.M. Stat. Ann. § 43–1–6E; N.C. Gen. Stat. § 122–55.2(b)(4); N.D. Cent. § 25–03.1–40.7.

164. Cal. Welf. & Inst. Code § 5006; Ill. Ann. Stat. § 2–102(b); Mo. Ann. Stat. § 630.180; S.D. Codified Laws § 27A–12–22; Wash. Rev. Code § 71.05.070; Wyo. Stat. § 25–3–124(e).

165. Cal. Welf. & Inst. Code § 5009; Mass. Gen. Laws, 111 § 70E.

166. Conn. Gen. Stat. § 19–575(e)(8); Haw. Rev. Stat. § 334E–2(14); Mo. Ann. Stat. § 630.115.1(13); Mont. Code Ann. § 53–21–142(12); N.M. Stat. Ann. 43–1–6F1; Okla. Stat. Ann. 43A § 91.

167. Kan. Stat. § 59–2929(a)(3); Mont. Code Ann. § 53–21–142(10); N.J. Stat. Ann. § 30:4–24.2(e)(10); Ohio Rev. Code Ann. § 5122.29(1).

168. Ariz. Rev. Stat. Ann. § 36–507; Mich. Comp. Laws Ann. § 330–1724; Mont. Code Ann. §§ 53–21–143, 144; S.D. Codified Laws § 27A–12–2–(1); Wis. Stat. Ann. § 51.61(10).

Chapter 10

Privacy and Confidentiality

Institutionalized patients, like all other persons, have a right to privacy and dignity.[1] JCAH standards provide that "each patient's personal privacy shall be assured and protected within the constraints of the individual treatment plan."[2] Statutes in 34 states provide some protection of the privacy of patients.[3] Nevertheless, because institutions "[are] often, unfortunately, overcrowded and understaffed,"[4] this right may prove very difficult to protect. One civilly committed patient, testifying against the superintendent of a Florida state institution, remarked that 60 persons slept in his "room" and that he had no place to go for privacy.[5] Mental health care personnel should make every effort to remedy similar physical problems that thwart patients' privacy.

Personnel must also try to protect institutionalized persons from intangible infringements on privacy rights. The attention focused on mental health care in recent years has given rise to documentary films and news broadcasts that detail the lives of institutionalized persons. Although the persons making these films and broadcasts hope that their projects will provide the catalyst for altering institutional conditions, they find themselves creating new privacy problems for their subjects.

In the late 1960s, a film maker requested permission from both the superintendent of a large Massachusetts institution and the commissioner of the Massachusetts Department of Mental Health to make an educational documentary film concerning the institution. He received permission, subject to the conditions that "the rights of the inmates and patients . . . [would be] fully protected"; that he would use only "photographs of inmates and patients . . . legally competent to sign releases"; that he would obtain a written release "from each patient whose photograph [he] used in the film"; and that the film would require the superintendent's and the commissioner's approval before it could be released.[6] The film maker then garnered the necessary "releases" and made his film.

The film's release, hailed by some critics as "art,"[7] elicited adverse reactions from the superintendent, the commissioner, and the state attorney general, in whose opinion ". . . the film constituted an invasion of the privacy of the inmates shown in the film . . . ."[8] The commonwealth brought suit to enjoin all showings of the film to any audience; the trial judge granted the injunction. On the film maker's appeal, the court supported the trial judge's fundamental ruling because "[t]he film shows many inmates in situations which would be degrading to a person of normal mentality and sensitivity. . . . There is a collective, indecent intrusion into the most private aspects of the lives of these unfortunate persons."[9] It recognized that the film maker had obtained releases from persons incompetent to understand a release and that the film maker had worked outside the scope of the permission granted. However, the court modified the trial court's sweeping injunction order and permitted the showing of the film to audiences ". . . of [a] specialized or professional character. . . ."[10]

More recently, an institutionalized mentally ill person sued a national television network and one of its employees to recover for an alleged false imprisonment and for violation of his privacy rights.[11] The court dismissed the patient's false imprisonment charge, but ruled that the network had made an "unprivileged invasion" upon the patient's right to privacy, as well as his right to publicity, by using his videotaped picture for trade purposes. Because the commissioner of the facility where the patient resided had never certified that the patient had sufficient mental capacity to consent to an interview or a photography session, the court could not find that the patient had competently granted the network the written "Consent for Patient Interview" required by New York law.

The defendants argued that, even if the patient had not validly consented to an interview, their intrusion into the patient's privacy right was *de minimus* (small, trifling).[12] Citing an earlier opinion, the court rejected this argument:

> While the argument appears persuasive on the surface, it does not, on deliberation, hold water. Assessing the degree of the intrusion against the newsworthiness of the story is a test that is too vague and subjective to counter balance the predominant interest served in protecting the rights of individuals in a free society against invasion of their privacy. . . .[13]

The court also noted that, even if the patient had given valid consent, the patient never authorized the defendants' distribution of the videotape nor any further use of the tape for commercialization. According to the court, "The mere fact that [the patient] may have voluntarily, on this one occasion, surrendered his right of privacy for monetary reward or gratuitously, does not forever forfeit his privacy right for all who would engage in commercial exploitation."[14]

JCAH standards require hospitals to have "written policies and procedures that protect the confidentiality of patient records and govern the disclosure of information in the records."[15] These policies must specify the conditions and procedures for the disclosure of information. A consent signed by the patient or the patient's representative must contain the name or organization to which the information is disclosed; specific information disclosed; purpose for the disclosure; date the consent was signed and the signature of the individual witnessing the consent; and a notice that the consent is valid for only a specified period of time.[16] The consent of a patient is valid only if the consent is in accordance with the law, if the patient has voluntarily consented, if the services are not contingent upon release, and if the patient's or the patient's authorized representative has been informed of the specific information requested and of the advantages and disadvantages of release.[17] All disclosures must be documented in the record, complete with date of release and the signature of the staff member who released the information.[18]

Pertinent medical information may be released in a life-threatening situation without consent. If information is released in an emergency, the following information must be recorded in the patient's record: date of disclosure; person to whom information was disclosed; reason for disclosure; reason written consent could not be obtained; and the specific information disclosed.[19]

The "maintenance of confidentiality of communications between patients and staff and of all information recorded in patient records shall be the responsibility of the staff."[20] Staff members who have access to patient records must be required to comply with hospital policies and the law.[21]

The MHS Act recommends that patient records be confidential and that patients have access to their records. The Act also recommends that patients' attorneys and legal representatives have reasonable access.[22]

All states except New Hampshire and the District of Columbia have statutes protecting the confidentiality of patient records and communications. In 39 states patients have access to their own records. Another 13 states provide access by a patient to records after discharge.[23]

Therapists have a statutory duty to keep communications and records confidential in the absence of consent by patients. There are exceptions to this rule. Some states make a blanket exception to testimony in criminal proceedings, while others make an exception where the defendant raises a claim or defense in the proceeding. Most states provide that the privilege exists with regard to civil proceedings except where the patient raises a claim or defense. Other exceptions to the privilege include involuntary hospitalization and guardianship proceedings, child abuse reporting, and peer review activities. Some states have made provision for the confidentiality of "personal notes" of the therapist, which are not discoverable so long as certain conditions are met.

The source of the privilege of confidentiality is the therapist-patient relationship.[24] The purpose of the privilege is to inspire confidence in patients and encourage them to disclose their problems fully, thereby increasing the effectiveness of therapy. The privilege extends to relationships between psychiatrists, psychologists, social workers, and nurses.[25] The Illinois statute extends the duty to "any other person not prohibited by law from providing such services or from holding himself out as a therapist if the . . . [patient] reasonably believes that such person is permitted to do so.''[26]

Generally, statutes frame the privilege in terms of all communications arising in the course of treatment, and sometimes diagnosis, or in terms of prohibiting disclosures that are necessary to treatment.[27] A number of exceptions to the privilege exist.

Some state statutes provide an exception in criminal proceedings[28] or in felony cases.[29] Others provide an exception only where the patient raises the issue, such as an insanity defense.[30] In Louisiana, the court reversed a robbery conviction where a physician had testified as to statements the defendant made during treatment in a hospital emergency room. The defendant told the physician he had been shot while attempting to rob a woman, and the physician related this information at trial. The court reversed the conviction because a privileged relationship had been established between doctor and patient.[31] When a defendant based his defense for drug possession in part on his participation in a treatment clinic program, the clinic was required to produce all records.[32] A Pennsylvania court refused to allow a psychologist to testify in a murder trial to impeach the credibility of the defendant's daughter, who the psychologist had examined.[33]

In Illinois disclosure may be made in any civil, criminal, or administrative proceeding in which the patient introduces his or her mental condition or any aspect of treatment administered as an element of a claim or a defense. Nevertheless, there are limits on such disclosures.

1. The court must find, after an *in camera* (in chambers) examination of testimony, or other evidence, that it is relevant, probative, not unduly prejudicial or inflammatory, and otherwise clearly admissible.
2. The court must find that other evidence is demonstrably unsatisfactory as evidence of the facts sought to be established.
3. The court must find that disclosure is more important to the interests of substantial justice than protection from injury to the therapist-patient relationship or to the patient or others whom disclosure is likely to harm.
4. Except with respect to insanity defenses to criminal charges, no record or communication between a therapist and a patient shall be deemed relevant except the fact of treatment, the cost of services, and the ultimate diagnosis unless the party seeking disclosure clearly establishes at trial a compelling need for its production.[34]

This exception specifically does not apply in divorce cases in which pain and suffering is an element of the claim unless the patient or a witness on the patient's behalf first testifies as to a communication or record.[35]

Where a psychiatrist or psychologist examines a patient pursuant to court order, the communication and records are not confidential and thus are admissible into evidence. Such examinations are commonly ordered in guardianship and involuntary hospitalization proceedings,[36] when determining fitness to stand trial,[37] when establishing criminal responsibility (insanity defense), and in child custody matters.[38] Disclosure is not necessarily restricted to information obtained during the examination. In a New Mexico case, a defendant wrote a letter to a physician who had conducted a court-ordered examination. The court held that the letter was not privileged, and therefore admissible into evidence.[39]

In Illinois, records and communications made to or by a therapist in court-ordered examinations may be disclosed in a civil, criminal, or administrative proceeding, but are admissible only as to issues involving the patient's physical or mental condition and only to the extent that these are germane to the proceeding.[40]

In addition, when patients in Illinois file malpractice claims, disclosure may be made to attorneys giving advice and providing representation to the therapist and persons working under their supervision. Testimony may be given as to records or communications in any administrative, judicial, or discovery proceeding for the purpose of preparing or presenting a defense against the claim or action.[41]

Disclosure may be made in proceedings to determine competency or need for a guardian, provided that the disclosure is made only with respect to that issue;[42] in proceedings to determine whether a person is fit to stand trial;[43] to determine in a civil or administrative proceeding the validity of or benefits under life, health, accident, or disability insurance policies, where the patient's mental condition or treatment is a material element of any claim or defense of any party; to provide information in a patient's application for benefits; and to comply with abuse and neglected child reporting requirements.[44]

In a Washington case, the court held that child abuse reporting statutes required the employer of a mental health clinic to report and testify as to acts of child abuse by a patient despite the statutory privileges for confidential communication in the course of treatment and counseling.[45] A psychiatrist was allowed to testify in a wardship case based on neglect, which involved child abuse charges.[46]

In Illinois, a therapist may disclose a record or communication without consent to a consulting therapist, the therapist's supervisor, members of the staff team, the record custodian, or a person acting under the supervision and control of the therapist. In addition, disclosure may be made to persons conducting peer review activities or attorneys or advocates consulted by a therapist concerning the legal rights or duties of the therapist or agency in relation to the patient. Such information may be disclosed only "to the extent that knowledge of the record or communication is essential to the purpose for which disclosure is made and only after the patient is informed that such disclosure may be made."[47]

In Illinois, the "personal notes" of a therapist are confidential so long as certain conditions are met. Personal notes are defined as:

1. information disclosed to the therapist (psychiatrist, physician, psychologist, social worker, or nurse) in confidence by other persons on condition that such information would never be disclosed to the patient or other persons;
2. information disclosed to the therapist by the patient that would be injurious to the patient's relationship to other persons; and
3. the therapist's speculations, impressions, hunches, and reminders.

Such personal notes are the confidential work product and personal property of the therapist and may not be disclosed under the Mental Health and Developmental Disabilities Confidentiality Act or subject to discovery in judicial proceedings. However, if the "personal notes" are disclosed to anyone except the therapist's supervisor, consulting therapist, or attorney, they are then considered part of the patient's record and protected only to the extent a record is ordinarily protected.[48]

Some statutes provide that the therapist as well as the patient may assert the privilege if the patient has not given instructions to permit disclosure,[49] but generally, only the patient or the patient's attorney may exercise the privilege.[50] After the patient's death, generally those who stand in his or her place may waive the privilege.[51]

Some state statutes, like Georgia's, expressly afford "every patient . . . the right to examine all medical records kept in the patient's name by the department or facility where the patient [was] hospitalized or treated."[52] Other states have statutes like Florida's, which permits only physicians, attorneys, and government agencies to examine a patient's records if the patient, his or her guardian, or his or her attorney has so consented.[53] In 1977, the Florida Court of Appeals ruled that this statute also allows a patient access to his or her own records because "the legislature clearly intended that the patient have access to the record in order to determine whether and to whom he [or she] wished the reports to be released."[54] Presumably, states with similar statutes would follow this reasoning.

Many reasons exist for requiring that mental health patients' records remain confidential. As a Washington court remarked:

> . . . one way to encourage a clinical approach, maintain a clinical atmosphere, and sublimate any penal aspects of mental illness, is to avoid making public spectacles of the mentally ill and to close the files. There are other reasons, too . . . not the least of which is that witnesses, members of the family, and others interested in the proceeding may act and speak with candor and forthrightness under the statutory theory that in most instances the proceeding is undertaken for the good of the subject and with the intention of getting a sick person into a hospital where he [or she] may receive medical care. . . .[55]

In a famous New York case,[56] a psychiatrist and her psychologist husband

> published a book which reported verbatim and extensively the patients' thoughts, feelings, and emotions, their sexual and other fantasies and biographies, their most intimate personal relationships and the disintegration of their marriage. Interspersed among the footnotes are [the psychiatrist's] diagnoses of what purport to be the illnesses suffered by the patients and one of their children.[57]

The therapists alleged that the patient-plaintiff consented to the publication. There was no written consent, and, in the psychiatrist's own words, consent "was there one day and not there another day. That was the nature of the illness I was treating, unreliable."[58]

As soon as she heard of the publication, the patient protested orally through a mutual friend and in writing through her attorney. The attorney received misleading and evasive answers. Before a restraining order could be obtained, 220 copies of the book had been published. The identities of the patients were not sufficiently concealed to protect them from recognition by friends, fellow employees, or employers.

The court stated:

> Every patient, and particularly every patient undergoing psychoanalysis, has such a right of privacy. Under what circumstances can a person be expected to reveal sexual fantasies, infantile memories, passions of hate and love, one's most intimate relationship with one's spouse and others except upon the inferential agreement that such confessions will be forever entombed in the psychiatrist's memory, never to be revealed during the psychiatrist's lifetime or thereafter? The very needs of the profession itself require that confidentiality exist and be enforced. . . . [A] large segment of the psychiatric profession concurs in Dr. Lifschutz's strongly held belief that an absolute privilege of confidentiality is essential to the effective practice of psychotherapy.[59]

The court found a contract to be created between the therapist and the patient:

> I too find that a physician, who enters into an agreement with a patient to provide medical attention, impliedly covenants to keep in confidence all disclosures made by the patient concerning the patient's physical or mental condition as well as all matters discovered by the physician in the course of examination or treatment. This is particularly and necessarily true of the psychiatric relationship, for in the dynamics of psychotherapy . . . [t]he patient is called upon to discuss in a candid

and frank manner personal material of the most intimate and disturbing nature. . . . He is expected to bring up all manner of socially unacceptable instincts and urges, immature wishes, perverse sexual thoughts—in short the unspeakable, the unthinkable, the repressed. To speak of such things to another human being requires an atmosphere of unusual trust, confidence and tolerance.

Patients will be helped only if they can form a trusting relationship with the psychiatrist.[60]

The court awarded the patient $20,000 in compensatory damages. It granted no punitive damages because the publication of the book was not "willful, malicious or wanton—merely stupid."[61] The patient suffered acute embarrassment on learning the extent to which her friends, colleagues, employer, students, and others had read or read of the book. "Her livelihood was threatened, her health suffered."

The defendants argued that confidentiality is not absolute and must give way to the public interest. The court agreed that courts have recognized a duty to protect their parties from danger, to disclose the existence of a contagious disease, and to report the use of controlled substances in certain situations. The court stated that "in no case, however, has the curiosity or education of the medical profession superseded the duty of confidentiality."[62]

In Illinois, a psychiatrist at a state institution stated the name of a client in a television interview and added that the patient was suffering from schizophrenia and had homosexual tendencies. The patient had not authorized such disclosures and filed an action against the psychiatrist.[63] The patient died before the matter went to trial, and his estate refused to authorize continuation of the action. It was dismissed.

Confidential information concerning other patients may not be disclosed to a patient in a malpractice action against a psychologist. In Texas, two patients filed suit against their psychologist alleging that during the course of their therapy the psychologist had "gained their complete cooperation and that when they were psychologically powerless to resist the psychologist [he] had sexual intercourse with them." Each patient alleged malpractice, assault and battery, fraud and deceit, and intentional infliction of emotional harm. The psychologist admitted sexual relations with the patients at his office but denied that sexual intercourse was a part of his professional treatment. Although the psychologist admitted charging for the therapy sessions in question, he denied charging for the particular time span during which sexual intercourse occurred. The two patients filed interrogatories (written questions under oath) asking the psychologist the names of all patients with whom he had intimate relations, the type of relations ranging from touching to sexual intercourse, and where such activity took place. The psychologist refused to answer, citing confidentiality as the reason. The trial court held the psychologist in contempt for his refusal to answer.

The Supreme Court of Texas reversed, stating that such disclosure would violate the confidentiality rights of the psychologist's other patients.[64]

Most state statutes allow limited disclosure of information to the U.S. Secret Service for the protection of public officials. For example, in Illinois disclosure by hospitals may be made to the Secret Service or to Department of Law Enforcement to protect a public official from death or injury. Such information must be limited to the patient's name, address and age, date of admission to or discharge from a facility, and any information that would indicate whether the patient has a history of violence or presents a danger of violence to the person under protection. The information may be used for investigative purposes only.[65]

> The [Mental Health and Developmental Disabilities Confidentiality]
> Act specifically states that it does not prohibit a facility director who
> has reason to believe that a violation of criminal law or other serious
> incident has occurred within a mental health facility from reporting
> such violation or incident and the identity of individuals with personal
> knowledge of the facts related to the violation or incident, to the
> appropriate law enforcement and investigating agencies.[66]

In the course of an investigation "any person with personal knowledge of the incident or the circumstances surrounding the incident may disclose such information to the individuals conducting the investigation." Such information regarding a patient "must be limited solely to information relating to the factual circumstances of the incident."[67] Information may also be furnished to law enforcement officials to determine an individual's eligibility to receive or retain a Firearm Owner's Identification Card.[68]

NOTES

1. Wyatt v. Stickney, 344 F. Supp. 373, 379 (M.D. Ala. 1972), *aff'd. sub. nom* Wyatt v. Aderholt, 503 F.2d 1305 (5th Cir. 1974).

2. JCAH, *Consolidated Standards Manual for Child, Adolescent, and Adult Psychiatric, Alcoholism, and Drug Abuse Facilities* (Chicago: JCAH, 1981 ed.), ¶ 14.2.4.

3. *See* Appendix E, "Treatment Rights."

4. Youngberg v. Romeo, 102 S.Ct. 2452 (1982).

5. R. Emery and B. Ennis, *The Rights of Mental Patients* (New York: Avon Books, 1978), pp. 122–125, citing Donaldson v. O'Connor, 493 F.2d 507 (5th Cir.), *vacated*, 422 U.S. 563 (1975).

6. Commonwealth v. Wiseman, 356 Mass. 251, 249 N.E.2d 610 (1969).

7. *Id.* at 614, n.5.

8. *Id.* at 613.

9. *Id.* at 615.

10. *Id.* at 618.

11. Delan v. CBS, Inc., 445 N.Y.S.2d 898 (1981).

12. *Id.* at 907.

13. *Id.*, citing Anderson v. WROC-TV, 109 Misc. 2d 904, 909, 441 N.Y.S.2d 220 (1981).

14. Delan v. CBS, Inc., *supra* note 11, at 908.

15. JCAH, *supra* note 1, at § 15.2.8.

16. *Id.* at § 15.2.8.2.

17. *Id.* at § 15.2.8.3.

18. *Id.* at § 15.2.8.6.

19. *Id.* at § 15.2.9.

20. *Id.* at § 14.5.

21. *Id.*

22. Mental Health Systems Act of 1980, 94 Stat. 1564, 501(1)(H), (1)(I).

23. *See* Appendix G, "Information and Records Rights."

24. 81 Am. Jur. 2d § 238 (1982).

25. Perry v. Fiumano, 403 N.Y.S.2d 382, 61 A.D.2d 512 (1978).

26. Ill. Ann. Stat., ch. 91–172, § 802(9) (Smith-Hurd Supp. 1982–1983).

27. 81 Am. Jur. 2d § 340 (1982).

28. Gibson v. Commonwealth, 215 Va. 412, 219 S.E.2d 845 *cert. denied*, 425 U.S. 994 (1976).

29. State v. Humphrey, 217 Kan. 352, 537 P.2d 155 (1975).

30. 81 Am. Jur. 2d § 247 (1982).

31. State v. Carter, 383 So.2d 357, S.Ct. La. (1980).

32. People v. Still, 48 A.D.2d 366, 369 N.Y.S.2d 759 (App. Div. 1975).

33. Commonwealth v. Garcia, 478 Pa. 406, 387 A.2d 46 (1978).

34. Ill. Ann. Stat. ch. 91–½, § 810(1) (Smith-Hurd Supp. 1982–1983).

35. *Id.*

36. In re Farrow, 41 N.C. App. 680, 255 S.E.2d 777 (1979).

37. State v. Mayhand, 298 N.C. 418, 259 S.E.2d 231 (1979).

38. In Interest of Westland, 48 Ill. App. 3d 172, 362 N.E. 1153 (1977).

39. State v. Milton, 86 N.M. 639, 526 P.2d 436 (1974).

40. Ill. Ann. Stat., ch. 91–½, § 810(4) (Smith-Hurd Supp. 1982–1983).

41. *Id.* at § 810(3).

42. *Id.* at § 810(5).

43. *Id.* at § 810(6).

44. *Id.* at § 810(7).

45. State v. Fagaide, 85 Wash. 2d 730, 539 P.2d 86 (1975).

46. In re Jackson, 81 Ill. App. 3d 136, 400 N.E.2d 1087 (1980).

47. Ill. Ann. Stat. ch. 91–½, § 809 (Smith-Hurd Supp. 1982–1983). In Missouri it has been held that the privilege cannot be asserted to records by a peer review committee reviewing the qualifications of the therapist. Klinge v. Lutheran Medical Center, 518 S.W.2d 157 (Mo. App. 1975).

48. Ill. Ann. Stat., ch. 91–½, §§ 802(4), (7), 803 (Smith-Hurd Supp. 1982–1983).

49. Am. Jur. 2d § 261 (1982).

50. *Id.* at § 264.

51. *Id.* at § 265.

52. Ga. Code Ann. §§ 88–502.13 (Supp. 1981); *see* Ariz. Rev. Stat. § 36–507(2)(3) (Supp. 1981); Wis. Stat. Ann. § 51.30(3) (d) (Supp. 1981); *see also* 9 State Health Legislation Report 1 (May 1981), pp. 13–23.

53. Fla. Stat. § 394.459(9)(a) (1975).

54. Sullivan v. State, 352 So.2d 1212 (Fla. Dist. Ct. App. 1977).

55. State ex rel. Carroll v. Junker, 79 Wash. 2d 12, 482 P.2d 775 (1971).

56. Doe v.Roe, 400 N.Y.S.2d 668 (N.Y. Sup. Ct. 1977).

57. *Id.* at 671.

58. *Id.*

59. *Id.* at 676.

60. *Id.* at 674, 675.

61. *Id.* at 679.

62. *Id.* at 677.

63. Friedman v. Escalona, No. 75C 4414, N.D. Ill., *dismissed*, May 5, 1976.

64. Ex Parte Abell, 613 S.W.2d 255 (Sup. Ct. of Texas 1981).

65. Ill. Ann. Stat., ch. 91–½, § 812(a) (Smith-Hurd Supp. 1982–1983).

66. *Id.* at § 812(b).

67. *Id.*

68. *Id.*

Chapter 11

Responsibility for the Safety of Patients

Therapists and the hospital staff have a duty to exercise reasonable care to safeguard a patient from any known or reasonably apprehensible danger, including suicide. A breach of this duty occurs when the conduct of the therapist or hospital staff falls below the standard of care provided by the ordinary, reasonable, and prudent professional or hospital acting under the same or similar circumstances in the same or a similar community. Liability of state institutions for the violation of a patient's constitutional right to safety under the federal Civil Rights Act occurs only where the departure from professional judgment has been substantial.

PROTECTION FROM SELF

When a therapist or hospital staff member knows or should know that a patient has suicidal tendencies, reasonable care must be taken to prevent suicide.[1] Some groups, such as alcoholics, schizophrenics, chronically ill older men, medical personnel, and the depressed have a high percentage of suicides. Nevertheless, identifying suicidal individuals within these groups remains very difficult. Unlike taking an x-ray to determine whether a person has a broken leg, there is no definitive test to determine whether a person has suicidal tendencies.

Courts are recognizing the difficulty of predicting and preventing suicide, as well as the problems in the contemporary practice of treating patients with the least restrictive means practicable. They are hesitant to impose liability in suicide or attempted-suicide cases absent a showing of clear negligence in the therapist's (or the hospital's) failure to detect and/or properly treat a patient's suicidal tendencies.[2]

Knowledge of suicidal tendencies is based on threats to commit suicide,[3] past attempts to commit suicide,[4] intentional self-injury,[5] medical diagnosis of suicidal tendencies,[6] and general environmental conditions suggestive of severe depression and potential suicide. Information concerning suicidal tendencies may be contained in psychiatric recommendations, court papers (petitions and certificates in involuntary admission proceedings), interviews with family, friends, and others, and medical records. Suicide cases point out the need for a careful review by professionals of the patient's history, particularly regarding any previous suicide attempts.[7] Where the therapist or hospital staff knows that a patient has actually attempted suicide or where a suicide threat or attempt is considered serious enough to require some precautionary action, the therapist or hospital staff is presumed to have actual knowledge of suicidal tendencies.[8]

In a case where the patient was placed alone in a locked room and subsequently strangled herself using plastic tubing, the court held that the psychiatrists had a duty to exercise reasonable care to safeguard the patient from suicide. The patient had been admitted to the hospital for attempting suicide.[9]

A New York court held a hospital liable for failure to take precautions against a patient's suicide, in spite of its knowledge of the patient's three previous attempts, and the patient's own request to be placed in a locked ward. The hospital had permitted the patient to leave the hospital grounds unaccompanied three days after his request to be restrained, and while he was still depressed. The patient jumped in front of a subway train and was killed. The court found ample evidence that the hospital knew of the patient's suicidal tendencies and that its failure to restrain him properly was the cause of his death.[10]

Recently, mental health professionals and the courts have recognized a strong therapeutic value in maintaining an "open door" policy in the treatment of mentally ill patients. Even in the case of potentially suicidal patients, overly restrictive confinement can be detrimental to the patient's mental health. Thus, mental health institutions and professionals may consider whether the patient is more likely to improve without restrictive confinement; the law will not mandate the use of only those treatment methods that are certain to ward off the danger of the patient's committing suicide.

The therapeutic principle that hospitalized psychiatric patients should be subject to as few physical restraints as possible is generally accepted. Permanent confinement and constant observation have been deemed antitherapeutic and perhaps more likely to evoke suicide than a less restrictive approach.[11] The therapist must balance two considerations: the extent to which restrictive care is necessary to avoid the danger of suicide, and the extent to which such restrictions will be detrimental to recovery. As with all therapeutic decisions, a mistake in judgment resulting in suicide or attempted suicide will not incur liability. The therapist or the mental health institution will incur liability only if treatment prescribed or administered involved acts of malpractice or negligence. Courts tend to accept the view that a nonrestrictive approach to treatment of mental patients is reasonable in light of contemporary psychiatric practice.

A finding of reasonableness, however, is not guaranteed. In a case where the patient escaped from a closed ward and jumped out of a window to his death, the court held that the psychiatric hospital was negligent in having only laminated safety glass in the window through which the patient leaped to his death. The hospital argued that close confinement and restraint were antitherapeutic and that the taking of a calculated risk was necessary to allow the patient to deal with the crisis in his life. By implication, the failure to have boards on windows was one such calculated risk.[12] The court stated:

> The planners of the hospital had to balance risk of patient suicide against the antitherapeutic impact of devices that could prevent suicide only at the cost of reminding patients that they were considered incapable of assuming full responsibility for their own behavior. The jury could not assess the reasonableness of the decision reached without an understanding of the risk of suicide among mental patients, the best methods preventing suicide—whether by physically restraining the suicidal patient or by treating the illness which made him suicidal—and the importance of an open, unrestricted environment for treatment.[13]

The plaintiffs in this case presented no expert testimony on the issue of whether the hospital was negligent in its selection of window glass. Nevertheless, the court found that the hospital had negligently allowed the patient to escape from the closed ward.

A Missouri court found no liability where a patient who was a potential suicide case committed suicide after being placed on an open ward. The court based its decision on testimony that the therapeutic value of an open ward outweighed the risk of suicide.[14] Courts in California and New York have agreed.[15] In New York a court that found the hospital not liable stated:

> The state could not have provided an employee to watch every move made by this unfortunate man during 24 hours of the day. . . . If institutions for the mentally ill are required to take all the precautions contended for in this case, and to be held liable for such delicate mistakes in judgment, patients would be kept in straitjackets or in some other form of confinement which would hardly be conducive to recovery. . . . An ingenious patient harboring a steady purpose to take his own life cannot always be thwarted.[16]

Psychiatrists, as well as hospitals, can be sued for negligence. In one such case, the plaintiff alleged that the negligent failure of two psychiatrists to prescribe proper supervision for the patient caused the patient's death by suicide. The hospital's alleged negligence was its failure to prevent the suicide. The patient had entered the hospital, and the resident who conducted the original examination diagnosed him as psychotic, depressive reaction, with discerned suicidal thoughts. The hospital did not take suicide precautions; it did not place the patient in a locked ward but rather in a double room near an unguarded window. One staff psychiatrist concluded from the patient's suicidal thoughts that he was suffering from an "acute anxiety state" and should be in a locked ward, but no beds were available, so transfer did not occur. Another psychiatrist had concluded, based on a one-hour interview early in the patient's hospitalization, that the patient was not a suicidal risk. The patient jumped from an unboarded window to his death. The court found the psychiatrists diligent and skillful in their efforts and not negligent even though in retrospect their assessments proved wrong. The hospital was free from liability because it had a right to rely on the instructions of the defendant psychiatrists as to what, if any, suicide precautions were necessary.[17]

Most cases involving psychiatrists have been limited to the issues of confinement and taking steps to physically protect the patient, but psychiatrists also could be held liable for prescribing a large quantity of medication for a suicidal patient or permitting such patient to regress so far in treatment that a danger arises that he will attempt suicide.

In one case, a patient was admitted to an Air Force hospital with depression. The depression apparently was a side effect of the drug Reserpine, which he had been taking for high blood pressure. His doctors had ordered that he not leave the psychiatric unit without a staff support escort. On the fourth day of his confinement, the nurses began to allow him to go to specific places in the hospital without an escort. On the fifth day he went to breakfast unescorted and was found dead soon thereafter on the ground below the window of an unsupervised seventh-floor lounge.

After his death, a note was added to his medical chart indicating that two days earlier the doctor's orders had been changed to permit him to leave the ward unescorted. The doctor testified that in fact he had authorized such a change in the patient's status. Nevertheless, the court did not accept the inserted note as a proper medical order, concluding that the doctor had not changed the patient's status and that the staff was negligent for failure to follow security requirements prescribed by the treating physician. The court also found that even if the doctor did change the patient's status, the hospital would still be liable because of the manner in which the psychiatrist changed the patient's status. The psychiatrist's "failure to maintain contemporary notes, orders or other records adequately recording and explaining his action in reclassifying the patient fell below the applicable standard of care."[18]

In Virginia, a prison inmate with a history of severe psychiatric problems is suing the state for physical and psychological injuries he suffered when he castrated himself with a razor in his cell. He alleged the state failed to provide him with medical care and security. The inmate had been transferred to a state mental institution several times, had been placed in "suicide precaution" for several months, and had engaged in self-mutilating behavior on three separate occasions. The inmate's sister and guardian, a psychiatric nurse, had warned prison officials that her brother was on the verge of a psychiatric breakdown. None of this information was entered in his record, and the inmate was allowed to take a safety razor into his cell without supervision.[19]

A Massachusetts federal court held the federal government not liable for the apparent suicide of a Navy recruit who, after having made one unsuccessful suicide attempt, climbed to a rooftop from which he either jumped or fell and died. Navy psychiatrists had diagnosed him as having a depressed neurosis and deemed him unfit for further service. His death occurred while he was awaiting the processing of his medical discharge.[20]

In a case where the patient set fire to herself in an attempt at suicide, the court stated that her assignment by the psychiatrist to a unit where she could have access to smoking materials without limitation and subsequent permission to go unattended about the institution "were medical judgments on his [psychiatrist] part as to the proper balance of freedom and confinement most likely to be therapeutic. . . ." Proof of a breach of this standard, said the court, must be established by expert testimony.[21]

A hospital is liable for the negligence of psychiatric nurses who are employees. Experienced psychiatric nurses should recognize the importance of close supervision of suicidal patients. When a shift is short-staffed, priority must be given to those patients on suicide precautions. Hospitals usually maintain their own policies regarding suicide precautions or close observation. Policies dictate how the staff should behave with a patient on such precaution.[22]

It is clear that hospital personnel must limit access by patients to instruments such as knives and other sharp objects and all items of clothing such as belts and shoelaces.[23] This issue can be complicated. In one case, a person removed a bandage from his own arm and used it to hang himself.[24]

Where nurses and psychiatric aides follow the specific orders of the psychiatrist as to the extent or degree of supervision, they are not negligent "in the absence of any unusual behavior on the part of [the patient] which would give them reason to depart from those orders."[25]

In the case of *State v. Washington Sanitarium and Hospital* a patient had been scheduled for hydrotherapy, but at the appointed time he had wandered off and was playing checkers. The hydrotherapy department took another patient. A short time later, the patient jumped from the sixth floor and killed himself. The plaintiff argued that the failure of the supervising nurse to insist that the patient receive hydrotherapy as scheduled was negligence. The court said that the physician's orders provided that the patient was not to be restrained and that no special attendant was necessary or desirable. There was no indication that the hospital staff had been put on notice that the patient was contemplating suicide. "It was not incumbent upon the nurses and attendants to apply restraints or supervision which the attending physician did not desire, at least in the absence of anything to indicate a change in the patient's condition."[26]

Where a patient's conduct should warn nurses and attendants that the patient may have suicidal tendencies, failure to take action may result in liability. The court in *Mounds Park Hospital v. Von Eye* said that a "hospital has a duty with reference to the nursing and care of its patients and in the performance of these it must exercise ordinary care which must be determined by the circumstances attending each case."[27] The physician in that case had ordered that the patient be "observed closely." The patient left the ward and went to the obstetrics ward where she jumped from a window and was injured.

In *Youngberg v. Romeo*,[28] the U.S. Supreme Court held that involuntarily admitted residents of state mental retardation institutions have a constitutional right to personal security.[29] The court seems to have adopted an extremely restrictive standard for violation of this right. The high court said that liability does exist where there is "substantial departure" from accepted professional judgment.[30] The result of this standard, one commentator has suggested, is that patients filing actions under the Civil Rights Act against state institutions will prevail only in the "most egregious violations."[31]

Nevertheless, a state hospital in Delaware[32] was found liable for the suicide of an involuntarily admitted patient who had made several suicide attempts. The patient was found dead from self-induced suffocation in the closet of his room one week after his admission. The court found that under *Romeo*, the hospital had a constitutional duty to provide for the safety of the patient unless "their failure to do so can be justified on the basis of accepted professional judgment, practice or standards."[33]

Mental health professionals also have a duty to protect patients from unintentional harm to themselves. In New York two residents of a New York drug rehabilitation center drank printing fluid; one patient died and the other was blinded. The court held that the hospital should have prevented access to the fluid. The court stated that although the patients had some realization of danger, they could not resist the impulse to drink the fluid.[34]

PROTECTION FROM OTHERS

Hospitals have a duty to protect patients from foreseeable harm from others such as hospital employees, other patients, and even unrelated third parties. In a New York case, a patient sued the state hospital when she was raped by a male technician who was giving her an EEG. The hospital argued that because the conduct was outside the scope of employment of the employee, it could not be held liable. The court disagreed, holding that the hospital was liable for failure to comply with its own rule that a female patient not be left alone with a male under those circumstances. "The conduct complained of was completely foreseeable. Its foreseeability undoubtedly was one of the very reasons for the requirement that female patients be accompanied by a female staff member."[35]

In Colorado, a female patient filed suit against a state hospital for sexual assault by a male patient. She alleged that state officials had failed to secure an environment free from physical and mental abuse. She was "attacked and kissed and 'felt up' without her consent while both persons were fully clothed." While acknowledging that mental hospitals owe a duty to protect patients from injury by another patient,[36] the court stated that the patient must allege "more than an isolated event of unconsented touching" to have a valid claim under the Civil Rights Act. In addition, the defendants not only had no part in producing a pattern of sexual assaults, but they had also prosecuted the assailant and acted in a reasonable manner to prevent future harm.[37]

A Missouri court awarded damages to a teen-age patient who had been placed on an open ward containing both sexes. Patients were free to leave their rooms and meet in hallways and lounges. The patient had sexual relations with male patients and claimed deterioration of her mental condition. The court instructed the jury that the hospital's conduct should be measured against the skill and learning ordinarily used under the same or similar circumstances by other hospitals.[38]

In Louisiana, a court held a state hospital liable for the death of a mentally retarded resident who, while returning records to a storage area, was hit by a drunken driver. The hospital breached its duty to supervise by failing to have someone accompany the resident to the storage area. The court awarded $35,000 to the resident's father.[39]

NOTES

1. Pietrucha v. Grant Hospital, 447 F.2d 1029, 1033 (7th Cir. 1971); Vistica v. Presbyterian Hospital and Medical Center, 67 Cal. 2d 465, 469, 432 P.2d 193, 196 (1976); Slater v. Missionary Sisters of the Sacred Heart, 20 Ill. App. 3d 464, 314 N.E.2d 715 (1974). *See also* Note, "Custodial Suicide Cases: An Analytical Approach to Determine Liability for Wrongful Death," *Boston U. L. Rev.* 62 (1982):177.

2. Gregory v. Robinson, 338 S.W.2d 88 (Mo. 1960); Baker v. United States, 226 F. Supp. 129 (S.D. Iowa 1964) *aff'd*, 343 F.2d 222 (8th Cir. 1965); Meier v. Ross General Hospital, 69 Cal. 2d 420, 445 P.2d 519, 71 Cal. Rptr. 903 (1968) (*en banc*); Hirsh v. State, 8 N.Y.2d 125, 168 N.E.2d 372, 202 N.Y.S.2d 296 (1960); Lucy Webb Hayes National Training School for Deaconesses and Missionaries v. Perotti, 419 F.2d 704 (D.C. Cir. 1969); Dimitrijevic v. Chicago Wesley Memorial Hospital, 92 Ill. App. 2d 265, 236 N.E.2d 309 (1968).

3. Maricopa County v. Cowart, 106 Ariz. 69, 70, 471 P.2d 265, 266 (1970); City of Belen v. Harrell, 93 N.M. 601, 602, 603 P.2d 711, 719 (1979); McBride v. State, 52 Misc.2d 880, 884, 277 N.Y.S.2d 80, 85 (Ct. Cl. 1967), *aff'd*, 30 A.D.2d 1025, 294 N.Y.S.2d 265 (App. Div. 1968).

4. Logue v. United States, 334 F.Supp. 322, 324 (S.D. Tex. 1971), *revd. on other grounds*, 459 F.2d 408 (5th Cir 1972), *vacated*, 412 U.S. 521 (1973); Maricopa County, *supra* note 3 at 471 P.2d 266; Johnson v. Grant Hospital, 32 Ohio St. 2d 169 291 N.E.2d 440 (1972); Broussard v. State, 356 So.2d 94, 95 (La. Ct. App.), *cert. denied*, 358 So. 2d 639 (La. 1978).

5. Logue v. United States, *supra* note 4; McBride v. State, *supra* note 3; Johnson v. Grant Hospital, *supra* note 4.

6. Pietrucha v. Grant Hospital, *supra* note 1, at 1030, 1031; Meier v. Ross General Hospital, *supra* note 2, at 522–523 (1968); Vistica v. Presbyterian Hospital and Medical Center, *supra* note 1, at 432 P.2d at 194.

7. Dinnerstein v. United States, 486 F.2d 34 (2d Cir. 1973); Pietrucha v. Grant Hospital, *supra* note 1; Cohen v. State, 51 A.D.2d 494, 382 N.Y.S.2d 128 (N.Y. App. Div. 1976); Patrick v. Hillside Hospital, 45 A.D.2d 708; 356 N.Y.S.2d 105 (N.Y. App. Div. 1974); *aff'd mem.*, 36 N.Y.2d 736, 368 N.Y.S.2d 161 (1965); Kent & Whitaker, 58 Wash. 2d 569; 364 P.2d 556 (1961). *Cf.* Carling v. State, 30 A.D.2d 987, 294 N.Y.S.2d 30 (N.Y. App. Div. 1968).

8. Logue v. United States, *supra* note 4, at 324; Broussard v. State, *supra* note 4, at 95.

9. Kent v. Whitaker, 58 Wash. 2d 569, 364 P.2d 556 (1961).

10. Comiskey v. New York, 71 A.D.2d 699, 418 N.Y.S.2d 233 (N.Y. App. Div. 1979).

11. Lucy Webb Hayes National Training School for Deaconesses and Missionaries v. Perotti, *supra* note 2, at 707–708.

12. *Id.*

13. *Id.* at 709.

14. Gregory v. Robinson, *supra* note 2.

15. Hirsh v. State, *supra* note 2. Meier v. Ross General Hospital, *supra* note 2.

16. Hirsh v. State, *supra* note 2, at 168 N.E.2d 372, 373.

17. Dimitrijevic v. Chicago Wesley Memorial Hospital, *supra* note 2.

18. Abille v. United States, 482 F.2d 703 (N.D. Cal. 1980).

19. Moe v. Virginia Department of Corrections, No. 80311 (E.D. Va., filed April 23, 1980), discussed in 4 *Mental Disability L. Rep.* (ABA) 4 (1980):251.

20. Becton v. United States, 489 F. Supp. 134 (D. Mass. 1980).

21. Payne v. Milwaukee Sanitarium Foundation, Inc., 81 Wis.2d 264, 260 N.W.2d 386, 391 (1977).

22. Pamela D. Andrade and John C. Andrade, "Malpractice of Psychiatric Nurse," POF 2d 26 (1981):393.

23. Dezort v. Village of Hinsdale, 35 Ill. App. 3d 703, 342 N.E.2d 468 (1976), *appeal following reconsideration*, 77 Ill. App. 3d 775, 396 N.E.2d 855 (1979); City of Belen v. Harrell, 93 N.M. 601, 603 P.2d 711 (1979).

24. Logue v. United States, *supra* note 4.

25. *Id.* State v. Washington Sanitarium and Hospital, 233 Md. 554, 165 A.2d 764 (1960).

26. *Id.* at 165 A.2d 767, 766 (1960).

27. Mounds Park Hospital v. Von Eye, 245 F.2d 756, 763 (8th Cir. 1957).

28. 73 L. Ed.2d 28 (1982).

29. *Id.* at 37.

30. *Id.* at 40.

31. "Developments in Mental Disability Law in 1982," *Clearinghouse Review* 16 (Jan. 1983):815, 816.

32. Gann v. Delaware State Hospital, 543 F. Supp. 268 (D.Del. 1982).

33. *Id.*

34. Padula v. New York, 48 N.Y.2d 366 (1979).

35. Cucalon v. New York, 103 Misc. 2d 808, 427 N.Y.S.2d 149 (N.Y. Ct. Cl. 1980).

36. Knight v. Colorado, 496 F. Supp. 799 (D. Colo. 1980).

37. *Id.*

38. M.W. v. Jewish Hospital Association of St. Louis, 637 S.W.2d 74 (Mo. Ct. App. 1982).

39. Daniels v. Conn, 378 So.2d 451 (La. Ct. App. 1979).

Chapter 12

Premature Discharge and Elopement

PREMATURE DISCHARGE

Nothing generates more public anger than the release of a dangerous patient who kills or seriously injures another person. In Alabama, a jury returned a verdict of $25 million against state mental health officials for the release of a violence-prone patient who is alleged to have killed the brother of the plaintiff. The patient had been institutionalized in the past following an earlier killing. The patient stabbed the plaintiff's brother to death on the street. The jury stated that it granted the plaintiff the full amount of damages sought in the hope of sending a message across the state and nation.[1]

Therapists have a duty to use reasonable care in the release of patients. They may be liable for the release of a patient if the decision deviates from professional standards (or is one that a reasonably prudent therapist would not have made under the same or similar circumstances), and such release results in the proximate cause of injury to another person or to the patient.[2] It is not sufficient merely to show that the released patient suffered from a mental illness[3] or that the therapist made an honest error in judgment.[4] Most of the reported cases involve liability of hospitals for the acts of their employees. In many cases the discharge or release may meet professional standards, but failure to provide appropriate follow-up outpatient care may deviate from professional standards.

Most often, the decision to release involves a consideration by therapists of whether a person is dangerous to himself or herself[5] or to others. This involves a thorough evaluation, including a careful review of the patient's records. Similarly, warnings from other persons such as relatives, friends, judges, and law enforcement officers may place a mental health professional on notice as to the dangerousness of a patient being considered for release.[6] In addition to the consideration of dangerousness, courts have recognized that certain calculated risks must be taken in the rehabilitation of a patient. It cannot be known with absolute certainty that a patient will not commit a dangerous act upon release, but home visits and conditional releases are a necessary part of the rehabilitative process.[7]

In Georgia, the children of a patient filed a wrongful death action against a hospital alleging malpractice in a physician's temporary release of their father, who subsequently killed his wife. The children agreed that their mother's murder was reasonably foreseeable by the institution, that their mother's death was proximately caused by the hospital's lack of reasonable care in allowing their father to leave the hospital, and that the hospital failed to exercise proper control over their father's freedom to leave. The hospital argued that Georgia law requires a physician-patient relationship as an element of a malpractice action. The court stated that the duty did not arise out of a "consensual transaction." "The legal duty in this case arises out of the general duty one owes to all the world not to subject them to an unreasonable risk of harm."[8]

A federal court in Illinois held the Veterans' Administration liable for the negligent release of a patient and improper follow-up. The patient had a history of hospitalization and violent behavior. In 1972 he had been committed after a court found him not guilty of murder by reason of insanity. In 1976, he was released while still suffering from "severe paranoid schizophrenia," with no follow-up. Several months later a friend of the patient informed the hospital psychiatrist that the patient was becoming increasingly belligerent. The psychiatrist advised the friend to hospitalize the patient. The next day—five months after his release—the patient killed an O'Hare airport security guard.[9]

The court found the Veterans' Administration hospital liable for deviation from standards of the "psychiatric community as guided by common sense and sound judgment" while taking "into account the difficulty of definitive diagnosis." The court concluded that the psychiatric examination and preparation of the medical records had been faulty and that the patient should not have been released "without first conducting a complete home investigation and ordering and establishing a plan for outpatient follow up care." The need for follow-up was established by the testimony of several psychiatrists, although two psychiatrists testified that such follow-up was unnecessary based on the information in the hospital records at the time. Without intensive follow-up, it was foreseeable that, with the stresses of community life, the patient might "suffer a recurrence of active symptoms."[10]

In California, a public institution released a patient on condition that he receive outpatient treatment and periodically report to the court. His condition deteriorated, and he stopped outpatient treatment. The center did not report this to the court. A month later he attempted to rob a bank, wounding a person who subsequently filed an action alleging the state and county were negligent. Based on a California statute[11] that "shields public entities from all direct and vicarious liability for injury proximately caused by a patient of a mental institution except for specific malpractice situations "[12] the court found no liability.

In South Carolina, a hospital gave a man an afternoon pass so that he could attend to some personal business with his mother. The man did not return to the hospital. The hospital had not thought him to be suicidal or homicidal. Five weeks later, he murdered his young daughter. The court, stressing the difficulties of predicting a psychiatric episode, held that the hospital was not liable because there was no causal connection between the man's departure and the death of his daughter.[13]

In New York, an educable mentally retarded patient burned down a barn on a dairy farm where he had been sent to work on convalescent leave. Because the patient's record had shown no propensity toward pyromania and because he had been responding well to treatment, release for convalescent leave did not fall below professional standards.[14] In a similar case in Michigan, state officials who had no occasion to know that a mentally retarded worker had fire-setting tendencies were held not liable when the worker set fire to a farmer's barn. The worker was on work-convalescent status in preparation for possible release from the state hospital.[15]

In North Dakota, a government hospital released a man for work leave despite the fact that the local mental health board, local doctors, the man's wife, a local judge, and others had warned the psychiatrist that the patient was dangerous. The patient subsequently killed his wife. The administrator of the wife's estate was allowed to recover.[16]

A patient was released from a government nursing home after a cursory and inadequate psychiatric examination. The patient, an army officer, returned to the nursing home and shot a student nurse and two guards. The court held that if the facts were proved, liability could be imposed.[17]

In a case involving a military hospital, a patient was admitted for two months after having attacked his wife with a crowbar. Hospital psychiatrists found the patient maladjusted, anxious, and depressed. He was released and returned to work as an airman without any restrictions on his activities. Two weeks later he withdrew a .45 automatic from the armory and shot his wife. The court found liability and granted damages to the wife's father because the patient's record was incomplete. The treating psychiatrist had failed to include information regarding the patient's first attack on his wife; thus it was not available to the psychiatrist who authorized his release.[18]

In Minnesota, a patient in a state hospital took a passkey from a supervisor's unlocked office and let himself out of the hospital. He set fire to a lumberyard, causing extensive damage. The hospital's policy was to account for patients on locked wards every 30 minutes. The court held the state liable (the state had waived sovereign immunity up to $75,000), stating that under Minnesota law, liability did not depend on whether the hospital could foresee the patient's pyromaniacal tendencies. It was enough to establish a foreseeable risk of harm, and the patient had demonstrated a tendency to engage in violent acts.[19]

In South Carolina, a government hospital released a patient who subsequently shot and killed a man. The release had been made without an adequate review of the patient's history of violence and without notification to law enforcement authorities who had made a specific request. The court stated that "a hospital cannot be charged with the responsibility of insuring the physical safety of the public from all harmful acts committed by patients who have been discharged." The court also said that "any claim of negligence against the hospital must be considered in light of the elusive qualities of mental disorders and the likelihood that honest errors in judgment will, from time to time occur."[20]

Nevertheless, the court found the hospital liable and concluded:

> . . . in light of [the patient's] . . . past history of hostile behavior and chronic alcoholism, it was entirely foreseeable that if released without supervision and left to his own devices, [he] . . . might have become intoxicated after he left the hospital and initiate an argument with a stranger. It was foreseeable, too, that the victim of such unprovoked hostility might attempt to repel [the patient's] . . . aggressive overtures by pushing [him] . . . away. Finally in light of [his] . . . history of violence, it was entirely foreseeable that he might make a violent, even fatal attack upon another.[21]

The court also stated that failure to notify the sheriff, who would have taken custody of the patient for pending charges, was a substantial factor in the death.

In an unreported New York case, a private psychiatrist discharged a patient from a private hospital. The patient, while in a conference with his estranged wife and her lawyer, attacked and bit off the nose of the lawyer. The lawyer recovered a large judgment, apparently because the patient was dangerous and likely to injure someone if not supervised.[22]

In Ohio, a state institution released a patient who shot and killed a man three months later. The victim's widow filed suit alleging that the hospital staff was negligent in failing to hospitalize the patient involuntarily. The court held that: (1) a state hospital has a duty toward third persons not to release a dangerous mental patient unreasonably; and (2) mental hospitals and doctors are not generally under a legal duty to third persons for decisions not to admit or readmit a patient because lay people are the principal source of information in the determination of whom to commit.[23] An earlier Ohio case held that a two-year gap barred liability.[24]

In Pennsylvania, an apartment house hired a former state hospital patient as a maintenance man. He sexually assaulted a tenant who recovered $175,000 from the apartment house owners. The apartment house owners filed an indemnity action against the hospital and some of its doctors.[25] The court dismissed this action based on sovereign immunity, but because the doctrine of sovereign immunity was later abolished the case was reinstated.[26]

In some states—Illinois, for example—statutory immunity exists for state-employed psychiatrists and psychologists who recommend the release of criminally insane persons where such persons subsequently commit other violent felonies.[27] However, it has been argued that such immunity should be abolished.[28]

In an Illinois case, a federal court of appeals held that state officials had no enforceable duty to protect the public under the Civil Rights Act, where no constitutional right or federal statute was violated. The complaint alleged that the patient was dangerous when the hospital released him and that the state acted recklessly in releasing him. The court noted that the suit could be filed in state court under Illinois common law.[29]

ELOPEMENT

The liability to third parties for injury inflicted by dangerous patients who escape is closely related in legal concept to a discharge or release that is negligence or malpractice. An Indiana case illustrates this close relationship. A patient escaped from an Indiana state institution and kidnapped and killed a child in Illinois. The complaint alleged that hospital personnel knew or should have known that the patient "was a criminal sexual deviant dangerous to the community," that he was in the custody of the state, that he was released or escaped from the custody of the state, and that the release or escape was negligence and the direct or proximate cause of the child's death.[30]

The court held that under Indiana law, "the state is under a duty to exercise reasonable care in restraining and controlling dangerous persons committed to its custody so that they will not have the opportunity to inflict foreseeable injury upon others. . . . This is the same duty as would apply to a private person or private institution caring for a mentally ill person." The court also cited the *Restatement of Torts*: "One who takes charge of a third party whom he knows or should know to be likely to cause bodily harm to others if not controlled is under a duty to exercise reasonable care to control the third person to prevent him from doing such harm."[31]

Applying the doctrine of *res ipsa loquitur*, the court also held that the parents of the victim need only show that the patient had escaped; the hospital then has the burden of showing that the escape was not due to its negligence. No immunity protected Indiana in this situation.[32]

In California, a former inpatient of a state hospital, who was on an unauthorized leave of absence, kidnapped and sexually abused a mother and her son. The court held the state hospital immune from liability based on statutory immunity, but stated that liability may be imposed on certain named employees.[33]

NOTES

1. *Chicago Tribune*, Nov. 10, 1982, sec. 1, page 18.

2. "Negligence—Release of Mental Patient," 38 A.L.R.3d 699 (1971).

3. Higgins v. State, 265 N.Y.S.2d 254 (1965).

4. St. George v. State, 127 N.Y.S.2d 147, *aff'd*, 308 N.Y. 681, 124 N.E.2d 320 (1954).

5. For a discussion of patients who were released and committed suicide, *see* Chapter 9.

6. For other factors to be considered when assessing whether a person is dangerous, *see* Chapter 3.

7. Eanes v. U.S., 407 F.2d 823 (4th Cir. 1969); Seavy v. State, 250 N.Y.S.2d 877 (1964), *aff'd*, 216 N.E.2d 613, 269 N.Y.S.2d 455 (1966).

8. The Bradley Center, Inc. v. Wessner, 250 Ga. 199, 296 S.E.2d 693 (1982).

9. Valenti v. United States, No. 78 C 5198 (N.D. Ill. July 3, 1982), *reported*, 6 *Mental Disability L. Reptr.* 387, 888 (1982).

10. *Id.*

11. Cal. Govt. Code, §§ 815.2, 855.8.

12. Guess v. California, 157 Cal. Rptr. 618 (Cal. Ct. App. 1979).

13. Ellis v. United States, 484 F. Supp. 4 (D. S.C. 1978).

14. Seavy v. State, *supra* note 7.

15. Knight v. Michigan, 297 N.W.2d 889 (Mich. Ct. App. 1980).

16. Merchants Nat'l. Bank and Trust Co. v. United States, 272 F. Supp. 409 (D.C. N.D. 1967).

17. Fair v. United States, 234 F.2d 288 (5th Cir. 1956).

18. Underwood v. United States, 356 F.2d 92 (5th Cir. 1966); *see also* Higgins v. State, *supra* note 3.

19. Rum River Lumber Co. v. Minnesota, 282 N.W.2d 882 (Minn. 1979).

20. Williams v. United States, 450 F.Supp. 1040, 1044 (D.C. S.C. 1978).

21. *Id.* at 1046.

22. Ronald J. Cohen, *Malpractice* (New York: The Free Press, 1979), p. 213.

23. Leverett v. Ohio, 399 N.E.2d 106 (Ohio Ct. App. 1978).

24. Harris v. Ohio, 358 N.E.2d 639 (Ohio Ct. Claims 1976).

25. Heifetz v. Philadelphia State Hospital, 393 A.2d 1160 (Pa. 1978).

26. Heifetz v. Philadelphia State Hospital, No. 3896, Jan. Term 1979 (Pa. Ct. C.P. Nov. 26, 1979).

27. Ill. Rev. Stat., ch. 85, § 6–107(a) (Smith-Hurd Supp. 1982–1983).

28. John Palincsar, "Should We Allow Tort Liability for State Employed Psychotherapists Who Recommend the Release of Criminally Insane Persons? " *Chicago Bar Record* (July/Aug. 1980):37.

29. Bowers v. DeVito, 686 F.2d 616 (7th Cir. 1982).

30. Maroon v. Indiana Department of Mental Health, 411 N.E.2d 404 (Ind. Ct. App. 1980).

31. *Id.* at 411.

32. *Id.*

33. Buford v. California, 164 Cal. Rptr. 264 (Cal. Ct. App. 1980).

Part V

Expert Witnesses

Chapter 13

Expert Witnesses

Psychiatrists and psychologists testify as expert witnesses in a variety of legal proceedings. Most commonly, they appear in involuntary hospitalization proceedings. They also appear as experts in other civil proceedings that determine whether persons are competent to manage their own person or estate (guardianship), are fit parents (custody), have the capacity to make a will, can transfer property or designate a beneficiary on an insurance policy, are disabled for purposes of Social Security disability benefits, or are entitled to special education. Psychiatrists, psychologists, and psychiatric nurses testify as experts in malpractice cases on the professional standards of care, deviations from such standards, and the extent of injuries suffered by patients. In the criminal area, they render opinions in proceedings to determine whether defendants are fit to stand trial, are responsible for their actions (insanity), or are treatable under habitual sexual offender acts.

EXPERT WITNESS DEFINED

The judge or jurors hearing a case decide questions involving matters of common knowledge and experience based on concrete facts that are derived from the testimony of witnesses, documentary evidence (e.g., medical records), and physical evidence (e.g., EEG results). They exercise personal judgment and reasoning powers without the assistance of expert opinion.[1] Normally, a witness is not allowed to give an opinion regarding matters that require no special knowledge or training.[2]

Where the judge or jurors need help to understand questions that inexperienced persons are not likely to decide correctly, an expert is called to testify.[3] Experts occupy the same position as other witnesses, except that within certain limits, they possess a superior knowledge, which enables them to understand, as one without special knowledge could not, what they have observed or the significance of certain facts. An "expert" is a person qualified by actual experience or careful study that enables him or her to form a definite opinion respecting a division of science, a branch of law, or a department of trade about which persons having no particular training or study cannot form accurate opinions or deduce direct conclusions.[4]

One court defined the expert witness as follows:

> An observer is qualified to testify because he has firsthand knowledge which the jury does not have of the situation or transaction at issue. The expert has something different to contribute. This is a power to draw inferences from the facts which a jury would not be competent to draw. To warrant the use of expert testimony, then, two elements are required. First, the subject of the inference must be so distinctively related to some science, profession, business or occupation as to be beyond the ken of the average layman, and second, the witness must have such skill, knowledge or experience in that field or calling as to make it appear that his opinion or inference will probably aid the trier in his search for truth. The knowledge may in some fields be derived from reading alone, in some from practice alone, or as is more commonly the case, from both.[5]

The Federal Rules of Evidence primarily provide three possible sources of opinion testimony by experts. They are: (1) opinions based on a witness' firsthand observation; (2) opinions based on the expert's having attended the trial and heard the testimony establishing the facts; and (3) opinions of the expert based on data presented and reviewed outside of court and other than by the expert's own perception.[6]

QUALIFICATIONS OF EXPERT WITNESSES

One court, which held that "some psychologists are qualified to render expert opinion in the field of mental disorders,"[7] analyzed the qualifications necessary for expert witnesses generally, and psychologists specifically, in this way:

> The test . . . is whether the opinion offered will be likely to aid the trier in the search for truth. In light of that purpose, it is hardly surprising that courts do not exclude all but the very best kind of witness. . . . The general rule is that "anyone who is shown to have special knowledge and skill in diagnosing and treating human ailments is qualified to testify as an expert if his learning and training show that he is qualified to give an opinion on the particular question at issue.
> "It is not essential that the witness be a medical practitioner." . . .
> Thus, nonmedical witnesses who have had experience in electrical

work may testify to the effects of electrical shock upon the human body. . . . Optometrists, whose training includes instruction in the symptoms of certain eye diseases, may testify to the presence of cataract discovered in the course of fitting glasses . . . and to the effect of a scar upon vision. . . . A toxicologist has been permitted to testify to the effect of oxalic acid, a poison, upon the human eye. . . . The kinds of witnesses whose opinions courts have received, even though they lacked medical training and would not be permitted by law to treat the condition they describe, are legion. The principle to be distilled from the cases is plain: if experience or training enables a proffered expert witness to form an opinion which would aid the jury, in the absence of some countervailing consideration, his testimony will be received. Suggesting the diagnostic category into which an accused's condition fits, and relating it to his past behavior, require skill far in excess of that possessed by laymen. Lest the jury be misled into relying on opinions which are not based upon relevant learning and experience, we must examine the reality behind the title "psychologist." Many psychologists may not qualify to testify concerning mental disease or defect. Their training and experience may not provide an adequate basis for their testimony. Some psychologists, for example, teach and engage in theoretical research in fields unrelated to the diagnosis and treatment of mental disease. . . . Such experience does not ordinarily provide the skill essential to offer expert testimony concerning mental disorders. . . .

On the other hand, the Ph.D. in Clinical Psychology involves some—and often much—training and experience in the diagnosis and treatment of mental disorders. . . . [M]any clinical psychologists administer and interpret diagnostic tests which elicit the patient's intellectual level, defenses, personality structure, attitudes, feelings, thought, and perceptual processes. . . . In many institutions and clinics their reports, which regularly include opinions concerning the presence or absence of mental disease or defect, are important aids to psychiatrists who customarily have the final responsibility for diagnosis. Some psychologists, moreover, regularly administer psychotherapy and related non-organic therapies in the treatment of certain types of mental disorders.

The determination of a psychologist's competence to render an expert opinion based on his findings as to the presence or absence of mental disease or defect must depend upon the nature and extent of his knowledge. It does not depend upon his claim to the title "psychologist." And that determination, after hearing, must be left in each case to the traditional discretion of the trial court subject to appellate review.

* * *

. . . We hold only that the lack of a medical degree and the lesser degree of responsibility for patient care which mental hospitals usually assign to psychologists, are not automatic disqualifications. Where relevant, these matters may be shown to affect the weight of their testimony, even though it be admitted in evidence. The critical factor in respect to admissibility is the actual experience of the witness and the probable probative value of his opinion. The trial judge should make a finding in respect to the individual qualifications of each challenged expert. Qualifications to express an opinion on a given topic are to be decided by the judge alone. The weight to be given an expert opinion admitted in evidence by the judge is exclusively for the jury. They should be so instructed.[8]

In general, psychiatrists, psychiatric nurses, and clinical psychologists establish their qualifications to testify by a showing of their education, training, subsequent learning, and experience related to the subject upon which an opinion is needed. This may include a description of articles and books written, licensure, and certification.

Psychiatrists

Psychiatrists are qualified as expert witnesses by their M.D. degrees. Standing alone, however, such a credential may result in little weight being given the opinion. Generally, psychiatrists testifying as experts are certified by the American Board of Psychiatry and Neurology or the American Board of Forensic Psychiatry. Experience that might enhance a psychiatrist's qualifications depends on the issues in the case. For example, in a malpractice case, the experience of a testifying psychiatrist may include: being chairman of a department of psychiatry in a hospital or a professor of psychiatry at a medical school; participation in peer review; quality assurance or risk management activities of a hospital;[9] or participation in the drafting of model standards by the American Psychiatric Association for a particular treatment.

Clinical Psychologists

A clinical psychologist holding a Ph.D. is generally held qualified by courts to testify as an expert witness.[10] Some courts have held a master's degree with extensive experience sufficient. For example, in California, a clinical psychologist with a master's degree and nine years' experience in the state hospital system was held qualified to testify on issues of sanity.[11]

In Virginia, a court excluded a witness who had a master's degree in counseling psychology but who was neither certified nor a clinical psychologist and had not testified as an expert witness before. He had counseled the defendant as a minister in a pastoral relationship rather than as a psychologist and had not conducted any psychological tests on the defendant.[12] Normally, a psychologist with only a bachelor's degree is held not qualified.[13] A federal court held that a professor of economics who was certified as a psychoanalyst by an institute and who had treated people for a number of years was not qualified to testify as an expert because he had no medical training.[14]

Some states have certification statutes that generally prohibit use of the terms "psychologist" and "psychological services." Other states have licensing acts that define the practice of psychology and limit such practice to those who possess a license.[15]

Some states continue to limit the testimony of psychologists. For instance, Maryland courts limit such testimony to interpretations of psychological tests and exclude testimony as to causes of psychological deficiencies.[16] In a murder prosecution in Illinois, a psychologist's opinion as to the defendant's limited mental ability and as to the results of tests performed were held properly excluded. The court stated that only a qualified psychiatrist could give an opinion as to the sanity of the defendant.[17] A Louisiana court held that an unlicensed practicing psychologist was unqualified to testify as an expert at a murder trial as to the sanity of the defendant at the time of the crime, although he could testify concerning the psychological test he had given the defendant and as to other facts within his special competence.[18]

In addition to qualifications and the kinds of cases in which a psychologist can give expert testimony, questions have been raised to the social status of the psychologist in the courtroom.[19] Judges and juries tend to think of psychologists as second-class experts when compared to medical experts.[20] Thus, when possible, attorneys frequently engage psychiatrists rather than psychologists on the theory that psychiatrists' testimony will be given more weight.

Psychiatric Nurses

In malpractice actions, nurses may testify as expert witnesses.[21] In a Connecticut case three psychiatric nurses gave their opinions as experts to establish the standard of care where a patient was placed in seclusion. The qualifications of those nurses, as described to the court, demonstrate the types of experience and training that make nurses acceptable experts. The qualifications of the first nurse testifying were:

. . . Registered Nurse, is chairman of the Psychiatric Mental Health Nursing Program at the Yale School of Nursing. From 1974 through 1977 she held the position of clinical specialist and assistant supervisor of the department of psychiatric nursing at Yale-New Haven Hospital, together with being an instructor of psychiatric nursing at the Yale University School of Nursing. In January of 1977 she had the responsibility for making sure that the psychiatric standard of care was being adhered to at the Yale-New Haven Hospital, and was responsible for the in-service education of the psychiatric nursing staff and the direct supervision of the nursing staff at the psychiatric unit. Since July 1978, she has been assistant professor in psychiatric nursing at the Yale School of Nursing, which has trained the present directors of psychiatric nursing at Waterbury Hospital, Griffin Hospital, Middlesex Memorial Hospital and Park City Hospital, in what is known as the "Yale Model." She testified that she was familiar with the "Yale Model" in January of 1976. Previous testimony in the case indicated that the defendant relied on the "Yale Model" for its standard of care for nurses.

The qualifications of the second nurse testifying were:

. . . Registered Nurse, is the supervisor of nursing for the department of psychiatry at St. Raphael's Hospital. She is the chairman of the General Hospital Psychiatric Nurse Managers Group, which is a group of nursing supervisors throughout the state of Connecticut who are concerned with the proper standard of care for psychiatric nursing in the state. She testified that she had personal knowledge of the care, skill and diligence ordinarily possessed and exercised by registered nurses, licensed practical nurses, and psychiatric technicians in the care of psychiatric patients in psychiatric units at general hospitals in the state of Connecticut as of January of 1976.

The qualifications of the third nurse testifying were:

. . . Registered Nurse, is a licensed nurse in the state of Connecticut. She completed her nursing program at the City University of New York and obtained her master's degree in psychiatric nursing from Yale University School of Nursing in 1972. She later became supervisor of psychiatric nursing at the Yale-New Haven Hospital and was on the faculty of the Yale School of Nursing and the Yale School of Medicine. She established the general psychiatric nursing procedures and policies for the opening of the psychiatric unit at Yale-New Haven Hospital, which policies are still in effect. She is presently the director of nursing and assistant director of the hospital for clinical services at the Western Psychiatric Institute and Clinic in Pittsburgh, Pennsylvania, a 120-bed hospital affiliated with the University of Pittsburgh School of Medicine, department of psychiatry. She testified that she was aware of the standard of care, skill and diligence ordinarily possessed and exercised by nurses, licensed practical nurses, and psychiatric technicians in Connecticut as of January of 1976 and by general hospital psychiatric units. She gained this familiarity because she spent six years in Connecticut working in psychiatric nursing and has maintained professional contact with psychiatric nurses still working in Connecticut in various capacities, as well as an awareness of the national standard of care in reference to nurses in general hospitals.[22]

VALIDITY AND RELIABILITY OF PSYCHIATRIC AND PSYCHOLOGICAL OPINIONS

The courts and others are raising doubts concerning the validity and reliability of psychiatric and psychological expert opinions. In 1967, Judge David L. Bazelon, former Chief Judge, U.S. Court of Appeals, District of Columbia, after proposing an instruction to be given to the expert witnesses in cases involving the insanity defense, stated:

> It may be that this instruction will not significantly improve the adjudication of criminal responsibility. Then we may be forced to consider an absolute prohibition on the use of conclusionary legal labels. Or it may be that psychiatry and the other social and behavioral sciences cannot provide sufficient data relevant to a determination of criminal responsibility no matter what the rules of evidence are. If so, we may be forced to eliminate the insanity defense altogether or refashion it in a way which is not tied so tightly to the medical model.[23]

In 1973, the same court, in considering the diagnosis of mental disorders and the prediction of dangerousness in involuntary admission proceedings, stated that psychiatric testimony "is far from satisfactory" and "has never been characterized by a high degree of accuracy."[24] In 1975, Chief Justice Burger stated in his concurring opinion in *O'Connor v. Donaldson* that, "The Court appropriately takes notice of the uncertainties of psychiatric diagnosis and therapy and the reported cases are replete with evidence of the divergence of medical opinion in this vexing area."[25] He also said, "There can be little responsible debate regarding the uncertainty of diagnosis in this field and the tentativeness of professional judgment."[26]

In discussing psychiatric evaluations the California Supreme Court stated:

> The assumption is that predictive judgments are truly valid and that the probability of error in such judgments is significantly less than probability of error in judgment determining that specific past events occurred. As sometimes happens to our most cherished preconceptions reality is otherwise. In the light of recent studies, it is no longer a

heresy to question the reliability of psychiatric predictions. Psychiatrists themselves would be the first to admit that however desirable an infallible crystal ball might be, it is not among the tools of their profession. It must be conceded that psychiatrists still experience considerable diagnosing difficulty in confidently and accurately diagnosing mental illness. Yet those difficulties are multiplied when the psychiatrists venture from diagnosis to prognosis and undertake to predict the consequences of such illness.[27]

One author has written a two-volume work "to demonstrate that despite the ever increasing utilization of psychiatric and psychological evidence in the legal process such evidence frequently does not meet reasonable criteria of admissibility and should not be admitted in a court of law, and if admitted, should be given little or no weight."[28]

It is likely that lawyers, when cross-examining psychiatric and psychological experts, will rely on court opinions and publications such as those mentioned here when attempting to discredit testimony. Thus, expert witnesses might profitably read materials intended as aids to attorneys preparing for cross-examination. Such materials will familiarize experts with approaches attorneys are likely to take. Of course, the lawyers for both sides should prepare their own experts to face such cross-examination techniques.

THE ROLES OF PSYCHIATRISTS, PSYCHOLOGISTS, AND PSYCHIATRIC NURSES AS EXPERT WITNESSES

Psychiatrists, psychologists, and psychiatric nurses appear as expert witnesses in various roles. First, psychiatrists appear as treating psychiatrists and testify as to the diagnosis, prognosis, and treatment of their patients. Clinical psychologists also appear as treating psychotherapists in such proceedings as involuntary admission hearings and special education hearings. Psychiatric nurses also diagnose and practice psychotherapy independently, although no cases have been found where nurses appeared as expert witnesses in this capacity.

Second, psychiatrists, psychologists, psychiatric nurses, and social workers give expert opinions based on examinations of individuals made at the request of an attorney or by order of the court in a variety of cases (for example, involuntary hospitalization, mental condition of a defendant in a criminal case, and capacity of an individual to enter into a contract or execute a will or trust).

Third, psychiatrists, psychologists, and psychiatric nurses opine on the standard of care, deviations from the standard of care, and the extent of injuries in malpractice actions involving members of their respective professions. Such opinions are based on hypothetical questions, or evidence such as the testimony of other witnesses, medical records, and EEG results.

The expert's role is to give an independent, objective opinion based on the facts. While an expert opinion generally favors one party over the other, it does not mean that the expert testifies "for" one or the other party in a proceeding. The expert's role is not to advocate the position of one party over the other. This does not mean that they are not advocates, but rather, that they are advocates for their own expert opinion, not for one of the parties.[29]

When an expert agrees to render an opinion in a case, care should be taken to ensure that the expert maintains an independent, objective posture during the evaluative stage. The attorney who retains the expert is generally looking for an opinion that will support his or her case. Therefore, it is important for the expert to ensure that all of the information, and not a selected portion, is made available. After reviewing all of the relevant data—clinical review, psychological testing, and all historical information—the expert should render an objective opinion.[30]

Once an objective opinion is formed, the expert witness may then become an advocate for the opinion in the sense that the expert must be persuasive by "demonstrating how his opinion [was] . . . formed, how its trustworthiness is based on the reliability of his data and on his reasoning about the data."[31] The credibility of the opinion depends upon the reliability of the data, the reasoning that links the data to the legal issue, the ability of the witness to communicate and demonstrate this to the judge or jury making the decision. In the demonstration and communication of an opinion it is appropriate to collaborate with the attorney to present the opinion in its most persuasive light.[32] This is part of the adversary process. The impact of an expert witness may depend more on persuasion than on the substantial aspects of his or her presentation.[33]

Some experts fail to form objective opinions. Rather they evaluate the available data with a view toward supporting the position of those who have retained them. Still others render opinions based on inadequate data. These problems reflect a lack of professionalism or incompetence; they are not inherent problems of the adversary process.

PRELIMINARY CONFERENCE

After reaching a tentative agreement to perform an evaluation, the expert and the attorney should hold a preliminary conference before the expert examines the individual who is the subject of the case. The attorney should outline the facts, explain the specific type of legal proceeding, the substantive standard of law involved, and the specific issues presented. The expert should describe his or her area of expertise and experience to ensure that he or she is qualified to give an opinion. If the expert is a psychiatrist, it may be appropriate to recommend psychological testing to corroborate findings.

Knowledge of the proceeding, the specific standard involved, and the questions to be addressed is essential if the expert is to form a useful opinion. One question is the impact of the mental illness on the individual's ability to function in a particular area either in the past, the present, or the future. The expert must understand the legal standard applied in that area to formulate an opinion. The standards overlap but are distinct. For example, the standard for appointment of a guardian or a conservator is whether the person is competent at present to manage his or her personal affairs or estate. The standard for whether a person is competent or fit to stand trial in a criminal proceeding is whether that person understands the charges and is capable of cooperating with his or her lawyer in the preparation of a defense. The attorney should give the expert specific questions that relate to the particular standard.

The expert should make it clear to the lawyer that available information about the individual related to the legal action is needed, including personal history and any expert opinions obtained by the other side. The lawyer should know that if the expert bases an opinion on selective data and this comes out at trial, the expert opinion will be compromised. One psychiatrist who testified for John Hinckley, Jr. had access to his previous psychiatric records, physical examinations, his writings over the past six or seven years, and the CT scan of his brain.[34]

The lawyer and the expert should clearly agree on what the expert is expected to do, e.g., conduct an examination, examine records and documents, assist counsel in preparing the case, testify, sit with counsel during the trial when opposing expert testimony is given, and advise counsel regarding possible cross-examination approaches.

A fee agreement should be reached at the preliminary conference. In most states an expert witness may be paid in excess of the statutory witness fee. Some states have specific statutory regulations, but most do not. An expert witness is entitled to be compensated for time spent on the case, but there should never be a contingent fee based on a favorable result in the case. The witness may be questioned about it on cross-examination, and the results would be disastrous.[35]

It is not uncommon for opposing counsel to ask a witness on cross-examination: "Doctor, how much are you being paid for your testimony (or your opinion)?" The witness should be prepared for such a question and answer it honestly: The compensation is for the time spent on the case, not for the opinion.

DIAGNOSIS AND EVALUATION

The type of diagnosis and evaluation depends upon the legal issue and relationship of the therapist to the individual who is a party to the proceeding. If the expert is the treating therapist, much of the information for an opinion is already available. A fresh examination is generally desirable and sometimes necessary to comply with statutory requirements. Guardianship reports and certificates for involuntary hospitalization require a personal examination within a certain time limit. For example, in Illinois, an evaluation for a guardianship report must be conducted within three months of the date of the filing of the report,[36] and the person executing a certificate for involuntary admission must conduct a personal examination within 72 hours prior to admission of the individual.[37]

Obviously, no current evaluation is possible where the subject of the litigation is deceased. The legal issue may involve the capacity of an individual when he or she executed a will sometime in the past. This type of case requires a reconstruction of the mental state of an individual at that particular time in the past. It would be fortunate if the expert had conducted a therapy session on the day the will was signed or near that time. Other assessments may involve a psychiatric or psychological interview with an individual where a case has been instituted to set aside a contract, lease, trust, or other instrument on the grounds that the individual lacked capacity. In cases involving the past mental state of an individual, it is important to obtain all the data possible. In any event, where the expert is the treating therapist, there is a tendency to give more weight to the opinion because there has been a greater opportunity to evaluate the individual over a longer period of time.

Most often, where an expert is retained by counsel or by order of the court to evaluate an individual, the proceeding involves involuntary admission to a psychiatric program, fitness to stand trial, or criminal responsibility (sanity).

In most cases at least two separate interviews constituting a minimum of approximately two hours is necessary to produce adequate data upon which to base an evaluation. Some highly complex psychiatric problems may require an evaluation extending to several days or even weeks in an inpatient institutional setting.[38] One of the psychiatrists who testified for John Hinckley, Jr. interviewed him for 35 hours over a one-year period.[39]

In most cases an opinion should include a complete psychiatric evaluation with a full past and present history of the client. It should also include a mental status examination. This includes assessment of intelligence, competence, organic brain functioning, symptoms of mental disorder, patterns of coping with stressful situations, and levels of anxiety and depression. An opinion on the ability of an individual to respond to treatment requires detailed knowledge of the specific individual, his or her mental disorder, motivation for therapy, response activity of the particular disorder to known treatment techniques, and available treatment resources. If resources permit, the parties may have a team of experts, generally led by a psychiatrist. Psychological tests using a variety of diagnostic techniques should supplement the psychiatric evaluation. Each evaluation is highly individualized; yet it lies within a broad framework used each time.

A physical examination may or may not be required in a particular evaluation. It may be performed by a physician other than the expert. Whenever a question concerning organic brain functioning has been raised, a physical examination is necessary, and it must include a complete neurological examination. Indicated laboratory procedures should also supplement the examination. Such laboratory procedures include serological testing, skull x-rays, electroencephalogram (EEG), spinal fluid examination, and other specialized tests on a clinical indication. Hospitalization for each detailed neurological test may be necessary in order to study adequately the functioning of the central nervous system.[40] A psychiatrist who testified for John Hinckley, Jr. also used the results of a computed axial tomography scan of Hinckley's brain.[41]

A detailed history is essential as part of the psychiatric evaluation. Such a complete history may be difficult to obtain from the individual undergoing evaluation because of concern about revealing certain information that might be related either to his or her attorney or to the court. It is therefore very helpful for the expert to obtain additional information from outside sources such as family, friends, and other significant persons in the individual's life (co-workers, teachers, religious leaders, etc.). In the area of criminal law, confessions, police statements, and various statements made to others may be very useful. Such materials may constitute hearsay evidence that cannot be used as a specific basis for forming an opinion admissible into evidence, but this information is still important to help the expert focus on areas that otherwise might be overlooked and that can serve as corroboration of the opinion.

At the beginning of an interview with an individual under evaluation, the expert should state the reason for the examination and the relationship of the expert to the client. The individual should be clearly informed that statements made to the expert are not confidential and that such statements made and information revealed may be disclosed in the court proceeding. This will begin the relationship between the expert and the individual on a straightforward, honest basis.

Psychiatrists, psychologists, or psychiatric nurses are engaged to testify in malpractice or negligence actions either on behalf of a patient, another professional, or a hospital. The expert will render an opinion on the standard of care involved in the particular incident, whether there was a deviation from that standard, and perhaps the extent of any injury suffered by the patient.

After evaluation and consideration of all available data, the expert arrives at a written opinion on the specific legal problem presented by the individual. Questions posed by the attorney prior to the evaluation are answered as fully as possible in this opinion. The report must be lucid and concise; it should contain minimal technical language. Such technical terms as may be used should be fully defined. Psychiatric and psychological jargon should be avoided. Once the report has been completed, the lawyer and the expert should hold a pretrial conference.

PRETRIAL CONFERENCE WITH LAWYER

The purpose of the pretrial conference is to clarify the issues and prepare the expert for testimony and for cross-examination. The specific legal issues and the specific psychiatric and psychological findings should be reviewed. Such a process will also educate the lawyer on the best approach to cross-examination of adverse expert witnesses. The lawyer needs all the specific information available on the client's illness. It is important that the expert understand his or her involvement with the legal system and the various rules of procedure and evidence that will govern testimony. Any questions or doubts that the expert may have regarding how the adversary system works should be asked of the lawyer. The attorney should also brief the expert on any particular attitudes or views that the presiding judge may have on the testimony of expert witnesses.

The expert is reminded that no confidentiality restriction exists on the information received during the evaluation. This may be important in obtaining optimum testimony from the expert, and it will prevent the expert from being guarded.

Direct Testimony

The most effective witness is one who presents his or her views in a straightforward, honest manner, being as concise and lucid as possible, and who communicates in language understood by the jury or the judge rather than in technical terms. In other words the expert witness should try to avoid professional jargon and present testimony in an unbiased manner.

The judge controls the trial by ensuring that the rules of evidence and procedure are followed. The judge decides whether evidence will be admitted, whether a witness is qualified to testify as an expert, and whether questions asked witnesses will be answered.

When a witness takes the stand to testify as an expert, the lawyer's first step is to establish the qualifications of the witness to give an expert opinion. (In bench trials, where the psychiatrist or psychologist regularly testifies before the court as an expert—for example, in involuntary admission proceedings—the qualifications of the witness are often stipulated.) The lawyer qualifies the witness by asking questions on education and experience. It is an opportunity to impress the decision makers with the quality of the background and learning of the witness. The questions and answers are reviewed at this pretrial conference.

Second, the attorney lays the foundation for the expert's testimony. The lawyer establishes that the expert conducted an evaluation by asking whether interviews were conducted, when, where, how long they lasted, and other circumstances surrounding the interviews. If the testimony is based solely on a review of medical records or on a hypothetical question, this is brought out. At the pretrial meeting, the questions and answers should be reviewed by the expert and the lawyer.

Experts are sometimes confused about the actual content of testimony. Basically, it is a function of the expert to present the mental state of the examined party at relevant times in issue. The psychodynamic base of any relevant behavior, including both conscious and unconscious processes, should be described. This includes presentation of the mental processes, forces, and motivations that result in specific behavior, although different situations will call for different kinds of testimony. Generally, an expert's opinion is directed at answering the ultimate legal questions presented in the case. Nevertheless, on January 19, 1983, the American Psychiatric Association issued a 6,000-word position paper on the insanity defense stating, among other things, that psychiatrists should not be asked their opinion as to whether a defendant was sane or insane at the time of the act: "Insanity is a legal, not a medical concept, and responsibility is a moral, not a medical concept."[42] An expert who has examined a party and testifies concerning the party's mental condition will be permitted to make a statement as to the nature of the examination and his or her diagnosis of the mental condition of the individual at the relevant time for the purposes of the subject matter of the litigation. The expert will be allowed to make any explanation reasonably certain to clarify the diagnosis and opinion.

The name, the chief characteristics, and the symptoms of the mental illness—with particular emphasis on its effect on judgment, knowledge and appreciation of the circumstances, social behavior, and self-control—should be given. The emphasis is determined by the ultimate issues in the case. The opinion must be supported by facts from the interview or medical records or from other testimony, and the expert must be able to articulate these facts. Opposing counsel will often try to elicit inconsistent statements.

The expert witness may be asked a hypothetical question framed to permit consideration of all pertinent facts in the case that are useful to the attorney's position. It may appear to the expert that this question does not adequately reflect the facts as they pertain to the person examined. It is important that the expert know that he or she is to give an opinion based on those facts presented in the hypothetical question and that other information the expert knows about the client should not enter into the answer. It is not the role of the expert to determine whether the facts adequately support the hypothetical question. The lawyer and the trier of fact will deal with this question according to the rules of evidence and civil procedure.

The lawyer may seek assistance from the expert in preparing any hypothetical question intended for the adverse expert witness. In a hypothetical question, the attorney presents the facts upon which opinion testimony is desired by hypothetical questions—questions that, for the purpose of the trial, assume a state of facts based on the evidence of other witnesses—and asks the expert to form an opinion based on those facts.

Opposing counsel may object to questions asked. If the judge upholds the objection, the expert should not answer, but rather should wait for the next question from the lawyer. If the objection is overruled, the question may be answered.

Cross-Examination

The purpose of cross-examination is to test the opinion and credibility of the expert witness by asking appropriate, but very direct and pointed, questions. Sometimes opposing counsel will become aggressive and hostile. The expert witness should remain courteous under the attack. The judge or other lawyer will intervene when the questions become inappropriate or repetitious. An expert should always pause before responding to give the lawyer with whom he or she is working time to object to an inappropriate question.

Cross-examination often makes a witness apprehensive. Adequate preparation, frank objectivity, and familiarity with the legal procedures will alleviate this apprehension. The purpose of cross-examination should be explained in the pretrial conference. It is to test the accuracy and value of the witness' opinion or the witness' credibility.[43]

A number of specific techniques are used on cross-examination to discredit an expert's opinion or testimony. The opposing counsel may attempt to show that the expert is biased because of his or her relationship with the hiring attorney from whom the expert will receive substantial fees. Another technique is to ask questions designed to show that an expert's education and experience are not actually relevant to the situation at hand. The attorney should review questions of this nature that can be anticipated on cross-examination with the expert and discuss the proper way to answer them. Opposing counsel may refer to specific sources to indicate conflicting points of view in the literature. An appropriate response by the expert to this line of questioning is a statement that his or her knowledge is based on many sources, including training and personal experience, and that he or she did not rely upon any specific source in forming the opinion. The expert should be prepared to testify specifically as to the experience upon which the opinion is based. The expert should frankly acknowledge differences of opinion between the experts testifying in the case. Care should be taken to ensure that earlier statements made on direct examination are not distorted, misquoted, or taken out of context during cross-examination. This can be done by carefully concentrating on the questions asked and simply pointing out misstatements as to the opinion given on direct examination.

The expert witness should not attempt to engage in legal debate with opposing counsel while under cross-examination. Counsel is likely to be far more expert in this area. Questions should not be answered with a categorical "yes" or "no" if a qualification is necessary for a complete answer. Efforts by the attorney to limit an answer to "yes" or "no" may be resisted by the witness who needs to clarify a response to make it complete, and the court will ordinarily allow this.

Thorough examination of the alleged offender, careful preparation for testimony, knowledge of the legal procedure, and a helpful, impartial demeanor in the courtroom ordinarily will lead to good testimony on direct examination, and, with this pattern as a base, the expert need not fear cross-examination.[44]

It is the duty of counsel for the opposing side to cross-examine the witness, revealing these distortions and biases, attempting to impeach the witness' testimony. It is legitimate to impeach the testimony through an attack upon the witness, that is, by eliciting evidence to show that the witness is not the expert he or she claims to be, that the clinical facts upon which the expert bases an opinion are not complete or may not even be true, that the professional skill and knowledge of the expert are deficient, that the expert's opinions are faulty and unwarranted. Under such cross-examination, or through redirect examination, the expert is expected to defend his or her status, clinical facts, and professional knowledge, and to justify any opinions rendered.

The witness should remember the importance of maintaining composure on the stand. Displays of sarcasm or petulance may antagonize the jury and make the witness appear to be excessively partisan and unprofessional. The witness should not offer smart or flip answers. The witness should never answer a question he or she does not understand or that includes unacceptable premises. The witness should always answer the question asked and not offer gratuitous comments either in the direct testimony or on cross-examination.

LIABILITY FOR MISDIAGNOSIS

Generally, an expert who testifies to an opinion pursuant to a court order is immune so long as the opinion is given in good faith and without malice. An expert who testifies in other capacities, for example, as a treating therapist or on retainer to analyze records or testify in a malpractice case, will not be liable so long as reasonable care is used.[45]

Plaintiffs in Texas brought a malpractice action against a psychiatrist because he testified that a criminal defendant had a sociopathic personality solely because he was "an individual who continues to break the rules and has no feeling of remorse." Another psychiatrist testified that a reasonable practitioner would have used 16 enumerated "standard criteria" in making such a diagnosis, and would know that the necrophiliac and sadistic tendencies that the person had exhibited were disorders separate and distinct from a sociopathic personality. Counsel for the defendant argued that improper expert testimony would occur less frequently if experts were held liable for damages for such misdiagnosis. The court rejected this argument based on its belief that the goal of unrestrained access to the courts and full development of the facts is best achieved by providing that any communication made in the course of a judicial proceeding is absolutely privileged and immune from client liability for damages.[46]

The parents of a child who was classified as emotionally handicapped by a school committee filed a malpractice action against a psychiatrist who the school district had retained to examine the child and provide an opinion on the child's condition. The parents alleged in their malpractice action that the opinion of the psychiatrist was erroneous and that it was based on a negligent examination. The court dismissed the malpractice action saying that:

> [I]n a typical malpractice action there was a breach of a duty which was owed to the patient who retained the physician. Here the school district had retained the physician for the sole purpose of furnishing a professional opinion to the school committee and not to diagnose the student for treatment purposes or to treat the student.[47]

The court said that the psychiatrist's testimony in the role of expert witness was offered to assist in the resolution of a dispute. It was not binding on anyone, it was tested by cross-examination, and it did not control the committee's judgment. The court stated that any attempt to impose liability on the witness called upon to express her opinion based on whatever observations she made would strike a serious blow at our adversary system of deciding disputes on the basis of testimony or evidence. No civil action is available against a witness for adverse testimony, even in cases of perjury.[48]

In Maryland a court held that a psychiatrist was not liable for defamation when he advised the attorney of the mother in a divorce proceeding that the father should not be given the right to visit his child. The psychiatrist included this opinion in a letter to the mother's attorney. The court stated:

> The attorney had solicited the psychiatrist's evaluation of the truthfulness of the child's allegation that his father had abused him, as well as the psychiatrist's opinion as to the advisability of continuing the father's visitation rights. The psychiatrist's evaluation and recommendation were sought for the purpose of determining whether there were probative facts and opinions sufficient to justify raising . . . the issue of a modification of the father's visitation rights. Despite the fact that this [letter] had not been filed in the pending divorce proceeding, it was nonetheless a document prepared for use in connection with the pending divorce proceeding. Under these circumstances, it is manifest that the psychiatrist's letter was directly related to that judicial proceeding, and that the allegedly defamatory statement contained in the letter was published during the course of that judicial proceeding. Accordingly, an absolute privilege applies to the allegedly defamatory statement published in the psychiatrist's letter to the attorney.[49]

Expert witnesses raised the question in a Delaware case of their potential civil liability to a third person arising from their special judgment and opinions expressed in sexually-dangerous-person procedures. The court opined that it was highly unlikely any liability would be imposed by Delaware courts. At most, the courts would probably only require reasonable care and skill in their rendering of psychiatric opinions.[50]

A psychiatrist owes a duty to a patient's insurance company to exercise reasonable care in performing medical services, making diagnoses, and transmitting them to the company, even though the psychiatrist has no contract with the insurance company. Accordingly, a trial court improperly ruled in favor of the psychiatrist in an insurance company's action against him for his allegedly negligent diagnosis. The company had relied on the diagnosis in paying disability payments to the patient.[51]

NOTES

1. 31 Am. Jur. 2d 496.

2. *Id.* at 497.

3. *Id.* at 511.

4. *Id.* at 494.

5. Jenkins v. United States, 307 F.2d 637, 643 (D.C. App. 1962), citing McCormick, Evidence § 13 (1954).

6. Fed. Rules of Evid. § 703.

7. Jenkins v. United States, *supra* note 5, at 643.

8. *Id.* at 643–646.

9. Pisel v. Stamford Hospital, 180 Conn. 314, 430 A.2d 1, 13 (1980).

10. *See, e.g.,* United v. Riggleman, 411 F.2d 1190 (4th Cir. 1969).

11. People v. Pennington, 66 Cal. 2d 508, 58 Cal. Rptr. 374, 426 P.2d 942 (1967).

12. Landis v. Commonwealth, 241 S.E.2d 749 (Va. 1978).

13. Smith v. State, 141 Ga. App. 720, 234 S.E.2d 385 (1977); In re Wellington, 34 Ill. App. 3d 515, 340 N.E.2d 31 (1975).

14. United States v. Huber, 603 F.2d 387 (2d Cir. 1979).

15. *E.g.,* Cal. Bus. & Prof. Code, Ch. 66, Sec. 2903.

16. Spann v. Bees, 327 A.2d 801 (Md. Ct. Spec. App. 1974), *cert. denied,* 327 A.2d 801 (1975).

17. People v. Strange, 81 Ill. App. 3d 81, 36 Ill. Dec. 486, 400 N.E.2d 1066 (1980); *see also* People v. Gillian, 16 Ill. App. 3d 659, 306 N.E.2d 352 (1974).

18. State v. Alexander, 252 La. 564, 211 So. 2d 650 (1968).

19. Michael L. Perlin, "The Legal Status of the Psychologist in the Courtroom," *Mental Health Disability Law Reporter* 4 (1980):194.

20. *Id.* at 196, 197.

21. Mundt v. Alta Bates Hospital, 223 Cal. App. 2d 413, 35 Cal. Rptr. 848 (1963); Hiatt v. Groce, 215 Kan. 14, 523 P.2d 320 (1974); Robert v. Chodoff, 259 Pa. Super. 332, 393 A.2d 853 (1978); Thompson v. United States, 368 F. Supp. 466 (W.D. La. 1973); Maslonka v. Hermann, 173 N.J. Super. 566, 414 A.2d 1350 (1980).

22. Pisel, *supra* note 9, at 13, 14.

23. Washington v. United States, 390 F.2d 444, 457 (D.C. Cir. 1967).

24. In Re Ballay, 482 F.2d 648 (D.C. Cir. 1973).

25. O'Connor v. Donaldson, 422 U.S. 563, 579 (1975).

26. *Id.* at 422 U.S. at 584 (quoting Greenwood v. U.S., 350 U.S. 366, 375 (1956)).

27. People v. Burnich, 14 Cal.3d 306, 325 (1975).

28. Zay Ziskin, *Coping With Psychiatric and Psychological Testimony* (3rd ed.) (Venice, Cal.: Law and Psychology Press, 1981), p. vii; *see also* Bruce J. Ennis and Thomas R. Litwack, "Psychiatry and the Presumption of Expertise: Flipping Coins in the Courtroom," *Calif. L. Rev.* 62 (1974): 693.

29. Seymour Pollack, "The Role of Psychiatry in the Rule of Law," *reprinted in Psychiatrists and the Legal Process: Diagnosis and Debate* (New York: Insight Communication, Inc., 1977), p. 16 [hereinafter cited as Pollack]. One psychiatrist stated that it is absurd to pretend that the psychiatric expert remains neutral in such a legal proceeding. For the sake of the expert's own ego and integrity, he or she must identify with his or her own opinion and become the advocate of those opinions. Bernard L. Diamond, M.D., "The Fallacy of the Impartial Expert," *Archives of Criminal Psychodynamics*, 3 (Spring 1959):221–236.

30. Comment on Pollack, *supra* note 29, at 23.

31. Pollack, *supra* note 29, at 16.

32. Comment on Pollack, *supra* note 29, at 23.

33. Steven C. Bank and Norman J. Poythren, Jr., "The Elements of Persuasion in Expert Testimony," *J. Psychiatry & Law* 173, 10 (1983).

34. David Bear, M.D., quoted in "Was John Hinckley Insane? Yes," *Chicago Tribune*, July 11, 1982, sec. 2, p. 1 [hereinafter cited as Bear].

35. Richard C. Allen, Elcye Z. Ferster, and Jesse G. Rubin, "The Psychiatrist and Psychologist as Expert Witnesses," *reprinted in Readings in Law and Psychiatry* (Baltimore, Md.: Johns Hopkins Press, 1975) p. 182.

36. Ill. Rev. Stat., ch. 110½, ¶ 11a–9(a).

37. Ill. Rev. Stat., ch. 91½, ¶ 3–602 (Smith-Hurd Supp. 1982–1983).

38. Leigh M. Roberts, M.D. "Some Observations on the Problems of the Forensic Psychiatrist," 1965 *Wisc. L. Rev.*:240–267.

39. David Bear, M.D., *supra* note 34.

40. Roberts, *supra* note 38, at 213.

41. Bear, *supra* note 34.

42. American Psychiatric Association, Position Paper on Insanity, Jan. 19, 1983.

43. 31 Am. Jur. 550.

44. *Id.* at 217.

45. Liability for misdiagnosis in involuntary admission proceeding is discussed in Chapter 5.

46. Clark v. Grigson, 579 S.W.2d 263 (Tex. Civ. App. 1979). *But see,* James v. Brown, 63 S.W.2d 91 (Tex. Sup. Ct. 1982), where the decision was criticized and an action for malpractice was allowed based on an evaluation of an individual for involuntary hospitalization.

47. Davis v. Tirrell, 443 N.Y.S.2d 136 (N.Y. Sup. Ct. Broome County, 1981).

48. *Id.*

49. Adams v. Peck, 415 A.2d 292 (Md. Ct. App. 1981).

50. Delaware v. Tarbutton, 407 A.2d 538 (Del. Super. Ct. 1979).

51. Berger v. North American Company for Life and Health Insurance, 648 F.2d 305 (5th Cir. 1981).

Chapter 14

Civil Proceedings

GUARDIANSHIP/INCOMPETENCY

The purpose of guardianship is to protect a disabled person by appointing a guardian to make personal decisions and/or decisions concerning the estate. When possible a family member or relative is appointed guardian of the person. If the person has substantial assets, a bank may be appointed "guardian of the estate." If the assets are modest, a family member or public agency may be appointed.

A "guardian of the person" makes personal decisions concerning living arrangements, consent for medical treatment, and the daily decisions of living. A situation in which the disabled person refuses to cooperate can be very frustrating for the guardian because guardians have no power to force implementation of their decisions.

If a public agency is guardian, the responsibilities are limited. For example, a public guardian in Illinois is mandated to visit the ward four times a year to review care received. The guardian of an estate manages the financial affairs of the disabled person.

Sometimes guardianship proceedings are quests for the control of wealth as much as concern for the individual involved. Heirs often wish to preserve their inheritance, and they may feel that Uncle Harry is not acting his age and is spending his money in a frivolous way. It also has been suggested that guardians sometimes overprotect disabled persons.[1]

Standards

State statutes describe individuals who are disabled or incompetent and in need of a guardian or a conservator. For example, Illinois defines a disabled person as:

A person 18 years or older who (a) because of mental deterioration or physical incapacity is not fully able to manage his person or estate, or (b) is mentally ill or developmentally disabled and who because of his mental illness or developmental disability is not fully able to manage his person or estate, or (c) because of gambling, idleness, debauchery or excessive use of intoxicants, or drugs, so spends or wastes his estate as to expose himself or his family to want or suffering.[2]

In California the standard under the mental health code is whether a person is gravely disabled as a result of mental disorder or impairment by chronic alcoholism.[3] Under the probate code, a conservator may be appointed for the person and/or property of "any adult person who by reason of advanced age, illness, injury, mental weakness, intemperance, addiction to drugs or for any other cause is unable to properly care for himself or for his property, or who for said causes or for any other cause is likely to be deceived or imposed upon by artful or designing persons. . . ."[4]

In New Hampshire a petition must contain "specific factual allegations as to the proposed ward's financial transactions, personal actions or actual occurrences which are claimed to demonstrate his or her inability to manage an estate or to provide for personal needs."[5] The purpose of this requirement is to allow the proposed ward the opportunity to prepare a defense.[6]

In Missouri, an individual was found incompetent due to his habitual drunkenness. The court said that the individual's life:

has been marred by numerous periods of drunkenness requiring hospitalization on many occasions and incarceration on others . . . and supports the finding that . . . [he] is and has for some time been an habitual drunkard and is incapable by reason thereof of "caring for himself." The mere fact that during periods of sobriety he is able to feed and dress himself does not diminish the threat to himself and others.

The standard was whether the individual was "incapable of understanding and acting with discretion in the ordinary affairs of life."[7]

Incompetency requiring appointment of a guardian or conservator should not be confused with incompetency or fitness to stand trial on criminal charges which involves the defendant's understanding of the charge and ability to cooperate with counsel in the preparation of a defense.[8]

In most states the standard for involuntary admission to a psychiatric program and the standard for guardianship differ. Standards for involuntary admission require a showing that individuals are mentally ill and that as a result of this mental illness, they are dangerous either to themselves or to others or unable to care for their own personal physical needs. Guardianship proceedings require a showing that individuals are unable to manage their own personal and/or financial affairs. While the evidence necessary to meet these standards generally overlaps, the standards themselves are separate and distinct. Nevertheless, in some states, for example, Utah, the involuntary admission statute encompasses the standard for guardianship. One of the criteria for involuntary admission in Utah is the inability to make rational treatment decisions,[9] which is similar to the inability to manage personal affairs.

Procedures

Procedures will vary somewhat from state to state. In general, an alleged disabled person must be served with a copy of the petition and a summons containing where and when the matter will be heard in court. A *guardian ad litem* is generally appointed to represent the best interests of the person. In Illinois, the *guardian ad litem* files a written report after a personal interview with the person. If the alleged disabled person opposes the guardianship, an attorney will be appointed to defend. Some states will provide a court-appointed independent expert if the person is indigent. Most states provide the right to a jury trial.

At the hearing, the petitioner introduces evidence that the alleged disabled person is in need of a guardian of the person or estate or both. Family members, friends, and others who have observed conduct indicating that the alleged disabled person is unable to manage his or her affairs testify to what they have observed. A physician will testify to the alleged disabled person's mental or physical condition that causes the inability to manage his or her affairs. The defense may call witnesses to counter this evidence, including a psychiatrist, clinical psychologist, psychiatric nurse or social worker who testifies as an expert. The *guardian ad litem* participates by questioning witnesses and making recommendations as to what is in the best interests of the disabled person to the court.

Expert Evaluation

State statutes generally require the opinion of a physician. Clinical psychologists often participate in the evaluation. In Illinois, the petition must be accompanied by a report that contains:

> . . . (1) a description of the nature and type of the respondent's disability; (2) evaluations of the respondent's mental, physical and educational condition, adaptive behavior and social skills; (3) an opinion as to whether guardianship is needed, the type and scope of the guardianship needed, and the reasons therefor; (4) a recommendation as to the most appropriate treatment or habilitation plan and living arrangement for the respondent and the reasons therefor; (5) the signatures of

all persons who performed the evaluations upon which the report is
based, one of whom shall be a licensed physician.[10]

The evaluation upon which the report is based must have been performed within
three months of the date of the filing of the petition.[11]

In an Illinois case two psychiatrists testified on behalf of a woman alleged to
be a disabled person, and an internist testified on behalf of the petitioner, the
woman's son.

> [The first psychiatrist] . . . stated that she had an obvious memory
> defect when questioned about her financial affairs; that she required
> the assistance of another in order to refresh her memory; that she did
> not know of her assets unless reminded of them; that as a result of this
> defect and of her desire to please others, she could be relatively easily
> led to conclusions which the assisting party desired her to reach. None-
> theless, in . . . [the psychiatrist's] opinion the . . . [woman] could
> make a reasonable judgment if supplied with the forgotten facts and
> she was capable of managing her own affairs if she was apprised of
> those affairs. [The] . . . examination [by the psychiatrist] consisted of
> one 45-minute session.[12]

The second psychiatrist basically agreed with the first:

> . . . In response to examination by the court, [the second psychiatrist]
> testified that without being reminded . . . [the woman] would not have
> independent knowledge of the nature or extent of her assets. However,
> [he] . . . believed this to be due essentially to the fact that throughout
> her life others had managed her affairs and not due to her memory
> defect. In his opinion [she] . . . was able to manage her affairs because
> she was able to obtain the help she needed, knew where to turn for
> such help, and knew whom to choose for such help, and knew whom
> to . . . entrust with those decisions. Nevertheless, [he] . . . further
> testified that [she] . . . could not independently "know where every-
> thing is, and make all the decisions, make them in a way that was
> necessarily in her best interests," relative to the management of her
> estate or financial affairs.[13]

The internist performed a medical examination pursuant to court order. He
testified that the woman suffered from a generalized sclerotic disease and exhibited signs of altered mental capacity commensurate with her age of 78. In
his opinion she would require help in managing her financial affairs.

> [His report] . . contained a brief evaluation of [the woman's] . . .
> physical condition and stated that [she] . . . had impaired memory

recall, impaired conjugative ability (the ability to draw conclusions from several factors); impaired mathematical skills and physical debility of old age in keeping with her chronological age. The report further stated that [she] . . . was only partially capable of making personal and financial decisions; incapable of being custodian of her assets. . . . Although capable of minor housekeeping and personal grooming decisions, she was incapable of making decisions regarding her health and safety. . . . On cross examination [the internist] . . . admitted that although he had presented [the woman] . . . with simple mathematical problems, he had asked [her] . . . no questions concerning her financial affairs. [14]

The finding of incompetency was upheld on appeal.

A finding of incompetency and appointment of a conservator was overturned in Illinois where an affidavit by an osteopath stated that he had examined the individual involved, when in fact no examination had taken place. [15]

Effect of Appointment of Guardian or Conservator

Traditionally, to be found incompetent is to be deprived of all personal decision-making power. A person found incompetent cannot enter into contracts, leases, marriage, etc. Some old court opinions state that, in terms of legal capacity, a person who has been found incompetent is dead. All legal capacity to act is transferred to the guardian or conservator. A person who has been declared incompetent lacks the legal capacity to file a petition for divorce. By statute, in Kansas, a conservator or guardian may file suit on behalf of the ward. [16] In Maine the state supreme court affirmed a finding that a marriage contract entered into by an incompetent adult was invalid because he did not have permission from his guardian. The court held that a ward is statutorily incapable of making a contract. [17]

There is a trend toward a limited guardianship tailored to the disability of the individual. For example, Illinois and Texas provide that a guardianship may be ordered only to the extent necessitated by the individual's actual mental, physical, and adaptive limitations. [18] In practice, there are few limited guardianships in Illinois. The situation cited as most appropriate for a limited guardianship is where an individual has a substantial sum of money that he or she is unable to manage; otherwise the individual is capable of making responsible decisions. A guardian would be appointed to manage this person's estate but not his or her person, leaving intact the individual's power to manage nonfinancial matters.

Under most state statutes a person who is involuntarily admitted to a hospital does not lose civil rights. For example, a New York statute that denied involuntarily admitted patients the right to vote was held unconstitutional because involuntary admission hearings, unlike adjudications of incompetency, do not involve findings of an individual's inability to conduct personal or business affairs.[19] Illinois law provides that no person involuntarily admitted to a hospital is "deprived of any rights, benefits, or privileges guaranteed by law."[20]

While a finding of incompetency or a need for a guardian may take away all the rights of the incompetent, the guardian or conservator appointed does not automatically have the power to make all personal decisions on behalf of the ward or incompetent. Some decisions are considered too personal for the guardian to make. For example, in New Jersey it was held that the mother of a comatose, mentally incompetent adult could not be appointed guardian to bring a divorce action on her son's behalf for the alleged adultery of his wife. The court said that divorce is too personal a matter to delegate to another person.[21] Nevertheless, in Colorado, a mentally retarded, mentally incompetent child can be sterilized with the approval of the parents or legal guardian if the detailed procedures are followed to ensure that sterilization is "medically necessary." The procedure requires a court order of representation of the child by a *guardian ad litem*, a full judicial hearing, consideration of the incompetent's point of view, and clear and convincing evidence that the operation is medically essential.[22] A guardian or conservator cannot give up parental right to a child. A *guardian ad litem* must be appointed and a court hearing held.[23]

In New York the court granted the application of a conservatee who wanted to compel the conservator to sell her apartment building and give the proceeds to her children or, alternatively, simply to convey the apartment building to them. The conservator opposed the transaction. Nevertheless, the court held that it had the discretion to grant the application notwithstanding the conservator's opposition. The court said that there was substantial proof that the conservatee could think rationally with regard to the disposition of her property and there was no reason to intrude upon her individual right by substituting someone else's judgment.[24] The court held that a conservator in Illinois has the authority to file suit to invalidate the marriage of a ward on the grounds that the ward lacked the mental capacity to enter into a marriage contract. The conservator or guardian believed that the wife was taking advantage of the husband-ward.[25]

In choosing a conservator or guardian the paramount concern is the selection of someone who will look out for the best interests and well-being of the disabled or incompetent person.[26] Generally, a family member or relative is chosen. When there is no family member or relative or none are willing to serve, a state agency is often the guardian of last resort.

PROPERTY MATTERS—WILLS, CONTRACTS, AND TRUSTS

The basic issue in property cases is whether the individual has the capacity to make a will, enter into a contract, set up a trust, designate a beneficiary on an insurance policy, or make some other property arrangement at the time of execution. When considering past events, several questions should be considered. Did the individual know and understand what he or she was doing when the document was signed? With regard to a will, does the individual understand the nature, size, and value of his or her property? Does the individual know the natural acts of his or her bounty and relatives? Does the individual understand the effect of the will?

Such actions require a reconstruction of the past event to determine whether the individual had sufficient capacity. The lack of capacity to complete a transaction is similar to the question of whether a person is competent to manage his or her estate. A person declared incompetent or in need of a guardian legally does not have the power to complete a transaction. However, a finding of incompetency is not retroactive and does not negate a transaction completed before the finding. Nevertheless, a transaction may be set aside where the individual lacked capacity without regard to a finding of competency.

There is a presumption that an individual is capable of entering into a contract or other agreement. Evidence to the contrary must be produced to overcome the presumption. In New Mexico a potential heir contested the trust agreement of an 87-year-old man. The trust was upheld because the heir was unable to overcome the presumption of competency by "clear, satisfactory and convincing proof." The court found the testimony of the attorney who drafted the trust that the man, who was now deceased, had experienced a lucid interval on the day the trust was made, to be more persuasive than the psychiatrist's who had not examined the deceased on the day the trust was made.[27]

In Pennsylvania it was held that "a signed document yields a presumption that it accurately expresses the state of mind of the signing party." The individual argued that a release given to her by an insurance company should be overturned because she was mentally incapacitated at the time she signed it. The court held evidence that the woman had suffered a head injury to be insufficient. "It is well settled that mere weakness of intellect resulting from sickness or old age is not legal grounds to set aside a secured contract if intelligence remains to comprehend the nature and care for the transaction."[28]

A promissory note and car loan were invalidated in Louisiana because a party was found insane. To annul a contract on the ground of insanity in that state, the party must be incapacitated at the time the contract was made and such incapacity must be generally known in the community. The record in this case established that the party had been receiving psychiatric care and medication from the time he had been discharged from the Army. He had lived in the community for many years, and it was generally known that he was incapable of handling his affairs.[29]

A quitclaim deed was set aside in Alabama where it was argued that the person signing the deed was under duress and undue influence because he was afflicted with Parkinson's disease. Deeds were canceled where a mentally retarded woman entered into a series of real estate exchanges involving a trailer park. The court held that she was unable to manage her own financial affairs and that the other party used that weakness in its long association with the woman to promote its own financial advantage.[30]

A man was found to have had the capacity to execute a contract for the purchase of three mobile homes in Arkansas. The contract had been signed ten days before he was adjudicated incompetent. The guardian sought to set aside the contract on the grounds that the man was incompetent. The court stated that the only evidence available other than his adjudication was testimony from his physician, who had not seen him for a month prior to the signing of the contract. The man discussed the sale with colleagues in a reasonable way and had plans to move the trailers and rent them. The court held that he had the necessary capacity.[31]

In Florida, a 71-year-old illiterate man was hospitalized and under heavy medication for 16 of the 19 days prior to the transfer of 318 acres of land to a son under terms that were exceptionally favorable to the son, both in price and in arrangements for mortgage. The court overturned the contract when the son failed to meet his burden of proof that he had not taken advantage of his father's weakened condition.[32]

A court refused to postpone a divorce proceeding in Connecticut even though a psychiatrist testified that a woman's judgment was impaired. The trial judge said that her discharge from the hospital, her success at university courses, her part-time job, and the fact that she qualified for a civil service position were all evidence that she understood the nature and consequences of the divorce proceedings and, therefore, the proceeding would not be postponed.[33]

The fact that an individual is found incompetent or in need of a guardian does not raise a presumption that the individual lacked capacity prior to the finding. A son exercised the power of attorney given to him by his mother to sell a farm. Subsequently, his mother was found incompetent, and the son was named the guardian. The son then tried to void the contract of sale on the ground that his mother was incompetent at the time of the execution. He offered no evidence except the adjudication of incompetency, and the court refused to set aside the sale saying that adjudication of incompetency is only prospective and is not evidence of prior disability.[34]

In a Florida case a man retained an attorney to defend him in a criminal case in which he raised the defense of insanity. The man was then adjudicated incompetent, and his guardian moved to ratify the contract with the attorney. After he was restored to competence, the man objected to the payment of attorney's fees. The court upheld the agreement with the attorney because the finding of incompetency was subsequent to the agreement.[35] Similarly, in Illinois, a woman hired an attorney to overturn an irrevocable trust that she had executed, naming her church as beneficiary. The attorney concluded that the trust could not be overturned and that his services should be terminated. Subsequently, the woman was adjudicated an incompetent, and the guardian appointed for her challenged the payments made to the attorney on the ground that the woman was incompetent when she retained him. The guardian was the minister of the church that was the beneficiary of the trust. Because she was adjudicated incompetent more than two months after the retainer agreement with the attorney had been signed, the court found that the evidence was insufficient to support a finding that she had no capacity to contract with the attorney.[36]

FAMILY CASES

Child Custody

In general, the custody of children may be terminated where the state proves by clear and convincing evidence that the child is suffering serious mental or emotional harm as a result of parent failure to carry out responsibilities, that such harm is likely to continue unremedied for the foreseeable future, and that termination is the least restrictive alternative.

The U.S. Supreme Court has held that the termination of the rights of natural parents to their children requires a clear and convincing evidence standard of proof.[37] The court stated:

> The fundamental liberty interest of natural parents in the care, custody, and management of their child does not evaporate simply because they have not been model parents or have lost temporary custody of their child to the state. Even when blood relationships are strained, parents retain a vital interest in preventing the irretrievable destruction of their family life. . . . When the state moves to destroy weakened familial bonds, it must provide the parents with fundamentally fair procedures.[38]

Three factors must be balanced: private interests, risk of error in the proceedings, and the countervailing governmental interest. As to private interest, the court stated that the termination of the rights of natural parents to their children is a state action that is both severe and irreversible in terms of its effect on the private interest of the parties involved. Such interest "favors heightened procedural protection."[39]

The risk of mistakes is great. Imprecise standards leave determinations open to the judge's subjective values. "In appraising the nature and quality of the complex series of encounters among the agency, the parents, and the child, the court possesses unusual discretion to underweigh probative facts that might favor the parent. Because parents subject to termination proceedings are often poor, uneducated, or members of minority groups . . ., such proceedings are often subject to judgments based on cultural or class value." In addition, the resources of the two parties are often unequal, the state having no limits on the "sums [it] may spend in prosecuting a given termination proceeding." The state may initiate or reinstate termination proceedings without violating double jeopardy provisions that only apply to criminal cases. Further, the use of the fair preponderance of the evidence standard "reflects the judgment that society is nearly neutral between erroneous termination of parental rights and erroneous failure to terminate those rights." The court concluded that the consequence of an erroneous termination is the unnecessary destruction of a natural family. Hence, a standard that allocates the risk of error equally between those two outcomes does not properly reflect their relative severity.[40]

The governmental interests involved in the termination of parental rights to children are the "*parens patriae* interests in preserving and promoting the welfare of the child and a fiscal administrative interest in reducing the cost and the burden of such proceedings." A standard of proof more strict than preponderance of the evidence is consistent with both interests. A clear and convincing evidence standard would reduce the chance of error and yet not increase the administrative burden because the state already uses the higher standard in other situations without "apparent effect upon the speed, form or cost of their fact-finding proceedings." Finally, the court said that the standard of beyond a reasonable doubt is too high; "like civil commitment hearings, termination proceedings often require the fact finder to evaluate medical and psychiatric testimony, and to decide issues difficult to prove to a level of absolute certainty, such as lack of parental motive, absence of affection between parent and child, and failure of parental foresight to progress."[41]

Standards

The standards to terminate parental rights to children differ in language from state to state. Nevertheless, they generally require a condition (often a mental illness that renders the parent unable to carry out his or her responsibilities) causing harm to the child that will continue for the foreseeable future. To terminate parental rights to children in Colorado, a determination must be made that: (1) under no reasonable circumstances could the welfare of the child be served by a continuation of the parental relationship; (2) no less drastic alternatives to termination were available to rectify the situation; (3) prior conduct of the parent constitutes "a form of severe and continuous neglect that warrants termination"; and (4) there is a substantial probability of future deprivation to the child in the event the parent-child relationship is not terminated.[42]

The Oklahoma Supreme Court has held that the state cannot terminate the parental rights of a father suffering from schizophrenia without giving him specific notice as to what norms of conduct are expected of him so that he can correct the condition that made his son a deprived child. The state must prove by clear and convincing evidence that harm will come to the child by abuse and neglect.[43] A parent is entitled to the minimum statutory period of three months to conform to those standards.[44] In North Dakota the standard is: (1) the child is a deprived child; (2) the condition and causes of the deprivation are likely to continue and will not be remedied; and (3) by reason of the continuous or irremediable condition and causes, the child suffers or will probably suffer serious physical, mental, moral, or emotional harm.[45] Basically, the standard is that there must be clear and convincing evidence of mental illness, of the parent's inability to care for his or her child due to that mental illness, and that the situation will continue for the foreseeable future.[46]

Parental termination is not based on the mere existence of a mental illness or a mental deficiency. The Nebraska statute also requires a condition "which renders the parent unable to discharge parental responsibility."[47] In Alabama, an appeals court held that the state must "establish not only the permanent incompetency and unsuitability of the parent by clear and convincing evidence, but that it presents a viable alternative to better preserve the future welfare of the children."[48]

Expert Testimony

The impact of the conduct of mentally impaired parents on their children is often established by the testimony of psychiatrists and psychologists. Evaluations must be fresh. For example, a psychiatric evaluation ten months before the hearing was too old to provide an accurate assessment of the mother's present capacity to care for her child.[49]

The following case summaries illustrate the factors considered by the courts. In Michigan, a mentally ill woman who had a prior history of drug and alcohol abuse had the rights to her children terminated. The woman had a history of severe psychiatric disturbances and hospitalizations since she was 15 years old. She also had a history of drug and alcohol abuse and problems raising her children. Several expert witnesses testified that she was mentally ill, that her children had been traumatized while living with her, and that her children would not benefit by being in her care. The court held that the decision was supported by clear and convincing evidence that she was "unfit and unable to become fit within a reasonable period of time."[50]

In a California case, one of the factors was the testimony of a psychiatrist that it would be harmful for a child who had been in a foster home for three years to return to his mother.[51]

In Nebraska, the court said that the termination of parental responsibilities due to mental illness must be based on reasonable grounds to conclude that the condition will continue for a "prolonged, indeterminate period." The court said there was sufficient evidence that the mother in this case was unfit to perform the duties imposed by the relationship or had forfeited that right. The evidence showed she had "a long history of psychiatric problems," that she "suffers from a paranoid type of schizophrenia'' and hallucinations, refused to take medication, did not maintain proper diet or personal hygiene, and was erratic and unpredictable and on occasion she became violent.[52]

The Supreme Court of Minnesota affirmed the termination of the parental rights of an American Indian who had a long history of psychiatric disturbances and drug and alcohol abuse. The evidence met the beyond-a-reasonable-doubt standard required by the Indian Child Welfare Act of 1978. The evidence included testimony from a qualified expert witness that the continued custody by the parents was likely to result in serious emotional and physical injury to the child. The mother had a long history of chemical abuse, instability, hospitalization, and attempted suicide. At the trial the psychiatrist testified that the mother could not care for the child due to her emotional problems and that her condition would not change for the better in the foreseeable future.[53]

Not all states require a showing of harm to a child. Some allow termination based on past harm. In Missouri, the state supreme court affirmed that the giving of temporary custody of an 18-month-old infant to the county division of family service was based on the mother's mental and physical illness that made her— at the time—unable to care for her daughter. The evidence was inconclusive as to whether the child had been harmed. It was shown that the mother had *grand mal* seizures, that she was mentally incapable of caring for the child, and that she had neglected her three other children.[54]

In the state of Washington, parental rights were terminated where the parents were diagnosed as schizophrenic and hospitalized, and in the past had lost custody of their six-month-old girl and lost all parental rights to their older children. The court found that the children lacked adequate food, shelter, and clothing. Living conditions were crowded, dirty, and cockroach-infested, and the apartment lacked heat. Parenting classes and counseling were provided to the parents, but they made almost no progress at all. The parents challenged these findings, claiming that they could not have abused or neglected the infant because the infant had been removed from them at birth. The court based the pattern of the behavior that rendered the parents unfit on the treatment of the children whose custody had been removed from them earlier. The court said that this pattern of treatment with the other children showed that the infant was in a clear and present danger and that there was no need to allow the parents to have custody pending actual damage to the child.[55]

In Georgia, a parental termination order was reversed because, while the evidence established that between 1974 and 1979 the mother suffered from an emotional breakdown that led to her drug and alcohol abuse and that from 1977 to 1978 she engaged in actions that were harmful to her children, the evidence also showed that after 1978 she changed her life style for the better. Therefore, the court held that there was insufficient evidence that the alleged parental unfitness would continue.[56]

In New York, the court reversed a termination of parental rights because it had not been shown that the conditions would continue in the "foreseeable future."[57] However, one year later the trial court terminated the mother's right based on permanent neglect. Permanent neglect consisted of repeatedly failing to make contact or plan with the state agency or to plan for the future of the child.[58]

Termination of parental rights in the state of Washington was based on a finding that the mother's progress and rehabilitation program was so slow that the children faced indefinite foster care.[59]

In Illinois, three severely mentally retarded youths were placed in a private educational facility over the objections of their mother. The evidence indicated that the mother refused to cooperate in the children's education and was making no progress in educating them at home. The court said that placing children in a residential facility would be in their best interests and was not "against the manifest weight of the evidence." Further, the court said that assuming the doctrine of least restrictive alternative applied, the state had met this requirement because the residential setting was the least restrictive viable alternative.[60]

Divorce and Separation

Mentally disabled persons sometimes receive no notice of a divorce proceeding, or they enter into agreements that they do not understand. In Indiana, a husband obtained a divorce from his wife, who was in a hospital. The service of summons was made on the hospital, but there was no evidence that the wife ever received notice of the proceeding. The husband was awarded all the property of the parties and custody of the children. The divorce was set aside because the wife did not have an opportunity to defend herself.[61]

In Delaware a court voided a separation agreement that was signed while the husband was just emerging from an acute psychotic state and was heavily medicated. The evidence showed that the medication affected his reasoning abilities and that he was very dependent on his wife. He hoped that signing the agreement would facilitate reconciliation. Under the agreement, 70 percent of the husband's salary would go to the wife, and he would not receive a tax deduction for the payments. The court held that "even if the mental weakness of the [husband] in this case did not rise to a level of contractual incapacity, such weakness is a circumstance that operates to make the separation agreement voidable and coupled with the evidence of lack of independent counsel, undue influence and the unfairness in the transaction present in this case."[62]

A California appeals court held that a court could not include in a divorce and custody settlement agreement an order that a wife make herself and her children available for therapy or counseling. The court said that this amounted to involuntary psychiatric treatment, which could only be court-ordered under a mental health act.[63]

SOCIAL SECURITY MENTAL DISABILITY BENEFITS

The Social Security Administration (Administration) is responsible for two disability programs: the Old Age Survivors and Disability Insurance Program (OASDI) and Supplemental Security Income (SSI). They are identical for the purposes of establishing a mental disability.[64] The basic difference between the programs is that under OASDI the recipient must have "insured" status, which means that the recipient or a certain person in his or her family has worked a sufficient amount of time to have a designated number of quarters of earnings credit. Under SSI the recipient must meet certain income criteria. These criteria include resources other than income.

Standards

To receive disability income, an individual must be disabled within the statutory definition. "Disability" is defined as "[t]he inability to do any substantial gainful activity by reason of any medically determinable . . . mental impairment . . . which has lasted or can be expected to last for a continuous period of not less than 12 months."[65]

The impairment "must result from anatomical, physiological, or psychological abnormalities which can be shown by medically acceptable clinical and laboratory diagnostic techniques."[66] A mental impairment "must be established by medical evidence consisting of signs, symptoms, and laboratory findings," and not just by an individual's statement of his or her symptoms.[67] Psychiatric signs are defined as "medically demonstrable phenomena which indicate specific abnormalities of behavior, affect thought, memory, orientation and contact with reality. They must also be shown by observable facts that can be medically described and evaluated."[68] "Laboratory findings" are anatomical, physiological, or psychological phenomena which can be shown by the use of medically acceptable laboratory diagnostic techniques such as EEG and psychological tests.[69]

A psychiatric or psychological evaluation

> requires consideration of the nature and clinical manifestation of the medically determinable impairment(s) as well as consideration of the degree of limitation such impairment(s) may impose on the individual's ability to work as reflected by (1) daily activities both in the occupational and social spheres; (2) range of interests; (3) ability to take care of personal needs; and (4) ability to relate to others. This evaluation must be based on medical evidence consisting of demonstrable clinical signs (medically demonstrable phenomena, apart from the in-

dividual's symptoms which indicate specific abnormalities of behavior, affect, thought, memory, orientation, or contact with reality) and laboratory findings (including psychological tests) relevant to such issues as restriction of daily activities, constriction of interest, deterioration of personal hygiene, and impaired ability to relate to others.[70]

To meet this disability requirement, individuals must have a "severe impairment" that makes them unable to do their previous work "or any other substantial gainful activity which exists in the national economy."[71] A mental impairment is severe if it meets the duration requirement and is an impairment listed by the Administration[72] or an impairment equal to one on the list.[73] An impairment is not considered severe if it does not significantly limit an individual's physical or mental abilities to do basic work activities. Confinement to an institution does not *per se* mean that the impairment is severe. Similarly, release from an institution does not necessarily establish that the individual's impairment is improved.[74] If an individual has a severe impairment (listed or equal), the Administration will find that person disabled without regard to age, education, or work experience.[75]

However, if the Administration cannot make a decision based on an individual's current work activity or on medical facts alone (impairment not listed), and the impairment is severe, the Administration will review the individual's "residual functional capacity" and the mental and physical demands of past work. If it is determined that the individual can still do this kind of work, it will find the person not disabled.[76]

The introductory paragraphs of Appendix J (List of Mental Impairments for Social Security Disability Benefits) concerning mental disorders list specific medical findings that are essential to establishing the existence of mental impairment. Each category of impairment sets forth the medical findings necessary to establish the requisite level of severity for a finding of disability.[77] The standard of functional restriction is the same for all psychiatric disorders. Claimants must show that due to mental illness, their daily activities are markedly restricted; their interests are constricted; their personal habits and hygiene have deteriorated; and their ability to relate to others is seriously impaired. These restrictions will be considered only to the extent that they are imposed by claimants' psychopathology.[78]

Impairments should be documented by the results of psychological tests such as the Minnesota Multiphasic Personality Inventory (MMPI). In additon to functional restrictions, a claimant must demonstrate the existence of one or more of the clinical signs listed under each of the three categories of mental disorders: chronic brain syndrome; functional psychotic disorders; and functional nonpsychotic disorders. The clinical manifestations are abnormalities of either behavior, affect, thought, memory, orientation, or contact with reality. They must be demonstrated by medical evidence apart from the claimant's own statements.[79]

Many claimants suffer from multiple disorders, none of which standing alone serves the requisite severity of a listed impairment. However, operating in conjunction, these disorders may have a disabling impairment as severe or more severe than that of a single listed impairment. A claimant who can successfully demonstrate the medical equivalence should be found disabled without consideration of vocational factors just as if the claimant had established existence of a listed impairment.[80] In addition to establishing the necessary impairment, the impairment must be expected either to result in death or to last for 12 continuous months. Certain psychiatric impairments by definition will not meet the 12-months duration requirement. For example, acute brain syndrome is by definition a condition of short duration that can be reversed by medical intervention.[81]

Disability benefits will also be denied where the mentally disabled claimant willfully refuses treatment that has been medically prescribed for the impairment and that could be expected to restore the claimant's ability to perform his or her former work.

Expert Opinions

Claimants with mental disorders encounter more difficulty in establishing an impairment because diagnoses of mental disorders are less precise and more vulnerable to attack than those used to determine the existence of physical impairments. Most courts will allow a claimant's impairment to be demonstrated by any means that is generally acceptable within the fields of psychiatry and psychology. It is important that an expert's statement address the existence of a listed impairment, its probable duration, and the severity of the impairment in functional terms. Where appropriate, the doctor's statement should address the effect of the interaction of a combination of impairments. It is particularly important in mental disability cases to have the doctor address the immediate and long-range effect of both current medications and those the claimant has taken in the past, if that should relate to the claimant's functional abilities, both physical and mental. To be current, medical reports should reflect examinations, findings, and prognoses made within three months prior to the disability hearing. Conclusions in the report should be supported by medical and diagnostic findings as directed by the regulations. In the case of mental disability, the examination should be conducted by a psychiatrist, preferably board certified, or by a licensed clinical psychologist.

The expert medical opinion of a treating or examining physician regarding the overall impact of the impairment of the claimant's physical and mental functioning is essential to the claimant's case. The administrative law judge must weigh the conclusions of expert witnesses to the extent that they are supported by specific and complete clinical findings and are consistent with other evidence relating to the severity of the impairments.[82]

In general, the trier of fact may exercise discretion in weighing conflicting medical evidence.[83] Nevertheless, judicial opinions create certain guidelines for ranking one medical opinion over another. For example, a generally accepted standard is that the opinion of the claimant's own psychiatrist or psychologist is entitled to greater weight because it reflects an expert judgment based on continuous observation of the claimant's condition over a prolonged period. The length of this period and the number of times the psychiatrist or psychologist has seen the claimant are relevant to the therapist's familiarity with the claimant's overall condition.[84] One court held that an administrative law judge's decision to dismiss the testimony of a physician who had treated the claimant for 15 years as being unsupported by adequate medical data was totally without foundation.[85] The argument that a treating physician's report should be viewed with skepticism because the claimant's physician is inclined to be sympathetic toward the patient and because the physician's reimbursement may be affected by the outcome of the disability claim has also been rejected.[86] Nevertheless, it is widely accepted that the opinion of the claimant's own physician should never be completely insulated from attack, especially where it is controverted by other respectable and persuasive medical evidence.[87] In general, a specialist's opinion is given greater weight than that of a general practitioner. Similarly, the opinion of a child psychologist regarding the mental condition of an adolescent SSI claimant should carry greater weight than the opinion of a psychiatrist who treats only adults. However, there are exceptions to this rule.[88] In *Eli* the court noted that in a case of multiple impairment the opinion of the general practitioner may be more reliable than that of the medical specialist because the family doctor is better able to take into account the overall condition of the claimant.

Three types of medical evidence must be considered when making a disability determination: (1) the objective medical facts, which are clinical findings of treating or examining physicians divorced from their expert judgments or opinions as to the significance of the clinical finding; (2) the expert diagnoses and opinions and subsidiary questions of fact; and (3) the subjective evidence obtained and disability testified to by the claimant and corroborated by his or her family, friends, and neighbors.[89]

Clinical findings in psychiatry consist of assessments of abnormalities in thought behavior, affect, and personality. Expert opinion concerning psychiatric disorders need not be supported by strictly objective clinical or laboratory findings. The courts recognize that it is more difficult to establish a psychiatric disorder than it is to establish a physical disorder.[90]

A waitress who was disabled by a bad back condition from vigorous physical activity was denied a claim for widow's benefits. The administrative law judge rejected a psychiatric diagnosis that the claimant's infirmity was complicated by an anxiety reaction with depressive features. The court held that the absence of medical evidence controverting the testimony that she had a significant psychological problem that complicated her physical levitation was a factor in the order for further proceedings.[91]

A doctor's report stated that the claimant "was suffering from depression and real and disabling complaints of pain" but contained no references to medically acceptable clinical or laboratory findings. The administrative law judge refused to consider the report. While pain and subjective symptoms should be considered under the statute, they must be linked to a "medically determinable impairment" to support a finding of disability.[92]

Disability benefits were denied where a claimant had recurring bouts of schizophrenia and manic-depressive reaction for more than ten years because he was capable of substantial gainful activity during periods of remission and his condition was not expected to last for a continuous 12-month period. Further, the court found that medication did not prevent his working during periods of remission.[93]

A claimaint was found to be able to work, but the findings did not take into consideration that she had taken Librium for many years, sometimes in large doses. The court sent the case back to determine if such use of Librium either by itself or in conjunction with her physical ailments prevents her from engaging in substantial gainful activity.[94]

Whether a claimant's confinement because of a mental impairment, regardless of its severity, is sufficient to constitute disability is determined by establishing: (1) whether the claimant could have performed substantial gainful activity despite confinement; (2) whether during the relevant period the claimant had a mental impairment; or (3) whether the mental impairment was not the real reason for the claimant's confinement.[95]

Where a claimant bases a disability on alcoholism, the test of whether such a claim is adequate is (1) whether the claimant lost self-control to such a degree that the claimant will not benefit from treatment and (2) whether the claimant's impairment is the medical equivalent of an impairment listed in the Widower's Disability Act.[96] The court gave little weight to the opinion of the doctor, which concluded that the impairment was not severe enough, because the doctor had not personally examined the claimant.[97]

SPECIAL EDUCATION

The Education for All Handicapped Children Act of 1975[98] provides for special education to students between the ages of 3 and 20 who suffer from an impairment or impairments that interfere with learning or social development. The act entitles handicapped children to an education that gives each child the opportunity for academic achievement and is at least comparable to the opportunity given to nonhandicapped children.[99] The program in which a child is placed for a severe learning disability need not be the best possible placement, but it must be effective enough to adequately meet the individual's needs.[100] In passing the Education for All Handicapped Children Act:

> Congress did not attempt to provide detailed substantive content to the concept of an "appropriate" education. Instead, emphasizing the uniqueness of each handicapped child's educational requirements, Congress defined appropriate education as "special education and related services which . . . are provided in conformity with the individualized education program." The IEP is thus at the heart of the congressional scheme. It is a document to be developed by parents and educators working together that states the child's present level of performance, the objectives of this program and the services that will achieve them, and "appropriate objective criteria" for determining success.[101]

In addition to individualized educational programs, school districts must "mainstream" handicapped children to the greatest extent possible in order to integrate them with nonhandicapped children.[102]

An appropriate educational program is one that requires

> an education for each handicapped child that would enable the child to be as free as reasonably possible from the dependency on others, would enable the child to become a productive member of society, and would hopefully promote academic achievement by the child that would roughly approximate that of his or her nonhandicapped classmates. A child's unique needs are met whenever the child's IEP enables the child to meet these goals.[103]

Under the act school districts are required to pay for psychological counseling or therapy when the individualized treatment plan calls for it. This includes social work services,[104] psychological services, or any of the services required by statute and regulation. It is characterized as "related services."[105] Psychologists evaluate students and testify at administrative hearings on diagnoses and appropriate individualized education programs.[106]

NOTES

1. Timothy Jost, "The Illinois Guardianship For Disabled Adults Legislation of 1978 and 1979: Protecting the Disabled from Their Zealous Protectors," *Chi.-Kent L. Rev.* 56 (1980):1087.

2. Ill. Rev. Stat., ch. 110–1.2, § 11a–2.

3. Lanterman-Petris-Short, Cal. Welf. & Inst. Code, § 5350 *et seq.*; *see* Mitchell v. County of Los Angeles, 170 Cal. Rptr. 758 (Cal. Ct. App. 1981).

4. Cal. Probate Code, § 1751.

5. N.H. Rev. Stat. Ann. 464–A:4, II(e) (Supp. 1979).

6. In re De Lucca, 426 A.2d 32 (N.H. 1981).

7. Compton v. Compton, 606 S.W.2d 436 (Mo. Ct. App. 1980).

8. *See* Chapter 13.

9. A.E. & R.R. v. Mitchell, No. C–78–466 (D. Utah June 16, 1980), *Mental Disability Rptr.* 5 (1981):154.

10. Ill. Rev. Stat., ch. 110–1.2, ¶ 11a–9(a).

11. Ill. Rev. Stat., ch. 110–1.2, ¶ 11a–9(a).

12. In re Estate of Malloy, 96 Ill. App. 3d 1020, 422 N.E.2d 76, 78 (1981).

13. *Id.*

14. *Id.* at 79.

15. In re Estate of Knutson, 404 N.E.2d 1003 (Ill. App. Ct. 1980).

16. Brice-Nash v. Brice-Nash, 625 P.2d 836 (Kan. Ct. App. 1980).

17. Knight v. Radonski, 414 A.2d 1211 (Me. 1980).

18. Ill. Rev. Stat., ch. 110–1.2, § 11a3(b); Tex. Prob. Code Ann. § 130A–O (Vernon Supp. 1978–1979).

19. Manhattan State Citizens' Group, Inc. v. Bass, 81 Civ. 5883 (G.L.G.) (L.D. N.Y. Oct. 30, 1981), *Mental Disability Law Rptr.* 6 (1982):25.

20. Ill. Rev. Stat., ch. 91½, ¶ 2–100 (Smith-Hurd Supp. 1982–1983).

21. In re Jennings, No. P. 35–81 (N.J. Super Ct. Oct. 9, 1981), *Mental Disability Law Rptr.* 6 (1982):16.

22. In re A.W., 80 S.A. 175 (Colo. Sup. Ct. Nov. 30, 1981), *Mental Disability Law Rptr.* 6 (1982):10.

23. South Carolina Dept. of Social Services v. McDow, 280 S.E.2d 208 (S.C. 1981).

24. In re Kurnyk, 441 N.Y.S.2d 328 (N.Y. Sup. Ct. 1981).

25. Payton v. Payne, 414 N.E.2d 33 (Ill. App. Ct. 1980).

26. In re Brown, 370 N.E.2d 148 (Ill. App. Ct. 1977), 65 A.L.R. 3rd 991; In re Vicic, 398 N.E.2d 420 (Ill. App. Ct. 1979).

27. In re Estate of Head, 615 P.2d 71 (N.M. Ct. App. 1980).

28. Taylor v. Abi, 415 A.2d 894 (Pa. Super. Ct. 1979).

29. Fidelity Financial Services, Inc. v. McCoy, 392 So. 2d 118 (La. Ct. App. 1980).

30. Meriwether v. Brown, 390 So. 2d 1042 (Ala. 1980).

31. Wright v. Garrison, 609 S.W.2d 111 (Ark. Ct. App. 1980); Alley v. Rodgers, 599 S.W.2d 739 (Ark. 1980).

32. Bryant v. Bryant, 379 So. 2d 382 (Fla. Dist. Ct. App. 1980).

33. Ridgeway v. Ridgeway, 429 A.2d 801 (Conn. Sup. Ct. 1980).

34. Cohen v. Krumpacker, 586 S.W.2d 370 (Mo. Ct. App. 1979).

35. Owen v. Owen, 376 So. 2d 26 (Fla. Dist. Ct. App. 1979).

36. Dalcarenchi v. Moenningu, 395 N.E.2d 113 (Ill. App. Ct. 1979).

37. Santosky v. Kramer, 455 U.S. 745 (1982).

38. *Id.* at 753.

39. *Id.* at 761.

40. *Id.* at 762–765.

41. *Id.* at 766–769.

42. In re E.A., 638 P.2d 278 (Colo. 1982).

43. In re C.G., No. 53281 (Okla. Sup. Ct. Nov. 10, 1981).

44. *Id.*

45. Interest of R.W.B., 241 N.W.2d 546 (N.D. 1976), *aff'd*, Kleingartner v. D.P.A.B., 310 N.W.2d 575 (N.D. 1981).

46. In re Sylvia M. & Alicia M., 443 N.Y.S.2d 214 (N.Y. App. Div. 1981).

47. In re Holley, 308 N.W.2d 341 (Neb. 1981).

48. Glover v. Alabama Department of Pensions and Security, 401 So. 2d 786 (Ala. Ct. Civ. App. 1981).

49. Louise Wise Services v. Phoebe D., 403 N.E.2d 451 (N.Y. Ct. App. 1980).

50. Department of Social Services v. Atkins, 316 N.W.2d 477 (Mich. Ct. App. 1982).

51. Alameda County Social Service Agency v. Katherine C., 181 Cal. Rptr. 188 (Cal. Ct. App. 1982).

52. Nebraska v. Farmer, 315 N.W.2d 454 (Neb. 1982).

53. In re R.M.M., III, 316 N.W.2d 538 (Minn. 1982).

54. In re C.L.M., 625 S.W.2d 613 (Mo. 1981).

55. In re Frederiksen, 610 P.2d 371 (Wash. Ct. App. 1980).

56. McCormick v. EEPT of Human Resources, 288 S.E.2d 120 (Ga. Ct. App. 1982).

57. Jewish Child Care Assn. v. Elaine S.Y., 418 N.E.2d 1305 (N.Y. Ct. App. 1981).

58. Jewish Child Care Assn. v. Elaine S.Y., 455 N.Y.S.2d 114 (N.Y. Ct. App. 1981).

59. In re Young, 600 P.2d 1312 (Wash. Ct. App. 1979).

60. Illinois v. White, 429 N.E.2d 1383 (Ill. App. Ct. 1982).

61. Munden v. Munden, No. 1–279A56 (Ind. Ct. App. Dec. 26, 1979), *discussed* in *Mental Disability Law Reporter* 4 (1980):107.

62. G.A.S. v. S.I.S., 406 A.2d 253 (Del. Dam. Ct. 1978).

63. Mathews v. Mathews, 161 Cal. Rptr. 879 (Cal. Ct. App. 1980).

64. OASDI: 42 U.S.C. § 405(a)(b) (1974) 20 C.F.R. Part 404 (1982); SSI: 42 U.S.C. § 423(d)(1)–(d)(5) (1974); 20 C.F.R. Part 416 (1982). *See generally* ABA Commission on the Mentally Retarded, Social Security Disability Benefits, Reprinted in *Mental Disability Law Reporter* 4 (1980):356 for a discussion of the administrative process.

65. 20 C.F.R. § 404.1505 (1982).

66. 20 C.F.R. § 404.1508 (1982).

67. *Id.*

68. 20 C.F.R. § 404.1528(b) (1982).

69. 20 C.F.R. § 404.1528(c) (1982).

70. Department of Health and Human Services, "Disability Evaluation under Social Security, A Handbook for Physicians" (Washington, D.C.: DHHS, August 1979).

71. 20 C.F.R. § 404.1505 (1982).

72. *See* Appendix J.

73. 20 C.F.R. § 404.1521 (1982).

74. Handbook, *supra* note 70.

75. 20 C.F.R. § 404.1520(d) (1982).

76. 20 C.F.R. § 404.1520(e) (1982).

77. *See* Appendix J.

78. *Id.*

79. *Id.*

80. 20 C.F.R. § 404.1522 (1982).

81. *Id.*

82. Underwood v. Ribicoff, 298 F.2d 850, 851 (4th Cir. 1962).

83. 20 C.F.R. § 404.1526 (1982).

84. Richardson v. Perales, 402 U.S. 389, 399 (1971).

85. Eli v. Weinberger, (1979) Unempl. Ins. Rep. (CCH) § 12429.56 (W.D. Va. Oct. 16, 1973).

86. Bitek v. Finch, 438 F.2d 1157 (4th Cir. 1971).

87. Whitson v. Finch, 437 F.2d 720 (6th Cir. 1971).

88. Halsey v. Richardson, 441 F.2d 431 (6th Cir. 1971).

89. Eli v. Weinberger, *supra* note 85.

90. Underwood v. Ribicoff, 298 F.2d 850, 851 (4th Cir. 1962).

91. Cutler v. Weinberger, 516 F.2d 1282 (2d Cir. 1975).

92. Aquino v. Harris, 516 F. Supp. 265 (E.D. Pa. 1981).

93. Ware v. Schweiker, 651 F.2d 408 (5th Cir. 1981).

94. Couise v. Harris, 510 F. Supp. 534 (W.D. Mo. 1981).

95. Schmoll v. Harris, 636 F.2d 1146 (7th Cir. 1980).

96. Doe v. Harris, 495 F. Supp. 1161 (S.D. N.Y. 1980).

97. Veal v. Califano, 610 F.2d 495 (8th Cir. 1979).

98. 20 U.S.C. § 1400, *et seq.*, 34 C.F.R. § 300 *et seq.*

99. Campbell v. Galladega County Board of Education, 518 F. Supp. 47 (N.D. Ala. 1981).

100. Morris v. Massachusetts Department of Education, 529 F. Supp. 759 (D. Mass. 1981).

101. Campbell v. Galladega County Board of Education, *supra* note 99, at 52.

102. Rowley v. Board of Education, 632 F.2d 945 (2d Cir. 1980).

103. *Id.*

104. Garby B. v. Cronin, No. 79 C 5383 (N.D. Ill. July 18, 1980).

105. 20 U.S.C. § 1401(17); 45 C.F.R. §§ 121a.13(a) and (b)(a).

106. Krip and Krip, "The Legalization of the School Psychologists' World" *J. School Psychol.* 14 (1976):83; Katz and Bonfield, "The Right to Education: Due Process and the Inner City Child," *Bull. Am. Acad. Psych. & L.* 3 (1976): 70; Krip, Bun and Kuriloff, "Legal Reform of Special Education: Empirical Studies and Procedural Proposals," *Calif. L. Rev.* 62 (1974):40; Goolow, "The School Psychologist as Expert Witness in Due Process Hearings," *J. School Psychol.* 13 (1975):311.

Chapter 15

Criminal Proceedings

Psychiatrists and psychologists testify as experts on a variety of issues in criminal proceedings, among them fitness to stand trial, insanity defenses or mentally ill but guilty pleas, and habitual sex offender acts. Psychiatrists and psychologists also present expert opinions in sentencing proceedings. [1]

FITNESS TO STAND TRIAL

Standards

"Fitness" or "competency" to stand trial is a determination of whether a defendant in a criminal proceeding understands the crime with which he or she has been charged and whether the defendant is presently able to cooperate with counsel in preparing a defense. If a physical or mental disability renders the defendant unable to cooperate with counsel or to appreciate the charges, then the defendant is "unfit" or "incompetent" to stand trial. [2]

Issue of Fitness Raised

To try an unfit defendant is a violation of due process because the defendant is unable to assist in his or her own defense and does not understand or appreciate the charges. Where a question of the defendant's mental capacity to proceed is raised, criminal prosecution should be halted until the defendant is found to have the mental capacity to proceed. [3] Due process requires an evidentiary hearing any time there is "substantial evidence" that a defendant may be mentally unfit to stand trial. Evidence is substantial if it raises reasonable doubt about the defendant's trial fitness. [4] Knowledge of the defendant's past psychiatric history is not sufficient under this standard. [5] Nevertheless, a California court held that where a psychiatrist or qualified psychologist testifies that a defendant is unable to understand the nature of proceedings or assist in the defense substantial evidence exists that the defendant's competency should be reviewed in a hearing.[6] Circumstances that cast doubt on the defendant's fitness to stand trial in this case were: (1) the trial court was unsure enough itself to order a psychiatric evaluation; (2) the defendant had eight previous admissions to the state mental hospital; (3) a doctor testified that the defendant had brain damage; and (4) the defendant was so disruptive at trial that he had to be removed from the courtroom.[7]

A conviction in a California case was reversed where there were bizarre outbursts by the defendant during questions by the court about his ability to assist counsel. The defense attorney requested a further examination to see if his client was capable of cooperation. He told the judge that one of the psychiatrists who had examined the defendant earlier and found him competent now believed that he was incompetent. The judge denied the request for another exam. The denial was reversed, and a new trial ordered. The court stated that mental competency is not decided by whether the defendant was oriented to time and place.[8]

An Illinois court held that the defendant's due process rights had been violated when the trial judge failed to hold a fitness hearing when a bona fide doubt existed. There was evidence of irrational behavior by the defendant just after the crime, and there were psychiatric reports indicating that the defendant had been under continuous psychiatric care.[9]

Nevertheless, a hearing is necessary only where a reasonable doubt exists as to the defendant's fitness to stand trial. A reasonable doubt was not raised in a case where there was no medical evidence on fitness, no history of irrational behavior, and a calm demeanor at trial.[10] The court had granted a motion for a fitness examination, which was supported by claims that the defendant had blackouts causing memory difficulties. The defendant failed to attend the examination, and his counsel never pursued it.[11] In Arizona, it was held that a fitness examination was unnecessary even though a doctor found that the defendant had "severe mental problems" and his presentence report recommended that he enroll in a mental health program and indicated he had a serious drinking problem. The court said that an examination is required only if reasonable grounds exist to believe that a defendant is unable to understand the proceedings or to assist counsel.[12]

Where an examination to determine fitness resulted in a diagnosis of "transient situational disturbance; adjustment reaction to adult life," but indicated no psychosis, the defense attorney took no further action on the matter. It was held that failure to conduct a hearing was not error.[13] The defendant, charged with rape and burglary, engaged in some bizarre acts. All three of his victims were named Patricia. He gave his gun to one victim and told her to shoot him. He asked another if she would freak out if he committed suicide, and then he fell asleep. The court quoted the U.S. Supreme Court: "[T]here are, of course, no fixed or immutable signs which invariably indicate need for further inquiries to determine fitness to proceed.'' The defendant was a chronic drug addict which may have explained his complaints and bizarre behavior. The court emphasized defense counsel's silence on the matter.

Relevant Factors Considered To Determine Fitness

In 1975, the U.S. Supreme Court set guidelines for the type of evidence that may be used to prove a defendant incompetent to stand trial. The factors to be considered are a history of irrational behavior, demeanor at trial, and medical opinion.[14] Expert opinions on fitness are not restricted to psychiatrists. In Illinois, psychologists are permitted to testify regarding fitness to stand trial.[15]

The Chief Justice of the Nebraska Supreme Court has set out factors to be considered in determining whether a defendant meets the test of fitness:

> (1) That the defendant has sufficient mental capacity to appreciate his presence in relation to time, place, and things; (2) That his elementary mental processes are such that he understands that he is in a court of law charged with a criminal offense; (3) That he realizes there is a judge on the bench; (4) That he understands that there is a prosecutor present who will try to convict him of a criminal charge; (5) That he has a lawyer who will undertake to defend him against the charge; (6) That he knows that he will be expected to tell lawyers all he knows or remembers about the events involved in the alleged crime; (7) That he understands that there will be a jury present to pass upon evidence in determining his guilt or innocence; (8) That he has sufficient memory to relate answers to questions posed to him; (9) That he has established rapport with his lawyer; (10) That he can follow the testimony reasonably well; (11) That he has the ability to meet stresses without his rationality of judgment breaking down; (12) That he has at least minimal contact with reality; (13) That he has the minimum intelligence necessary to grasp the events taking place; (14) That he can confer coherently with some appreciation of proceedings; (15) That he can both give and receive advice from his attorneys; (16) That he can divulge facts without paranoid distress; (17) That he can decide upon a plea; (18) That he can testify, if necessary; (19) That he can make simple decisions; and (20) That he has a desire for justice rather than undeserved punishment.[16]

A defendant must be fit at the time of trial. A new trial was given a defendant who had been found competent to stand trial in November based on a hospital report made the previous April. There was evidence that his condition changed. While in jail he was observed eating off the floor and washing in the commode. A new inquiry was ordered.[17]

Expert Opinions

The fact that a defendant refuses to cooperate with the experts conducting an evaluation is not evidence sufficient to support a finding of unfitness. In Louisiana, two physicians who examined the defendant testified that they could not tell if the unresponsiveness was the result of an inability to comprehend or intentional malingering, and both recommended longer observation. The trial court interviewed the defendant and found him fit.[18] There was no indication that he was unfit to stand trial. The court stated that "a defendant cannot establish his unfitness to stand trial merely by having stymied the efforts of the sanity commission."[19] The trial judge also based his finding on his observation of the defendant at various pretrial hearings.[20]

There is a difference, however, between refusal to cooperate and not being able to cooperate with experts. In a New York case, two psychiatrists testified that the defendant's thought disorder and paranoid schizophrenia prevented him from assisting his attorney. The hospital staff reported that, "he was still very belligerent, uncooperative, extremely hostile, negative, unresponsive, very irrational and illogical" so that they could not reasonably converse with him. He had murdered his wife because of a delusion that she had abused their children.[21]

Past hospitalization,[22] a diagnosis that a defendant is a pathological liar,[23] a diagnosis of a personality disorder,[24] or a diagnosis of a mental disorder[25] have been held insufficient by themselves to establish unfitness to stand trial. Nevertheless, "One need not be catatonic, raving or frothing, to be unable to understand the nature of the charges against him and to be unable to relate realistically to the problems of his defense."[26] "It is unnatural" for a defendant not to try to favorably impress the jury in his testimony, and such behavior is "indicative of one who is not operating in a world of reality."[27] The defendant had a long history of hospitalization, escapes, and shock treatment. This history was not counterbalanced by the testimony of the arresting officer and custodial officers and one medical doctor who was trained in neither psychiatry nor psychology, all of whom testified that he seemed sane to them. The court held that the testimony of the lay witnesses who observed his conduct was not of value because they lacked prolonged and intimate contact with the defendant.

The Iowa Supreme Court held that a defendant who was unable to assist counsel effectively because of a mental illness was unfit to stand trial. The defendant had a history of hospitalization, drug abuse, and livestock mutilation and led a nomad-like existence. Both the state's doctor and the defendant's doctor agreed that the defendant had a mental disorder, although they disagreed as to what type. The defense doctor took that position that the defendant "had pronounced negativism and also delusions that his case had to be dismissed if not tried within 30 days." This combination prevented the defendant from either assisting or accepting counsel in the view of the expert physician. When the defendant refused to accept counsel after the judge made several attempts to convince him to do so, the trial went on with no defense being offered. The supreme court said that the defendant's lack of responsiveness and outbursts during the trial indicated the delusional nature of the defendant's behavior. Based on the opinions of the two psychiatrists who testified regarding his behavior during and after trial, the conviction was reversed and sent back for further proceedings.[28]

In Tennessee, a defendant was held competent to stand trial where she was taking medication for epilepsy. The examination to determine if the prescription affected her ability to stand trial or her condition at the time of the trial indicated that the medication had no effect on her fitness.[29] A codefendant who was also found competent was denied a psychiatric evaluation to determine competency. He was a drug addict with a liver ailment. He had suffered withdrawal symptoms in jail and had made two earlier suicide attempts. The court stated that this was not evidence that he was incompetent to stand trial.[30]

Neither amnesia nor memory lapse necessarily renders a defendant unfit. A defendant's fitness "depends upon his rational, as well as factual, understanding of the proceedings against him and his sufficient present ability to consult with his lawyer with a reasonable degree of rational understanding."[31] The defendant suffered from Binswanger's Disease, which causes blackouts and memory lapses. Defendant had not claimed that this disorder affected his understanding of the charges or his ability to consult with counsel, but only that he could not remember all the events underlying the charges and could not provide his counsel with all the facts from his perspective. "Partial memory loss does not substantially impair defendant's ability to consult with counsel and to understand the proceedings against him."[32]

The Kentucky Supreme Court has held that amnesia about a crime due to mental disease does not render a defendant incompetent. Amnesia does not preclude the defendant from receiving a fair trial, because memory is only one source of ascertaining facts concerning a criminal offense. The defendant, diagnosed as suffering from "paranoid schizophrenia with fixed delusional beliefs," was found by a trial judge to understand the nature and consequences of the trial proceedings but not to have the capacity to participate rationally in his defense due to his distorted thinking based on his poor memory of events surrounding the charged offenses.[33]

The Iowa Supreme Court reversed a plea of guilty where the 16-year-old defendant had been tried as an adult. The defendant had a borderline I.Q., slow emotional development, limited grasp of reality, and poor memory about basic events of his life, such as how long he went to school.[34]

In California, a finding of competency was reversed as not supported by substantial evidence. Five psychiatrists, three psychologists, a medical doctor, a nurse, and three psychiatric technicians testified regarding the patient's lack of competence based on four psychiatric reports that concluded he suffered from chronic schizophrenia, some degree of mental retardation, and some organic dysfunction that caused very bizarre speech and thought patterns. The defendant had a long history of mental illness, extremely high tolerance of massive doses of psychotropic drugs, extremely regressive behavior, low intelligence, and involuntary physiological symptoms.[35]

Once a defendant has been found unfit, there must be another hearing, with the same protection, to restore competence.[36]

CRIMINAL RESPONSIBILITY—THE INSANITY DEFENSE

Insanity is a defense raised against felony charges, most commonly murder. In essence, it is a defense that states the defendant did not have the intent to commit the act—the defendant either did not know the act was wrong or could not control his actions—a requisite element that must be proved in criminal cases. All states allow the defense.[37] Montana has a limited defense that does not permit psychiatric testimony at trial unless it is necessary to show that the defendant was so insane that the requisite *mens rea* (intent) did not exist.[38] There is a presumption that the defendant was sane when the crime was committed. This presumption is overcome as soon as the defendant introduces the slightest evidence tending to prove a lack of capacity at the time of the crime. At that point twenty-three states require that the prosecution prove beyond a reasonable doubt that the defendant is sane.

One state, Texas, requires that the state prove the defendant is sane by a preponderance of the evidence.[39] Twenty-two states and the District of Columbia require the defendant to prove insanity by a preponderance of the evidence. One state requires that the defendant proves insanity "to the satisfaction of the jury" and another requires proof "to the reasonable satisfaction of the jury." One state requires "preponderance of the greater weight of evidence" and another requires "reasonable certainty by the greater weight of credible evidence." Only one state, Maryland, requires the defendant to prove insanity "beyond a reasonable doubt."[40]

The question is whether the defendant was sane at the time the crime was committed. The testimony of lay witnesses who observed the defendant during the act or shortly thereafter may be more persuasive as to the mental state of the defendant than psychiatric opinion based upon an evaluation conducted months after the crime. In an Oklahoma case the defense presented detailed evidence of repeated hospitalizations for a recurring mental condition. The father of the defendant and the chief county jailer both presented incidents of bizarre behavior by the defendant both before and following the offense. The arresting officer testified that the suspect seemed lucid fifteen minutes after the robbery. The court upheld the finding of sanity stating that the only moment for the purpose of the trial is when the crime was committed. Even though the evidence in question was consistent with the doctor's diagnosis, its value for determining the defendant's condition at the time of the robbery was for the jury to decide.[41]

In Illinois a court held that the prosecution carried its burden of proving that the defendant was sane even though it presented no expert witnesses of its own to rebut the views of medical experts who testified for the defense. In the opinion of the defense experts, the defendant suffered brain damage and epilepsy from a gunshot wound to the head that had occurred several years prior to the sexual assault with which he had been charged. An internist diagnosed the defendant as having a "psychopathic personality and as being unable to conform his conduct or actions to the requirements of the law." Psychiatrists label the disorder as organic brain syndrome, leaving the defendant "unable to appreciate the criminality of his conduct or control to the requirements of the law." The prosecution relied on the observations of the victim and her fiance indicating "no evidence of defendant having the speech or difficulty attributed to him by his expert witnesses."[42]

Standards

Federal and state courts apply a number of tests to determine whether the defendant is responsible for the criminal act committed.

M'Naughton Rule

The *M'Naughton* rule, or the *M'Naughton* rule plus irresistible impulse, remains the law of most American jurisdictions. The *M'Naughton* rule is:

> that every man is to be presumed to be sane, and to possess a sufficient degree of reason to be responsible for his crime, until a contrary be proved to their satisfaction; and that to establish a defense on the ground of insanity, it must be clearly proved, at the time of the committing of the act, the party accused was laboring under such a defective reason, from disease of the mind, as not to know the nature and quality of the act he was doing; or, if he did know it, that he did not know he was doing what was wrong. The mode of putting the latter part of the question to the jury on these occasions has generally been, whether the accused at the time of doing the act knew the difference between right and wrong . . . in respect to the very act with which he is charged.[43]

The irresistible impulse test is a formula stating that a person is not responsible for a crime if the act was compelled by an irresistible impulse. In other words, "an irresistible impulse means an impulse to commit an unlawful or criminal act which cannot be resisted or overcome because mental disease has destroyed the freedom of will, the power of self-control and the choice of actions."[44] This is usually construed to mean a psychotic or obsessive compulsive (neurotic) impulse and not a simple reaction of rage. Currently, 14 states accept irresistible impulse tests; the remaining 36 reject them.

Pennsylvania and Indiana have declined to reexamine and abrogate the *M'Naughton* rule in light of recent advancements in the field of psychology.[45]

American Law Institute Test

The American Law Institute (ALI) test used by the federal courts is that "if as a result of mental disease or defect he [the defendant] lacks substantial capacity either to appreciate the wrongfulness of his conduct or to conform his conduct to the requirement of law. The terms 'mental disease or defect' do not include abnormality manifested only by repeated criminal or otherwise antisocial conduct."[46]

A person is not responsible for criminal conduct if at the time of such conduct, as a result of mental disease or defect, that person "lacks substantial capacity either to appreciate the criminality [wrongfulness] of his conduct or to conform his conduct to the requirements of the law." Some states use a variation of the ALI Model Penal Code: "The jury must be satisfied that at the time of committing the prohibited act, defendant, as a result of mental disease or defect, lacks substantial capacity to conform his conduct to the requirements of the law which he is alleged to have violated. . . ."[47]

In connection with the ALI's test, courts use the term "diminished responsibility." A federal court stated:

> Our decision accompanies the redefinition of when a mental condition exonerates a defendant from criminal responsibility with the doctrine that expert testimony as to a defendant's abnormal mental condition may be received and considered, as tending to show, in a responsible way, that defendant did not have the specific mental state required for a particular crime or degree of crime—even though he was aware that his act was wrongful and was able to control it, and hence was not entitled to complete exoneration. Some of the cases following this doctrine use the term "diminished responsibility," but we prefer the example of the cases that avoid this term.[48]

The diminished responsibility doctrine, also known as partial insanity, refers to the defendant's lack of capacity to achieve the state of mind requisite for the commission of a crime. It "permits the trier of fact to regard the impaired mental state of the defendant in mitigation of the punishment or degree of the offense even though the impairment does not qualify as insanity under the prevailing test."[49] For example, "in some jurisdictions, mental retardation and extremely low intelligence will, if proved, serve to reduce first degree murder to manslaughter."[50] The Arkansas Supreme Court reduced a death sentence to life imprisonment due to defense counsel's failure to alert the jury at sentencing to the significance of the evidence of his client's diminished capacity.[51]

Rhode Island has adopted the ALI's view of criminal responsibility. As the majority of jurisdictions have adopted ALI, Rhode Island recognizes the diminished capacity concept that allows a defendant a chance "to establish the existence of a mental defect or obstacle to the presence of the state of mind that is an element of the crime." The jury is free to believe or disbelieve the testimony given on the issue.[52]

Federal courts in 13 states recognize the defense of diminished responsibility,[53] as do the state courts in Alaska, Colorado, Connecticut, Hawaii, Iowa, Kansas, Nebraska, New Mexico, Ohio, Pennsylvania, Washington, Wisconsin, and Vermont.[54] Maine, Missouri, and Montana recognize the diminished capacity defense by statute.[55] Arizona, Delaware, the District of Columbia, Louisiana, Maryland, Massachusetts, Nevada, North Carolina, and West Virginia do not recognize this defense.[56]

In a robbery case it was held that the compelling desire to obtain drugs occasioned by drug withdrawal does not negate the intent element of the robbery, kidnapping, and extortion that took place. The withdrawal pains are neither an abnormal condition of the mind or "intoxication" rising to the level of diminished capacity nor insanity.[57]

Evaluation of Defendant by Experts

Both sides generally introduce psychiatric expert opinion at trial to establish whether the defendant was sane at the time of the crime. It is common for psychiatrists to answer the ultimate question of sanity in terms of the legal standard used in a particular jurisdiction. The psychiatric opinion is not conclusive. The judge or jury makes the ultimate finding. An Illinois appeals court refused to reverse a murder conviction on the grounds of insanity even though there was enough evidence to sustain a finding of insanity. In considering "the totality of the evidence," the judge or jury is allowed "to waive testimony and determine the credibility of the witnesses, both lay and expert without being required by law to accept the opinions of psychiatrists. . . . A finding of sanity will not be disturbed unless it is so erroneous as to indicate that it was based upon prejudice or passion."[58]

Claiming insanity, a woman in Alabama with a history of mental problems failed to overturn her conviction for the shooting of three members of a family on whose property she lived. The psychiatric report indicated that she suffered from paranoid schizophrenia. Nevertheless, her calmness just prior to the attack, her drinking that day, and her fleeing the scene of the crime helped the jury to conclude that she was not insane. Given the presumption of sanity, the expert's testimony alone did not establish insanity by the required preponderance of the evidence. There were ample facts to justify the jury's sanity finding in this admittedly close case.[59]

Even though there is a conflict in testimony regarding the defendant's ability to understand the nature of his or her acts and to know whether the act was wrong (*M'Naughton* standard), where there is enough evidence to decide that the state had proved insanity beyond a reasonable doubt and by the same evidence that the defendant had not acted in the heat of passion, the weight to be given evidence is up to the trier of facts.[60]

While a majority of the courts that have passed upon the issue have rejected the claim that the defendant has a right to the presence of counsel at a court-ordered psychiatric examination,[61] an Alaska court held that it was error to refuse defense counsel permission to be present at a state-ordered psychiatric exam. The court observed that a tape recording of such psychiatric exam in its entirety would offer "a potentially adequate alternative to the physical presence of the defense counsel during the psychiatric interview."[62]

In a federal case the prosecution's psychiatric expert witness based his testimony on reports received from other physicians who took part in the interviews and other staff members who observed the patient. The psychiatrist also relied on test results, FBI reports, and information from the U.S. Attorney's office. None of this information was put into evidence, but the defendant was provided copies of it. The chief of psychiatry at the Federal Medical Center where the defendant underwent three months of examination admitted that he had only limited contact with the defendant, had had no private interviews except informal ones, and took part in only two staff interviews of the defendant. The court held that, because the defendant had access to most of his data and was provided with an adequate opportunity to cross-examine and confront the witnesses, there was no violation of constitutional rights.[63]

In Massachusetts, a psychiatrist for the prosecution attempted to discredit the defendant's psychiatrist by testifying about what the defendant's wife had told him in an interview. It was inadmissible hearsay for the prosecution's expert to reveal the wife's view of her husband's relationship with the psychiatrist, which she described as "bizarre and unprofessional." The relationship had nothing to do with the defendant's sanity when he committed the specific offenses. A defendant's psychiatrist should not be put on trial, nor should a trial be allowed to become merely a war between the experts.[64]

In New York, an appeals court ordered an in-chambers inspection of a murder defendant's 38-page statement, which was written at his counsel's request prior to the time the defense decided to rely on the insanity defense. The prosecution sought discovery of this document based on a waiver of any privilege because of a proposed insanity defense. The court held that the prosecutor be allowed to discover portions of this document relevant to the insanity defense; the court would protect the remainder from discovery based on the attorney-client privilege. The court stated that the defense psychiatrist would aid the court, if necessary, in making a determination of which portions of the document were relevant to the insanity plea.[65]

In New York, the court ruled that a forensic psychiatrist may question on the record a seriously disturbed youth who allegedly assaulted his sibling. Using the right to linguistic interpretive services as a basis for its holding, the court allowed a forensic specialist to assist in communicating with this defendant, whose thought processes were so convoluted that such a specialized interpreter was needed to conduct the statutorily required questioning necessary to accept the insanity plea.[66]

Insanity Defense in General

"Emotional insanity or temporary mania, not associated with a disease of the mind, does not constitute insanity."[67] A defendant who was convicted of an escape from jail argued that he had become insane at the time he escaped because he had just been convicted of robbery.[68] The Supreme Court of Pennsylvania obtained the murder conviction of a mother for killing her 6-year-old son despite evidence that she was insane. The psychiatrist's diagnosis of "chronic schizophrenia, acute type" was outweighed by the state's testimony about the mother's acts and statements at the time of the son's drowning and her state of mind at the time of her confession. "Mental illness alone cannot absolve appellant from criminal responsibility."[69] Nor will drug abuse by itself prove insanity; there must be psychosis.[70]

The sanity of the defendant was affirmed where a clinical psychologist testified that the defendant lacked the ability to distinguish right from wrong and was incapable of understanding the consequences of his acts. However, the psychologist admitted there was no evidence of psychosis; she did acknowledge that intellectual impairment is not equivalent to insanity and also rejected the view that intoxication and insanity are synonymous.[71]

Recommendations of the American Bar Association and of the American Psychiatric Association

In the wake of the Hinckley verdict in June 1982 the country became embroiled in public, professional, and legislative debates regarding the insanity defense. Bills were introduced to modify or abolish this defense.[72] In December 1982, the American Psychiatric Association (APA) issued a statement on the insanity defense. In February 1983, the American Bar Association (ABA) made recommendations on the defense.[73]

Recommendations of the American Bar Association

The American Bar Association recommended "in principle, a defense of nonresponsibility for crime, which focuses solely on whether the defendant, as a result of mental disease or defect, was unable to appreciate the wrongfulness of his or her conduct at the time of the offense charged."[74]

In effect, this is a modification of the ALI's Model Penal Code test. The cognitive part of the test is retained while the volitional part of the test is rejected. The ABA report stated that:

> The drafters of the Model Penal Code used the term "appreciate" rather than "know" to take into account the emotional or "effective" dimensions of severe mental disorder and thereby meant to facilitate a full clinical description of the defendant's perception and understanding at the time of the offense. We believe that this was an important and valuable suggestion and we endorse it in our proposed language "unable to appreciate the wrongfulness of that defendant's conduct. . . ." This formulation will allow proper and necessary expert testimony regarding "appreciation." We also emphasize, however, that the overly vague "substantial capacity" language of the ALI test does not appear within our formulation. We choose instead to employ the term "unable." In our judgment the formulation of our proposed test poses for the jury a more concrete question and reduces the risk that juries won't interpret the test too loosely. To the extent that the drafters of the Model Penal Code use a "substantial capacity" formulation to achieve flexibility we think the term "appreciate" adequately accomplishes this objective.[75]

The ABA rejected the volitional part of the ALI test because "experience confirms that there is still no accurate scientific basis for measuring one's capacity for self-control or for calibrating the impairment of such capacity."[76] Thus, the irresistible-impulse and the diminished-capacity prong of the ALI test was rejected. The report stated:

> The principal problem with the continuing utilization of the volitional or "control" test is that the test is combined with vague or broad interpretations of the term "mental disease." And there is a mixing of these two ephemeral notions that result inevitably in unstructured expert speculation regarding the psychological causes of criminal behavior. This is the result especially in cases where defendants have a personality disorder, an impulse disorder, or any other diagnosable abnormality short of clinically recognized psychoses. Our proposal will eliminate expert speculation in these highly subjective areas and will, we submit, help psychiatrists, counsel and courts focus on these legitimate and more objective psychiatric factors which should be taken into consideration in determining responsibility for crime.[77]

The second recommendation of the ABA is that the allocation of the burden of proof in insanity defense cases should be that:

> [I]n any jurisdictions utilizing any test for insanity which focuses solely on whether the defendant, as a result of mental disease or a defect, was unable to know, understand or appreciate the wrongfulness of his or her conduct at the time of the offense charge, the prosecution should have the burden of disproving the defendant's claim of insanity beyond a reasonable doubt; and, secondly, that in jurisdictions utilizing the ALI-Model Penal Code Tests for insanity the defendant should have the burden of proving by a preponderance of the evidence his or her claim of insanity.[78]

Currently, federal practice allocates the burden of proof to the prosecution in insanity defense cases on a beyond-a-reasonable-doubt standard. Within the states, the allocation of the burden of proof is split. Twenty-six states and the District of Columbia place the burden on the defendant, and the bulk of these states utilize a ''preponderance of evidence'' standard. The remaining 24 states place the burden on the prosecution and require the prosecution to prove sanity beyond a reasonable doubt. The ABA's recommendation provides that the burden should fall upon the prosecution to disprove a defendant's claim of insanity in those states using a test that focuses solely on whether the defendant, as a result of mental disease or defect, was unable to know, understand, or appreciate the wrongfulness of his or her conduct. In those jurisdictions employing the combined cognitive-volitional tests, the burden of proof shifts to the defendant because the defendant is the recipient of the possible benefits flowing from an expanded insanity test. The shift is thus a *quid pro quo* for the greater latitude implicit within the volitional part of the test.[79]

Finally, the ABA opposed the enactment of statutes that supplement the verdict of ''not guilty by reason of insanity'' with an alternative verdict of ''guilty but mentally ill.''[80]

The ''guilty but mentally ill'' verdict is currently provided for in eight states. It presents an additional verdict option for the jury. Such an approach has two ''apparent and different objectives.'' One relates to an assessment of the defendant's criminal responsibility at the time of the offense, and the other relates to the disposition of the defendant after criminal adjudication. The ABA concluded that:

> Determinations regarding the defendant's criminal responsibility for the act are, in essence, backward-looking and based on moral criteria. The dispositional determinations are forward-looking and dependent primarily upon predictive judgment about the defendant's future behavior and a possibility of successful treatment.[81]

Further, says the ABA, this approach offers no help in the difficult question of assessing a defendant's criminal responsibility. This determination in insanity cases is essentially a moral judgment. If in fact the defendant is so mentally diseased or defective as to be not criminally responsible for the offending act, it would be morally obtuse to assign criminal responsibility.[82] The report characterized the guilty but mentally ill verdict "as a moral-sleight-of-hand which simply will not do."

In its report the ABA also rejected the so-called "*mens rea*" limitation. The *mens rea* limitation was characterized as the abolitionist's approach and would do away with an independent exculpatory defense of insanity. This approach eliminates "any criterion of exculpation based on mental disease which is independent of the elements of particular crimes." The report said:

> [This] overly harsh narrowing of the extent to which mental disease or defect would be taken into account in establishing non-responsibility for crime would require those who administer and apply the law to condemn as criminal the acts of some mentally ill defendants who were uncontrovertibly psychotic and mostly out of touch with reality. To label as criminal those so severely disturbed that they could not appreciate the wrongfulness of their acts offends the moral tenets of the criminal law and, we submit, would offend the moral intuition of the community.[83]

This approach has been adopted in Montana and Idaho.

Recommendations of the American Psychiatric Association

The APA made several suggestions with regard to the insanity standard. First, as to the substitution of the word "appreciate" for "knowing" or "understanding" in the ALI standard, the APA does not believe this will necessarily "expand the insanity dialogue to include a broader and more comprehensive view of human behavior and thinking."[84] The ABA statement did make a significant comment relevant to the ABA's recommendation that the volitional prong of the ALI's standard be dropped:

> Many psychiatrists . . . believe that psychiatric information relevant to determining whether a defendant understood the nature of his act, and whether he appreciated its wrongfulness, is more reliable and has a stronger scientific basis than, for example, does psychiatric information relevant to whether a defendant was able to control his behavior. The line between an irresistible impulse and an impulse not resisted is probably no sharper than that between twilight and dusk. Psychiatry is a deterministic discipline that views all human behavior as, to a

good extent, "caused." The concept of volition is the subject of some disparagement among psychiatrists. Many psychiatrists therefore believe that psychiatric testimony (particularly that of a conclusory nature) about volition is more likely to produce confusion for jurors than is psychiatric testimony relevant to a defendant's appreciation or understanding.[85]

The APA suggested that insanity defense standards should clearly "indicate that mental disorders potentially leading to exculpation must be *serious*. Such disorders should usually be of the severity (if not always of the quality) of conditions that psychiatrists diagnose as psychoses."[86]

The APA endorsed a standard that permits relevant psychiatric testimony to be introduced on the issue of the insanity defense:

A person charged with a criminal offense should be found not guilty by reason of insanity if it is shown that as a result of mental disease or mental retardation he was unable to appreciate the wrongfulness of his conduct at the time of the offense.

As used in this standard, the terms mental disease or mental retardation include only those severely abnormal mental conditions that grossly and demonstrably impair a person's perception or understanding of reality and that are not attributable primarily to the voluntary ingestion of alcohol or other psychoactive substances.[87]

As to the testimony of psychiatrists, the APA stated:

[The APA] is not opposed to legislatures restricting psychiatric testimony about the aforementioned ultimate legal issues concerning the insanity defense. We adopt this position because it is clear that psychiatrists are experts in medicine, not the law. As such, the psychiatrist's first obligation and expertise in the courtroom is to "do psychiatry," i.e., to present medical information and opinion about the defendant's mental state and motivation and to explain in detail the reason for his medical psychiatric conclusions. When, however, "ultimate issue" questions are formulated by the law and put to the expert witness who must then say "yea" or "nay," then the expert witness is required to make a leap in logic. He no longer addresses himself to medical concepts but instead must infer or intuit what is in fact unspeakable, namely, the *probable relationship* between medical concepts and legal or moral constructs such as free will. These impermissible leaps in logic made by expert witnesses confuse the jury.[88]

As to the release of a person acquitted by reason of insanity, the APA set out guidelines for legislation:

1. Special legislation should be designed for those persons charged with violent offenses who have been found "not guilty by reason of insanity."
2. Confinement and release decisions should be made by a board constituted to include psychiatrists and other professions representing the criminal justice system—akin to a parole board.
3. Release should be conditional upon having a treatment supervision plan in place with the necessary resources available to implement it.
4. The board having jurisdiction over released insanity acquittees should have clear authority to reconfine.
5. When psychiatric treatment within a hospital setting has obtained the maximal treatment benefit possible but the board believes that for other reasons confinement is still necessary, the insanity acquittee should be transferred to the most appropriate nonhospital facility.[89]

The APA expressed skepticism about the "guilty but mentally ill" approach. Such an approach is an alternative to the traditional insanity defense. If this were the only verdict besides guilty or innocent, says the APA, it would be the abolitionist approach in disguise. As an alternative, it offers a compromise for the jury. "Persons who might otherwise have qualified for an insanity verdict may instead be siphoned into a category of guilty but mentally ill."[90] This may become the easy way out. "Juries may avoid grappling with the difficult moral issues inherent in adjudicating guilt or innocence, jurors instead settling conveniently on "guilty but mentally ill.""[91]

Finally, this approach presupposes that meaningful mental health treatment is given defendants found guilty but mentally ill. In fact, funds for such treatment are not available.

Guilty But Mentally Ill

Michigan,[92] Indiana,[93] Illinois,[94] Kentucky,[95] Delaware,[96] Alaska,[97] New Mexico,[98] and Georgia[99] have implemented a guilty-but-mentally-ill plea. Under this alternative, a defendant who pleads not guilty by reason of insanity may be found not guilty, not guilty by reason of insanity, guilty but mentally ill, or guilty. In Illinois and Michigan a person was not sane at the time of the crime if as a result of mental illness the defendant "lacks substantial capacity to appreciate the wrongfulness of his conduct or to conform his conduct to the requirements of the law." If the defendant had "substantial capacity," but also had "a substantial disorder of thought or mood that significantly impairs judgment, behavior, capacity to recognize reality or ability to cope with the ordinary demands of life," he or she may be found "guilty but mentally ill." If found "guilty but mentally ill," the defendant may be sentenced as if convicted of the crime charged and placed in either the corrections department or the mental health department. The defendant can be held only for the time that would have been imposed under a straight finding of guilty. Under either alternative the defendant must receive treatment from the corrections or mental health department. One commentator has expressed skepticism over the possibility of such treatment, given the overcrowded conditions, turmoil, brutality, and racial tension that pervade prisons.[100]

Michigan law provides that persons found guilty but mentally ill shall undergo further evaluation and be given treatment as is psychiatrically indicated for the defendant's mental illness or retardation. The defendant in *Michigan v. Mack* had pled guilty but mentally ill to a manslaughter charge in exchange for the prosecution's dropping of an earlier assault charge. The trial court directed the corrections department to provide intensive individual counseling, including alcohol therapy. The defendant appealed, contending she had not received the required psychiatric care. The appellate court said that because her record failed to reveal whether the defendant was receiving proper care, the case would be sent back to the trial court to determine the appropriate psychiatric treatment and assure that it is provided.[101]

Mentally Disordered Sex Offenders

State statutes provide for the involuntary admission of sexual offenders or sexual psychopaths in order to deal with the problems of those individuals who, because of psychopathic disorders, commit or have a tendency to commit sex offenses. These statutes aim to protect society by detaining such individuals as long as they remain a danger to others and to provide treatment. While state statutes differ, they generally provide for a separate hearing to determine whether the person charged with a criminal offense falls within the purview of the statute.[102]

The statutes recognize that the sexual psychopath is mentally ill, but not legally insane, and requires special consideration. Not criminal laws, such statutes provide for civil commitment, segregation from other mental patients, and treatment. Psychiatrists and psychologists testify at the hearing on the mental condition of the individual. The alleged sexual psychopath is entitled to be present at the hearing, have counsel, and have a jury trial in some states.[103]

It must be established that the individual is irresponsible about sexual matters and, because of this fact, is dangerous to others. If the person is found to be a sexual psychopath, he or she is committed for specialized treatment. In some states, he or she may be required by the court to stand trial on criminal charges.[104]

Discharge from confinement depends on the particular statute. Some provide for release when the hospital superintendent finds he or she has recovered sufficiently so as not to be dangerous. Others provide that such recovery must be established at a hearing. Some states provide that the individual may be required to stand trial on the criminal charges after release. Other states provide that the finding of sexual psychopathy precludes further prosecution and, upon recovery, the individual is free.[105]

In Massachusetts, a sexually dangerous person is defined as one whose conduct in sexual matters reflects a lack of control in sexual impulses by "repetitive or compulsive behavior and either violence or aggression by an adult against a victim under the age of sixteen."[106] A defendant who challenged his denial of a discharge after 16 years of confinement as a patient told two psychiatrists that he was sent to the facility for at least three acts of fellatio on a 12-year-old boy. One psychiatrist's report characterized the patient's sexual behavior both outside and within the center as "repetitive and compulsive, gauged his repetition likelihood as very high and found him still a sexually dangerous person." The other psychiatric report cited a lack of control over impulses and continued attraction to children as sex objects and found a very strong likelihood of repeat offenses if released. Both psychiatrists commented on the subject's sexual misbehavior in the institution. The court said that the evidence sustained an inability to refrain from future sexual advancements toward children, which was sufficient to justify continuation of his commitment.[107]

An Illinois court ruled that it is unfair for a psychiatrist "to totally ground his diagnosis on an assumption that the defendant committed the act alleged in the charging instrument." In that case, however, the doctor also based his findings on his interview with the defendant and the results of psychological tests. "Thus, on balance there is no prejudice to defendant doctor's diagnosis. . . . Evidence of a prior sex crime was clearly relevant as the state is required to prove that the defendant has a propensity to commit sex crimes and that his mental disorder had existed for more than one year."[108]

Mentally disordered sex offenders diagnosed as "fixated pedophiles" or "regressed offenders"—the major categories of molesters—are often diverted from the correctional system to the mental health system on the basis of psychiatric or psychological opinion that child molestation is a treatable mental illness. A movement is afoot that opposes such diversion. Proponents of the movement argue that the best way to treat child molesters is to keep them locked away from their prey.[109] California has abolished its Mentally Disordered Offender Act.[110]

A federal court held that persons who are sentenced as sexually dangerous persons have a constitutional right to individualized treatment that will provide them with a realistic chance to be cured or to improve their mental condition.[111]

An Illinois court held that a defendant charged with taking indecent liberties with a child—a person who had been convicted previously of a similar offense and who suffered from the mental disorder of pedophilia, coupled with criminal propensities to commit sex crimes—was properly adjudicated a sexually dangerous person.[112]

NOTES

1. A psychiatric opinion that a defendant is basically incapable of rehabilitation may justify a particularly severe sentence. People v. Darnell, 94 Ill. App. 3d 830, 419 N.E.2d 384, 389 (1981). There are not many reported cases involving psychiatric testimony at the hearing on sentencing.

2. *See, e.g.*, State v. Guatney, 207 Neb. 501, 299 N.W.2d 538, 543 (1980); Smith v. Indiana, 427 N.E.2d 1156 (Ind. Ct. App. 1981).

3. Louisiana v. Harris, 406 So. 2d 128, 129 (Sup. Ct. La. 1981).

4. Lindhorst v. United States, 658 F.2d 598, 607 (8th Cir. 1981).

5. *Id.*

6. California v. Amremi, 180 Cal. Rptr. 471, 474–475 (Cal. Ct. App. 1982).

7. Pate v. Smith, 637 F.2d 1068, 1071 (6th Cir. 1981).

8. California v. Sundberg, 177 Cal. Rptr. 734, 740 (Cal. Ct. App. 1981).

9. United States ex Rel. Mireles v. Greer, 528 F. Supp. 1122 (N.D. Ill. 1981).

10. Collins v. Housewright, 664 F.2d 181 (8th Cir. 1981).

11. *Id.*

12. Arizona v. Romero, 634 P.2d 954 (Ariz. 1981).

13. Owens v. Sowders, 661 F.2d 584 (6th Cir. 1981).

14. Drope v. Missouri, 420 U.S. 162 (1975).

15. Illinois v. Lewis, 393 N.E.2d 1380 (Ill. App. Ct. 1979).

16. State v. Guatney, *supra* note 2, at 545.

17. Williams v. Alabama, 386 So. 2d 506 (Ala. Ct. Crim. App. 1980).

18. Louisiana v. Holmes, 393 So. 2d 670, 674 (La. 1981).

19. *Id.*

20. *Id.* at 673.

21. New York v. Berwid, No. 49856 (N.Y. Nassau County Ct. Oct. 3, 1980), discussed at *Mental Disability Law Reporter* 4 (1980):392.

22. Colorado v. Lopez, 640 P.2d 275 (Colo. Ct. App. 1982).

23. Pennsylvania v. Sourbeer, 422 A.2d 116 (Pa. 1980).

24. Louisiana v. Freeman, 409 So.2d 581 (La. 1982).

25. Pennsylvania v. Powell, 439 A.2d 203 (Pa. Super. Ct. 1981).

26. Lokos v. Kapps, 625 F.2d 1258 (5th Cir. 1980).

27. *Id.*

28. Iowa v. Petersen, 309 N.W.2d 490 (Iowa 1981).

29. Tennessee v. Robinson, 622 S.W.2d 62 (Tenn. Ct. Crim. App. 1980).

30. *Id.*

31. United States v. Alley, 661 F.2d 718 (8th Cir. 1981).

32. *Id.*

33. Kentucky v. Griffin, 622 S.W.2d 214 (Ky. 1981).

34. Iowa v. Kemps, 282 N.W.2d 704 (Iowa 1979).

35. California v. Samuel, 174 Cal. Rptr. 684 (Cal. 1981).

36. Illinois v. Williams, 415 N.E.2d 1192 (Ill. App. Ct. 1980); *See* Chavez v. United States, 641 F.2d 1253 (9th Cir. 1981), for a review of evidence in incompetency cases.

37. "Table on Current Tests for Insanity, Allocation of Burden and Quantum of Proof within Federal Jurisdictions and Several States," 7 *Mental Disability Law Reptr.* 140 (1983) [hereinafter cited as "Table"].

38. *Id.*

39. *Id.*

40. *Id.*

41. McFarthing v. Oklahoma, 630 P.2d 324 (Okla. Ct. Crim. App. 1981).

42. Illinois v. Gardner, *supra* note 39.

43. *M'Naughton's case*, 8 Eng. Rep. 718 (1843).

44. *Black's Law Dictionary* (5th ed. 1979):744.

45. Pennsylvania v. Oblek, 437 A.2d 1162 (Pa. 1981); Johnson v. Indiana, 426 N.E.2d 1312 (Ind. 1981).

46. Model Penal Code. 4.01.

47. United States v. Curran, 290 F.2d 751 (3rd Cir. 1961).

48. United States v. Brawner, 471 F.2d 969 (D.C. Cir. 1972).

49. *Black's Law Dictionary*, *supra* note 44, at 412.

50. *Id.*

51. Neal v. Arkansas, 623 S.W.2d 191 (Ark. 1981).

52. Rhode Island v. Correra, 430 A.2d 1251 (R.I. Sup. Ct. 1981).

53. United States v. Zinc [Zink], 612 F.2d 511 (10th Cir. 1980) (Arizona, Colorado, Kansas, New Mexico, Oklahoma, Utah, and Wyoming); United States v. Busic, 592 F.2d 13 (2d Cir. 1978) (Connecticut, New York and Vermont); Hughes v. Mathews, 576 F.2d 1250 (7th Cir. 1978) (Illinois, Indiana and Wisconsin); United States v. Brawner, 471 F.2d 969 (D.C. Cir. 1972) (District of Columbia).

54. Hensel v. Alaska, 604 P.2d 222 (Alaska 1979); California v. Cruz, 605 P.2d 830 (Cal. 1980); Becksted v. Colorado, 292 P.2d 189 (Colo. 1956); Connecticut v. Donahue, 109 A.2d 364 (Conn. 1954); Hawaii v. Moeller, 433 P.2d 136 (Hawaii 1967); Iowa v. Gramenz, 126 N.W.2d 285 (Iowa 1964); Kansas v. Dargatz, 614 P.2d 430 (Kan. 1980); Starkwether v. Nebraska, 93 N.W.2d 619 (Neb. 1958); New Mexico v. Chambers, 502 P.2d 999 (N.M. 1972); Ohio v. Nichols, 209 N.E.2d 750 (Ohio 1956); Pennsylvania v. Walzack, 360 A.2d 914 (Penn. 1976); Washington v. Ferrick, 506 P.2d 860 (Wash. 1973); Schimmel v. Wisconsin, 267 N.W.2d 271 (Wis. 1978); Vermont v. Smith, 396 A.2d 125 (Vt. 1978).

55. Maine v. Burnham, 406 A.2d 889 (Me. 1979); Missouri v. Anderson, 515 S.W.2d 534 (Mo. 1974); Montana v. McKenzie, 608 P.2d 428 (Mont. 1980).

56. Arizona v. Doss, 568 P.2d 1054 (Ariz. 1977); Bates v. Delaware, 386 A.2d 1139 (Del. 1978); Bethea v. United States, 365 A.2d 64 (D.C. 1976); Louisiana v. Jones, 359 So. 2d 95 (La. 1978); Armstead v. Maryland, 175 A.2d 24 (Md. 1961); Massachusetts v. Mazza, 313 N.E.2d 875 (Mass. 1974); Fox v. Nevada, 361 P.2d 924 (Nev. 1957); North Carolina v. Harris, 228 S.E.2d 424 (N.C. 1976); West Virginia v. Flint, 96 S.E.2d 677 (W.Va. 1957). *See* 22 A.L.R.3d 1228 (1968).

57. Maine v. Mishne, 427 A.2d 450 (Me. 1981).

58. Illinois v. Johnson, 428 N.E.2d 1133 (Ill. Ct. App. 1981).

59. Bullard v. Alabama, So. 2d 164 (Ala. Ct. Crim. App. 1981).

60. Pennsylvania v. Roberts, 437 A.2d 948 (Pa. 1981).

61. People v. Larsen, 361 N.E.2d 713 (Ill. App. 1977).

62. Houston v. Alaska, No. 3339 (Alaska Sup. Ct. Nov. 16, 1979).

63. United States v. Lawson, 653 F.2d 299 (7th Cir. 1981).

64. Massachusetts v. Kendall, 399 N.E.2d 1115 (Mass. App. Ct. 1980).

65. New York v. Hairston, 444 N.Y.S.2d 853 (N.Y. Sup. Ct. 1981).

66. New York v. Johnny, 445 N.Y.S.2d 1007 (N.Y. Crim. Ct. 1981).

67. McKinnon v. Alabama, 405 So. 2d 78 (Ala. Ct. Crim. App. 1981).

68. *Id.*

69. Pennsylvania v. Tempest, 437 A.2d 952 (Pa. 1981).

70. Dorsey v. Missouri, 586 S.W.2d 810 (Mo. Ct. App. 1979).

71. Rogers v. Oklahoma, 634 P.2d 743 (Okla. Ct. Crim. App. 1981).

72. American Psychiatric Association, Statement on the Insanity Defense, Dec. 1982 [hereinafter cited as APA].

73. American Bar Association, Recommendations and Report on the Insanity Defense, Feb. 1983.

74. *Id.* at 1.

75. *Id.* at 4.

76. *Id.* at 4, 5

77. *Id.* at 5.

78. *Id.* at 1, 2.

79. *Id.* at 6.

80. *Id.* at 2.

81. *Id.*

82. *Id.*

83. *Id.* at 3.

84. APA, *supra* note 74, at 10.

85. *Id.* at 11.

86. *Id.*

87. *Id.* at 12.

88. *Id.* at 14.

89. *Id.* at 17.

90. *Id.* at 9.

91. *Id.*

92. Mich. Comp. Law Ann. § 768–36(3); Mich. Stat. Ann. § 28.1059. These statutes have been held constitutional. Michigan v. McLeod, 407 Mich. 632, 288 N.W.2d 909 (1980).

93. Ind. Code, § 35–5–2.

94. Public Act 82–0553.

95. Ky. Rev. Stat. § 504.130 (1982 Cum. Supp.).

96. Del. Code Ann. Tit. 11, § 408 (1982 Cum. Supp.).

97. Alaska Stat. § 12–47.030, 1982/SLA Ch. 143, p. 461.

98. N.M. Stat. Ann. §§ 31–9–3, 31–9–4 (1982 Cum. Supp.).

99. Ga. Code Ann. § 17–7–131 (1983 Cum. Supp.).

100. Norvel Morris, *Madness and the Criminal Law* (Chicago: The University of Chicago Press, 1983).

101. Michigan v. Mack, 305 N.W.2d 264 (Mich. Ct. App. 1981).

102. "Commitment of Sexual Offenders," 96 ALR 3d 842 (1980).

103. 41 Am. Jur 2d § 49 (1980).

104. *Id.* at §§ 50–52.

105. *Id.* at § 54.

106. Mass. Gen. Laws, ch. 123A, §§ 1, 9.

107. In re Davis, 421 N.E.2d 441 (Mass. 1981).

108. Illinois v. Studdard, 403 N.E.2d 68 (Ill. App. Ct. 1980).

109. The move is spearheaded by a California-based organization called Society's League Against Molestation (SLAM). "Beware of Child Molesters," *Newsweek*, Aug. 9, 1982, p. 45. Ohlinger v. Watson, 652 F.2d 775 (9th Cir. 1982).

110. Cal. Penal Code §§ 1210.

111. Ohlinger v. Watson, 652 F.2d 775 (9th Cir. 1981).

112. Illinois v. Pettit, 423 N.E.2d 513 (Ill. App. Ct. 1981).

State Involuntary Admission Statutes

State	Criteria	Maximum Length of Disposition
Alabama Code (1982 Cum. Supp.)	Mental illness and as a consequence poses a real and present threat of substantial harm to himself or others as evidenced by a recent overt act. § 22–52–10(a).	None
Alaska Stat.	Mentally ill and likely to injure self or others or in need of immediate care or treatment, and because of illness lacks sufficient insight or capacity to make responsible decisions concerning hospitalization. § 47.30.070(i).	Indeterminate § 47.30.070(i).
Arizona Rev. Stat. Ann.	Mental disorder and as a result poses a danger to himself or others or is gravely disabled. § 36–540.	Variable: 60 days to one year. § 36–540.
Arkansas Stat. (1981 Cum. Supp.)	Person has a mental illness, disease or disorder and as a result is homicidal, suicidal or gravely disabled. § 59–1410. Homicidal means the person poses a significant risk of physical harm to others as manifested by recent overt behavior evidencing homicidal or other assaultive tendencies toward others. § 59–1401(a). Suicidal means the person "poses a substantial risk of physical harm to himself as manifested by evidence of threats of, or attempt at suicide or serious self-inflicted bodily harm, or by evidence of other behavior or thoughts that create a grave and imminent risk to his physical condition." § 59–1401(b).	Initial 45 days § 49–1409. Additional 120 days. § 49–1410. New proceeding must be initiated for additional time beyond 165 days. § 49–1410.

Source: Information is taken from the respective statutes listed under each state.

State	Criteria	Maximum Length of Disposition
Arkansas (cont.)	Gravely disabled "refers to a person who is likely to injure himself or others if allowed to remain at liberty or is unable to provide for his own food, clothes, or other shelter by reason of mental illness or disorder." § 59–1401(c).	
California (Welf. & Inst. Code)	Mental disorder and as a result attempted, inflicted, or made a substantial threat of physical harm upon the person of another (§§ 5300, 5304), or himself (§ 5213), or is gravely disabled (§ 5358) ("a condition in which a person, as a result of mental disorder, is unable to provide for his basic personal needs for food, clothing or shelter"). § 5008(h)(i).	194 days for persons dangerous to others (§ 5300); 28 days for suicidal persons (§ 5260); and no limit for gravely disabled, except dissolution of conservatorship.
Colorado Rev. Stat. Ann.	Mentally ill and as a result person is dangerous to others, himself or is gravely disabled. "Mentally ill person" means a person who is of such mental condition that he is in need of medical supervision, treatment, care, or restraint. § 27–10–101(7). "Gravely disabled" means a condition in which a person, as a result of mental illness, is unable to take care of his basic personal needs, or is making irrational or grossly irresponsible decisions concerning his person and lacks the capacity to understand this is so. § 27–10–101(5).	12 months. § 27–10–109.
Connecticut Gen. Stat. Ann.	Mentally ill and dangerous to himself or others or gravely disabled. "Mentally ill person" means any person who has a mental or emotional condition which has substantial adverse effects on his or her ability to function and who requires care and treatment excluding drug dependence and alcoholism. § 17–176. "Dangerous to self or others" means there is a substantial risk that physical harm will be inflicted by an individual upon his or her own person or upon another person. § 17–176. "Gravely disabled" means that a person, as a result of mental or emotional impairment, is in danger of serious harm as a result of an inability or failure to	Duration of mental illness. § 17–178(c).

State	Criteria	Maximum Length of Disposition
Connecticut (cont.)	provide for his or her own basic human needs such as essential food, clothing, shelter, or safety and that hospital treatment is necessary and available and that such person is mentally incapable of determining whether or not to accept such treatment because his judgment is impaired by his mental illness. §§ 17–176, 17–178(c).	
Delaware Code Ann. (Title 16) (1982 Cum. Supp.)	Mental disease and poses a real and present threat to self or others, or to property. Threat must be based upon manifest indication that person is likely to commit or suffer serious harm to himself or others or property if immediate care and treatment are not given. "Mentally ill person" means a person suffering from a mental disease or condition which requires such person to be observed and treated at a mental hospital for his own welfare and which either (1) renders such person unable to make responsible decisions with respect to his hospitalization, or (2) poses a real and present threat, based upon manifest indications, that such person is likely to commit or suffer serious harm to himself or others or to property if not given immediate hospital care and treatment. §§ 5001, 5010.	6 months to indefinite. §§ 5010, 5012.
District of Columbia Code	Mental illness and likely to injure himself or others. § 21–545(b). "Mental illness" means a psychosis or other disease which substantially impairs the mental health of a person. § 21–501.	Indeterminate. § 21–545(b).
Florida Stat. Ann. (West)	Suffers from an apparent or manifest mental illness: has refused voluntary placement, is unable to determine for himself whether placement is necessary. "Is manifestly incapable of surviving alone or with the help of willing and responsible family or friends, or alternative services, and without treatment is likely to suffer from neglect or refuse to care for himself and such neglect or refusal poses a real and present threat of substantial harm to his well-being or it is more likely than not	Initial 6-month periods with additional 6-month periods. § 394.467(2)(d).

State	Criteria	Maximum Length of Disposition
Florida (cont.)	that in the near future he will inflict serious harm on another person, as evidenced by behavior causing, attempting, or threatening such harm, including at least one incident thereof within 20 days prior to initiation of proceedings." § 394.467. "Mental illness" means an impairment of the emotional processes, of the ability to exercise conscious control of one's actions, or of the ability to perceive reality, or to understand which impairment substantially interferes with a person's ability to meet the ordinary demands of living regardless of etiology, excluding developmental disabilities, simple alcoholism, or conditions manifested only by antisocial behavior or drug addiction. § 394.455(3).	
Georgia Code Ann.	Mental illness and a substantial risk of imminent harm to self or others (as manifested by either recent overt acts or recent expressed threats of violence which present a probability of physical injury to himself or others) or is unable to care for his physical health and safety as to create an imminently life-threatening crisis. § 37–3–1(11), (12). "Mental illness" means having a disorder or thought mold which significantly impairs judgment, behavior, capacity to recognize reality or ability to cope with the ordinary demands of life. § 37–3–1(11), (12).	Up to 20 months. § 37–38–3(d).
Hawaii Rev. Stat.	Mental illness or substance abuse and dangerous to self or others or to property and in need of care and treatment. § 334–60(b) (1). Must also be least restrictive alternative. "Mentally ill person" means a person having psychiatric disorder or other disease which substantially impairs his mental health and necessitates treatment or supervision. § 334–1. "Dangerous to others" means likely to do substantial physical or emotional injury on another, as evidenced by a recent act, attempt, or threat. § 334–1.	90 days. § 334–60(b) (5)

State	Criteria	Maximum Length of Disposition
Hawaii (cont.)	"Dangerous to self" means likely to do substantial physical injury to one's self, as evidenced by a recent act, attempt, or threat to injure one's self physically or by neglect or refusal to take necessary care for one's own physical health and safety together with incompetence to determine whether treatment for mental illness or substance abuse is appropriate. § 334–1. "Dangerous to property" means inflicting, attempting, or threatening imminently to inflict damage to any property in a manner which constitutes a crime, as evidenced by a recent act, attempt, or threat. § 334–1.	
Idaho Code	Mentally ill and either likely to injure himself or others or is gravely disabled. § 66–329(k). "Mentally ill" shall mean a person who as a result of a substantial disorder of thought, mood, perception, orientation, or memory, which grossly impairs judgment, behavior, capacity to recognize and adapt to reality, requires care and treatment at a facility. "Likely to injure self or others" means: (1) A substantial risk that physical harm will be inflicted by the proposed patient upon his own person, as evidenced by threats or attempts to commit suicide or inflict physical harm upon himself; or (2) A substantial risk that physical harm will be inflicted by the proposed patient upon another as evidenced by behavior which has caused such harm or which places another person or persons in reasonable fear of sustaining such harm. "Gravely disabled" shall mean a person who, as a result of mental illness, is in danger of serious physical harm due to the person's inability to provide for his essential needs. § 66–317(l), (m), and (n).	3 years. § 66–329(k).
Illinois Ann. Stat. (ch. 91–½) (Smith-Hurd	Mental illness and as a result the person is reasonably expected to inflict serious physical harm on self or another in the	180 days. § 3–813.

State	Criteria	Maximum Length of Disposition
Supp. 1982–1983)	near future, or is unable to provide for his basic physical needs. § 1–119.	
Indiana Stat. Ann. (Burn's)	Mentally ill and gravely disabled or dangerous and in need of custody, care or treatment. § 16–14–9.1–10(d).	Indeterminate. § 16–14–9.1–10(d).
	"Mental illness" means a psychiatric disorder which substantially disturbs a person's thinking, feeling, or behavior and impairs the person's ability to function. It includes mental retardation, epilepsy, alcoholism, or addiction to narcotics or dangerous drugs. § 16–14–9.1–1(b).	
	"Gravely disabled" means a condition in which a person as a result of a mental illness is in danger of coming to harm because of his inability to provide for his food, clothing, shelter, or other essential needs. § 16–14–9.1–1(b).	
	"Dangerous" means a condition in which a person as a result of mental illness presents a substantial risk that he will harm himself or others. § 16–14–9.1–1(c).	
Iowa Code Ann.	Seriously mentally impaired and is likely to injure himself or herself or other persons if allowed to remain at liberty.	Indeterminate. § 229.14.3.
	"Seriously mentally impaired" means "a mental illness (every type of mental disease or disorder except mental retardation) and because of illness lacks sufficient judgment to make responsible decisions with respect to his or her hospitalization or treatment, and who:	
	"(a) is likely to physically injure himself or herself or others if allowed to remain at liberty without treatment; or	
	"(b) is likely to inflict serious emotional injury on members of his or her family or others who lack reasonable opportunity to avoid contact with the afflicted person if the afflicted person is allowed to remain at liberty."	
	"Serious emotional injury" is an injury which does not necessarily exhibit any physical characteristics but which can be recognized and diagnosed by a licensed physician or other qualified mental health professional and which can be causally	

State	Criteria	Maximum Length of Disposition
Iowa (cont.)	connected with the act or omission of a person who is, or is alleged to be, mentally ill. §§ 299.1.1, .2.	
Kansas Stat. Ann. (1982 Cum. Supp.)	Mentally ill person who is dangerous to himself or others or who is unable to meet his or her own basic physical needs. (1) "Mentally ill person" means any person who is mentally impaired to the extent that such person is in need of treatment and who is dangerous to himself or herself and others and (a) who lacks sufficient understanding or capacity to make responsible decisions with respect to his or her need for treatment, or (b) who refuses to seek treatment; proof of a person's failure to meet his or her basic physical needs, to the extent that such failure threatens such person's life, shall be deemed as proof that such person is dangerous to himself or herself; except that no person who is being treated by prayer in the practice of the religion of any church which teaches reliance on spiritual means alone through prayer for healing shall be determined to be a mentally ill person unless substantial evidence is produced upon which the district court finds that the proposed patient is dangerous to himself or herself or others. § 59–2902(a).	90 days. § 59–2917a.
Kentucky Rev. Stat.	Mentally ill person who presents a danger or threat of danger to self, family, or others and can reasonably benefit from treatment. § 202A.026. "Mentally ill person" means a person with substantially impaired capacity to use self control, judgment, or discretion in the conduct of his affairs and social relations, associated with maladaptive behavior or recognized emotional symptions where impaired capacity, maladaptive behavior, or emotional symptoms can be related to physiological, psychological, or social factors. § 202A.011(8).	360 days. § 202A.051.

State	Criteria	Maximum Length of Disposition
Kentucky (cont.)	"Danger" or "threat of danger to family or others" means substantial physical harm or threat of substantial physical harm upon self, family, or others, including actions which deprive self, family, or others of the basic means of survival including provision for reasonable shelter, food, or clothing. § 202A.011(2).	
Louisiana Stat. Ann. (ch. 28)	Mental illness or substance abuse which causes a person to be dangerous to self or others or gravely disabled. § 55(E). "Mentally ill person" means any person with a psychiatric disorder which has substantial adverse effects on his ability to function and who requires care and treatment. It does not include persons suffering from mental retardation, epilepsy, alcoholism, or drug abuse. § 28:2(14). "Dangerous to others" means the condition of a person whose behavior or significant threats support a reasonable expectation that there is a substantial risk that he will inflict physical harm upon another person in the near future. § 28:2(3). "Dangerous to self" means the condition of a person whose behavior, significant threats or inaction supports a reasonable expectation that there is a substantial risk that he will inflict physical or severe emotional harm upon his own person. § 28:2(4).	Mental illness, indeterminate; alcoholism, 45 days (initial) and up to two 60-day periods thereafter. § 28.56.
Maine Rev. Stat. Ann.	Mental illness and poses a likelihood of serious harm and inpatient hospitalization is best available means of treatment. § 2234(5). "Mentally ill individual" means an individual having a psychiatric or other disease which substantially impairs his mental health. Does not include mentally retarded or sociopathic individuals. Does include persons suffering from drugs, narcotics, hallucinogens, or intoxicants, including alcohol. 34 § 2251(5). "Likelihood of serious harm" means: A substantial risk of physical harm to the person himself as manifested by evidence of recent threats of, or attempts	1 year. 34 § 2334(6)(A).

State	Criteria	Maximum Length of Disposition
Maine (cont.)	at, suicide or serious bodily harm to himself, and, after consideration of less restrictive treatment settings and modalities, a determination that community resources for his care and treatment are available; or	
	A substantial risk of physical harm to other persons as manifested by recent evidence of homicidal or other violent behavior or recent evidence that others are placed in reasonable fear of violent behavior and serious physical harm to them and, after consideration of less restrictive treatment settings and modalities, a determination that community resources for his care and treatment are available; or	
	A reasonable certainty that severe physical or mental impairment or injury will result to the person alleged to be mentally ill as manifested by recent evidence of his actions or behavior which demonstrate his inability to avoid or protect himself from such impairment or injury, and, after consideration of less restrictive treatment settings and modalities, a determination that suitable community resources for his care are available. 34 § 2251(7).	
Maryland Ann. Code	A person who has a mental disorder and needs inpatient care or treatment for the protection of self or others. Individual presents a danger to the life or safety of the individual or others. § 10–617.	Indeterminate. §§ 10–805, 10–806.
Massachusetts Ann. Laws (ch. 123)	Person is mentally ill and discharge would create a likelihood of serious harm. § 8. "Likelihood of serious harm" means (1) substantial risk of physical harm to the person himself as manifested by evidence of threats of, or attempts at, suicide or serious bodily harm; (2) a substantial risk of physical harm to other persons as manifested by evidence of homicidal or other violent behavior or evidence that others are placed in reasonable fear of violent behavior and serious physical harm to them; or (3) a very substantial risk of physical	1 year. § 8.

State	Criteria	Maximum Length of Disposition
Massachusetts (cont.)	impairment or injury to the person himself as manifested by evidence that such person's judgment is so affected that he is unable to protect himself in the community and that reasonable provision for his protection is not available in the community.	
Michigan Stat. Ann.	A mentally ill person who can reasonably be expected within the near future to intentionally or unintentionally seriously physically injure himself or another and who has engaged in an act or acts or made significant threats that are substantially supportive of the expectation or is unable to attend to basic physical needs such as food, clothing, or shelter that must be attended to in order for him to avoid serious harm in the near future, and who has demonstrated that inability by failing to attend to those basic physical needs. § 14.800(401a,b). "Mental illness" means a substantial disorder of thought or mood which significantly impairs judgment, behavior, capacity to recognize reality, or ability to cope with the ordinary demands of life. § 14.800(400a). A mentally ill person is one whose judgment is so impaired that he is unable to understand his need for treatment. One whose continued behavior is the result of mental illness can reasonably be expected on the basis of competent medical opinion to result in significant physical harm to self or others. § 14.800(401(c)).	Unspecified following commitment periods of 60 and 90 days. § 14.800(472)(3).
Minnesota Stat. Ann.	Mentally ill, mentally retarded, or chemically dependent person. § 253B.09. "Mentally ill person" means a substantial psychiatric disorder of mood, perception, orientation or memory which grossly impairs judgment, behavior, capacity to recognize reality, or to reason or understand, which: (1) is manifested by instances of grossly disturbed behavior or faulty perceptions;	6 months. § 253B.09(5).

State	Criteria	Maximum Length of Disposition
Minnesota (cont.)	(2) poses a substantial likelihood of physical harm to self or others as demonstrated by: (a) a recent attempt or threat to physically harm himself or others; or (b) a failure to provide necessary food, clothing, shelter or medical care for himself, as a result of the impairment. § 253B.02(13). "Mentally ill person" means any person who has a substantial psychiatric disorder of thought, mood, perception, orientation, or memory which grossly impairs judgment, behavior, capacity to recognize reality, or to reason or understand, which (a) is manifested by instances of grossly disturbed behavior or faulty perceptions; and (b) poses a substantial likelihood of physical harm to himself or others as demonstrated by (i) a recent attempt or threat to physically harm himself or others; or (ii) a failure to provide necessary food, clothing, shelter or medical care for himself, as a result of the impairment. This impairment excludes (a) epilepsy, (b) mental retardation, (c) brief periods of intoxication caused by alcohol or drugs, or (d) dependence upon or addiction to any alcohol or drugs. § 253B.02(13). "Chemically dependent person" means any person (a) determined as being incapable of managing himself or his affairs by reason of the habitual and excessive use of alcohol or drugs; and (b) whose recent conduct as a result of habitual and excessive use of alcohol or drugs poses a substantial likelihood of physical harm to himself or others as demonstrated by (i) a recent attempt or threat to physically harm himself or others, (ii) evidence of recent serious physical problems, or (iii) a failure to provide necessary food, clothing, shelter, or medical care for himself. § 253B.02(2).	
Mississippi Code Ann.	Person afflicted with mental illness if reasonably expected at the time determination is made or within	Indeterminate. § 41–21–83.

State	Criteria	Maximum Length of Disposition
Mississippi (cont.)	reasonable time thereafter to intentionally or unintentionally physically injure himself or others or is unable to care for himself so as to guard himself from physical injury or to provide for his own physical needs. It does not include mental retardation. § 41–21–61.	
Missouri Ann. Stat. (Vernon's)	Mental disorder which causes the likelihood of serious physical harm to himself or others. § 632.300.	1 year, 3 months. §§ 632.340, 632.355.
Montana Code Ann.	"Seriously mentally ill" which means suffering from a mental disorder that has resulted in self-inflicted injury to self or others or the imminent threat thereof or which has deprived the person afflicted of the ability to protect his life or health. For this purpose, injury means physical injury. No person may be involuntarily committed because he is epileptic, mentally deficient, mentally retarded, senile, or suffering from a mental disorder unless the condition causes him to be seriously mentally ill. § 53–21–102(14).	One year, thereafter new involuntary proceedings must be initiated for additional detention. §§ 53–21–127, 128
Nebraska Rev. Stat.	Mentally ill dangerous person who poses a substantial risk of serious harm to himself or others. Mentally ill dangerous person shall mean any mentally ill person or alcoholic person who presents: (1) a substantial risk of serious harm to another person or persons in the near future, as manifested by evidence of recent violent acts or threats of violence by placing others in reasonable fear of harm, or (2) a substantial risk of serious harm to himself within the near future, as manifested by evidence of recent attempts at or threats of, suicide or serious bodily harm, or evidence of inability to provide for his basic human needs, including food, clothing, shelter, essential medical care or personal safety. § 83–1009.	Indeterminate. §§ 83–1046, 83–1079.
Nevada Rev. Stat.	A person who is mentally ill and who exhibits observable behavior that he is likely to harm himself or others if allowed	6 months. § 433A.310(2).

State	Criteria	Maximum Length of Disposition
Nevada (cont.)	to remain at liberty, or that he is gravely disabled. § 433A.310(1).	
New Hampshire Rev. Stat. Ann.	Person in such mental condition as a result of illness as to create a potentially serious likelihood of danger to himself or others. § 135–B:26. "Mental illness" means a substantial impairment of emotional processes, or of the ability to exercise conscious control of one's actions, or of the ability to perceive reality or to reason, which impairment is manifested by instances of extremely abnormal behavior or extremely faulty perceptions; it does not include impairment primarily caused by: (a) epilepsy; (b) mental retardation; (c) continuous or noncontinuous periods of intoxication caused by substances such as alcohol or drugs; (d) dependence upon or addiction to any substance such as alcohol or drugs. § 135–B:2X1 (1981 Cum. Supp.).	2 years. § 135–B:38.
New Jersey Stat. Ann.	Person so afflicted with mental disease that he requires care and treatment for his own welfare or the welfare of others or of the community. §§ 30:4–44, 30:4–23.	Indeterminate. N.J. Court Rule, 4:74–7(f).
New Mexico Stat. Ann.	Client with mental disorder that presents a likelihood of serious harm to himself or others; the client needs and is likely to benefit from proposed treatment consistent with least restrictive alternative. "Mental disorder" means a substantial disorder of the person's emotional processes, thought or cognition which grossly impairs judgment, behavior or capacity to recognize reality. "Likelihood of serious harm to oneself" means that it is more likely than not that in the near future the person will attempt to commit suicide or will cause serious bodily harm to himself by violent or other self-destructive means including but not limited to grave passive neglect as evidenced by behavior causing, attempting or threatening the infliction of serious bodily harm to self.	1 year. § 43–1–12(C).

State	Criteria	Maximum Length of Disposition
New Mexico (cont.)	"Likelihood of serious harm to others" means the person will inflict serious, unjustified bodily harm on another person or commit a criminal sexual offense as evidenced by behavior causing, attempting or threatening such harm, which behavior gives rise to a reasonable fear of such harm from said person. §§ 43–1–13(E), 43–1–3(L), (M), (N).	
New York Mental Hygiene Law (McKinney)	Person who has a mental illness for which care and treatment as a patient in a hospital is essential to such person's welfare and whose judgment is so impaired that he is unable to understand the need for such care and treatment. § 9.01. Mental illness for which immediate inpatient care and treatment in a hospital is appropriate and which is likely to result in serious harm to himself or others; "likelihood of serious harm" shall mean: (1) substantial risk of physical harm to himself as manifested by threats of or attempts at suicide or serious bodily harm or other conduct demonstrating that he is dangerous to himself; or (2) a substantial risk of physical harm to other persons as manifested by homicidal or other violent behavior by which others are placed in reasonable fear of serious physical harm. §§ 9.37, 9.39.	2 years. § 9.33(D).
North Carolina Gen. Stat.	Mentally ill, mentally retarded or inebriate person who, because of an accompanying behavior disorder, is dangerous to himself or others, or is mentally retarded, and because of an accompanying behavior disorder, is dangerous to others. § 122–58.7. a. "Dangerous to himself" shall mean that within the recent past: 1. The person has acted in such manner as to evidence: I. That he would be unable without care, supervision, and the continued assistance of others not otherwise	90 days. § 122–58.8.

State	Criteria	Maximum Length of Disposition

North Carolina (cont.)	available to exercise self-control, judgment, and discretion in the conduct of his daily responsibilities and social relations, or to satisfy his need for nourishment, personal, or medical care, shelter, or self-protection and safety; and
	  II. That there is a reasonable probability of serious physical debilitation to him within the near future unless adequate treatment is afforded pursuant to this Article. A showing of behavior that is grossly irrational or of actions which the person is unable to control or of behavior that is grossly inappropriate to the situation or other evidence of severely impaired insight and judgment shall create a *prima facie* inference that the person is unable to care for himself; or
	  2. The person has attempted suicide and that there is reasonable probability of suicide unless adequate treatment is afforded under this Article; or
	  3. The person has mutilated himself or attempted to mutilate himself and that there is a reasonable probability of serious self-mutilation unless adequate treatment is afforded under this Article.
	  b. "Dangerous to others" shall mean that within the recent past, the person has inflicted or threatened to inflict serious bodily harm on another or has acted in such a manner as to create a substantial risk of serious bodily harm to another and that there is a reasonable probability that such conduct will be repeated. § 122.58.2.	

North Dakota Cent. Code	Mentally ill persons requiring treatment. "Mentally ill person" means an individual with an organic, mental, or emotional disorder which substantially impairs the capacity to use self-control, judgment, and discretion in the conduct of personal affairs and social relations. Does not include mental retardation. "Person requiring treatment" means either: A person who is mentally ill, an alcoholic, or a drug addict and who as a result of such condition can reasonably be	90 days. § 25–03.1–22.

State	Criteria	Maximum Length of Disposition
North Dakota (cont.)	expected within the near future to intentionally or unintentionally seriously physically harm himself or another person, and who has engaged in an act or acts or made significant threats that are substantially supportive of this expectation; or A person who is mentally ill, an alcoholic, or a drug addict and who as a result of such condition is unable to attend to his basic physical needs, such as food, clothing, or shelter that must be attended to for him to avoid serious harm in the near future, and who has demonstrated that inability by failing to meet those basic physical needs. § 25–03.1–02.	
Ohio Rev. Stat. Ann. (Baldwin's)	Mentally ill person who creates a substantial risk of physical harm to himself or others, or who would benefit from treatment. (A) "Mental illness" means a substantial disorder of thought, mood, perception, orientation, or memory that grossly impairs judgment, behavior, capacity to recognize reality, or ability to meet the ordinary demands of life. (B) "Mentally ill person subject to hospitalization by court order" means a mentally ill person who, because of his illness: (1) Represents a substantial risk of physical harm to himself as manifested by evidence of threats of, or attempts at, suicide or serious self-inflicted bodily harm; (2) Represents a substantial risk of physical harm to others as manifested by evidence of recent homicidal or other behavior, evidence of recent threats that place another in reasonable fear of violent behavior and serious physical harm, or other evidence of present dangerousness; (3) Represents a substantial and immediate risk of serious physical impairment or injury to himself as manifested by evidence that he is unable to provide for and is not providing for his	2 years. § 5122.15(H).

State	Criteria	Maximum Length of Disposition
Ohio (cont.)	basic physical needs because of his mental illness and that appropriate provision for such needs cannot be made immediately available in the community; or (4) Would benefit from treatment in a hospital for his mental illness and is in need of such treatment as manifested by evidence of behavior that creates a grave and imminent risk to substantial rights of others or himself. § 5122.01.	
Oklahoma Stat. Ann. (West)	A person who has a mental illness and in the near future can be expected to intentionally or unintentionally harm himself or others or is unable to care for his basic physical needs. (c) "Mentally ill person" means any person afflicted with a substantial disorder of thought, mood, perception, psychological orientation or memory that significantly impairs judgment, behavior, capacity to recognize reality or ability to meet the ordinary demands of life; (o) "Person requiring treatment" means either: (1) A person who has a demonstrable mental illness and who as a result of that mental illness can be expected within the near future to intentionally or unintentionally seriously and physically injure himself or another person and who has engaged in one or more recent overt acts or made significant recent threats that substantially support that expectation; or (2) A person who has a demonstrable mental illness and who as a result of that mental illness is unable to attend to those of his basic physical needs such as food, clothing or shelter that must be attended to in order for him to avoid serious harm in the near future and who has demonstrated such inability by failing to attend to those basic physical needs in the recent past; but (3) Person requiring treatment shall not mean a person whose mental processes have simply been weakened or impaired	Indeterminate. 43A § 73.

State	Criteria	Maximum Length of Disposition
Oklahoma (cont.)	by reason of advanced years, a mentally deficient person or a person with epilepsy unless the person also meets the criteria set forth in this paragraph. However, the person may be hospitalized under the voluntary admission provisions of this act if he is deemed clinically suitable and a fit subject for care and treatment by the person in charge of the facility. 43A § 54.3(o).	
Oregon Rev. Stat.	Mentally ill person who is dangerous to himself or others or is unable to provide for his own basic personal needs. A mentally ill person means a person who, because of a mental disorder, is either: (a) dangerous to himself or others; or (b) unable to provide for his basic personal needs and is not receiving such care as is necessary for his health or safety. § 426.005.	180 days. § 426.130.
Pennsylvania Stat. Ann. (Purdon's)	A severely mentally disabled person who poses a clear and present danger to others or himself. (a) Whenever a person is severely mentally disabled and in need of immediate treatment, he may be made subject to involuntary emergency examination and treatment. A person is severely mentally disabled when, as a result of mental illness, his capacity to exercise self-control, judgment and discretion in the conduct of his affairs and social relations or to care for his own personal needs is so lessened that he poses a clear and present danger of harm to others or to himself. (1) Clear and present danger to others shall be shown by establishing that within the past 30 days the person has inflicted or attempted to inflict serious bodily harm on another and that there is a reasonable probability that such conduct will be repeated. If, however, the person has been found incompetent to be tried or has been acquitted by reason of lack of criminal responsibility on charges arising from conduct involving	90 days; up to 1 year if criminal charges involving dangerous acts. 50 § 7304(g).

State	Criteria	Maximum Length of Disposition
Pennsylvania (cont.)	infliction of or attempt to inflict substantial bodily harm on another, such 30-day limitation shall not apply so long as an application for examination and treatment is filed within 30 days after the date of such determination or verdict. In such case, a clear and present danger to others may be shown by establishing that the conduct charged in the criminal proceeding did occur, and that there is a reasonable probability that such conduct will be repeated. For the purpose of this section, a clear and present danger of harm to others may be demonstrated by proof that the person has made threats of harm and has committed acts in furtherance of the threat to commit harm.	

(2) Clear and present danger to himself shall be shown by establishing that within the past 30 days:

(i) the person has acted in such manner as to evidence that he would be unable, without care, supervision and the continued assistance of others to satisfy his need for nourishment, personal or medical care, shelter, or self-protection and safety, and that there is a reasonable probability that death, serious bodily injury or serious physical debilitation would ensue within 30 days unless adequate treatment were afforded under this act; or

(ii) The person has attempted suicide and that there is a reasonable probability of suicide unless adequate treatment is afforded under this act. For the purposes of this subsection, a clear and present danger may be demonstrated by the proof that the person has made threats to commit suicide and has committed acts which are in furtherance of the threat to commit suicide; or

(iii) the person has substantially mutilated himself or attempted to mutilate himself substantially and that there is the reasonable probability of mutilation unless adequate treatment is afforded under this act. For the purposes of this subsection, a clear and present danger

State	Criteria	Maximum Length of Disposition
Pennsylvania (cont.)	shall be established by proof that the person has made threats to commit mutilation and has committed acts which are in furtherance of the threat to commit mutilation. 50 § 7301.	
Rhode Island Gen. Laws	A person who is so insane as to be dangerous to the peace or safety of the people of the state or so as to render his restraint and treatment necessary for his own welfare. § 40.1–5.1–1.	Indeterminate. § 40.1–5.1–3.
South Carolina Code	A person who is mentally ill, needs treatment and because of his condition: (1) lacks sufficient insight or capacity to make responsible decisions with respect to his treatment; or (2) there is a likelihood of serious harm to himself or others. § 44–17–580 (1982 Cum. Supp.).	Indeterminate. § 44–17–820 (1982 Cum. Supp.).
South Dakota Codified Laws	Mentally ill person who lacks sufficient understanding and capacity to meet the ordinary demands of life or is dangerous to himself or others. § 27A–1–1. The term "mentally ill" as used in this title includes any person whose mental condition is such that his behavior establishes one or more of the following: (1) He lacks sufficient understanding or capacity to make responsible decisions concerning his person so as to interfere grossly with his capacity to meet the ordinary demands of life; or (2) He is a danger to himself or others.	Indeterminate. § 27A–9–18.
Tennessee Code Ann.	A person is mentally ill and poses a likelihood of serious harm and is in need of care and treatment. § 33–604(a), (d). "Likelihood of serious harm" means (1) a substantial risk of physical harm to the person himself as manifested by evidence of threats of, or attempts at, suicide or serious bodily harm; or (2) a substantial risk of physical harm to other persons as manifested by evidence of homicidal or other violent behavior or evidence that others are placed in a reasonable fear of violent behavior and serious physical harm to them; or (3) a reasonable certainty that severe impairment or injury will result to the	

State	Criteria	Maximum Length of Disposition
Tennessee (cont.)	person alleged to be mentally ill as manifested by his inability to avoid or protect himself from such impairment or injury and suitable community resources for his care are unavailable. § 33–604.	
Texas Rev. Civ. Stat. Ann.	A person who is mentally ill and requires hospitalization for his own welfare and protection or the welfare and protection of others. § 5547–52(b). Mentally ill person means a person whose mental health is substantially impaired. § 5547–4(k).	Indefinite. § 5547–52(b).
Utah Code Ann.	(a) The proposed patient has a mental illness; and (b) Because of the patient's illness the proposed patient poses an immediate danger of physical injury to others or self, which may include the inability to provide the basic necessities of life, such as food, clothing, and shelter, if allowed to remain at liberty; and (c) The patient lacks the ability to engage in a rational decision-making process regarding the acceptance of mental treatment as demonstrated by evidence of inability to weigh the possible costs and benefits of treatment; and (d) There is no appropriate less restrictive alternative to a court order of hospitalization. § 64–7–36(10). "Mental illness" means a psychiatric disorder as defined by the current *Diagnostic and Statistical Manual of Mental Disorders* which substantially impairs a person's mental, emotional, behavioral, or related functioning. § 64–7–28(1).	Indefinite. § 64–7–36(11)(a).
Vermont Stat. Ann. (Title 18) (1982 Cum. Supp.)	(17) "A person in need of treatment" means a person who is suffering from mental illness and, as a result of that mental illness, his capacity to exercise self-control, judgment, or discretion in the conduct of his affairs and social relations is so lessened that he poses a danger of harm to himself or others; (A) A danger of harm to others may be shown by establishing that:	Indeterminate. § 7621.

State	Criteria	Maximum Length of Disposition
Vermont (cont.)	(i) he has inflicted or attempted to inflict bodily harm on another; or (ii) by his threats or actions he has placed others in reasonable fear of physical harm to themselves; or (iii) by his actions or inactions he has presented a danger to persons in his care. (B) A danger of harm to himself may be shown by establishing that: (i) he has threatened or attempted suicide or serious bodily harm; or (ii) he has behaved in such a manner as to indicate that he is unable, without supervision and the assistance of others, to satisfy his need for nourishment, personal or medical care, shelter, or self-protection and safety, so that it is probable that death, substantial bodily injury, serious mental deterioration or serious physical debilitation or disease will ensue unless adequate treatment is afforded. (14) "Mental illness" means a substantial disorder of thought, mood, perception, orientation or memory, any of which grossly impairs judgment, behavior, capacity to recognize reality, or ability to meet the ordinary demands of life, but shall not include mental retardation. § 7101(17), (14).	
Virginia Code (1982 Cum. Supp.)	A person who (a) presents an imminent danger to himself or others as a result of mental illness, or (b) has otherwise been proven to be so seriously mentally ill as to be substantially unable to care for himself, and (c) that there is no less restrictive alternative to institutional confinement and treatment and that the alternatives to involuntary hospitalization were investigated and were deemed not suitable. § 37.1–67.3.	180 days. § 37.1–67.3.
Washington Rev. Code Ann.	A person who has threatened, attempted, or inflicted: (a) Physical harm upon the person of another or himself, or substantial damage upon the property of another, and (b) as a result of mental disorder presents a likelihood of serious harm to others or himself; or	180 days. § 71.05.320.

State	Criteria	Maximum Length of Disposition
Washington (cont.)	(2) Such person was taken into custody as a result of conduct in which he attempted or inflicted harm upon the person of another or himself, and continues to present, as a result of mental disorder, a likelihood of serious harm to others or himself. (1) Such person has been determined to be incompetent and criminal charges have been dismissed and has committed acts constituting a felony, and as a result of a mental disorder, presents a substantial likelihood of repeating similar acts. In any proceeding pursuant to this subsection it shall not be necessary to show intent, willfulness or state of mind as an element of the felony; or (2) such person is gravely disabled. § 71.05.280. "Gravely disabled" means a condition in which a person, as a result of a mental disorder: (a) is in danger of serious physical harm resulting from a failure to provide for his essential human needs of health or safety, or (b) manifests severe deterioration in routine functioning evidenced by repeated and escalating loss of cognitive or volitional control over his or her actions and is not receiving such care as is essential for his or her health or safety. § 71.05.020(1). "Mental disorder" means any organic, mental, or emotional impairment which has substantial adverse effects on an individual's cognitive or volitional functions. § 71.05.020(2). "Likelihood of serious harm" means either: (a) a substantial risk that physical harm will be inflicted by an individual upon his own person, as evidenced by threats or attempts to commit suicide or inflict physical harm on one's self, (b) a substantial risk that physical harm will be inflicted by an individual upon another, as evidenced by behavior which has caused such harm or which places another person or persons in reasonable fear of sustaining such harm or (c) a substantial risk that physical harm will be	

State	Criteria	Maximum Length of Disposition
Washington (cont.)	inflicted by an individual upon the property of others, as evidenced by behavior which has caused substantial loss or damage to the property of others. § 71.05.020(3).	
West Virginia Code Ann.	Mental illness, retarded or addicted and is likely to cause serious harm to himself or to others. Mental illness means a manifestation in a person of significantly impaired capacity to maintain acceptable rules of functioning in the areas of intellect, emotion and physical well-being. § 27–1–2. "Likely to cause serious harm" refers to a person who has: (1) A substantial tendency to physically harm himself which is manifested by threats of or attempts at suicide or serious bodily harm or other conduct, either active or passive, which demonstrates that he is dangerous to himself; or (2) A substantial tendency to physically harm other persons which is manifested by homicidal or other violent behavior which places others in reasonable fear of serious physical harm; or (3) A complete inability to care for himself by reason of mental retardation; or (4) Become incapacitated. § 27–1–12.	2 years. § 27–5–4(k)–4.
Wisconsin Stat. Ann. (West)	(1) A person who is mentally ill, drug dependent, or developmentally disabled and is a proper subject for treatment: and . . . (2) Is dangerous because . . . the individual: (a) Evidences a substantial probability of physical harm to himself or herself as manifested by evidence of recent threats of or attempts at suicide or serious bodily harm . . . (b) Evidences a substantial probability of physical harm to other individuals as manifested by evidence of recent homicidal or other violent behavior, or by evidence that others are placed in reasonable fear of violent behavior and serious physical harm to them, as	1 year. § 51.20(13)(g).

State	Criteria	Maximum Length of Disposition
Wisconsin (cont.)	evidenced by a recent overt act, attempt or threat to do . . . serious physical harm . . . (c) Evidences such impaired judgment, manifested by evidence of a pattern of recent acts or omissions, that there is a . . . substantial probability of physical impairment or injury to himself or herself. The probability of physical impairment or injury . . . is not substantial under this subparagraph if reasonable provision for the subject individual's protection is available in the community . . . . The subject individual's status as a minor does not automatically establish a . . . substantial probability of physical impairment or injury under this subparagraph; or (d) Evidences behavior manifested by recent acts or omissions that, due to mental illness, he or she is unable to safisfy basic needs for nourishment, medical care, shelter or safety without prompt and adequate treatment so that a substantial probability exists that death, serious physical injury, serious physical debilitation or serious physical disease will imminently ensue unless the individual receives prompt and adequate treatment for this mental illness. § 51.20(1).	
Wyoming Stat. Ann.	Person is mentally ill based on evidence of recent overt acts or threats. § 25–10–110. A mentally ill person means a person who presents an imminent threat of physical harm to himself or others as a result of a physical, emotional, mental or behavioral disorder which grossly impairs his ability to function socially, vocationally or interpersonally and who needs treatment and who cannot comprehend the need for or purposes of treatment and with respect to whom the potential risk and benefits are such that a reasonable person would consent to treatment. § 25–10–101.	Indeterminate. § 25–10–116.

§ 405.1037 Condition of Participation—Special Medical Record Requirements for Psychiatric Hospitals

The medical records maintained by a psychiatric hospital permit determination of the degree and intensity of the treatment provided to individuals who are furnished services in the institution.

(a) *Standard; medical records.* Medical records stress the psychiatric components of the record including history of findings and treatment rendered for the psychiatric condition for which the patient is hospitalized. The factors explaining the standard are as follows:

(1) The identification data include the patient's legal status.

(2) A provisional or admitting diagnosis is made on every patient at the time of admission and includes the diagnoses of intercurrent diseases as well as the psychiatric diagnoses.

(3) The complaint of others regarding the patient is included as well as the patient's comments.

(4) The psychiatric evaluation, including a medical history, contains a record of mental status and notes the onset of illness, the circumstances leading to admission, attitudes, behavior, estimate of intellectual functioning, memory functioning, orientation, and an inventory of the patient's assets in descriptive, not interpretative, fashion.

(5) A complete neurological examination is recorded at the time of the admission physical examination, when indicated.

(6) The social service records, including reports of interviews with patients, family members and others, provide an assessment of

Source: 42 C.F.R. § 405.1037.

home plans and family attitudes, and community resource contacts as well as a social history.

(7) Reports of consultations, psychological evaluations, reports of electroencephalograms, dental records and reports of special studies are included in the record.

(8) The individual comprehensive treatment plan is recorded, based on an inventory of the patient's strengths as well as his disabilities, and includes a substantiated diagnosis in the terminology of the American Psychiatric Association's Diagnostic and Statistical Manual, short-term and long-range goals, and the specific treatment modalities utilized as well as the responsibilities of each member of the treatment team in such a manner that it provides adequate justification and documentation for the diagnoses and for the treatment and rehabilitation activities carried out.

(9) The treatment received by the patient is documented in such a manner and with such frequency as to assure that all active therapeutic efforts such as individual and group psychotherapy, drug therapy, milieu therapy, occupational therapy, recreational therapy, industrial or work therapy, nursing care and other therapeutic interventions are included.

(10) Progress notes are recorded by the physician, nurse, social worker and, when appropriate, others significantly involved in active treatment modalities. Their frequency is determined by the condition of the patient but should be recorded at least weekly for the first 2 months and at least once a month thereafter and should contain recommendations for revisions in the treatment plan as indicated as well as precise assessment of the patient's progress in accordance with the original or revised treatment plan.

(11) The discharge summary includes a recapitulation of the patient's hospitalization and recommendations from appropriate services concerning follow-up or aftercare as well as a brief summary of the patient's condition on discharge.

(12) The psychiatric diagnoses contained in the final diagnoses are written in the terminology of the American Psychiatric Association's Diagnostic and Statistical Manual.

Appendix C

State Voluntary Admission Statutes

State	Initiation	Release
Alabama Code	No provision.	No provision.
Alaska Stat.	Application of individual, including a minor with consent of parent or guardian. § 47.30.020.	Release immediately upon request with consent of individual or parent or guardian if minor. Release may be postponed up to 5 days for initiation of involuntary proceeding. § 47.30.050.
Arizona Rev. Stat. Ann.	Adult may apply. Minor over 14 may apply if application is signed by minor and a parent, guardian, or custodian, and a parent, guardian, or custodian of minor under 14 may apply. § 36–518.	Discharge within 24 hours of request except on weekends or holidays or where involuntary proceedings are initiated. § 36–519.
Arkansas Stat. (1981 Cum. Supp.)	Application signed by any person in the presence of two witnesses. § 59–1403.	Release upon request. May be held for initiation of involuntary proceedings. § 59–1403.
California (Welf. & Inst. Code)	Adult or parent, guardian, conservator, or other persons entitled to custody of minor may apply. § 6000.	May leave at any time. § 6000.

Source: Information is taken from the respective statutes listed under each state.

State	Initiation	Release
Colorado Rev. Stat. Ann.	Person over 15 may apply and parent or legal guardian of minor may apply. § 27–10–103.	No provision.
Connecticut Gen. Stat. Ann.	Any person may apply. § 17–187.	Release within 5 days of written notice except may be detained for involuntary proceedings. § 17–187.
Delaware Code Ann. (tit. 16) (1982 Cum. Supp.)	Person over 16 or parent, spouse, or legal guardian of person under 18 may apply. § 5123(a), (c).	Discharge within 5 days of request unless involuntarily admitted. § 5123(e).
District of Columbia Code	Any person over 18 or spouse, parent or legal guardian of person under 18 may apply. § 21–511.	Discharge within 48 hours of request. § 21–512.
Florida Stat. Ann. (West)	Any person 18 or older or parent or guardian of person 17 or under may apply. § 394.465(1).	Discharge within 3 days of delivery of written request. § 394.465(2).
Georgia Code Ann.	Any person 12 or older or parent or guardian of person under 18 or guardian of legally incompetent can apply. § 88–503.1.	Discharge within 72 hours of delivery of written request excluding Sundays and holidays. § 88–503.3.
Hawaii Rev. Stat.	Voluntary application in accordance with the usual standards for hospital admissions. Parent or guardian may apply for individual under 15. § 334–60(a).	Discharge upon written request. State has 24 hours or until noon of the next court date to initiate involuntary proceedings. § 334–60(a).
Idaho Code	Application by person over 14 years of age, emancipated minors, persons under 14 years of age with consent of parent or guardian and any individual who lacks capacity to make informed decisions about treatment upon application of the individual's guardian. § 66–318(a).	Release upon application with consent of parent or guardian if 16 years of age or under. State may detain 3 days to initiate involuntary proceedings. § 66–320.

State	Initiation	Release
Illinois Ann. Stat. (Smith-Hurd Supp. 1982–1983) (ch. 91½)	Application by person over 16, or any interested person 18 or older. § 3–401.	Discharge within 5 working days of request. § 3–403.
Indiana Stat. Ann. (Burn's)	Application by anyone over 18 or by parent or legal guardian of individual under 18. § 16–14–9.1–2(a).	Upon request. § 16–14–9.1–2(b).
Iowa Code Ann.	Application by any person or by parent, guardian, or custodian of minor. § 229.2.	Release "forthwith" upon request except where involuntary proceedings initiated. § 229.4.
Kansas Stat. Ann.	Voluntary admission: Application by person over 18 years of age. Persons 14 to 18 years of age may apply or their parent or guardian may make application. If person is under 14 years of age, parent or guardian must make application. Whenever a person between the ages of 14 and 18 makes application, the parent or guardian must be informed. § 59–2905 (1982 Cum. Supp.). Informal admission: Any person may be admitted on an informal basis. § 59–2904.	Voluntary patient must be released within a reasonable time not to exceed 3 working days. § 59–2907 (1982 Cum. Supp.). Informed patient is free to leave on any day between the hours of 9 a.m. and 5 p.m. § 59–2904.
Kentucky Rev. Stat. Ann.	Any person may apply. A parent or guardian may apply for a person under 18. A child 14 or older may apply, but parent must be notified. § 202A.21.	Release upon written request. § 202A.21.
Louisiana Stat. Ann. (ch. 28)	Any person may request a formal voluntary or informal voluntary admission. §§ 28:52.1, .2.	Release within 72 hours of request. Informed voluntary patients may leave any time during normal day shift hours of operation. § 28:52.2B.
Maine Rev. Stat. Ann. (tit. 34)	Any person may apply. A person under 18 must have consent of parent or guardian and in the case of a nonprivate hospital, the consent of the Commissioner of Mental Health and Corrections. 34 § 2290.	Free to leave at any time. 34 § 2290.
Maryland (Health-General)	Any person 16 or older or any parent or guardian of a minor may formally apply. §§ 10–609, 610.	Release within 3 days of request. § 10–803.

State	Initiation	Release
Massachusetts Ann. Laws (ch. 123)	Application by anyone over 16, by a parent or guardian of a person under 18, or by guardian of a person under guardianship. § 10.	Free to leave at any time during normal working hours. 3 days' notice may be required. § 11.
Michigan Stat. Ann.	Any person 18 years or over or the parent, guardian or person *in loco parentis* may apply for voluntary admission. §§ 14.800 (411, 415).	An informal voluntary patient may leave the hospital at any time during the normal day shift hours of the hospital. § 14.800 (412). A voluntary patient is released within 3 days of request. § 14.800 (419).
Minnesota Stat. Ann.	Any person may apply for informal admission. § 253A.03.	Free to leave within 12 hours of request. Drug dependent person released in three days. § 253A.03.
Mississippi Code	Any person 18 or over or married, any immediate relative or attorney, any parent, guardian, or other person standing *in loco parentis*, or any guardian of adult incompetent may apply. § 41–21–103(2).	Release 5 days excluding Saturdays, Sundays, and holidays, after written request. § 41–21–103(3).
Missouri Ann. Stat. (Vernon's)	Any person 18 or older or a parent or other legal custodian may apply for a minor. §§ 632.105, 632.110.	Immediate release upon request unless meets standard for involuntary admission. §§ 632.150, 632.155.
Montana Code Ann.	Person 16 or older may apply. §§ 53–21–111, 53–21–112.	Release within 5 days of request excluding weekends and holidays. §§ 53–21–111, 53–21–112.
Nebraska Rev. Stat.	Any person may apply. § 83–1019.	Unconditional discharge within 48 hours after delivery of written request. § 83–1019.
Nevada Rev. Stat.	Any person or any spouse, parent, or legal guardian or a minor may apply. § 433A.140(1).	Release within the normal working day of request. § 433A.140(3).

State	Initiation	Release
New Hampshire Rev. Stat. Ann.	Anyone over the age of majority may apply. Minors covered by regulations. § 135–B:11.	Right to withdraw immediately during business hours. § 135–B:15. Maximum voluntary admission of two years. § 135–B:17.
New Jersey Stat. Ann.	Application by person 18 or older or by a parent, guardian, grandparent, or adult brother or sister of a minor under 21 years of age. § 30:4–46.	Release within 72 hours of request. § 30:4–48.
New Mexico Stat. Ann.	Any person and any minor over 12 may apply. §§ 43–1–14A, 43–1–16B.	Immediate release upon request unless person meets criterion for involuntary admission. § 43–1–14C.
New York (Mental Hyg. Law)	Any person may apply for voluntary or informal admission. §§ 9.13, 9.15, 9.17. If under 16, application of parent, legal guardian, next-of-kin, or certain specified officials is required. § 9.13(A).	"Prompt" release upon request. § 9.13(B).
North Carolina Gen. Stat.	Any person may apply for treatment of mental illness or inebriety. A parent or guardian or person standing *in loco parentis* shall act for a minor. §§ 122–56.3, 122–56.5.	Applicant may be held for 72 hours after written request. § 122–56.3.
North Dakota Cent. Code	Application by any person or application on behalf of minor by parent or guardian of any person who is mentally ill, alcoholic, or a drug addict or who has symptoms of such illnesses. § 25–03.1–04.	Immediate release upon request. § 25–03.1–06.
Ohio Rev. Stat. Ann. (Baldwin's)	Any person 18 or older may apply. A parent, guardian, or one having custody of a minor or incompetent may apply. § 5122.02.	Release "forthwith" after request. § 5122.03.
Oklahoma Stat. Ann. (tit. 43A) (West)	Any person 18 or older may apply and any person 16 to 18 may apply with consent of parent or guardian. 43A § 53.	Release within 15 days of written request. 43A § 53.
Oregon Rev. Stat.	Anyone may apply. Minors must have adult next-of-kin or legal guardian apply. § 426.220.	Release within 72 hours of request to leave. § 426.220.
Pennsylvania Stat. Ann. (tit. 50) (Purdon's)	Any person 14 or older may apply. A parent, guardian, or one standing *in loco parentis* may apply for a child under 14. § 7201.	Release within 72 hours. § 7206.

State	Initiation	Release
Rhode Island Gen. Laws	Any person may make application. § 40.1–5.1–18.	Release within 3 days after giving notice in writing. § 40.1–5.1–18.
South Carolina Code	Any person over 16 may apply. A parent or legal guardian of child under 16 may apply. § 44–17–310 (1982 Cum. Supp.).	Discharge "forthwith" upon request. 14 days' notice may be required of parent or guardian. § 44–17–330.
South Dakota Codified Laws	Application by anyone over 18 or by parent, guardian, or person *in loco parentis* if person is under 18. §§ 27A–8–1, 27A–8–2.	Release within at least 5 days excluding Saturdays, Sundays, and holidays from request. §§ 27A–8–10, 27A–8–11.
Tennessee Code Ann.	Any person 16 or older or the spouse, parent, or legal guardian on behalf of a person under 16 may apply. § 33–601(a).	Release within 48 hours of request excluding Saturdays, Sundays, and holidays. § 33–601(b).
Texas Rev. Stat. Ann. (Vernon's)	Application by any person if he is legally of age or by his parent, legal guardian, or the county judge if applicant is not legally of age. § 5547–23.	Release within 96 hours of request. § 5547–25.
Utah Code Ann.	Application by person over 16 or by parent or legal guardian of person under 16. § 64–7–29.	Release "forthwith" after request except release may be delayed 2 days to initiate involuntary proceedings. § 64–7–31.
Vermont Stat. Ann. (1982 Cum. Supp.) (tit. 18)	Application by person over 14 or if under the age of 14, the consent of the person and the parent or guardian. § 7503.	Released promptly upon request unless agreement at admission that release can be delayed. May be held up to 4 days for initiation of involuntary proceedings. § 8010.
Virginia Code	Any person may request admission. A parent or guardian of a mentally retarded incapable person may apply for that person. §§ 37.1–65, 37.1–65.1.	Discharge when no longer a proper case for treatment. § 37.1–98A4.

State	Initiation	Release
Washington Rev. Code Ann.	Any person may apply. § 71.05.050.	Immediate release upon request except if meets involuntary standard, may be detained to initiate such proceedings. § 71.05.050.
West Virginia Code Ann.	Any person over 18 or parent or guardian of person under 18 may apply. § 27–4–1.	Release "forthwith." § 27–4–3.
Wisconsin Stat. Ann. (West)	Any adult may apply or any parent or guardian of person under 14 may apply. If a person under 14 years of age does not consent, this will be a factor considered at review. §§ 51.10(1), 51.13(1).	Discharge upon request unless involuntary proceedings initiated. § 51.10(5) (6).
Wyoming Stat.	Application by competent adult or by parent or guardian of minor or incompetent adult. § 25–3–106(a)(i).	Release within 24 hours. § 25–3–109.

Appendix D

Mental Health Rights and Advocacy

§ 9501. BILL OF RIGHTS

It is the sense of the Congress that each State should review and revise, if necessary, its laws to ensure that mental health patients receive the protection and services they require; and in making such review and revision should take into account the recommendations of the President's Commission on Mental Health and the following:

(1) A person admitted to a program or facility for the purpose of receiving mental health services should be accorded the following:
  (A) The right to appropriate treatment and related services in a setting and under conditions that—
    (i) are the most supportive of such person's personal liberty; and
    (ii) restrict such liberty only to the extent necessary consistent with such person's treatment needs, applicable requirements of law, and applicable judicial orders.
  (B) The right to an individualized, written, treatment or service plan (such plan to be developed promptly after admission of such person), the right to treatment based on such plan, the right to periodic review and reassessment of treatment and related service needs, and the right to appropriate revision of such plan, including any revision necessary to provide a description of mental health services that may be needed after such person is discharged from such program or facility.
  (C) The right to ongoing participation, in a manner appropriate to such person's capabilities, in the planning of mental health services to be provided such person (including the right to participate in the development and periodic revision of the plan described in subparagraph

Source: Mental Health Systems Act of 1980, P.L. 96–398, 94 Stat. 1564 (1980).

(B)), and, in connection with such participation, the right to be provided with a reasonable explanation, in terms and language appropriate to such person's condition and ability to understand, of—

(i)   such person's general mental condition and, if such program or facility has provided a physical examination, such person's general physical condition;

(ii) the objectives of treatment;

(iii) the nature and significant possible adverse effects of recommended treatments;

(iv) the reasons why a particular treatment is considered appropriate;

(v)   the reasons why access to certain visitors may not be appropriate; and

(vi) any appropriate and available alternative treatments, services, and types of providers of mental health services.

(D) The right not to receive a mode or course of treatment, established pursuant to the treatment plan, in the absence of such person's informed, voluntary, written consent to such mode or course of treatment, except treatment—

(i)   during an emergency situation if such treatment is pursuant to or documented contemporaneously by the written order of a responsible mental health professonal; or

(ii) as permitted under applicable law in the case of a person committed by a court to a treatment program or facility.

(E) The right not to participate in experimentation in the absence of such person's informed, voluntary, written consent, the right to appropriate protections in connection with such participation, including the right to a reasonable explanation of the procedure to be followed, the benefits to be expected, the relative advantages of alternative treatments, and the potential discomforts and risks, and the right and opportunity to revoke such consent.

(F) The right to freedom from restraint or seclusion, other than as a mode or course of treatment or restraint or seclusion during an emergency situation if such restraint or seclusion is pursuant to or documented contemporaneously by the written order of a responsible mental health professional.

(G) The right to a humane treatment environment that affords reasonable protection from harm and appropriate privacy to such person with regard to personal needs.

(H) The right to confidentiality of such person's records.

(I) The right to access, upon request, to such person's mental health care records, except such person may be refused access to—

(i)   information in such records provided by a third party under assurance that such information shall remain confidential; and

(ii) specific material in such records if the healh professional responsible for the mental health services concerned has made a determination in writing that such access would be detrimental to such person's health, except that such material may be made available to a similarly licensed health professional selected by such person and such health professional may, in the exercise of professional judgment, provide such person with access to any or all parts of such material or otherwise disclose the information contained in such material to such person.

(J) The right, in the case of a person admitted on a residential or inpatient care basis, to converse with others privately, to have convenient and reasonable access to the telephone and mails, and to see visitors during regularly scheduled hours, except that, if a mental health professional treating such person determines that denial of access to a particular visitor is necessary for treatment purposes, such mental health professional may, for a specific, limited, and reasonable period of time, deny such access if such mental health professional has ordered such denial in writing and such order has been incorporated in the treatment plan for such person. An order denying such access should include the reasons for such denial.

(K) The right to be informed promptly at the time of admission and periodically thereafter, in language and terms appropriate to such person's condition and ability to understand, of the rights described in this section.

(L) The right to assert grievances with respect to infringement of the rights described in this section, including the right to have such grievances considered in a fair, timely, and impartial grievance procedure provided for or by the program or facility.

(M) Notwithstanding subparagraph (J), the right of access to (including the opportunties and facilities for private communication with) any available—

(i) rights protection service within the program or facility;

(ii) rights protection service within the State mental health system designed to be available to such person; and

(iii) qualified advocate;

for the purpose of receiving assistance to understand, exercise, and protect the rights described in this section and in other provisions of law.

(N) The right to exercise the rights described in this section without reprisal, including reprisal in the form of denial of any appropriate, available treatment.

(O) The right to referral as appropriate to other providers of mental health services upon discharge.

(2) (A) The rights described in this section should be in addition to and not in derogation of any other statutory or constitutional rights.

    (B) The rights to confidentiality of and access to records as provided in subparagraphs (H) and (I) of paragraph (1) should remain applicable to records pertaining to a person after such person's discharge from a program or facility.

(3) (A) No otherwise eligible person should be denied admission to a program or facility for mental health services as a reprisal for the exercise of the rights described in this section.

    (B) Nothing in this section should—

        (i) obligate an individual mental health or health professional to administer treatment contrary to such professional's clinical judgment;

        (ii) prevent any program or facility from discharging any person for whom the provision of appropriate treatment, consistent with the clinical judgment of the mental health professional primarily responsible for such person's treatment, is or has become impossible as a result of such person's refusal to consent to such treatment;

        (iii) require a program or facility to admit any person who, while admitted on prior occasions to such program or facility, has repeatedly frustrated the purposes of such admissions by withholding consent to proposed treatment; or

        (iv) obligate a program or facility to provide treatment services to any person who is admitted to such program or facility solely for diagnostic or evaluative purposes.

    (C) In order to assist a person admitted to a program or facility in the exercise or protection of such person's rights, such person's attorney or legal representatives should have reasonable access to—

        (i) such person;

        (ii) the areas of the program or facility where such person has received treatment, resided, or had access; and

        (iii) pursuant to the written authorization of such person, the records and information pertaining to such person's diagnosis, treatment, and related services described in paragraph (1)(I).

    (D) Each program and facility should post a notice listing and describing, in language and terms appropriate to the ability of the persons to whom such notice is addressed to understand, the rights described in this section of all persons admitted to such program or facility. Each such notice should conform to the format and content for such notices, and should be posted in all appropriate locations.

(4) (A) In the case of a person adjudicated by a court of competent jurisdiction as being incompetent to exercise the right to consent to treatment or experimentation described in subparagraph (D) or (E) of paragraph (1), or the right to confidentiality of or access to records described in subparagraph (H) or (I) of such paragraph, or to provide authorization as described in paragraph (3)(C)(iii), such right may be exercised or such authorization may be provided by the individual appointed by such court as such person's guardian or representative for the purpose of exercising such right or such authorization.

(B) In the case of a person who lacks capacity to exercise the right to consent to treatment or experimentation under subparagraph (D) or (E) of paragraph (1), or the right to confidentiality of or access to records described in subparagraph (H) or (I) of such paragraph, or to provide authorization as described in paragraph (3)(C)(iii), because such person has not attained an age considered sufficiently advanced under State law to permit the exercise of such right or such authorization to be legally binding, such right may be exercised or such authorization may be provided on behalf of such person by a parent or legal guardian of such person.

(C) Notwithstanding subparagraphs (A) and (B), in the case of a person admitted to a program or facility for the purpose of receiving mental health services, no individual employed by or receiving any remuneration from such program or facility should act as such person's guardian or representative.

(Oct. 7, 1980, P.L. 96–398, Title V, § 501.94 Stat. 1598.)

Treatment Rights

Source: Reprinted from Martha A. Lyon, Martin L. Levine, and Jack Zusman, "Patients' Bills of Rights: A Survey of State Statutes," *Mental Disability Law Reporter* 6 (1982):185–187. Used by permission of the American Bar Association.

	(1)(A)(i) Appropriate treatment and services	(1)(B) Individual treatment plan	(1)(B) Treatment based on plan	(1)(B) Periodic review	(1)(B) Aftercare plan	(1)(G) Humane treatment environment	(1)(G) Privacy for personal needs	(1)(G) Safety	(1)(O) Discharge referrals
Ala. Code	N	N	N	N	N	N	N	N	N
Alaska Stat.	§§ 47.30.655(2), (3)	§ 47.30.825(1)	See (1)(B)	P § 47.30.220	§ 47.30.825(8)	N	§§ 47.30.840(1)–(4)	N	N
Ariz. Rev. Stat. Ann.	§ 36-511(A)	§§ 36-511(B)1. 2	N	§§ 36-511(B)1-3	N	§ 36-507	N	N	See (1)(B)
Ark. Stat. Ann.	§ 59-1416(24)	N	N	§ 59-1416(12)	See (1)(O)	§ 59-1416(9)	§§ 59-1416(1), (3)	§ 59-1416(23)	§ 59-1416(22)
Cal. Welf. & Inst. Code	§ 5325.1(a)	§ 5352.6	N	§ 5352.6	P §§ 5020.1, 5152	§ 5325.1(b)	N	N	P See (1)(B)
Colo. Rev. Stat.	§§ 27-10-116(1)(a), 27-10-101(1)(a)	P § 27-10-116	N	N	N	§ 27-10-117(1)(c)	§ 27-10-101(1)(c)	N	N
Conn. Gen. Stat.	§§ 17-206c, 19-575a(b)	P § 17-206c	N	§ 17-206f	N	§ 17-206c	§ 17-206i(a)	§ 19-575e(e)(5)	N
Del. Code Ann.	16 § 5161(a)(1)	16 § 5161(2)(e)	N	16 §§ 5161(a)(2)(a), (b)	N	16 § 5161(a)(1)	16 § 5161(a)(4)	N	N
D.C. Code	§ 21-562	N	N	§§ 21-546, 548	N	N	See (1)(G)	See (1)(G)	N
Fla. Stat. Ann.	§ 394.459(1)	P § 394.459(4)	N	N	N	§ 394.459(4)(a)	See (1)(G)	N	N
Ga. Code Ann.	§ 88-502.4(a)	P § 88-501(w)	N	§ 88-506.6(a)	N	§ 88-502.2	§ 88-502.8	§ 88-502.5(a)	N
Hawaii Rev. Stat.	§ 334E-2(8)	N	N	§ 334-35(2)	N	§ 334E-2(4)	§ 334E-2(3)	N	N
Idaho Code	§ 66-344	N	N	See (1)(B)	N	§ 66-344	P § 66-346(a)(3)	N	N
Ill. Ann. Stat.	91½ § 2-102(a)	91½ § 2-102(a)	91½ § 3-209	N	N	N	91½ § 2-104	N	P See (1)(B)
Ind. Code Ann.	§ 16-14-1.6-2(a)(1)	N	N	See (1)(B)	P § 16-14-1.6-7	§ 16-14-1.6-2(a)(2)	§ 16-14-1.6-3(a)(1)	N	P See (1)(B)
Iowa Code Ann.	§ 229.23(1)	N	N	§ 229.15	P See (1)(O)	P § 229.23(3)	See (1)(G)	See (1)(G)	
Kan. Stat.	§ 59-2927		N	P § 59-2917(a)	P See (1)(O)	§ 59-2927	§ 59-2929(a)(1)	N	P § 59-2924
Ky. Rev. Stat.		§ 202A.180(1)	N	N	P See (1)(O)	N	§ 202A.180	N	P § 202A.180(12)
La. Rev. Stat. Ann.	§ 28:171(R)	§ 28:171(Q)	N	§ 28:171(Q)		N	§ 28:171(A), (G)	N	P § 28:100.1
Maine Rev. Stat.	34 § 2252	34 § 2004(B)	N	N	P 34 § 2375	34 § 2252	34 § 2004(F)	N	P See (1)(B)
Md. Ann. Code	59 § 2	59 § 3A	N	59 § 3A	59 § 32B	N	N	N	59 § 32B
Mass. Gen. Laws			N	123 § 4	N	N	111 § 70E(l)	N	
Mich. Comp. Laws Ann.	§ 330.1708	§ 330.1712	N	§ 330.1482	See (1)(O)	§ 330.1708	§ 330.1728	§ 330.1708	§§ 330.1478, 1209(a)
Minn. Stat. Ann.	§ 253A.17, subd. (19)	§ 253A.17, subd. (9)	N	§ 253A.17, subd. (7)	§§ 253A.15, subds. (12, 13)	N	N	N	See (1)(B)
Miss. Code Ann.	N	N	N	P § 41-21-99	N	N	N	N	N
Mo. Ann. Stat.	§§ 630.115(1), (2)	N	N	N	N	§§ 630.115(1), (3), (14)	§§ 630.110(1), (2)	§ 630.115(3)	N
Mont. Code Ann.	§ 53-21-142(11)	§ 53-21-162(2)	N	§ 53-21-163(5)	§ 53-21-163(3)	§ 53-21-142(13)	§ 53-21-142(1)	See (1)(G)	See (1)(B)
Neb. Rev. Stat.	§ 83-1066(2)	§ 83-1044	P See (1)(B)	§ 83-1045	N	N	§ 83-1066(5)	N	N
Nev. Rev. Stat.	§ 433.484(1)	§ 433.494(1)	N	§ 433.494(2)	N	N	§§ 433.484(2), (3)	N	See (1)(B)

State									
N.H. Rev. Stat. Ann.	§ 135-B:43	P § 135-B:44	N	N	N	§ 135-B:43	See (1)(G)	N	N
N.J. Stat. Ann.	§ 30:4-24.1	N	N	N	N	§§ 30:4-24.2(e)(1), (3), (4)	N	See (1)(G)	N
N.M. Stat. Ann.	§ 43-1-7	§ 43-1-9(A)	§ 43-1-7	§ 43-1-9(D)	N	§ 43-1-6(D)	§ 43-1-6(H)	N	N
N.Y. Mental Hyg. Law	§ 33.03(a)	§ 29.13	§ 29.13	§ 33.03(b)(1)	§§ 29.15(f), (g)	§§ 33.03(a), (b)	See (1)(G)	P § 33.07(a)	§§ 29.15(f), (g)
N.C. Gen. Stat.	§ 122-55.5	§§ 122-55.5, .6	N	N	§ 122-55.6	§ 122-55.1	N	See (1)(G)	§ 122-55.6
N.D. Cent. Code	§ 25-03.1-40(1)	N	N	§ 25-03.1-31	§ 25-03.1-30(5)	§ 25-03.1-40(3)	N	§ 25-03.1-40(7)	§ 25-03.1-30(5)
Ohio Rev. Code Ann.	§ 5122.27(F)	§ 5122.27(B)	§ 5122.27(C)	§ 5122.27(D)	§ 5122.231	§ 5122.27(F)(3)	N	§ 5122.29(G)	P See (1)(G)
Okla. Stat. Ann.	43A § 91	N	N	P 43A § 54.11(A)	P See (1)(O)	43A § 91	N	N	P 43A § 152
Or. Rev. Stat.	N	§ 426.385(11)(g)	N	§ 426.385(1)(g)	P § 426.500(2)	N	See (1)(G)	§§ 426.385(1)(b), (c)	P See (1)(B)
Pa. Stat. Ann.	50 § 7104	50 §§ 7106(a), 7107	N	50 § 7108	50 § 7116(a)	50 § 7104	N	See (1)(G)	50 § 7116(a)
R.I. Gen. Laws	§ 40.1-5-9	§ 40.1-5-9	§ 40.1-5-9	§ 40.1-5-5(7)	N	N	N	§ 40.1-5-5(6)(a)	N
S.C. Code	§ 44-17-650	P § 44-17-650	N	§ 44-17-820	N	N	N	§§ 44-23-1030(3), (4)	N
S.D. Codified Laws	P § 27A-12-18	§ 27A-12-11	§ 27A-12-10	§ 27A-12-13	N	N	N	§ 27A-12-1	N
Tenn. Code Ann.	§ 33-306(b)	N	N	N	§ 33-306(b)	§ 33-306(b)	N	N	N
Tex. Mental Health Code Ann.	92 § 5547-70	N	N	N	N	N	N	N	N
Utah Code Ann.	§ 64-7-46	N	N	§ 64-7-42	See (1)(O)	§ 64-7-46	N	N	§ 64-7-30
Vt. Stat. Ann.	N	N	N	18 § 7802	N	N	N	N	N
Va. Code	§ 37.1-84.1(2)	N	N	§ 37.1-84.2	§ 37.1-98A	§ 37.1-84.1(3)	N	N	§ 37.1-98A
Wash. Rev. Code	§ 71.05.360	P § 71.05.360(2)	N	P § 71.05.050	N	N	N	§§ 71.05.370(1), (3)	N
W. Va. Code Ann.	§ 27-5-9(b)	§ 27-5-9(d)	§§ 27-5-9(c)(1)-(4)	See (1)(B)	N	§ 27-5-9(b)	§ 27-5-9(b)	§ 27-5-9(b)	N
Wis. Stat. Ann.	§ 51.61(1)(f)	N	N	§ 51.20(17)	N	§ 51.61(1)(n)	N	N	N
Wyo. Stat.	§ 25-3-122	N	N	P § 25-3-120	§ 25-3-121(a)	N	N	N	§ 25-3-121(a)

Note: N = State law contradicts Mental Health Systems Act of 1980 subsection, or no corresponding provision of state law.
P = Partial compliance.

Consent and Communications Rights

Source: Reprinted from Martha A. Lyon, Martin L. Levine, and Jack Zusman, "Patients' Bills of Rights: A Survey of State Statutes," *Mental Disability Law Reporter* 6 (1982):188–190. Used by permission of the American Bar Association.

	(1)(C) Ongoing participation	(1)(D) Refuse treatment	(1)(E) Nonparticipation in experimentation	(1)(J) Converse privately	(1)(J) Telephone and mail	(1)(J) Visitors
Ala. Code	N	N	N	N	N	N
Alaska Stat.	§ 47.30.655(5)	§ 47.30.825(5)	§ 47.30.830		§§ 47.30.840(6), (7)	§ 47.30.840(5)
Ariz. Rev. Stat. Ann.	N	§§ 36-512, 513	P § 36-512	P § 36-514(2)	§§ 36-514(2), (3)	§ 36-514(1)
Ark. Stat. Ann.	N	P §§ 59-1416(7), (8), (23)	§ 59-1416(15)	P § 59-1416(20)	P §§ 59-1416(5), (6)	P §§ 59-1416(4), (17), (20)
Cal. Welf. & Inst. Code	N	P §§ 5325.1(c), 5325(f), (g)	P § 5325.1(l)	N	§§ 5325(d), (e)	§ 5325(c)
Colo. Rev. Stat.	N	P § 27-10-116(2)(a)	P § 27-10-116(2)(d)	P § 27-10-117(1)(c)	§§ 27-10-117(1)(a)-(c)	§ 27-10-117(1)(d)
Conn. Gen. Stat.	N	P §§ 17-206d(a), (b)		§ 19-575e(2)	§§ 19-575e(3)-(4)	§ 17-206(a)
Del. Code Ann.	N	P 16 § 5161(a)(2)d	16 § 5161(a)(2)d	16 § 5161(a)(3)	16 § 5161(a)(3)	16 § 5161(a)(3)
D.C. Code Ann.	N				§ 21-561	§ 21-561
Fla. Stat. Ann.	N	P §§ 394, 459(3)(a), (b)		§ 394.459(5)(a)	§ 394.459(5)(b), (c)	§ 394.459(5)(a)
Ga. Code Ann.	§§ 88-502.24(a), .4(b)	P §§ 88-502.6(b), (d)	§ 88-502.4(c)	§ 88-502.7(a)	§§ 88-502.7(b)-(d), (e), (h)	§§ 88-502.7(a), (e)
Hawaii Rev. Stat.	§ 334E-2(11)	§ 334E-1	N	§§ 334E-2(3), (6)	§ 334E-2(6)	§ 334E-2(6)
Idaho Code	N	§§ 66-346(a)(4), (c)	N	N	§§ 66-346(a)(1)	§§ 66-346(a)(2)
Ill. Ann. Stat.	91½ § 2-102(a)	91½ § 2-107	91½ § 2-110	91½ § 2-103	91½ §§ 2-103(a), (b)	91½ § 2-103
Ind. Code Ann.	N	P § 16-14-1.6-7	N		§ 16-14-1.6-3(a)(2)	P §§ 16-14-1.6-3(c)
Iowa Code Ann.	N	P § 229.23(2)	N	P § 229.23(3)	§ 229.23(3)	§ 229.23(3)
Kan. Stat.	N	§ 59-2929(a)(6), (b)	§§ 59-2929(a)(6), (7)	N	§§ 2929(a)(2), (b)	§§ 2929(a)(4)-(6)
Ky. Rev. Stat.	P § 202A.180(2)	P § 202A.180(3), (7)		N	P §§ 202A.170(4), 210.220	P § 202A.180(5)
La. Rev. Stat. Ann.	N	P §§ 28:171(F), 52(H), 52(K)	N	§ 28:171(C)	§ 28:171(C)	§ 28:171(C)
Maine Rev. Stat.	34 § 2004(B)	N	N	N	P 34 § 2254(1)	34 § 2254(2)
Md. Ann. Code	N	N	N	N	59 §§ 50(a)-(e)	59 § 50(d)
Mass. Gen. Laws	N	P 123 § 23	111 § 70E(i)	P 123 § 23	123 § 23	123 § 23
Mich. Comp. Laws Ann.	N	§§ 330.1716(1), (2), 1718(1), (2)		P §§ 330.1726(1), (6), (7)	§ 330.1726	§§ 330.1726(1), (6), (7)
Minn. Stat. Ann.	§ 253A.17 subd. (9)	N	N	§ 253A.05 subd. (1)	§ 253A.17 subds. (2)-(5)	§ 253A.17 subd. (6)
Miss. Code Ann.	N					
Mo. Ann. Stat.	N	§§ 630.130; 630.133; 630.115(12)	§§ 630.115(8); 630.192	P § 630.110(3)	§§ 630.110(1)(3), (1)(5)	§§ 630.110(1)(4), (3)
Mont. Code Ann.	N	§ 53-21-148	§ 53-21-147(2)	P § 53-21-142(3)	§§ 53-21-142(3)-(5)	§ 53-21-142(3)
Neb. Rev. Stat.	§ 83-1066(2)	§ 83-1066(3)			§ 83-1066(4)	§ 83-1066(4)
Nev. Rev. Stat.	N	§§ 433.534(1), 433.484(1)(d), 433.493(1)(e)	§ 433.484(1)(a)	P § 433.484(5)	§ 433.484(5), (6)	§ 433.484(4)
N.H. Rev. Stat. Ann.	N	§ 135-B:22	N	§ 135-B:45	§ 135-B:45	§ 135-B:45

N.J. Stat. Ann.	P § 30:4-24.1	§§ 30:4-24.2(d)(1), (2), 30:4-24.2(f)	§ 30:4-24.4(d)(2)	P § 30:4-24.2(e)(1)	§§ 30:4-24.2(e)(6), (7)
N.M. Stat. Ann.	P §§ 43-1-9(B), (D)	P §§ 43-1-6(1), 43-1-15(A), (F)	§ 43-1-15(A)	P §§ 43-1-6(A), (B)	§ 43-1-6(B)
N.Y. Mental Hygiene Law	§ 29.13(b)	§ 33.03(b)(4)	§ 33.03(b)(4)	§ 33.05(a)	§ 33.05(a)
N.C. Gen. Stat.	N	§ 122-55.6	§ 122-55.6	P §§ 122-55.2(b)(1), (6)	§§ 122-55.2(a), (b)(1)
N.D. Cent. Code	N	P §§ 25-03.1-40(10), (13); 25-03.1-24	§ 25-03.1-40	N	§§ 25-03.1-40(5), (6)
Ohio Rev. Code Ann.	N	§§ 5122.291(A), (D), (E)	N	N	§§ 5122.29(D)(2), (E)
Okla. Stat. Ann.	N	P 43A §§ 54.8(A), 96	N	N	43A § 93
Or. Rev. Stat.	N	P §§ 426.385(2), 426.710(1)	§§ 426.700(2), 426.715(2)	§ 426.385(1)(a)	§§ 426.385(1)(a), (f)
Pa. Stat. Ann.	P 50 § 7107	N	N	P 50 § 4423(1)	P 50 § 4423(4)
R.I. Gen. Laws	N	N	N	§ 40.1-5-5(6)(e)	§ 40.1-5-5(6)(f), (g)
S.C. Code	N	P § 44-23-1010	P § 44-23-1010	N	§ 44-23-1030(1)
S.D. Codified Laws	N	§§ 27A-12-2(1), 20	§§ 27A-12-2(1), 20	§ 27A-12-7	§ 27A-12-2(4)
Tenn. Code Ann.	N	P §§ 33-307(a), 33-320(a), (f)	N	N	P § 33-306(a)
Tex. Mental Health Code Ann.	N	N	N	N	P 92 § 5547-86(a)(3)
Utah Code Ann.	N	N	N	P § 64-7-48(1)(a)	§ 64-7-48(1)(a)
Vt. Stat. Ann.	N	P 18 § 7708	N	N	18 §§ 7705(a)(1), (2)
Va. Code	N	P § 37.1-84.1(5)	§ 37.1-235	N	P § 37.1-84.1(7)
Wash. Rev. Code	N	P § 71.05.370(7)	N	P § 71.05.370(5)	§§ 71.05.370(5), (6)
W. Va. Code Ann.	N	P § 27-4-4(b)	N	N	N
Wis. Stat. Ann.	N	P § 51.61(1)(h)	§ 51.61(1)(i)	N	§ 51.61(1)(c)
Wyo. Stat.	N	N	N	P § 25-3-124(a)(i)	§ 25-3-124(a)(i)

N.J. Stat. Ann.	§ 30:4-24.2(e)(5)
N.M. Stat. Ann.	§ 43-1-6(A)
N.Y. Mental Hygiene Law	§ 33.05(b)
N.C. Gen. Stat.	§ 122-55.2(b)(2)
N.D. Cent. Code	§ 25-03.1-40(5)
Ohio Rev. Code Ann.	§ 5122.29(D)(1)
Okla. Stat. Ann.	43A § 93
Or. Rev. Stat.	N
Pa. Stat. Ann.	P 50 §§ 4423(1), (2)
R.I. Gen. Laws	§ 40.1-5-5(6)(e)
S.C. Code	§ 44-23-1030(2)
S.D. Codified Laws	§ 27A-12-2(4)
Tenn. Code Ann.	§ 33-306(a)
Tex. Mental Health Code Ann.	P 92 § 5547-86(a)(1)
Utah Code Ann.	§ 64-7-48(1)(b)
Vt. Stat. Ann.	18 §§ 7705(a)(2), (6)
Va. Code	N
Wash. Rev. Code	§ 71.05.370(4)
W. Va. Code Ann.	N
Wis. Stat. Ann.	§ 51.61(1)(p)
Wyo. Stat.	§ 25-3-124(a)(ii)

Note: N = State law contradicts Mental Health Systems Act of 1980 subsection, or no corresponding provision of state law.

P = Partial compliance.

Information and Records Rights

Source: Reprinted from Martha A. Lyon, Martin L. Levine, and Jack Zusman, "Patients' Bills of Rights: A Survey of State Statutes," *Mental Disability Law Reporter* 6 (1982):191–193. Used by permission of the American Bar Association.

	(1)(C)(i), (iv), (vi) Explanation re: treatment	(1)(E) Explanation re: experimentation	(1)(H) Confidentiality of records	(1)(I) Access to records	(1)(K) Information re: rights	(2)(B) Confidentiality of records and access after discharge	(3)(D) Posted notice of rights
Ala. Code	N	N	§ 22–50–62	N	N	N	N
Alaska Stat.	P §§ 47.30.825(1), (2)	N	§ 47.30.845	§ 47.30.260(a)(1)	N	§ 47.30.260(a)	§§ 47.30.855, 860
Ariz. Rev. Ann.	N	N	§ 36–509	§ 36–507(3)	§ 36–528(D)	N	§ 36–504(A)
Ark. Stat. Ann.	§§ 59–1416(11), (13)	P §§ 59–1416(11)	§ 59–1416(14)	N	P §§ 59–1408, 1416(28)	N	§ 59–1418(28)
Cal. Welf. & Inst. Code	§ 5326.2	N	§ 5328	N	§ 5325(h)	§ 5328(k)	§ 5325
Colo. Rev. Stat.	N	P § 27–10–116(2)(d)	§ 27–10–120(1)	§ 27–10–120(1)(b)	§§ 27–10–117(1), (5)	N	P § 27–10–117
Conn. Gen. Stat.	N	N	§ 17–180	§§ 17–206i(b), 4–104	P § 19–575a(f)	§§ 17–206i(a), 4–104	§§ 19–575(f), 17–206i(c)
Del. Code Ann.	N	P § 16–5161(a)(2)d	§ 16–5161(a)(7)a	§ 16–5161(a)(7)c	§ 16–5161(a)	N	§ 16–5161(a)
D.C. Code Ann.		N		P § 21–562	P § 21–565	N	N
Fla. Stat. Ann.	P § 394.459(3)(a)	N	§ 394.459(9)		P § 394.459(5)(e)	N	P § 394.459(5)(e)
Ga. Code Ann.	P § 88–502.4(b)	N	§ 88–502.12(a)	§§ 88–502.12(a)(2), 88–502.4(b), 88–502.13(a)	P § 88–503.4	N	N
Hawaii Rev. Stat.	§ 334E–1(a)	N	§ 334–5	§§ 334–5, 334E–2(19)	P § 334E–2(20)	N	
Idaho Code	N	N	§ 66–348(a)	§§ 66–348(a)(1), 66–346(a)(7)	P § 66–346(d)	N	P § 66–346(d)
Ill. Ann. Stat.	N	P 91½ § 2–107	91½ §§ 803(a), 805, 813	91½ § 804	91½ §§ 2–200, 3–205	N	91½ §§ 2–200(A), 3–204
Ind. Code Ann.	P § 16–14–1.6–7	N	§ 16–14–1.6–8(b)	§ 16–14–1.6–8(c)	P § 16–14–1.6–11	N	N
Iowa Code Ann.		N	§ 229.24(1)		P § 229.23(3)	N	N
Kan. Stat.	P § 59–2929(a)(7), (b)	§ 59–2929(a)(7)	§ 59–2931(a)	§ 59–2931(a)(2)(A)	P § 59–2929(a)(10)	§ 59–2931(a)(2)(A)	N
Ky. Rev. Stat.	P § 202A.180(1)	N	§ 210.235	§ 210.235	P § 202A.170(1)	§ 210.235	P § 202A.170(1)
La. Rev. Stat. Ann.	N	N	§ 44:7(A)	§ 44:7(B)	P § 28:52(F)	P §§ 44:7(C), (B)	28:52(F)
Maine Rev. Stat.	N	N	34 §§ 2004(G), 1–B	34 § 1–B		N	N
Md. Ann. Code	N	N	59 § 19	N	59 §§ 13(a), (b), (e), (f)	N	N
Mass. Gen. Laws	N	111 § 70E(i)	111 § 70E(b)	111 § 70E(g)	P 111 § 70E(e)	N	P 111 § 70E
Mich. Comp. Laws Ann.	P § 330.1714	N	§ 330.1748	§ 330.1748(5)(b)	P § 330.1706	N	N
Minn. Stat. Ann.	P § 253A.17, subd. 9	N	P § 246.13		P §§ 253A.05, subds. (2), (3)	N	N
Miss. Code Ann.		N	P § 41–21–97	P § 41–9–65		N	
Mo. Ann. Stat.	P § 630.115(6)	§§ 630.115(8), .192	§ 630.140(1)	§§ 630.110(1), (6)	§ 630.125	N	§ 630.125(3)
Mont. Code Ann.		P § 53–21–147(2)	§ 53–21–166	§§ 53–21–166(2), 53–21–165	§§ 53–21–114(1), 53–21–168	N	§ 53–21–168

	1	2	3	4	5	6	7
Neb. Rev. Stat.	P § 83-1044	N		§ 83-1068	§ 83-1068(1)	P § 83-1068	N
Nev. Rev. Stat.	§ 433.484(1)(b)		§ 433.360	§ 433.504.360	§§ 433.504, 433, 534	P § 433.484	P § 433.484
N.H. Rev. Stat. Ann.	N	N	N	§ 30:4-24.3	§§ 30:4-24.3(1), (3)	P §§ 135-B:22, 24	P § 135-B:46
N.J. Stat. Ann.	N	N	§ 30:4-24.3	§ 30:4-24.3	§§ 30:4-24.3(1), (3)	P § 30:4-24.2(b)	§ 30:4-24.2(d)
N.M. Stat. Ann.	P §§ 43-1-9(c), (1), (3), (4)	N	§ 43-1-19(A)	§ 43-1-19(A)	§ 43-1-19(D)	N	N
N.Y. Mental Hygiene Law	N		§ 33.13(c)	§ 33.13(c)(3)	P § 9.07(a)	P § 33.14	§ 9.07(b)
N.C. Gen. Stat.	N	N	P § 122-56.8(a)		N	P § 122-56.8(c)	N
N.D. Cent. Code	N	N	§ 25-03.1-43	P § 25-03.1-43(2)	§ 25-03.1-27	P § 25-03.1-45	N
Ohio Rev. Code Ann.	P § 5122.27(F)(4)		§ 5122.31	§ 5122.31	§§ 5122.29(A), 5122.27(G)	§ 5122.31	
Okla. Stat. Ann.	N	N	43A § 54.4(M)				
Or. Rev. Stat.	N	§§ 426.700(2), 426.715(2)	§§ 426.385(L), 426.160, 192.525	§ 192.525	N	P § 426.070(5)	§ 426.395
Pa. Stat. Ann.	P 50 § 7107		50 § 7111	50 § 7111		P 50 § 7302(c)	N
R.I. Gen. Laws	P § 40.1-5-10(3)	N	§ 40.1-5-26	§§ 40.1-5-26(1), (3)	§§ 40.1-5-26(1), (3)	N	N
S.C. Code	N	P § 44-23-1090	§ 44-23-1090(1)	§ 44-23-1090(1)	§ 44-23-1090(1)	P § 27A-12-3	P § 27A-12-3
S.D. Codified Laws	N	N	§§ 27A-12-25, 26	§ 27A-12-28(2)	§ 27A-12-28(2)	P § 27A-12-3	P § 27A-12-3
Tenn. Code Ann.	N	N	§ 33-306(b)	§ 33-306(b)	§ 33-306(h)	§ 33-306(h)	N
Tex. Mental Health Code Ann.	N	N	92 § 5547-87(1)	§ 64-7-50(1)(a)	92 § 5547-24	P 92 § 5547-24	N
Utah Code Ann.	N	N	§ 64-7-50(1)	§ 64-7-50(1)(a)	§ 64-7-50(1)(a)	P § 64-7-48	§ 64-7-48(5)
Vt. Stat. Ann.	N	N	18 § 7103(a)	18 § 7103(a)(1)	18 § 7103(a)(1)	P 18 § 7701	P 18 § 7701
Va. Code	P § 37.1-84.1(2)	§ 37.1-234(6)	§ 37.1-84.1(8)	§ 37.1-84.1(8)	§ 37.1-84.1(8)	P § 37.1-84.1(8)	P § 71.05.370
Wash. Rev. Code	N	N	§ 71.05.390	§ 71.05.390	§ 71.05.390(6)	P § 71.05.050	§ 71.05.390(6)
W. Va. Code Ann.	N	N	§ 27-3-1(a)	§ 27-3-1(a)		P § 27-5-9	N
Wis. Stat. Ann.	P §§ 51.61(1)(j), 51.61(4)(a)	N	§ 51.61(n)	§ 51.61(n)	§ 51.61(n)	P § 51.61(1)(a)	P § 51.61(1)(b)
Wyo. Stat.	N		§§ 25-3-126(a)	§§ 25-3-126(a)(i), 25-3-126(b)	§§ 25-3-126(a)(i), 25-3-126(b)	N	§ 25-3-126

Note: N = State law contradicts Mental Health Systems Act of 1980 subsection, or no corresponding provision of state law.

P = Partial compliance.

Grievance and Access Rights

Source: Reprinted from Martha A. Lyon, Martin L. Levine, and Jack Zusman, "Patient's Bills of Rights: A Survey of State Statutes," *Mental Disability Law Reporter* 6 (1982):194–197. Used by permission of the American Bar Association.

	(1)(L) Assert grievances	(1)(L) Fair grievance procedure	(1)(M) Access to advocate	(3)(C) Access by legal representative
Ala. Code	N	N	N	N
Alaska Stat.	N	N	N	P § 47.30.150(a)(2)
Ariz. Rev. Stat. Ann.	P § 36–516	N	N	P §§ 36–514(1), 537(A)
Ark. Stat. Ann.	P § 59–1416(21)	N	P §§ 59–1417, 1408(A)(1)	P §§ 59–1416(14), (20)
Cal. Welf. & Inst. Code	P § 5326.9	P § 5326.9	P § 5326.9	P §§ 5325(c), 5328(i)
Colo. Rev. Stat.	N	N	N	P §§ 27-10–117(1)(d), 116(1)(a)
Conn. Gen. Stat.	§ 19–575(e)(7)	N	N	P §§ 17–206(h)(c), 17–180, 19–575(c)(10)
Del. Code Ann.	§ 21–549	N	N	P 16 §§ 5161(a)(3), (7)b
D.C. Code Ann.	N	N	N	P § 21–561
Fla. Stat. Ann.	N	N	N	P §§ 394–459(5)(a), (9)(a)
Ga. Code Ann.	P § 88–502.22	P § 88–502.22	N	P § 88–502.7(a)
Hawaii Rev. Stat.	N	§ 334E–2(2)	P § 334E–2	P §§ 334E–2(6), 334–5
Idaho Code	N	N	N	P §§ 66–346(a)(5), 66–348(a)(1)
Ill. Ann. Stat.	N	N	N	P 91½ §§ 3–609, 809(a)(3)
Ind. Code Ann.	P § 16–14–1.6–10	N	N	P §§ 16–14–1.6–2(a)(4), 16–14–1.6–8(e)(3)
Iowa Code Ann.	N	N	N	P §§ 229.24(2), 229.25(4)
Kan. Stat.	P §§ 59–2929(a)(8)	N	P § 59–2929(a)(8)	P §§ 59–2929(a)(9), 59–2931(a)(2)(D)
Ky. Rev. Stat.	P §§ 202A.180(8), (9)	N	P § 202A.170(4)	P § 210.235(1)
La. Rev. Stat. Ann.	N	N	P § 28:171(K)	P §§ 28:64(D), 28:53(E), 28:171(C)
Maine Rev. Stat.	P 34 §§ 2255, 2259	34 § 2004(K)	P 34 § 2004(J)	P 34 § 2254(2)
Md. Ann. Code	N	N	P 59 § 54	P 59 §§ 19, 50(d)
Mass. Gen. Laws	N	N	P 123 §§ 23	P 123 §§ 23, 36(2), 55(b)
Mich. Comp. Laws Ann.	P §§ 330.1484, 1486	N		P §§ 330.1726(7), 330.1748(4)(c)
Minn. Stat. Ann.	§ 253A.16, subd. (2)	§ 253A.16. subd. (2)	§§ 253A.22, subds. (3), (4)	P §§ 253A.05, subd. (1), 253A.17, subd. (6)
Miss. Code Ann.	N	N	N	
Mo. Ann. Stat.	§ 630.115(2)	N	P § 630.110(4)	P § 630.110(3), §§ 630.140(2)–(4)
Mont. Code Ann.	N	N	N	P §§ 53–21–142(3), 165
Neb. Rev. Stat.	§§ 83–1066(8), (9)	N	P §§ 83–1066(8), (9)	P §§ 83–1066(4), 83–1068(2)
Nev. Rev. Stat.	N	N	P § 433.534	P §§ 433.484(4), 433A.360(1)
N.H. Rev. Stat. Ann.	N	N	N	P § 155–B:45
N.J. Stat. Ann.	N	N	N	P §§ 30:4–24.2..3
N.M. Stat. Ann.	P § 43–1–23	N	N	P §§ 43–1–6(A), 19(A)
N.Y. Mental Hygiene Law	N	N	P §§ 33.05(a), 29.09	P §§ 33.05(a), 33.13(c)(3)
N.C. Gen. Stat.	P § 122–55.7	N	N	P §§ 122–55.2(a)(2), (d)
N.D. Cent. Code	N	N	P § 25–01–02.1	P § 25–03.1–40(5)
Ohio Rev. Code Ann.	§ 5122.30	N	P §§ 5122.29(C), 5123.60(B)	P §§ 5122.29(C), 5122.31(A)
Okla. Stat. Ann.	N	N	P 43A §§ 93, 98	P 43A §§ 93, 54.4

State				
Or. Rev. Stat.	N	N	N	N
Pa. Stat. Ann.	N	N	P 50 § 4423(1)	P 50 § 4423(1)
R.I. Gen. Laws	§ 40.1-5-5(6)(m)	Z	§ 40.1-5-5(6)(m)	P § 40.1-5-24(1)
S.C. Code	N	Z	P § 44-23-1030	P §§ 44-23-1030, 1090
S.D. Codified Laws	N	Z	P § 27A-7-4	P §§ 27A-12-8, 27
Tenn. Code Ann.	N	Z	P § 33-306(a)	P § 33-306(b)
Tex. Mental Health Code Ann.	N	Z	P 92 § 5547-86(a)(4)	N
Utah Code Ann.	N	Z	P § 64-7-48(4)	P §§ 64-7-48(3), 64-7-50(1)(a)
Vt. Stat. Ann.		N	P 18 § 7705(a)(1)	P 18 §§ 7710, 7103(b)
Va. Code	§ 37.1-84.1	§ 37.1-84.1(a)	N	P § 37.1-84.1(8)
Wash. Rev. Code	N	N	N	P § 71.05.370(4)
W. Va. Code Ann.	P §§ 51.61(2), (5), (7)	P §§ 51.61(2), 51.61(5)(a)	P § 27-4-4(c)	P § 27-5-9(e)(2)
Wis. Stat. Ann.	N	N	P § 51.61(1)(c)	P §§ 51.61(1)(t), 51.30(4)(b)11
Wyo. Stat.	N	N	P § 25-3-124(a)(i)	P § 25-3-124(a)(ii)

Note: N = State law contradicts Mental Health Systems Act of 1980 subsection, or no corresponding provision of state law.

P = Partial compliance.

Other Rights

Source: Reprinted from Martha A. Lyon, Martin L. Levine, and Jack Zusman, "Patients' Bills of Rights: A Survey of State Statutes," *Mental Disability Law Reporter* 6 (1982):197–199. Used by permission of the American Bar Association.

	(1)(A)(i), (ii) Treatment and least restriction of liberty	(1)(F) Freedom from restraint or seclusion	(2)(A) Other civil rights	(1)(N), (3)(A) No reprisals for assertion of rights
Ala. Code	N	N	N	N
Alaska Stat.	§§ 47.30.655(2), (3)	§§ 47.30.825.2(c), 4; § 47.30.140	§ 47.30.150(a)(3)	N
Ariz. Rev. Stat. Ann.	P § 36–511(A)	§ 36–513	§ 36–506	N
Ark. Stat. Ann.	§§ 59–1416(24), 1415(A)	§§ 59–1415(A), 59–1416(23)	§ 59–1416	N
Cal. Welf. & Inst. Code	§ 5325.1(a)	§ 5325.1(c)	§ 5005	P § 5326.5(b)
Colo. Rev. Stat.	§§ 27–10–101(1)(a), 27–10–116(1)(a)		§ 27–10–104	N
Conn. Gen. Stat.	P §§ 19–575a(b), 17–206c	§§ 19–575e(b), 17–206e	P §§ 17–206i(a), 4–104	§ 19–575e(7)
Del. Code Ann.	P 16 § 5161(a)(1)			N
D.C. Code Ann.	N	§ 21–563	P § 21–564(a)	N
Fla. Stat. Ann.	§§ 394.459(1), (2)(b)	§ 394.459(1)	§ 394.459(1)	N
Ga. Code Ann.	§§ 88–502.21, 88–502.4(a)	§ 88–502.5(b)	§ 88–502.1	N
Hawaii Rev. Stat.	§§ 334–35(1), 334–104	§ 334E–2	P § 334–61	N
Idaho Code	N	§ 66–345	P §§ 66–346(a), (b)	N
Ill. Ann. Stat.	91½ § 2–102(a)	91½ §§ 2–108, 109	91½ § 2–100	N
Ind. Code Ann.	N	§ 16–14–1.6–6	§ 16–14–1.6–4(a)	N
Iowa Code Ann.	P § 229.23(1)		§ 229.33(3)	N
Kan. Stat.	P § 59–2927	§ 59–2928	§ 59–2930	N
Ky. Rev. Stat.	P §§ 202A.180(12), (13)	§ 202A.180(10)	§ 202A.170(4)	N
La. Rev. Stat. Ann.	P § 28:171(Q)	§§ 28:171(D), (E)	28:171(A)	N
Maine Rev. Stat.	P 34 § 2004(1)(A)	34 § 2253	34 § 2254(3)	N
Md. Ann. Code	N	N	59 §§ 51, 57	N
Mass. Gen. Laws	P 123 § 4(3)	123 § 21	123 §§ 23, 25	N
Mich. Comp. Laws Ann.	N	§§ 330.1740, .1742, .1744	§ 330.1704	N
Minn. Stat. Ann.	P § 253A.17, subd. (9)	§ 253A.17, subd. (1)	N	253A.16, subd. (3)
Miss. Code Ann.	N	N	N	N
Mo. Ann. Stat.	§§ 630.115(1), (2), (7), (10)	§ 630.175	N	N
Mont. Code Ann.	§ 53–21–142(2)	§§ 53–21–145, 146	§ 53–21–141(1)	N
Neb. Rev. Stat.	§ 83–1044		N	N
Nev. Rev. Stat.	§ 433.494(1)	§ 433.484(7)		N
N.H. Rev. Stat. Ann.	P § 135–B:43		§ 135–B:42	N
N.J. Stat. Ann.	P § 30:4–24.2(c)(2)	§§ 30:4–24.2(d)(1), (3)	§§ 30:4–24.1; 30:4–24.2(a), (b)	N
N.M. Stat. Ann.	§§ 43–1–7, 43–1–9(C)(2)	N	§ 43–1–5	N
N.Y. Mental Hygiene Law	N	§ 33.04	§ 33.01	N
N.C. Gen. Stat.	§ 122–55.1	§§ 122–55.3, .6	P §§ 122–55.2(c), 122–55.7	N

N.D. Cent. Code	§§ 25–03.1–40(1)–(3)	P § 25–03.1–40(4)	§ 25–03.1–40	N
Ohio Rev. Code Ann.	§ 5122.27(F)	§§ 5122.27(F)(6), (7)	§§ 5122.42, 5122.301	N
Okla. Stat. Ann.	P 43A § 54.9(A)	P 43A § 92	N	N
Or. Rev. Stat.	N	P § 426.385(3)	§ 426.385(1)(m)	N
Pa. Stat. Ann.	50 § 7107	P 50 § 4422	50 § 7113	N
R.I. Gen. Laws	§ 40.1–5–9	P § 40.1–5–5(6)(1)	§ 40.1–5–5(6)	N
S.C. Code	N	§ 44–23–1020	§ 44–23–1040	N
S.D. Codified Laws	P §§ 27A–12–11–(2), (6)	§ 27A–12–6	§ 27A–12–33	N
Tenn. Code Ann.		§ 33–306(d)	P § 33–306(e)	N
Tex. Mental Health Code Ann.	P 92 § 5547–70	P 92 § 5547–71	92 § 5547–83(b)	N
Utah Code Ann.	P § 64–7–46	§ 64–7–47	§ 64–7–48(1)(c)	N
Vt. Stat. Ann.	P 18 § 7703(a)	P 18 § 7704	P 18 § 7705(a)(3)	N
Va. Code	§ 37.1–84.1(6)	P § 37.1–84.1(6)	§ 37.1–84.1(1)	N
Wash. Rev. Code	P §§ 71.05.010, 71.05.210	N	§ 71.05.060	N
W. Va. Code Ann.	P § 27–5–9		§ 27–5–9(a)	P § 27–3–2
Wis. Stat. Ann.	§§ 51.61(1)(e); 51.01(1), (2)	§ 51.61(1)(i)	§ 51.80	N
Wyo. Stat.	P § 25–3–122	P § 25–3–123	§ 25–3–125	N

Note: **N** = State law contradicts Mental Health Systems Act of 1980 subsection, or corresponding provision of state law.

P = Partial compliance.

List of Mental Impairments for Social Security Disability Benefits

11.00 NEUROLOGICAL

A. Convulsive Disorders

In convulsive disorders, regardless of etiology, severity will be determined according to type, frequency, duration, and sequelae of seizures. At least one detailed description of a typical seizure is required. Such description includes the presence or absence of aura, tongue bites, sphincter control, injuries associated with the attack, and postictal phenomena. The reporting physician should indicate the extent to which description of seizures reflects his own observations and the source of ancillary information. Testimony of persons other than the claimant is essential for description of type and frequency of seizures if professional observation is not available.

Documentation of epilepsy should include at least one electroencephalogram (EEG).

Under 11.02 and 11.03, a severe impairment is considered present only if it persists despite the fact that the individual is following prescribed anticonvulsive treatment. Adherence to prescribed anticonvulsant therapy can ordinarily be determined from objective clinical findings in the report of the physician currently providing treatment for epilepsy. Determination of blood levels of phenytoin sodium or other anticonvulsive drugs may serve to indicate whether the prescribed medication is being taken. Should serum drug levels appear therapeutically inadequate, consideration should be given as to whether this is caused by individual idiosyncrasy in absorption or metabolism of the drug. Where adequate seizure control is obtained only with unusually large doses, the possibility of impairment resulting from the side effects of this medication must also be assessed. Where documentation shows that use of alcohol or drugs affects adherence to prescribed

Source: Appendix to Social Security regulations, 20 C.F.R. 404.

359

therapy or may play a part in the precipitation of seizures, this must also be considered in the overall assessment of impairment severity.

B. Brain Tumors

The diagnosis of malignant brain tumor should be established under the criteria described in 13.00B for neoplastic disease.

In histologically malignant tumors, the pathological diagnosis alone will be the decisive criterion for severity and expected duration (see 11.05A). In cases of benign tumors (see 11.05B) the severity and duration of the impairment will be determined on the bases of the symptoms, signs, and pertinent laboratory findings.

C. Persistent Disorganization of Motor Function

In the form of paresis or paralysis, tremor or other involuntary movements, ataxia and sensory disturbances (any or all of which may be due to cerebral, cerebellar, brain stem, spinal cord, or peripheral nerve dysfunction) which occur singly or in various combinations, frequently provides the sole or partial basis for decision in cases of neurological impairment. The assessment of impairment depends on the degree of interference with locomotion and/or interference with the use of fingers, hands, and arms.

D. In Conditions Which Are Episodic in Character

Such as multiple sclerosis or myasthenia gravis, consideration should be given to frequency and duration of exacerbations, length of remissions, and permanent residuals.

11.01 Category of Impairments, Neurological

11.02 *Epilepsy–major motor seizures (grand mal or psychomotor), documented by EEG and by detailed description of a typical seizure pattern, including all associated phenomena; occurring more frequently than once a month, in spite of at least 3 months of prescribed treatment.* With:

A. Diurnal episodes (loss of consciousness and convulsive seizures); or

B. Nocturnal episodes manifesting residuals which interfere significantly with activity during the day.

11.03 *Epilepsy–minor motor seizures (petit mal, psychomotor, or focal), documented by EEG and by detailed description of a typical seizure pattern, including all associated phenomena; occurring more frequently than once weekly in spite of at least 3 months of prescribed treatment.* With alteration of awareness or loss of consciousness and transient postictal manifestations of unconventional behavior or significant interference with activity during the day.

11.04 *Central nervous system vascular accident*. With one of the following more than 3 months post-vascular accident:

A. Sensory or motor aphasia resulting in ineffective speech or communication; or

B. Significant and persistent disorganization of motor function in two extremities, resulting in sustained disturbance of gross and dexterous movements, or gait and station (see 11.00C).

11.05 *Brain tumors*.

A. Malignant gliomas (astrocytoma—grades III and IV, glioblastoma multiforme), medulloblastoma, ependymoblastoma, or primary sarcoma; or

B. Astrocytoma (grades I and II), meningioma, pituitary tumors, oligodendroglioma, ependymoma, clivus chordoma, and benign tumors. Evaluate under 11.02, 11.03, 11.04 A, or B, or 12.02.

11.06 *Parkinsonian syndrome* with the following signs: Significant rigidity, brady kinesia, or tremor in two extremities, which, singly or in combination, result in sustained disturbance of gross and dexterous movements, or gait and station.

11.07 *Cerebral palsy*. With:

A. IQ of 69 or less; or

B. Abnormal behavior patterns, such as destructiveness or emotional instability; or

C. Significant interference in communication due to speech, hearing, or visual defect; or

D. Disorganization of motor function as described in 11.04B.

11.08 *Spinal cord or nerve root lesions, due to any cause* with disorganization of motor function as described in 11.04B.

11.09 *Multiple sclerosis*. With:

A. Disorganization of motor function as described in 11.04B; or

B. Visual or mental impairment as described under the criteria in 2.02, 2.03, 2.04, or 12.02.

11.10 *Amyotrophic lateral sclerosis*. With:

A. Significant bulbar signs; or

B. Disorganization of motor function as described in 11.04B.

11.11 *Anterior poliomyelitis*. With:

A. Persistent difficulty with swallowing or breathing; or

B. Unintelligible speech; or

C. Disorganization of motor function as described in 11.04B.

11.12 *Myasthenia gravis*. With:

A. Significant difficulty with speaking, swallowing, or breathing while on prescribed therapy; or

B. Significant motor weakness of muscles of extremities on repetitive activity against resistance while on prescribed therapy.

11.13 *Muscular dystrophy* with disorganization of motor function as described in 11.04B.

11.14 *Peripheral neuropathies*. With disorganization of motor function as described in 11.04B, in spite of prescribed treatment.

11.15 *Tabes dorsalis*. With:

A. Tabetic crises occurring more frequently than once monthly; or

B. Unsteady, broad-based or ataxic gait causing significant restriction of mobility substantiated by appropriate posterior column signs.

11.16 *Subacute combined cord degeneration (pernicious anemia)* with disorganization of motor function as described in 11.04B or 11.15B, not significantly improved by prescribed treatment.

11.17 *Degenerative disease not listed elsewhere, such as Huntington's chorea, Friedreich's ataxia, and spino-cerebellar degeneration*. With:

A. Disorganization of motor function as described in 11.04B or 11.15B; or

B. Chronic brain syndrome. Evaluate under 12.02.

11.18 *Cerebral trauma*. Evaluate under the provisions of 11.02, 11.03, 11.04, and 12.02 as applicable.

11.19 *Syringomyelia*. With:

A. Significant bulbar signs; or

B. Disorganization of motor function as described in 11.04B.

12.00 MENTAL DISORDERS

A. Introduction

The evaluation of disability applications on the basis of mental disorders requires consideration of the nature and clinical manifestations of the medically determinable impairment(s) as well as consideration of the degree of limitation such impairment(s) may impose on the individual's ability to work, as reflected by (1) daily activities both in the occupational and social spheres; (2) range of interest; (3) ability to take care of personal needs; and (4) ability to relate to others. This evaluation must be based on medical evidence consisting of demonstrable clinical signs (medically demonstrable phenomena, apart from the individual's symptoms, which indicate specific abnormalities of behavior, affect, thought, memory, orientation, or contact with reality) and laboratory findings (including psychological tests) relevant to such issues as restriction of daily activities, constriction of interests, deterioration of personal habits (including personal hygiene), and impaired ability to relate to others.

The severity and duration of mental impairment(s) should be evaluated on the basis of reports from psychiatrists, psychologists, and hospitals, in conjunction with adequate descriptions of daily activities from these or other sources. Since confinement in an institution may occur because of legal or social requirements, confinement per se does not establish that impairment is severe. Similarly, release from an institution does not establish improvement. As always, severity and duration of impairment are determined by the medical evidence. A description of the individual's personal appearance and behavior at the time of the examination is also important to the evaluation process.

Diagnosis alone is insufficient as a basis for evaluation of the severity of mental impairment(s). Accordingly, the criteria of severity under mental disorders are arranged in four comprehensive groups: chronic brain syndromes (see 12.02), functional (nonorganic) psychotic disorders (see 12.03), functional nonpsychotic disorders (see 12.04), and mental retardation (see 12.05). Each category consists of a set of clinical findings, one or more of which must be met, and a set of functional restrictions, all of which must be met. The functional restrictions are to be interpreted in the light of the extent to which they are imposed by psychopathology.

The criteria for severity of mental impairment(s) are so constructed that a decision can be reached even if there are disagreements regarding diagnosis. All available clinical and laboratory evidence must be considered since it is not unusual to find, in the same individual, signs and test results associated with several pathological conditions, mental or physical. For example, an individual might show evidence of depression, chronic brain syndrome, cirrhosis of the liver, etc., in various combinations.

In some cases, the results of well-standardized psychological tests, such as Wechsler Adult Intelligence Scale (WAIS) and the Minnesota Multiphasic Personality Inventory (MMPI), may contribute to the assessment of severity of impairment. To provide full documentation, the psychological report should include key data on which the report was based, such as MMPI profiles, WAIS subtest scores, etc.

B. Discussion of Mental Disorders

1. *Chronic brain syndromes* (organic brain syndromes) result from persistent, more or less irreversible, diffuse impairment of cerebral tissue function. They are usually permanent and may be progressive. They may be accompanied by psychotic or neurotic behavior superimposed on organic brain pathology. The degree of impairment may range from mild to severe. Acute brain syndromes are temporary and reversible conditions with favorable prognosis and no significant residuals. Occasionally, an acute brain syndrome may progress into a chronic brain syndrome.

2. *Functional psychotic disorders* are characterized by demonstrable mental abnormalities without demonstrable structural changes in brain tissue. Mood disorders (involutional psychosis, manic-depressive illness, psychotic depressive

reaction) or thought disorders (schizophrenias and paranoid states) are characterized by varying degrees of personality disorganization and accompanied by a corresponding degree of inability to maintain contact with reality (e.g., hallucinations, delusions).

3. *Functional nonpsychotic disorders* are likewise characterized by demonstrable mental abnormalities without demonstrable structural changes in brain tissue (psychophysiologic, neurotic, personality and certain other nonpsychotic disorders).

a. *Psychophysiologic (autonomic and visceral) disorders* (e.g., cardiovascular, gastrointestinal, genitourinary, musculoskeletal, respiratory). In these conditions, the normal physiological expression of emotions is exaggerated by chronic emotional tensions, eventually leading to a disruption of the autonomic regulatory system and resulting in various visceral disorders. If the condition persists, it may lead to demonstrable structural changes (e.g., peptic ulcer, bronchial asthma, dermatitis).

b. *Neurotic disorders* (e.g., anxiety, depressive, hysterical, obsessive-compulsive, and phobic neuroses). In these conditions there are no gross falsifications of reality such as observed in the psychoses in the form of hallucinations or delusions. Neuroses are characterized by reactions to deep-seated conflicts and are classified by the defense mechanisms the individual employs to stave off the threat of emotional decompensation (e.g., anxiety, depression, conversion, obsessive-compulsive, or phobic mechanisms). Anxiety or depression occurring in connection with overwhelming external situations (i.e., situational reactions) are self-limited and the symptoms usually recede when the situational stress diminishes.

c. *Other functional nonpsychotic disorders*, including paranoid, cyclothymic, schizoid, explosive, obsessive-compulsive, hysterical, asthenic, antisocial, passive-aggressive and inadequate personality; sexual deviation; alcohol addiction and drug addiction. These disorders are characterized by deeply ingrained maladaptive patterns of behavior, generally of long duration. Unlike neurotic disorders, conflict in these cases is not primarily within the individual but between the individual and his environment. In many of these conditions, the patient may experience little anxiety and little or no sense of distress, except when anxiety and distress are consequences of maladaptive behavior.

4. *Mental retardation* denotes a lifelong condition characterized by below-average intellectual endowment as measured by well-standardized intelligence (IQ) tests and associated with impairment in one or more of the following areas: learning, maturation, and social adjustment. The degree of impairment should be determined primarily on the basis of intelligence level and the medical report. Care should be taken to ascertain that test results are consistent with daily activities and behavior. A well-standardized, comprehensive intelligence test, such as the Wechsler Adult Intelligence Scale (WAIS), should be administered and interpreted by a psychologist or psychiatrist qualified by training and ex-

perience to perform such an evaluation. In special circumstances, nonverbal measures, such as the Raven Progressive Matrices or the Arthur Point Scale, may be substituted.

Unfortunately, identical IQ scores obtained from different tests do not always reflect a similar degree of intellectual function. In this connection, it may be noted that on the WAIS, perhaps currently the most widely used measure of intellectual ability in adults, IQ's of 69 and below are characteristic of approximately the lowest 2 percent of the general population. In instances where other tests are administered, it will be necessary to convert the IQ to the corresponding percentile rank in the general population in order to determine the actual degree of impairment reflected by the IQ scores. Where more than one IQ is customarily derived from the test administered, i.e., where Verbal, Performance, and Full Scale IQ's are provided as on the WAIS, the lowest of these is to be used in conjunction with 12.05.

In cases where the nature of the individual's impairment is such that testing, as described above, is precluded, medical reports specifically describing the level of intellectual, social, and physical function should be obtained. Actual observations by district office or State DDS personnel, reports from educational institutions, and information furnished by public welfare agencies or other reliable, objective sources should be considered as additional evidence.

12.01 Category of Impairments, Mental

12.02 *Chronic brain syndromes* (organic brain syndromes). With both A and B:

A. Demonstrated deterioration in intellectual functioning, manifested by persistence of one or more of the following clinical signs:

1. Marked memory defect for recent events; or
2. Impoverished, slowed, perseverative thinking, with confusion or disorientation; or
3. Labile, shallow, or coarse affect;

B. Resulting persistence of marked restriction of daily activities and constriction of interests and deterioration in personal habits and seriously impaired ability to relate to other people.

12.03 *Functional psychotic disorders* (mood disorders, schizophrenias, paranoid states). With both A and B:

A. Manifested persistence of one or more of the following clinical signs:

1. Depression (or elation); or
2. Agitation; or
3. Psychomotor disturbances; or

4. Hallucinations or delusions; or
5. Autistic or other regressive behavior; or
6. Inappropriateness of affect; or
7. Illogical association of ideas;

B. Resulting persistence of marked restriction of daily activities and constriction of interests and seriously impaired ability to relate to other people.

12.04 *Functional nonpsychotic disorders* (psychophysiologic, neurotic, and personality disorders; addictive dependence on alcohol or drugs). With both A and B:

A. Manifested persistence of one or more of the following clinical signs:

1. Demonstrable and persistent structural changes mediated through psychophysiological channels (e.g., duodenal ulcer); or
2. Recurrent and persistent periods of anxiety, with tension, apprehension, and interference with concentration and memory; or
3. Persistent depressive affect with insomnia, loss of weight, and suicidal preoccupation; or
4. Persistent phobic or obsessive ruminations with inappropriate, bizarre, or disruptive behavior; or
5. Persistent compulsive, ritualistic behavior; or
6. Persistent functional disturbance of vision, speech, hearing, or use of a limb with demonstrable structural or trophic changes; or
7. Persistent, deeply ingrained maladaptive patterns of behavior manifested by either:
   a. Seclusiveness or autistic thinking; or
   b. Pathologically inappropriate suspiciousness or hostility;

B. Resulting persistence of marked restriction of daily activities and constriction of interests and deterioration in personal habits and seriously impaired ability to relate to other people.

12.05 *Mental retardation.* As manifested by:

A. Severe mental and social incapacity as evidenced by marked dependence upon others for personal needs (e.g., bathing, washing, dressing, etc.) and inability to understand the spoken word and inability to avoid physical danger (fire, cars, etc.) and inability to follow simple directions and inability to read, write, and perform simple calculations; or

B. IQ of 59 or less (see 12.00B4); or

C. IQ of 60 to 69 inclusive (see 12.00B4) and a physical or other mental impairment imposing additional and significant work-related limitation of function.

13.00 NEOPLASTIC DISEASE—MALIGNANT

A. Introduction

The determination of the level of severity resulting from malignant tumors is made from a consideration of the site of lesion, the histogenesis of the tumor, the extent of involvement, the apparent adequacy and response to therapy (surgery, irradiation, hormones, chemotherapy, etc.), and the magnitude of the posttherapeutic residuals.

B. Documentation

The diagnosis of malignant tumor should be established on the basis of symptoms, signs, and laboratory findings. The site of the primary, recurrent, and metastatic lesion must be specified in all cases of malignant neoplastic diseases. If an operative procedure has been performed, the evidence should include a copy of the operative note and the report of the gross and microscopic examination of the surgical specimen. If these documents are not obtainable, then the summary of hospitalization or a report from the treating physician must include details of the findings at surgery and the results of the pathologist's gross and microscopic examination of the tissues.

For those cases in which a disabling impairment was not established when therapy was begun but progression of the disease is likely, current medical evidence should include a report of a recent examination directed especially at local or regional recurrence, soft part or skeletal metastases, and significant posttherapeutic residuals.

C. Evaluation

Usually, when the malignant tumor consists only of a local lesion with metastasis to the regional lymph nodes which apparently has been competely excised, imminent recurrence or metastasis is not anticipated. Exceptions are noted in 13.02E, 13.03, 13.05B, 13.09B and E, 13.11A and F, 13.13B, 13.16B and C, 13.21B, 13.22A and B, and 13.24A. For adjudicative purposes, "distant metastasis" or "metastasis beyond the regional lymph nodes" refers to metastasis beyond the lines of the usual radical en bloc resection.

Local or regional recurrence after radical surgery or pathological evidence of incomplete excision by radical surgery is to be equated with unresectable lesions (except for carcinoma of the breast, 13.09C) and, for the purposes of our program, may be evaluated as "inoperable." These situations are usually followed by severe impairment within 6 months to 1 year.

Local or regional recurrence after incomplete excision of a localized and still completely resectable tumor is not to be equated with recurrence after radical surgery. In the evaluation of lymphomas, the tissue type and site of involvement are not necessarily indicators of the severity of the impairment.

When a malignant tumor has metastasized beyond the regional lymph nodes, the impairment usually will be considered to be severe. Exceptions are hormone-dependent tumors, isotope-sensitive metastases, metastases from seminoma of the testicles which are controlled by definitive therapy, or distant metastases which have apparently disappeared and have not been evident for 3 or more years.

D. Effects of Therapy

Significant posttherapeutic residuals, not specifically included in the category of impairments for malignant neoplasms, should be evaluated according to the affected body system.

Where the impairment is not listed in the Listing of Impairments and is not medically equivalent to a listed impairment, the impact of any residual impairment including that caused by therapy must be considered. The therapeutic regimen and consequent adverse response to therapy may vary widely; therefore, each case must be considered on an individual basis. It is essential to obtain a specific description of the therapeutic regimen, including the drugs given, dosage, frequency of drug administration, and plans for continued drug administration. It is necessary to obtain a description of the complications or any other adverse response to therapy such as nausea, vomiting, diarrhea, weakness, dermatologic disorders, or reactive mental disorders. Since the severity of the adverse effects of anticancer chemotherapy may change during the period of drug administration, the decision regarding the impact of drug therapy should be based on a sufficient period of therapy to permit proper consideration.

E. Onset

To establish onset of disability prior to the time a malignancy is first demonstrated to be inoperable or beyond control by other modes of therapy (and prior evidence is nonexistent) requires medical judgment based on medically reported symptoms, the type of the specific malignancy, its location, and extent of involvement when first demonstrated.

Index

369

About the Author

EDWARD B. BEIS, LL.B., is currently in private practice in St. Louis, Missouri. Formerly, he was a partner with Keck, Mahin, & Cate in Chicago, where he represented not-for-profit institutions, such as hospitals, colleges, and seminaries. Mr. Beis also has served as director of the Cook County Legal Assistance Foundation, Inc., a program providing free legal services to indigent persons, including the mentally disabled. He was a member of a lawyer/social worker team that provided representation in criminal and civil matters to patients in state institutions.

Mr. Beis received his bachelor's degree in English literature from St. Louis University and an LL.B. from the University of Missouri School of Law at Columbia.